T0299065

POLITICS AND TRADE COOPERATION IN THE NINETEENTH CENTURY

This book examines international trade cooperation from 1815 to 1914. Its theoretical analysis is grounded in the domestic political economy of states, on which Robert Pahre develops theories of international cooperation, the spread of trade cooperation, and the effect of trade regimes. It is the first book to examine trade politics around the world over the entire century from 1815 to 1914, using a new database of trade agreements. It will appeal to students of international relations, comparative political economy, economic history, trade law, and international organizations.

Robert Pahre is Professor of Political Science at the University of Illinois in Urbana-Champaign and Director of the European Union Center. He previously taught at the University of Michigan and the University of Rochester. Professor Pahre is the author of *Leading Questions: How Hegemony Affects the International Political Economy* (1999); editor of *Democratic Foreign Policy Making: Problems of Divided Government* (2006); coauthor with Fiona McGillivray, Iain McLean, and Cheryl Schonhardt-Bailey of *International Trade and Political Institutions: Instituting Trade in the Long Nineteenth Century* (2001); and, with Mattei Dogan, coauthor of *Creative Marginality: Innovation at the Intersection of Social Sciences* (1990). His research has appeared in academic journals in political science, sociology, and the philosophy of science.

Politics and Trade Cooperation in the Nineteenth Century

The "Agreeable Customs" of 1815–1914

ROBERT PAHRE

University of Illinois

CAMBRIDGE
UNIVERSITY PRESS

32 Avenue of the Americas, New York NY 10013-2473, USA

Cambridge University Press is part of the University of Cambridge.

It furthers the University's mission by disseminating knowledge in the pursuit of
education, learning and research at the highest international levels of excellence.

www.cambridge.org
Information on this title: www.cambridge.org/9780521872744

First published 2008
First paperback edition 2012

A catalogue record for this publication is available from the British Library

Library of Congress Cataloguing in Publication data

Pahre, Robert.
Politics and trade cooperation in the nineteenth century : the "agreeable customs"
of 1815–1914 / Robert Pahre.
p. cm.
Includes bibliographical references and index.
ISBN 978-0-521-87274-4 (hardback)
1. International trade – History – 19th century.   2. International trade – History –
20th century.   I. Title.   II. Title: Politics and trade cooperation in the 19th century.
HF1379.P344   2008
382.09′034–dc22   2007024346

ISBN 978-0-521-87274-4 Hardback

for
Janice Nikoline Pahre
Richard Neal Pahre

Contents

List of Figures

List of Tables

Preface

This is, unfortunately, a long book, and it has taken too long to write. It began as a claim in a footnote in a previous book that such a thing could be done, at least in principle. For good or ill, it turns out that this thing can also be done in practice.

Besides being too long, this book tramples rather too freely in disciplines and subfields where I am not expert, doubtless making errors along the way that will offend the local specialists. My only defense is the trite hope that the whole is greater than the sum of its parts.

This wandering over time and space requires some comments on spelling, orthography, and translation. These present tricky problems for which many solutions are possible (see Kann 1974: xiii). For the modern nation-states I use the common English name. For other places, I normally use native names and spelling unless an English or international substitute enjoys wide currency (i.e., Vienna not Wien). This principle also guided my use of *Zollverein* (Customs Union) for the major German economic union because that name is familiar to the political economy community. In contrast, I used the translation "Tax Union" for the less familiar *Steuerverein* in North Germany. Where differences are minor, I see no reason not to use the native spelling (Hannover not Hanover, México not Mexico, Perú not Peru, Württemberg not Wurttemberg or Wuerttemberg). I also use the native name where the English name would be unfamiliar to most Americans anyway (Kärnten not Carinthia, Pfalz not Palatinate, Sachsen-Weimar not Saxe-Weimar). In a few cases, the choice of name is political (Holsten versus Holstein, Alsace versus Elsaß); to the modern victors go the spoils. Finally, one apparently arbitrary decision reflects the fact that I always discuss the place as part of the German Confederation (namely, Luxemburg not Luxembourg or Letzeburg).

I have also tried to take a practical stance on translation. I favor loose translations over strict translations that try to remain close to the structure of the original text. Given the nature of good English style, this preference means that I will often take long sentences in the original and break them up into several sentences, each with a more direct writing style than the original. I also prefer translating idiom to idiom rather than being literal; for example, in Chapter 7 "freundig begrüßt" – literally, "greeted friendly" – becomes "warmly welcomed." This philosophy of translation is especially important because many of my sources are written in highly formal nineteenth-century German, where the average sentence "is a sublime and impressive curiosity" (Twain 1880: 441).[1] Given my looseness of translation, I always provide the original text in a footnote so that interested readers can choose their own translation.

I have benefited from many comments from a wide range of people. Parts of this book were presented at the conference on "Instituting Trade: Trade Policy and 19th Century Political Institutions," Center for Political Economy, Washington University, St. Louis, March 1997; at the "Rational International Institutions Project" conferences at the University of Chicago in May 1998 and in Boston in August 1998; at the Political Science Department of the University of Illinois in June 1998 and July 1999; at the annual meetings of the American Political Science Association in September 1998 and August 1999; at the conference on "Does International Cooperation Matter?" at the UCLA Center for Political Economy, Lake Arrowhead, California, February 2000; at the Ohio State University in February 2000; at the Institute for Government and Public Affairs at the University of Illinois at Urbana-Champaign in October 2000; and at the University of California at Berkeley and at Davis in December 2000. Each presentation yielded many helpful comments that have improved the final product.

The papers at those conferences also yielded several published articles. Parts of Chapters 10–12 have already appeared in *European Union Politics* and *International Organization*. The core of the model, now spread across Chapters 3, 7, and 8, first appeared in the *Journal of Conflict Resolution*. A summary of the main story appeared as a chapter in *International Trade and Political Institutions: Instituting Trade in the Long Nineteenth Century*, edited by Fiona McGillivray, Iain McLean, Robert Pahre, and Cheryl Schonhardt-Bailey.

Many people have read parts of this book, mostly in the form of stand-alone papers or partial chapters. Pradeep Chhibber, John Conybeare, I. M. Destler, George Downs, Zachary Elkins, Jeffry Frieden, Matthew Gabel,

---

[1] Twain (1880) also provides the seminal statement of the field of judgmental comparative linguistics, which still lacks a journal.

Robert Keohane, Barbara Koremenos, Ann Lin, Charles Lipson, Edward
Mansfield, Lisa Martin, Fiona McGillivray, Iain McLean, Brian Pollins,
Ronald Rogowski, Michael Ross, Cheryl Schonhardt-Bailey, Alastair Smith,
and Duncan Snidal have provided comments on parts of the manuscript.
Paul Diehl and Doug Dion read the whole darned thing and provided
valuable comments throughout. Four referees also provided thorough comments, and I wish I could thank them by name. I am grateful for them all.

My highest gratitude goes to the Department of Political Science at the
University of Iowa, which allowed me to present the entire book manuscript
to them. This entailed a summary presentation to the department and
extended sessions with graduate students, many of whom gave me valuable
and detailed critiques of the manuscript (in particular, Christiana Bejarano,
Benjamin Bergmann, Alex C. H. Chang, Min Ou Chon, Stephanie Duck,
Holley Hansen, Tanya Janulewicz, Karleen Jones, and Anoop Sarbahi). Special thanks also go to Doug Dion, who organized the visit – and who resisted
the temptation to exclaim, "One hears such sounds, and what can one say
but . . . Salieri!"

Some of this research was supported by a Rackham Graduate School
Faculty Fellowship at the University of Michigan and by a Research Board
Grant at the University of Illinois. The thorough and multilingual research
assistance of José-Raúl Perales Hernandez was indispensable for creating the
Trade Agreements Database. Other research assistants, especially Angelika
Mathur and Jennifer Shulman, were helpful with data collection and the
historiography. Burcu Ucaray helped bring the final manuscript to print
and compiled the index.

Finally, I am especially indebted to my parents and the value they have
always placed on education. That education is much to blame for the content
and breadth of this book. With love and thanks, this book is for them.

POLITICS AND TRADE COOPERATION IN THE NINETEENTH CENTURY

PART ONE

COOPERATION AND VARIATION

ONE

International Cooperation Across
Time and Space

"[M]orality after all is not founded upon self-sacrifice, but upon enlightened self-interest, a clearer and more complete understanding of all the ties that bind us the one to the other. And such clearer understanding is bound to improve, not merely the relationship of one group to another, but the relationship of all men to all other men, to create a consciousness which must make for more efficient human co-operation, a better human society."
    – Norman Angell, 1912 (cited in Keegan 1999: 11–12)

Economic relations between nations have grown increasingly cooperative in the last 200 years. Countries now depend on one another for staples, intermediate products, and consumer goods to an extent unimaginable 250 years ago. This cooperation rests on an extensive network of international organizations, less formal regimes, and treaties among states. Such institutions as the World Trade Organization (WTO), European Union (EU), North American Free Trade Area (NAFTA), and Southern Cone Common Market (MERCOSUR) play a central role in managing these international trade relations. As a result, we live in a highly institutionalized global economy.

Though its highly institutionalized form today dates only to the 1940s, extensive economic cooperation has been an important feature of international life since the middle of the nineteenth century. Scattered trade treaties appeared even earlier, including the Methuen Treaty between England and Portugal (1703), the Vergennes Treaty between England and France (1789), and the Ottoman capitulations (see Chapter 12). Such treaties have increased in density since then, often in a series of spurts or waves.

Despite this extended history of economic cooperation, most studies of cooperation have limited themselves to events since World War II. This narrow focus is unfortunate. This last half-century has been exceptional in many ways, characterized by postwar reconstruction, the Cold War, centralized

3

networks of formalized international organizations, and American leadership. Too many scholars have treated this context as if it were typical.

A lack of historical perspective means that many observers have feared the end of cooperation – first, at a time of declining American power in the 1970s and 1980s, and second, at the end of the Cold War in 1989–1990. Neither prediction came true. Similarly, many observers today believe that the political backlash against globalization today will threaten existing economic cooperation. This prediction will also be proven false, I believe.

This book represents a long justification for this more optimistic prediction. Perhaps paradoxically, its optimism about cooperation comes from studying *non*cooperation – or, more precisely, from studying variation between cooperation and noncooperation. Common forms of domestic politics, trade reciprocity, and decentralized international institutions can sustain globalization. The post-1945 pattern of globalization undergirded by the Cold War, military alliances, and all-encompassing institutions is by no means necessary for politically sustainable globalization. The bottom-up theory of trade cooperation developed here shows that domestic politics can provide the foundation for a stable international trade regime, a regime that is fairly resistant to economic shocks.

To understand both cooperation and noncooperation in trade, this book examines a historical period abundant in both: the "nineteenth century" of 1815–1914. This period also provides an interesting historical analogy for today. Though the media, pundits, policy wonks, and scholars all note the supposedly unprecedented scope of globalization today, one could argue that globalization in 2000 was no greater than in 1900, for example (see Bordo, Eichengreen, and Irwin 1999 for a critical review). This certainly varies by issue – globalization is probably greater today on most dimensions, but not in trade or the migration of people. The nineteenth century therefore provides an excellent subject for understanding these processes and a possible historical analogy for the twenty-first century (cf. O'Rourke and Williamson 1999). The period is especially relevant for thinking about economic cooperation in the twenty-first century, when the security underpinnings of the post-1945 system have largely fallen away.

This book seeks both a theory of trade cooperation and a fuller account of the nineteenth century trade regime. Together, theory and historical analogy can improve our understanding of the twenty-first century. Although intended as a general theory of trade cooperation, the book also provides an explanation of nineteenth-century trade cooperation on its own terms. Dialogue between theory and history plays a central role in the exposition.

Analytically, this book develops a theory of trade cooperation from the bottom up, moving from domestic politics to the relations between states and then up to the international system as a whole. It begins with the interaction between domestic groups and political leaders in Part II, using the theory of political support. Political-support theory provides a tool with which to examine how a variety of political factors, including a state's fiscal institutions and level of democracy, cause tariff levels to vary from one country to another. Though following conventional accounts in many parts, Chapters 2–5 also provide evidence and analysis contrary to common claims in the trade policy literature. For example, Chapter 4 shows that heavy reliance on tariffs for government revenue does not necessarily provide a constraint forcing the state to choose high tariffs, for revenue might be maximized at relatively low tariff levels. Chapter 5 revisits the literature on democracy and free trade, showing that democracy need not be associated with more liberal trade policy because democratization may empower protectionist voters.

Exogenous events, such as changes in world prices, disturb the equilibrium found in the political-support model and lead countries to raise or lower their tariffs. The effects of global changes can be complex because states respond not only to economic change but also react to one another's responses. For example, France's response to the Great Depression of 1873–1896 reflected not only the decline of world agricultural prices but also the move to protectionism in Germany and other countries, whose own choices affected world prices as well as one another.

These reactions between countries play a critical role in the overall theory of trade cooperation developed in Part III. States normally react to one another by doing the opposite – foreign protectionism breeds home liberalization, while foreign liberalization leads to home protectionism. As a result, global free trade cannot come from one country's "leadership," nor can general trends such as economic globalization produce uniform liberalization. Only international cooperation can produce mutually beneficial reductions in trade barriers, by which home liberalization is contractually linked to foreign liberalization.

To understand this, I examine the conditions that make cooperation more or less likely. The basic rule is that low-tariff countries are more likely to cooperate than are high-tariff countries. For this reason, the conditions that favor cooperation tend to be the same set of variables that affect a country's autonomous tariffs. Improving terms of trade, for example, makes tariffs go up and trade cooperation less likely. Heavy reliance on tariffs for government revenue often inhibits cooperation as well as leads to higher autonomous tariffs. Still, some specific effects vary. For example, democracy unambiguously encourages reciprocal trade liberalization, despite having ambiguous effects on unilateral trade policy. These chapters show the importance of separating the effects of these variables on autonomous tariffs from their possibly contrary effects on trade cooperation.

Though changing economic and political conditions may make countries either more or less likely to cooperate, once they have signed a trade treaty this cooperation will be relatively insulated from changes in these same conditions. As a result, cooperation can weather economic disturbances that would have led to protectionism without such cooperation. This stabilizing effect remains even if trade treaties make relatively small tariff concessions.

Cooperation also changes the incentives for other states. If discriminatory, outsiders who had been reluctant to cooperate may find it in their interests to join a network of cooperators. For this reason, after examining the two-country cooperation problem, I analyze general features of the global political economy as a whole in Part IV. The norm of most-favored nation (MFN) plays a leading role in the analysis, determining how cooperation between two countries affects their cooperation with outsiders as well as cooperation by other parties. Perhaps surprisingly, MFN makes cooperation more difficult and the concessions in trade treaties less deep. However, a network of MFN treaties – if it discriminates against outsiders – does make countries excluded from the network more eager to join it.

Thus, past cooperation helps structure further cooperation. This takes the theory to a systemic-level analysis of cooperation, norms, and regimes. A trade network, like the bilateral cooperation within it, can also weather economic storms that would have led to protectionism without it.

In summary, economic and political variables affect trade policy in a single country, the relations between pairs of countries, and system-wide patterns of interaction in this bottom-up theory of cooperation. The mode of analysis, moving from domestic politics up to regimes, resembles that found in some constructivist theories of international relations, though it is firmly rooted in rationalist theory. This bottom-up approach differs considerably from traditional approaches to international behavior among realists and liberals, who tend to begin with states acting in the international system, seeing domestic politics mostly as a confounding factor in their theories. The book's overall approach is rooted in the liberal institutionalist tradition in international political economy but, like Helen Milner's *Interests, Institutions, and Information* (1997a) and some other books, turns that tradition on its head by beginning with domestic politics.

Theories of International Cooperation

Explaining cooperation is a salient part of the study of international relations, and this focus helps make the field different from the study of domestic political systems. Whereas domestic politics takes place within some institutional framework set by a state with a monopoly over the legitimate use of force, international cooperation occurs between sovereign nations. For this reason, states must monitor and enforce cooperation themselves, without recourse to third-party enforcers. This concern with enforcement has pointed research toward looking at how states monitor compliance and how they improve information about compliance and about one another's preferences (Axelrod 1984; Keohane 1984; Koremenos, Lipson, and Snidal 2001; Lipson 1984; Martin 1992; Oye 1986; Pahre 1994, 1995a, 1999: Chapters 7–9; Stein 1983, 1991; Yarbrough and Yarbrough 1986). Much of this research finds that three variables explain the success or failure of cooperation: "mutuality of interest, the shadow of the future, and the number of players" (Axelrod and Keohane 1986: 227). Each variable makes enforcement easier or the incentive to cheat less.

This research has provided the foundational language for thinking about international cooperation. Because much of the literature poses the problem of cooperation as part of a theoretical critique of Realism – which more or less denies that meaningful international cooperation exists – it has given less attention to the nitty-gritty questions of data collection and hypothesis testing. For example, the shadow of the future is very difficult to measure (but see Chapter 8). It also has more ambiguous effects than scholars suspected at first. Research suggests that a high shadow of the future might make cooperation less likely by magnifying the distributional effects of a bargain (Fearon 1998; Snidal 1985a,b, 1991). A state will negotiate harder for a good deal if it believes this bargain will affect its payoffs for a long time to come, though the possibility of regular renegotiation tempers this problem somewhat (Koremenos 2001).

The second variable, the number of actors, is theoretically suspect (see Lohmann 1997; Pahre 1994, 1995a). Increasing the number of players may make international cooperation more likely, not less likely, by reducing each player's incentive to cheat. Including many states also increases the number of players available to punish a cheater. In addition, states facing a large-n environment can construct networks of bilateral cooperation to achieve multilateral ends (Lipson 1985).

The last independent variable in cooperation theory, mutuality of interest, is simply another way of saying that states' preferences affect their willingness to cooperate (cf. Moravcsik 1998).[1] It is notoriously difficult to specify these preferences independently of the outcomes they are trying to explain, as Duncan Snidal (1986) argued forcefully. The researcher must figure out a state's interests in cooperation while studying that cooperation itself, a research design that flirts with the fallacy of *post hoc, ergo propter hoc.* By looking at a single example of cooperation, case study methods face these inference problems in an especially severe form. Alternatives include specifying preferences deductively, and studying a large number of cases. I do both in this book.

Because of these problems, the major propositions of cooperation theory largely fail to explain variation in cooperation. This failing comes in part from this literature's rhetorical origins. Because it confronted the neo-Realist belief that international cooperation is unimportant, cooperation theory concentrated on explaining the *existence* of significant international cooperation (Axelrod 1984; Oye 1986 *inter alia*).[2] This approach analyzed a plethora of problems that might require international cooperation, including incomplete information, international market imperfections, inadequately specified property rights, power maximization, transactions costs, joint income maximization, and domestic political objectives (Conybeare 1987; Keohane 1984; Kindleberger 1973; Krasner 1976; Lake 1988; Milner 1997; see also Abbott and Snidal 1998 and Koremenos et al. 2001). Many theoretical elaborations of the theory have also focused on existence-type problems such as whether states might want to link two or more issues when cooperating, or whether multilateral cooperation makes sense (see Lohmann 1997; McGinnis 1986; Pahre 1994; Sebenius 1983; Tollison and Willett 1979).

These studies have been limited by their theoretical *problematique.* To show that Realism was wrong, it sufficed to argue abstractly that some class of problem demanded international cooperation, and then to show empirically that such a case existed in the real world, and that states did cooperate in such circumstances. Existence claims (Pahre 2005), and not

---

[1] Most scholars have assumed that increasing the benefits of cooperation makes cooperation more likely (Milner 1997a: Chapter 2), overlooking the fact that greater benefits also make cheating more likely. One solution is to look at a state's share of costs relative to benefits (Pahre 1999: Chapter 7).

[2] One exception, illuminating in itself, is the literature arguing that cooperation is easier in economic matters than in security affairs (Jervis 1983; Lipson 1984). A second exception attributes variation in economic cooperation to variation in security ties: the so-called relative gains theory (Grieco 1990; Morrow 1997; Morrow et al. 1998, 1999; Pahre 1999: Chapters 7–9; Snidal 1991; Stein 1984). For a thorough historical study of this question in this period, see Harvey (1938), who rejects these claims for most dyads.

studies of how the variables varied, thus dominated the arguments. For example, I am aware of no studies comparing a case in which two states enjoyed complete information about one another with another case in which they did not. Similarly, some scholars assume that transaction costs or power maximization are ubiquitous in international relations and therefore do not vary (i.e., Grieco 1990; Keohane 1984). Without variation in the independent variables, then, we can hardly be surprised that this literature overlooked variation in the dependent variable of cooperation.

By failing to look at variation between cooperation and noncooperation, most cooperation theory has also not considered the real possibility that the reversion point, the outcome when cooperation breaks down, might affect the likelihood of cooperation. If the reversion point is unattractive, states have a greater incentive to cooperate so as to avoid it; if the reversion point is not too bad, states are less likely to cooperate. Because reversion points are important, any study of cooperation must begin with trade policy in the absence of cooperation. Domestic politics also affects this reversion point, and understanding this effect requires greater attention to the domestic politics of trade. This provides the central task for Part II.

States also threaten to return to the noncooperative outcome in order to receive a more favorable treaty. These distributional issues have recently joined enforcement and monitoring issues as a central concern in cooperation theory (see Fearon 1998; Garrett 1992; Garrett and Tsebelis 1996; Krasner 1991; Oatley and Nabors 1998). Most distributional problems in trade policy rest on domestic political concerns. Customs unions and free trade areas (Milner 1997b), and discriminatory policies such as Super 301 actions all reflect domestic political demands. Studies that explain such discrimination therefore need to consider domestic distributional concerns as well as foreign policy considerations.

Domestic Politics and International Cooperation

While the effects of the international system on international cooperation remain a dominant concern in the literature on international political economy, theoretical research has not rested with traditional cooperation theory. Recent years have seen substantial research on how domestic politics affects international relations, increasingly using theories from comparative politics to explain trade policy and cooperation (i.e., Gilligan 1997; Mansfield, Milner, and Rosendorff 2000, 2002a; McGillivray 2004; Milner 1997a; O'Halloran 1994; Pahre 1997, 2001a; Schonhardt-Bailey 2006; Verdier 1994).

The literature on two-level games has gained particular prominence in this area. Robert Putnam (1988) first distinguished a "Level I" game between two governments from the "Level II" game between each government and any relevant domestic actors. Intentionally synthetic, the two-level literature responds to the eclecticism of many domestic-level theories in political science by attempting to combine the insights of systemic- and domestic-level theories.

Since Putnam, much of the literature has developed typologies of how foreign policy affects domestic politics or vice versa. For example, the nonformal literature has examined bargaining tactics, such as mobilizing foreign interest groups, changing foreign domestic political agendas, making side payments, or using international negotiations to avoid blocking actors at home (Friman 1993; F. Mayer 1992; Milner 1997a; Paarlberg 1993; Schneider 2000; Schoppa 1993). Like other literatures reviewed earlier, this one has developed a valuable theoretical language. At the same time, it has tended to emphasize both theoretical and empirical existence claims instead of examining variation between cooperation and noncooperation.

Instead of cataloging forms of influence, formal theorists in the two-level tradition have focused on how rational negotiators anticipate domestic actors' reactions. Many claim that domestic politics normally makes international cooperation less likely because a domestic legislature with ratification powers might reject an agreement (i.e., Iida 1993; Milner and Rosendorff 1996, 1997; Mo 1994, 1995; Schneider and Cederman 1993; but Pahre 2001a). Such obstacles become more likely as the difference between executive and legislative preferences increase, a difference known as the degree of divided government (Pahre 2006). Trying to satisfy an unpredictable legislature under conditions of uncertainty may also force an executive to maintain a hard-line stance abroad, preventing cooperation with foreigners (Milner 1997a).

While having a legislature with ratification power may make cooperation less likely, the two-level framework in its present state of theoretical development is of limited usefulness for explaining cross-national differences. It assumes that the executive and legislature have different preferences, but the reasons for these supposed differences are often misleading. In many countries, the legislature and executive do not have systematically different preferences because one branch of government chooses the other. In a pure parliamentary system, for example, the legislature chooses the executive, presumably selecting an executive with preferences near its own (Pahre 1997). In many dictatorships and monarchies, the executive chooses the legislature, and executives continue to play a role in choosing the members of many upper houses even in modern democracies. For these reasons, making any assumptions at all about the divergent preferences of an executive and legislature is likely to do violence to many cases and to be irrelevant for many others. In many cases we need model only a single actor, who chooses the other.

Such an actor lies at the center of the approach in this book, which studies the political incentives of a single political leader seeking to maximize support from domestic groups (see Chapter 3). I then consider variation in institutions and ratification problems as extensions of the basic model, with a legislature independent of the executive. Chapter 9, in particular, adds a two-level framework to the basic model. This modeling strategy, starting with a single politician and then adding executive-legislative relations, helps uncover the extent to which these complications explain variation in international cooperation.

In the theory of political support, an individual politician – and not interest groups, voters, legislators, or public opinion – makes policy. This politician seeks votes and other political support from as many groups as possible, balancing interests against each other. Focusing on the leader who supplies policy, instead of the groups who demand it, leads to some counterintuitive results. One surprising result is that gaining wealth makes a group *less* influential. As a group gains wealth, its marginal utility of wealth declines, so at the margin additional support from that group becomes less valuable to the political leader. Instead, the politician will give some policy reward to a weaker group that will value it more highly at the margin. As a result, political-support theory finds that leaders choose policy that compensates those people who are harmed by exogenous change, such as changes in the world economy. They pay for this compensatory policy by drawing off some of the benefits that would otherwise have gone to the "winners" from change.

To show how this balancing or compensatory mechanism works, most of this book is devoted to analyzing the domestic politics of trade when nations do not cooperate. Indeed, Chapters 3–5 could be classified as studies in comparative foreign policy more than international relations, for they examine the domestic sources of trade policy in a single state. Again, I argue that the noncooperative outcomes, analyzed in these chapters, critically affect cooperation and therefore must be part of our analysis. By proceeding in this way, the theory of political support helps bring together an explanation of both noncooperative trade policies and trade cooperation. Its bottom-up approach moves from the domestic institutional setting for trade policy to the interaction of states, international cooperation, and then international norms and regimes.

Issues of Research Strategy and Scope

Focusing on variation between cooperation and noncooperation among many countries over a long period represents a research strategy that differs from that found in many other studies of international cooperation. Most studies of international cooperation have examined a single institution such as the WTO or a single issue such as agricultural trade (see *inter alia* the contributions to Avery 1993; Krasner 1983; Oye 1986; Ruggie 1993a). Some works compare a small number of cases of cooperation (i.e., Keohane 1984; Milner 1997a), though a few collections reach larger numbers (i.e., Evans, Jacobson, and Putnam 1993; Koremenos et al. 2001).

Such research has provided an essential foundation for the study of international cooperation, including the very concept of "cooperation" itself. This body of research has also supplied key analytical concepts for understanding cooperation, most notably the metaphor of the Prisoners' Dilemma (PD). Critiques both internal and external to the literature have also played key roles in deepening our understanding of cooperation and delineating the limits of our theories – notably, again, the strengths and weaknesses of using PD as a metaphor for international cooperation.

Despite these contributions, much research has studied only those cases in which cooperation occurs. Cooperation theory shares this biased research design with many other subjects in political science, including studies of war that look only at wars, studies of revolutions that look only at revolutions, and studies of voter turnout interviewing only voters (King, Keohane, and Verba 1994: 129–132).[3] Unfortunately, this design makes it impossible to test certain kinds of arguments. For example, the literature often makes correlative claims, such as hypotheses that time horizons or the number of actors causes variation in cooperation. Testing these correlative hypotheses requires looking at many cases in which cooperation may or may not occur. Unfortunately, cases of noncooperation have received little or no attention.

Second, the lack of variation in most case studies complicates inference. When studying a single regime, an analyst normally finds features that make both it and its historical period unique. The scholar naturally attributes this regime to the peculiarities of its period, such as explaining post-1945 economic cooperation as a result of the Cold War or the New Deal political

---

[3] I should note that a study lacking variation in cooperation may still be appropriate for examining changing *forms* of cooperation. Examples of such research include those examining the changing depth of cooperation, changing memberships, greater or lesser issue scope, or the degree of centralization within cooperative institutions (i.e. Abbott and Snidal 1998; Aggarwal 1985; Downs, Rocke, and Barsoom 1998; Pahre 1995a).

coalition in the United States. While these historical idiosyncracies doubtless help shape any regime, this approach neglects the many other causes shared by a larger set of regimes.

Third, studying cooperation alone selects on the dependent variable. Although selecting on the dependent variable is appropriate for testing hypotheses about necessary conditions, it is a poor choice for arguments that rest on correlations or sufficient conditions (Dion 1998). Unfortunately, as mentioned earlier, most hypotheses on cooperation are correlative hypotheses in which selection on the independent variable would be appropriate (King et al. 1994). Although typical research designs would work for necessary conditions, these are not tested – even though the literature includes several necessary conditions. Specifically, many claim that repeated play is necessary for cooperation and, second, that incomplete information about domestic preferences is necessary for ratification failures. However, I am unaware of any tests of these claims, which would require that scholars operationalize difficult concepts such as "no repeated play" or "complete information."

As an example of the limits of existing research, one important collection of case studies provides excellent variation but poor research design. Evans et al. (1993) pair cases of cooperation and noncooperation in what they identify as a most-similar design. This design selects on the dependent variable, but one needs no cases of noncooperation to test a necessary condition about cooperation. Most contributors to the volume proposed either sufficient or correlative conditions for which selection on the independent variables would have been appropriate. Pairing cases in this way biases the study unless the population of all potentially cooperative dyads consists of outcomes that are exactly half successful, half unsuccessful.

Unlike this other research, this book uses the entire population of cases in an issue area to investigate both when cooperation takes place and when it does not. I use these data to test hypotheses drawn from a general theory of cooperation in trade. Studying this variation reveals the causes of cooperation better than just looking at successful cooperation.

I use trade treaties as a measure of trade cooperation. Trade treaties are a quintessential example of international cooperation, commonly defined as cases in which "actors adjust their behavior to the actual or anticipated preferences of others, through a process of policy coordination" (Keohane 1984: 51–52). In trade cooperation, two states adjust their trade policies – their tariffs and nontariff barriers to trade – in response to each other. This mutual adjustment takes many legal forms (see Table 6.2).

As I show in the next section, trade treaties in the period from 1815 to 1913 provide good variation between cooperation and noncooperation.

Some countries cooperated with many other states, while some countries rarely cooperated with anyone, thereby providing cross-national variation. Cooperation in trade treaties also varied intertemporally, both increasing and decreasing with time. Trade cooperation also supported cooperation in other economic areas, making it substantively as well as theoretically important.

In addition to being substantively important, trade cooperation also points us to the domestic foundations of foreign policy. Contemporary debates over NAFTA, the Maastricht Treaty, the Treaty for a European Constitution, and the Uruguay and Doha Rounds of the General Agreement on Trade and Tariffs (GATT) have highlighted the fact that domestic politics play a critical role in the success or failure of cooperation (Evans et al. 1993; Milner 1997a; Pahre and Papayoanou 1997; Pahre 2006; Putnam 1988). To capture this role, the bottom-up theory of cooperation here assumes that politicians choose trade policies as part of their efforts to maximize domestic political support. Because it abstracts from differences across countries, the theory is manageable for studying many countries. It also yields a variety of novel results that are largely supported by evidence from the set of nineteenth-century treaties.

Trade Cooperation in the Nineteenth Century

As discussed in the previous section, good research design requires a dependent variable providing variation between cooperation and noncooperation. The period since World War II will not suffice, for the major trading countries all joined the GATT, now the WTO, soon after World War II. The early establishment of the GATT eliminates any intertemporal variation between cooperation and noncooperation unless we look across the interval provided by World War II.[4] However, doing this would require considering how global war shapes the incentives for international cooperation, a question that is – we hope – distinct from the problems of cooperation the world faces today. Such a research design would also tend to focus on war itself as a cause of cooperation (i.e., Gilpin 1981) to the neglect of other causes. I do not doubt that another world war would have serious consequences for trade cooperation today, as it did in 1914, but it is also important to understand cooperation in times of peace.

---

[4] One might study intertemporal variation *within* the GATT, a task taken up by Aggarwal (1985), Finlayson and Zacher (1981), Keohane (1980), and others. Another possibility is to study the depth of cooperation, as is common in scholarship on the European Union (i.e., Pahre 1995a; Schneider and Cederman 1993).

In addition to the problems connected with global war, the GATT's wide membership rules out many studies of cross-national variation in cooperation. Communist countries remained outside the GATT until the 1970s, but this reluctance to join obviously depended on the Cold War. Many developing countries also remained outside the GATT for a decade or two. These decisions often reflected the Third World's role as a Cold War battleground, and nonmembers quickly signed up when the USSR fell apart. The historical peculiarity of the Cold War makes it hard to use this variation to generalize about trade cooperation in any period lacking such an intense security rivalry.

Instead of the postwar or contemporary period, then, this book investigates cooperation from 1815 to 1913. This century featured substantial cross-national and intertemporal variation in trade cooperation, both in Europe and the Americas. Data limitations, and, in some cases, the analytical problems of "unequal treaties" preclude systematic attention to most non-European countries. For this reason, the primary focus is on European treaties, with secondary study of the Western Hemisphere.

As an illustration of the intertemporal variation this century provides, consider an example of no particular substantive importance, Belgian-Venezuelan trade treaties. The United Netherlands signed a treaty of amity, commerce, and navigation with Gran Colombia on May 1, 1829. This treaty guaranteed reciprocity in navigation regulations and included clauses concerning tariffs that had effects similar to MFN status. The treaty was to remain in force for 12 years, and thereafter unless denounced. The Netherlands ratified the treaty on June 10, 1829, and Gran Colombia ratified it on September 10, 1829.

The treaty remained in effect as both countries split up in 1830–1832; Venezuela chose to ratify the treaty again on separation from Gran Colombia. The treaty lasted nearly 20 more years, until Venezuela denounced it on October 4, 1849. Belgian-Venezuelan trade relations presumably languished without a treaty, but the two states reached a new treaty ten years later in 1858. This treaty took effect after ratifications were exchanged on August 2, 1860, but this too was denounced ten years later, on October 2, 1870. No new treaty was concluded for almost 15 years. A treaty of friendship, commerce, and navigation signed on March 1, 1884, granted reciprocal MFN treatment and was to last for five years, and thereafter unless denounced. It took effect on April 8, 1886, and apparently lasted until World War I.

In short, Belgium and Venezuela alternated between periods of cooperation and noncooperation, cooperating in about two-thirds of this period and not cooperating in the remaining one-third. Aside from the fact that both nations succeeded larger countries in the early decades of our century, this pattern is in no way atypical. Yet, existing theories seem helpless to explain such variation. The literature has not yet provided basic hypotheses about how changing economic or political conditions might affect trade cooperation over time.

The limitations of existing theories become more evident when we consider a dyad of greater economic importance and one for which a historiography exists, Sweden and Germany. These natural trading partners did not sign a trade treaty until 1906.[5] Because Germany was a major participant in the trade cooperation system of the late nineteenth century, the responsibility for this noncooperation presumably lies with Sweden. This too presents a puzzle. Sweden did cooperate with France, Russia, and Switzerland. Existing theory provides no real guidance to explain either the variation in Swedish cooperation by target (Germany versus Russia) or over time (no cooperation with Germany until 1906).[6] This book's central goal is to develop hypotheses that can provide guidance in explaining any such case (see Chapter 8 in general and Chapter 9 for Sweden), hypotheses that are sufficiently general to serve as a starting point for any case that may be of interest.

Beyond the dyadic level, I also seek to explain systemic-wide patterns of cooperation. Again, the nineteenth century provides excellent variation that becomes evident when we look at the period on a grander scale. Trade cooperation varied intertemporally, coming roughly in three waves.[7] The first wave, from the 1820s to the 1850s, was dominated by the German customs union, the *Zollverein*. Domestic institutional factors such as government revenue needs and international economic changes such as a declining price for Prussia's grain exports combine to explain this wave. When other states cooperated, they often did so in response to developments in Germany (see Chapter 11). Both wider and deeper cooperation in the *Zollverein* had particularly significant effects on Austrian, British, Belgian, Dutch, and French trade policies.

---

[5] They did grant another's goods the conventional tariff despite the lack of a treaty. Chapter 11 shows how this practice might have inhibited cooperation.

[6] The Swedish historiography examines the intertemporal pattern with Germany without asking why Sweden successfully cooperated with France and Russia (Lindberg 1983; Y. M. Werner 1989). The German historiography treats Sweden as geographically and analytically peripheral to the empire's trade treaty system (i.e., Weitowitz 1978) without providing any more sophisticated explanation. A puzzle remains, for Germany signed treaties with many other "peripheral" countries. These lacunae suggest that theory can make a real contribution to understanding such cases.

[7] Interestingly enough, Lévy-Leboyer and Bourguignon's (1985) macroeconomic modeling of France in this century suggests a very similar periodization, with structural breaks in 1860 and 1887.

This first wave also coincided with a series of treaties in Latin America that established commercial relationships between newly independent countries and their trading partners. These treaties tended to guarantee reciprocal MFN treatment to signatories, while granting some mutual concessions on particular line items. These MFN clauses were much less common in purely European treaties, a fact that provides variation in the form of cooperation.

The second wave, and the most well known, began in 1860 with the Anglo-French treaty of commerce (also known as the Cobden-Chevalier treaty). Again, economic conditions in Europe and domestic political reforms – notably in Austria, France, Germany, and Italy – sparked greater cooperation. This treaty inaugurated a system of MFN treaties among Austria, Belgium, France, Italy, Prussia/Germany, and some other countries (Bairoch 1972, 1993; Marsh 1999). The symbolic transition between the first and second waves came in 1862, when Prussia gave up its hitherto preferential treatment of Austria by signing an MFN treaty with France; Austria was pulled into the new Western system by a new *Zollverein* treaty in 1865. Despite being in at its start, Britain played a relatively small role in this wave. Some countries, such as the Netherlands, the Ottoman Empire, Portugal, and Sweden, had only weak links to the system; Russia and Spain remained aloof. Because movements in Latin American terms of trade tended to mirror European changes, the Western Hemisphere did not find this middle period conducive for cooperation. Again, we have substantial cross-national variation.

The final wave began in the early 1890s and is often associated with Chancellor Leo von Caprivi's *Neue Kurs* in Germany, France's Méline tariff of 1892, and to a lesser extent the McKinley tariff of 1890 and the Dingley tariff of 1897 in the United States (Barkin 1970; Fay 1927; Fisk 1903; Gilligan 1997: Chapter 4; Lake 1988; Marsh 1999: Chapter 8; Snyder 1940; Weitowitz 1978; see Chapters 4 and 5). Several countries in this wave, most notably Italy, negotiated new treaties out of fears of foreign protectionism. Formerly peripheral countries in Europe also became more active in these decades, led by newly independent Bulgaria. This wave saw less cross-national variation because almost all European countries participated. However, many of these treaties were less far reaching than those of the 1860s, for reasons connected to the MFN norm (see Chapter 12).

Explaining this variation in waves of cooperation at the level of individual states, dyads, and the system as a whole is the task of this book, both theoretically and historically. The approach works from the bottom up. I begin with changes in domestic politics, particularly democratization and state capacity. Changes in the international economy, such as the terms of trade, business cycle, and declining transportation costs, also affect the noncooperative tariffs (see Chapters 3–5). Then I turn to cooperation per se. Variation in size, economic variables, and domestic political variables all affect a country's willingness to cooperate (see Chapters 7–9). At the system level, third-party cooperation affects each country's incentives to cooperate, leading to spread of the trade treaty regime from one dyad to another. Regime characteristics, including MFN clauses, also produce systemic-level features such as "clustering," the grouping of many negotiations together in time (see Chapters 11 and 12). Thus, the approach moves from inside each state to the interactions between them, and then to the international system as a whole.

The Golden Age of Tariff Politics and Tariff History

The nineteenth century provides a good object of study not only for the variation it exhibits but also because of its substantive importance. Economic and political modernization characterized the century in Europe and some other parts of the world. With the emergence of mass society, political leaders could and did mobilize the working class around tariffs. Germany's Chancellor Leo von Caprivi, for example, tried to mobilize the many class fractions created by industrialization on behalf of a new trade policy based on treaties (Barkin 1970). This mobilization gave the issue unprecedented political salience in many countries, from Austria-Hungary to the United States. Trade treaties also grew in importance with the end of mercantilism and the rise of an industrial society based on regional and global divisions of labor.

Studying tariff policy thus provides a window into the century's political economy (for overviews, see Bordo et al. 1999; O'Rourke and Williamson 1999; Pollard 1997). As H. Dietzel (1903: 384) argued a century ago, "Tariff questions are questions of might. The several occupations and parties do not trouble themselves about general interests. Each takes its position in tariff controversies according to its special interest."

Helen Milner (1988: 3) elaborated a similar idea 85 years later:

> The formulation of a nation's trade policy involves a struggle among domestic groups, the national government, and foreign governments. The complex interactions of these groups provide insights into the relationship between domestic and international politics. Furthermore, this struggle brings to light connections between politics and economics. It shows how the existing distribution of power among actors influences their ability to obtain the economic policies they desire and thereby affects the distribution of wealth.

In short, the pattern of winners and losers here can tell us a lot about politics in general. A period such as 1815–1913, in which tariffs were unusually salient, can tell us more than most.

With the politicization of the tariff in the age of mass politics, trade treaties also became politically divisive in many countries. Both protectionists and free traders mobilized politically on the treaty question in France (Haight 1941; M. S. Smith 1980). In many German states, tariffs were a central locus of struggle among different visions of the state (Hahn 1982: Chapter 1). Caprivi's tariff treaties were controversial in Imperial Germany (Barkin 1970; Dietzel 1903; Schonhardt-Bailey 1998a,b, 2006; Weitowitz 1978). Commercial policy divided the Austrian and Hungarian halves of the Dual Monarchy after 1866 (von Bazant 1894; von Bülow 1902: Matis 1973: 41–45; May 1951; Pahre 2001a; Weitowitz 1978: 53–55; K. H. Werner 1949). Treaties to secure exports for southern agricultural produce helped mitigate criticism that a unified Italy sought only the interests of its more industrialized North (Coppa 1970). Tariffs provided a major cleavage in the party system of the United States after the Civil War (Goldstein 1993: Chapter 3; Lake 1988), and were a central political question in Canada (Dunlop 1946). Legislative maneuvers on the tariff led to parliamentary government in Sweden in 1885 (Lewin 1988: 33–52), and the resulting protectionism provided a rallying point for Norwegian nationalists leading to independence in 1905 (Hodne 1983). Though its policy hardly changed after 1846, debates over trade policy regularly reemerged in the United Kingdom (Howe 1997; Marsh 1999).

Not surprisingly, then, the period was also a Golden Age for those writing tariff history. Economics had reached a level of sophistication that allowed for a sensible analysis of tariff policy. Participants in English debates over the repeal of the Corn Laws understood how factor immobility, the business cycle, and systems of political representation gave people incentives to mobilize for or against free trade (see Schonhardt-Bailey 1997). Many eminent Italians, including Antonio Gramsci, Gaetano Mosca, Vilfredo Pareto, Gaetano Salvemini, and Palmiro Togliatti, gave the tariff a prominent place in their writings on political economy at century's end (see Coppa 1971 for an overview). Students of and participants in public policy also added notable studies of reciprocity treaties in the first half of the twentieth century (i.e., Beckett 1941; Culbertson 1937; Kreider 1943; Laughlin and Willis 1903; Setser 1937; Tasca 1938/67; USTC 1920). Many of these older works remain the best available monographs on, say, Romanian (Antonescu 1915) or Belgian (Mahaim 1892) trade treaties. Despite its age, much of this writing would find the logic of modern political economy familiar (cf. Edwards 1970).

Subsequent generations of scholars have let these traditions fade. Political scientists lost interest in tariff history after World War II, which saw negotiations within international institutions replace unilateral tariff legislation as the driving force behind trade policy. As a result, writing on nineteenth-century trade policy since the 1930s has been largely confined to historians of a single country (i.e., Coppa 1971; Howe 1997; Lindberg 1983; Marsh 1999; Patterson 1968; Ratcliffe 1978; Sykes 1979a; Weitowitz 1978; Y. M. Werner 1989).

These historians have taken two approaches to studying trade treaties, essentially mirroring the levels-of-analysis distinction in political science. One group examines trade treaties as a form of foreign policy. For example, Carl-Axel Gemzell's project on "Sweden and the Great Powers, 1905–1945" ("Stormakterna och Sverige 1905–1945") at the Lund Historical Institute (Historiska Institutionen i Lund) has supported several dissertations and monographs examining Swedish trade treaties (published examples include Lindberg 1983; Y. M. Werner 1989). These studies view trade treaties as part of Swedish foreign policy more generally and as solutions to the problems facing a small state in a system dominated by great powers. Similarly, Barry Ratcliffe (1978) sees trade negotiations as part of the *Entente Cordiale* of the 1830s and thus part of foreign policy more generally. Asaana Iliasu's (1971) widely cited study of Cobden-Chevalier presents a similar analysis, tracing France's policy to its security interests in Italy. Judith Blow Williams's (1972: 142) study of British trade treaties from 1750 to 1850 also emphasizes the ties of foreign economic policy to diplomacy more generally:

The type of diplomacy depended upon circumstances, such as the general political situation, international or local, the degree of civilization of a land, its stage in economic development, its wants and resources, and the temper of its people. British policies were also influential factors; policies such as Britain's protection of its own colonial market through the Acts of Trade, its protection of agriculture through the Corn Laws, and of shipping through the Navigation Acts.

Finally, a long tradition of German historiography examines German nationalism, Prussian foreign policy objectives, national economic development, and the *Zollverein*. For example, Friedrich List (1844/1996) saw the *Zollverein* as a way to counter British industry, whereas Heinrich von Treitschke (1879–1894) saw Prussian leadership as the expression of German nationalism. These contending perspectives continue to shape historiographical debates (Dumke 1978; Hahn 1982: introduction).

A second group of historians have viewed trade treaties as part of tariff policy, and thus essentially a domestic political problem. Dunham (1930) examines the Cobden-Chevalier treaty, in the context of French economic development, as part of a package of internal and external reforms. Michael Stephen Smith (1980) and Peter Marsh (1999) see French and English trade treaties as part of domestic political battles over the tariff. In his classic *Bread and Democracy in Germany*, Alexander Gerschenkron (1943/1989) shows how political coalitions between agriculture and industry against labor lay behind the tariff in Germany. Even the small states saw important domestic struggles triumph over power politics. Hans-Werner Hahn (1982) argues that the *Zollverein* reflected the particularist economic interests of its member states in Hesse rather than being a simple manifestation of Prussian leadership toward inevitable German unification.[8]

For many countries, the historiography links trade policy to the process of state building. One of the eighteenth century's administrative battles was the creation of a single tariff unit coinciding with the boundaries of the nation-state, replacing many internal tariff boundaries (Hahn 1982: Chapter 1). This process remained incomplete, with *de jure* unification of the Austrian Empire coming only in 1850 and lasting only to 1866 (see Chapter 9).

Modern states used the development of an external tariff as part of the state-building process. They used protection to integrate previously excluded groups into the political system, a claim labeled here the "integrative thesis." For example, Vilfredo Pareto argued that Giolitti's "demagogic plutocracy" used the tariff to buy the support of organized northern workers and industrialists, a thesis that many Italian historians continue to support (see Coppa 1971: Chapter 1). Michael Stephen Smith (1980) argues that the bourgeoisie used the tariff to buy peasant support and to consolidate the Third Republic against opposition from both the Left and Right. According to Rolf Weitowitz (1978), Leo von Caprivi sought to integrate excluded workers and Catholics into the post-Bismarck Reich through a policy of commercial treaties. The political coalitions around trade treaty making were an early example of the corporatism that characterizes Sweden's political economy today (Lindberg 1983). Chapter 3 argues that this integrative thesis resonates in many ways with the theory of political support, giving the theory additional plausibility in this period.

For other countries, tariffs were often a tool to promote industrial development. This argument is most familiar from Alexander Hamilton in the United States and Friedrich List in Germany (Irwin 1996). It can also be found in Romania (Antonescu 1915) and in much of the Latin American literature (i.e., Bulwer-Thomas 1994; Cariola and Sunkel 1985; Leff 1982; McGreevey 1985; Ocampo 1981).

---

[8] Compare Alan Milward's (1984, 1992) revisionist accounts of regional cooperation in post-1945 Europe, which insist on European economic self-interest over American foreign policy leadership.

Tariffs also played an important role in consolidating the capitalist state into *organisierter Kapitalismus* ("organized capitalism"), which continues as the democratic corporatism that we see today (Milbourn 1992; Offe and Wiesenthal 1980; Rosenberg 1978; Wehler 1974; Winkler 1974). For whatever reason, German historiography has tended to follow Rudolf Hilferding in emphasizing the role of financial capital and not trade policy. However, trade cooperation was important to the close relationship between industry and the state in Sweden, argues Yvonne Maria Werner (1989: 8):

Contacts between the state bureaucracy and industrial life intensified, strengthening the state's influence over industry at the same time that industry obtained a greater ability to affect the decisions of the state authorities in economic matters. Interest groups played an important role in this connection as industry developed. Protectionism also helped strengthen popular representation because tariff changes and trade treaties required popular sanction to take effect.[9]

The same could be said of Italy, Austria-Hungary, France, and many smaller states.

For all their insight into particular countries, these tariff histories suffer from several distinct weaknesses. First, this literature tends not to distinguish among different kinds of tariff variation, such as variation from one good to another, from one country to another, or from one period to another (see Chapter 3). This oversight affects the historians' interpretation of trade policy because the apparent causes of tariff levels depend importantly on what kind of tariff variation a scholar investigates. Looking at variation between steel and textile tariffs points toward differences in each industry's domestic political strength, for example, while looking at variation by a good's country of origin points to general foreign policy issues. Thus, it is surprising that most studies of discriminatory trading areas such as the *Zollverein* stress foreign policy issues, while those interested in Bismarck's marriage of iron and rye stress sectoral politics. Each of these claims is "correct," but the nature of the research design limits our ability to generalize from them (see Chapter 2).

A second general limitation of the tariff historiography is that almost none of this literature compares one country to another. Very few works provide surveys of more than one country at a time (one classic exception, dated but still useful, is Ashley [1926]; Marsh [1999] is a more modern partial

---

[9] "Kontakterna mellan den statliga byråkratien och näringslivet intensifierades, vilket bidrog till att stärka statens inflytande över näringslivet samtidigt som detta erhöll ökade möjligheter att påverka de statliga myndigheternas beslut i ekonomiska angelägenheter. En betydande roll i detta sammanhang spelade de intresseorganisationer som bildats inom näringslivet. Protektionismen bidrog även till att stärka folkrepresentationes ställning, ty tullförändringar och handelsfördrag krävde dess sanktion för att träda i kraft."

exception). Most obviously, this focus tends to exclude cross-national differences in political institutions as an explanation of trade policy. However, intertemporal variation in a single country's trade policy receives significant attention in these studies and is often well explained by them.

Third, historians' single-country studies generally neglect the systematic ways in which one country's choices affect the choices of others. Without examining the incentives of other states, most scholars follow the contemporary conventional wisdom that the French trade treaties of the 1860s inaugurated a period of free trade that was reversed in the 1880s or 1890s (von Bazant 1894; Fay 1927; Rogowski 1989; Schmoller 1900; M. S. Smith 1980; Snyder 1940; Stein 1984; Verdier 1994; Viner 1924).[10] Only those studying Sweden and Finland seem to have examined exactly how the great powers shaped the incentives for smaller states (Alapuro 1988; Lindberg 1983; Y. M. Werner 1989), though one study of Italy also displays some sensitivity to the issue (Coppa 1970, 1971). While Scandinavia was peripheral to the system, Belgium and Switzerland played an important role in the network and have been largely overlooked (but see Marsh 1999: Chapters 3 and 8). I argue in Chapters 8, 11, and 12 that this international context has strong and systematic effects on trade policy and therefore should not be ignored.

By neglecting the international context, these studies also miss some ways in which the politics of trade treaties differs from the politics behind an autonomous tariff. For example, Michael Stephen Smith's (1980) landmark study of interest group politics and the French tariff handles the political battles over trade treaties in the same way as those over the 1881 or 1892 tariff bills.[11] This makes it puzzling that a large majority of French chambers of commerce in the 1870s supported trade treaties but also favored protectionism. In this approach, Smith represents a century-old tradition, for Émile Levasseur (1892: 29–31) also treats the politics behind France's general tariff of 1881 as analytically identical to the battle over the authority to negotiate trade treaties. Political struggles over German tariffs, whether autonomous or negotiated, also receive the same analytical treatment in German historiography (i.e., Dawson 1904; Gerschenkron 1943/1989; Hahn 1982; Lotz 1907; Weitowitz 1978). As I show, the political processes behind

---

[10] While following the conventional wisdom for the 1860s, Marsh (1999) rightly stresses the central role of Germany in the 1890s.

[11] Political scientists also neglect this distinction. For example, Cheryl Schonhardt-Bailey (1998b) finds that many industries and regions behave differently on a vote reducing tariffs than on a vote ratifying a trade treaty that reduces tariffs. Heavy industry in Düsseldorf and Aachen supported trade treaties but opposed lower autonomous duties, as did eastern regions such as Prussia and Posen.

these two differ, not least because treaties require negotiations with an outside party.

The bottom-up approach to trade policy and trade cooperation used in this book shows that we should expect the politics of trade cooperation to differ significantly from the politics of tariffs more narrowly defined (see also Gilligan 1997). Indeed, an important body of thought, "protectionist reciprocity," favored both protection and reciprocal liberalization (see Chapter 7).

These limitations of the historiography make the 25 years before World War I puzzling. Though characterized by imperialism and increasing protectionism, these years also saw the final wave of commercial treaties. These treaties dampened protectionist impulses and supported unprecedented levels of openness to the world in most countries. Tariff treaties responded to foreign protectionism, while it muted home protectionism. By reducing both home and foreign tariffs, these treaties encouraged unprecedented interdependence among nations. Part IV of this book, in particular, explains these apparent contradictions.

Again, these distinctions make an important difference for our understanding of the contemporary world. A surge of protectionism at home, as in the United States today, works differently within a world of treaty networks and institutions than in a less institutionalized world such as 1929. Many groups that will support package deals in trade would demand higher protection in an autonomous tariff. In this way, the WTO, like the nineteenth-century regime, keeps protectionist pressures from unmaking the trading system. Important as developments in a single country can be, they also occur within a wider international context that we must take into account.

A Formal Theory of Trade Policy and Cooperation

To examine this interaction between national and international political economy, much of this book uses a deductive model of trade policy. The basic model of trade policy is simple and general. These features make it easy to extend the model to the problem of several countries that may choose to cooperate with each other to lower tariff.

The major advantage of deductive theorizing is its logical consistency. When done correctly, the conclusions of a formal theory must follow logically from its premises, making it easier for others to replicate or criticize the logic of an argument. Deductive theorizing also provides a unified framework for theory building that is flexible enough to handle a variety of real-world events (Pahre and Papayouanou 1997).

Table 1.1. *Types of propositions in this book*

	Origin	Falsifiability	Falsifications challenge
Hypothesis	Deduced from model	High	Model or its operationalization
Corollary	Informal extension of hypothesis	High	Hypothesis or informal reasoning
Finding	Induced from evidence	None within same dataset	Not applicable
Result	Synthesis of hypothesis and finding	High	Underlying hypothesis, not finding

Formal theories can sometimes lead to conclusions that are contrary to intuition; it is hard to see how verbal reasoning can surprise its author in quite this way. The unexpected plays an important role in falsification, because scholars never really expect their own claims to be false. Finding an unexpected prediction in your model really forces you to take the evidence seriously – as a challenge to the model if the prediction is not supported, as a striking confirmation if the prediction pans out. Formal theory's relationship with falsification is key for some formalists, such as Bruce Bueno de Mesquita and David Lalman (1992: 20): "We model because we believe that how we look at the facts must be shaped by the logic of our generalizations. We are deeply committed to the notion that the evidence cannot be both the source of hypotheses and the means of their falsification or corroboration." Inductive theories, in which the data provide the source of hypotheses as well as their corroboration, are fatally flawed according to this view. Deduction too has its limitations, so most scholars combine induction and deduction in their research, as I do here.

Like anything else, formal models also have disadvantages. One salient disadvantage is incompleteness, in that no model based on a few assumptions can capture all the issues found in a particular substantive problem, such as trade cooperation. To understand this cooperation, then, I often go outside the model. These extensions of the model are often quite loose or speculative, which risks losing deduction's advantages in logical coherence.

To keep the advantages of deduction, however, I wish to be clear about when I am working inside or outside the formal model. To do this, I distinguish among "hypotheses," "corollaries," "findings," and "results." These terms are sometimes used interchangeably in various traditions of research, and my appropriation of more precise meanings here is entirely idiosyncratic (see summary in Table 1.1). The point of these distinctions is to aid in evaluating falsifications and their implications for the underlying core of the theory. The tightest deductions place the entire theory at risk, whereas the more speculative claims constitute a research agenda that may or may not pan out (compare the "hard" and "soft" research programs in Lakatos 1970).

I use the term *finding* to characterize an empirical generalization based on some evidence, lying outside the model. Findings need not relate two concepts, for a summary statistic, such as a mean or a standard deviation, would count as a finding. These findings can be purely atheoretical, though clearly a theory would like to incorporate as many findings as possible. Interestingly, many of the findings that I present contradict the conventional wisdom on various points, largely because this book focuses on all countries over a century and not on a shorter time period or set of countries. Because these findings are purely inductive generalizations taken from a population of cases, they cannot be "falsified" against that population any more than a summary statistic such as a mean could be falsified. However, a finding about one set of data could be shown not to fit a different set of data or not to hold for a larger and more inclusive dataset.

A *hypothesis* is a falsifiable statement about reality derived from the formal model, relating two or more concepts to one another. Because they are deductive claims, they are eminently falsifiable. *Corollaries*, which are looser extensions of hypotheses, are also falsifiable though it is easier to blame loose reasoning for any falsifications that result. I make extensive use of such loosely derived claims to explore how far the theory can be pushed, in the belief that, when two or more theories both explain the same evidence, we should prefer the theory with the most connections to other hypotheses explaining other facts. Testing these hypotheses and their corollaries presents the central evidence for the usefulness of the model.

At times I also synthesize a finding and a hypotheses to generate a *result*. For example, a hypothesis might make a prediction about countries that share some characteristic, whereas a finding tells us which countries have that characteristic. Putting these together yields a result that predicts how the behavior of those states will differ from others. For example, Chapter 4 shows inductively that the United States (to 1865) and Canada (to 1867), like some other countries, had taxation systems with an "exogenous" revenue constraint, and Chapter 8 shows deductively that such countries are less likely to cooperate with one another. The resulting synthetic claim that the United States and Canada are less likely to cooperate because of revenue constraints is falsifiable, but its validity rests on the quality of both the inductive finding and the deductive hypothesis.

As this discussion suggests, empirical questions are central to this book despite its deductive scaffolding.[12] This has consequences throughout the book. For example, my presentation of the model differs somewhat from the norm among formal theorists. After each hypothesis, I give one or more historical illustrations of its logic at work. These illustrations come, in principle, from all over the world, but readers will note that my illustrations have regional biases of various kinds. Although these anecdotes cannot provide a test of the hypotheses, they do show that the theory is plausible in at least some cases. They also make the abstract nature of formal hypotheses concrete.

Unfortunately, providing such illustrations does not help a scholar avoid formalizing the obvious, which is another major failing of contemporary mathematical theory. Scholars of a deductivist bent should ask whether we can help address any historiographical problems perceived by more inductivist historians. Looking at the historiography also provides a challenge to formal theory's usefulness that most formal theorists seem unwilling to face (cf. Hall 1995). This concern provides one motivation for my attention to the historiography in this introduction and for my proposal of a revisionist narrative of nineteenth-century trade cooperation. On more detailed points, each chapter points out whether the illustrations are consistent with, or contradictory to, the historiographies. A useful formal model should be consistent in part with the historiography, but also depart from it enough to make its own contribution. The reader can then judge the relative merits of the two explanations.

Research fails when it restates what is already known or so totally rejects earlier work that it is inherently implausible. Historically grounded formal theory seeks to avoid these twin dangers by working closely with inductive historiography. History should also help motivate our theories and shape the substantive problems that we address. Questions of political integration, reciprocity, national unification, coercive treaties, and the German *Zollverein* (customs union) served as more than data points for this book and in some cases helped organize it – notably in Chapter 11. These issues are brought together again in the historical summary in Chapter 13, where the reader can decide how well the theory succeeds. In principle, formal theory should play a role in political history no different from the role of economic theory

---

[12] It is ironic that formal theory has grown in political science just as deterministic and positivist epistemologies are under attack in the natural sciences (Fuller 1988; Knorr-Cetina and Mulkay 1983 *inter alia*). No rival philosophy of science presents a clearly superior alternative, however. I take a pragmatic position in such debates (see Pahre 1995b, 1996).

and econometrics in economic history – sometimes useful, sometimes not, but always a part of the field's toolkit.

The Analytical Plan of the Book

To explain why states sign trade treaties, we must first understand what happens when they do not cooperate. This points me toward domestic politics as an explanation of trade policy in Part II. This part begins with a methodological excursus in Chapter 2 that discusses the various ways that one might think about trade policy, how it varies over time and space, and how one might best measure a concept such as "protection." Drawing from the economic literature on endogenous tariff theory, Chapter 3 presents the theory of political support that underpins the book as a whole. It derives several hypotheses about how economic conditions affect trade policy. Some of these hypotheses are novel, and others are familiar; for example, the model derives the familiar result that declining import prices (improving terms of trade) leads to higher tariffs. The core logic of the theory of political support here differs somewhat from others, however, resting on the process by which politicians compensate economic losers by giving them favorable economic policies. This logic of compensation characterized much of the political discourse in the nineteenth century and can also be found today in the WTO.

Building on this economic foundation, I then turn to political factors that affect trade policy. In Chapters 4 and 5, I examine how state capacity in the form of revenue collection needs and domestic political institutions affects trade policy. These chapters respond to different literatures while providing indirect evidence for the theory of political support. Many historians, and some political scientists, argue that the state's need for revenue often precludes tariff liberalization, which would reduce the tax revenue collected from the tariff. If true, this would significantly limit the validity of the theory of political support. I find that revenue considerations of this sort, which I label "exogenous" revenue concerns, play an important role in only a relatively few countries. Most countries make an "endogenous" political choice to rely on tariffs instead of other sources of revenue, and this choice reflects the kind of distributional concerns that lie at the heart of the theory of political support. Some countries change from one to the other over time. The United States, for example, added new revenue instruments during the Civil War of 1861–1865, moving from an exogenous constraint that limited trade cooperation to an endogenous, politically dominated tariff.

The analysis of democracy and trade in Chapter 5 responds to a growing literature in political science claiming that democracies have lower tariffs and cooperate more than do nondemocracies (i.e., Mansfield et al. 2000, 2002a; Morrow, Siverson, and Tabares 1998, 1999; Mueller 1999; Rosendorff 2006; and indirectly, Hobson 1997). Though this literature has found strong evidence in its support in the post-1945 system, I show that democracy may be associated with either liberalization or protection in the nineteenth century. Because the theory of political support can encompass this variation, while this other literature cannot, I find that the theory of political support provides a better foundation for studying trade policy.

Both Chapter 4 (revenue concerns) and Chapter 5 (democracy) give explicit attention to explaining both cross-national and intertemporal variation in trade policy. Intriguingly, both chapters find that differences in these institutions across countries have a stronger effect on the tariff than do changes in a single country over time. This finding presumably reflects the fact that institutional changes, although important, occur only intermittently in a single country. In light of this finding, I suggest that comparative case studies of political economy can identify causal variation more effectively than the more common historical institutionalist studies of a single country.

The intermittent nature of institutional change also provides indirect justification for the theory of political support. The quest for domestic political support dominates policymaking between institutional changes. When seeking support, political leaders change their trade policy in response to external market conditions, so that tariffs vary with the business cycle and other economic variables examined in Chapter 3. Taken as a whole, then, Part II specifies the relationships between economic and political conditions and autonomous tariff policy, developing the theory of political support and examining its range of application.

After these single-country studies of trade policy, Part III investigates the conditions under which two states will cooperate with each other. Again, this requires one chapter giving attention to conceptual, definitional, and measurement issues. Chapter 6 also presents the Trade Agreements Database used as evidence throughout the book.

Chapter 7 turns to a theoretical analysis of cooperation within the theory of political support. It begins by showing that cooperation is rational; that is, that politicians will negotiate downward a tariff originally set higher by these same politicians. Political rhetoric in the nineteenth century, especially the ideology that I label "protectionist reciprocity," reflected a logic similar to that in the model. Chapter 8 then examines how the political and economic factors that determine the autonomous tariff also affect trade cooperation; countries with low tariffs are more likely to cooperate than countries with high tariffs, despite the greater potential gains for the high-tariff countries. In addition, the level of the tariff itself affects cooperation. Finally, one nation's policy will also change in response to other countries' policies, so that free trade abroad breeds protectionism at home, and vice versa. However, these changes can be muted by embedding trade policy in a network of trade cooperation.

The analysis so far treats each country as a unitary actor. Clearly, this can be unreasonable for many purposes. Domestic actors play various roles in trade policy. For example, some domestic actors – especially legislatures – may reject a treaty outright, an issue highlighted in the literature on two-level games. Though such rejection seems to pose a serious threat to cooperation, Chapter 9 shows that legislative obstacles matter for relatively few countries. In addition to ratification, legislatures play another role in determining the status quo, and this power affects cooperation indirectly. This chapter thus provides a foundation for extending the theory of political support toward the interaction between the legislature and executive in making trade policy, thereby building on existing theories, especially the literature on two-level games (Evans et al. 1993; Pahre 2006; Putnam 1988).

Not only the relations between states but third parties' relations with one another also affect cooperation. The very organization of the international system will shape these relations as well. To understand this impact, Part IV explores how international norms affect variation in trade cooperation. Like the others, this part begins with conceptual discussion, examining the notion of a "regime" and "norm" as well as the concrete example of the MFN norm (Chapter 10). I also argue that the MFN norm reflects political considerations, often related to foreign policy more generally.

Chapter 11 shows how variation in MFN affects variation in trade cooperation. First, the MFN regime affects whether states sign trade treaties. In contrast to the conventional wisdom, I argue that a trade regime spreads to new participants when states do *not* include MFN clauses in their trade treaties. In this way, the very existence of a trade treaty between two countries influences third parties' decisions on whether to cooperate.

The MFN clause also affects the timing of trade negotiations. Chapter 12 shows that states have an incentive to "cluster" their negotiations, signing many treaties in a short period of time, when they include MFN clauses in their treaties. Clustering also affects the distribution of benefits in agreements, in that clustering states gain distributional advantages over those states that do not. In this way, MFN leads indirectly to heightened distributional conflicts through clustering. These distributional conflicts became so severe from the 1890s that many historians have overlooked the real cooperation underlying these disputes.

Part IV also explores how the trade policies of many countries are inter-related. Although I emphasize European trade policies, they also shaped the policies of other countries. In particular, Latin American trade policies usu-ally depended on the evolution of the European political economy. However, Latin America was ahead of Europe in one critical respect: Latin American treaties almost always included an unconditional MFN clause, which did not become commonplace in Europe until 50 years later. Comparing Europe and Latin America therefore provides additional interregional and intertempo-ral variation in cooperation.

Finally, Part V reviews the argument and contribution of the book. The conclusion in Chapter 13 also steps back from the theory to summarize the book's interpretation of the nineteenth-century trade regime, which I discuss in the next section. Within this general theoretical and historical project, I develop more than four dozen specific propositions. The specificity of these hypotheses does not make for easy entry into the debates between "perspec-tives" in international relations, which often hinge on differences between two or three incompatible general claims. Because my hypotheses do not lend themselves to easy summary, they are listed in Chapter 13 instead of here (see Tables 13.1–13.3 and Figure 13.1). However, the central hypoth-esis is easily stated: countries with low tariffs are more likely to cooperate than countries with high tariffs, even though the gains from cooperation are greater for high-tariff countries. Explaining *why* some countries have low tariffs, while others do not, accounts for much of Part II. Both economic and political conditions determine the autonomous tariff, as do the actions of other countries. Cooperation is also directly affected by changing economic and political conditions, with democracy, higher import prices, and other variables making cooperation easier. Moreover, some variables – notably democracy – have different effects on tariffs than on cooperation.

A Preview of the Historical Account

Though the book follows the analytical organization described in the preced-ing section, it also represents a revisionist narrative of trade cooperation in 1815–1913. By looking systematically at all countries over the entire period, the data led me to focus on overlooked periods, such as the wave that began in the 1820s, and to highlight countries that have been overlooked by polit-ical scientists who have studied France or the United Kingdom. Central to this reinterpretation is a move eastward and toward the central economies of Austria-Hungary and Germany. Prussian leadership of the *Zollverein* and Austria-Hungary's eventual participation in the resulting German trade network both played a critical role in the growth of the nineteenth-century trade treaty system.

This book shows that a variety of political factors, including a state's fiscal institutions and level of democracy, cause tariff levels to vary. These factors should be at their most important when trade cooperation is infrequent, because treaties can keep tariff levels from varying. Thus, in roughly the first third of our century – from 1815 to 1848, say – revenue constraints, administrative obstacles, political institutions, and changes in world prices made tariffs relatively volatile in response to exogenous events. Countries also responded to one another's tariff changes, adding a level of complexity that is difficult to analyze.

As it turns out, a relaxation of the revenue constraint proved to be most important for the history of the trade regime. In the 1820s, Prussia depended on tariff revenue for 15 to 20% of its administrative expenditures; other German states were more dependent, such as Bavaria (25%) and Württemberg (43%). None could be called a democracy, but the need to collect revenue more effectively led Prussia to create a network of trade treaties. It began by dealing with its enclave states and territories.

Though cooperation remained low in the first third of the period, it came to dominate the middle part of the century, from 1848 into the 1870s. Cooperation began with those countries that already had relatively low tariffs, notably northern Germany, the low countries, Britain, Denmark, and then France. Various domestic political changes also encouraged cooperation in this period, including a peculiar change in Second Empire tariff-making rules, the executive-centered structure of the *Zollverein*, and, eventually, the 1867 *Ausgleich* in Austria-Hungary. The development of new revenue instruments in this period, often as a result of constitutional reform or war, also facilitated future cooperation for many countries.

The international price movements that made these decades favorable for European cooperation also made them less favorable for the Americas. However, it seems that Europe's political and economic power was able to counteract some of these factors, such that the international market variables that explain variation in European cooperation well tend not to explain cooperation in the Americas so well.

In the third period, the system-wide organization of the treaty network began to take on a life of its own, structured by the MFN norm. The unification of Germany and Italy provides a symbolic transition to the period lasting from the 1870s until World War I, as these unifications effectively raised the trade barriers that outsiders faced in these countries. Formal trade treaties also created barriers against outsiders, though the spread of the MFN norm ameliorated this discrimination if the treaties covered goods relevant to outsiders. Outsiders such as Russia began to enter the network until it became nearly universal.

The major significance of this late-century network seems to be its ability to constrain protectionism more than its ability to encourage liberalization. Treaties prevented exogenous economic and political changes from affecting the tariffs – to a point. That point was never quite reached in this century, even in the Great Depression of 1873–1896. However, the Great Depression of 1929–1939 clearly did reach that point, and countries denounced their treaties in the first half of that decade.

Conclusions and Implications

The backlash against globalization today, high unemployment and low growth in continental Europe, and the economic difficulties of Japan's "lost decade" all seem much more similar to the nineteenth century than to 1929. In today's environment, the WTO, like the more informal nineteenth-century system, keeps countries from turning to protectionism in response to economic hard times. Institutional innovations such as the dispute resolution mechanism do a better job providing an escape valve for protectionist demands. The WTO shares with the nineteenth-century regime widespread use of the MFN regime, which makes tariff concessions smaller and more difficult to reach, a feature that was most recently in evidence in the failure of the Doha Development Round to agree on new liberalizations. Within limits, regionalism may address these limitations, and interaction between regional blocs may provide a motor for global cooperation. The history of the German *Zollverein* again provides room for optimism.

Despite the challenges to the WTO, past concessions remain in force, and that may be the more valuable contribution of the WTO regime. If so, this contribution to stability is only visible against the counterfactual backdrop of how domestic politics affects trade policy in the absence of the regime.

This book also provides a reassessment of the relationship between democracy and freer trade. A growing community of neo-Kantians and neo-Cobdenites argues that democracy is associated with both international peace and international trade, and that peace and trade reinforce each other as well as democracy. Unlike paleo-Kantians and paleo-Cobdenites, these scholars can point to a sizable body of evidence on conflict since 1945 and on trade data since the 1940s or a little before. By going back further in time, my findings suggest a more nuanced view of democracy's effects on trade. Democracy does make international economic cooperation easier, but it has more ambiguous effects on noncooperative outcomes. Protectionists may thrive in a democracy, and expanding the suffrage to import-competing producers can strengthen protectionists. It is not coincidental that France's Third Republic (1871–1944) saw a surge of protectionism, though this was mitigated by trade treaties. The United States too was well known for both democracy and protectionism from the Jacksonian era on.

International economic cooperation is all the more important for globalization in an age of protectionist backlash because it constrains what local protectionists can do against global welfare. The semi-democratic world of 1890–1914 sustained a global economy through trade treaties that served as a bulwark against protectionists in countries of all political types. This has clear implications for today's world, which includes many fragile democracies characterized by contentious debates over globalization and participation in the WTO.

This history of the nineteenth-century trade regime suggests a more optimistic view of today's trading system than we would expect from such events as the Seattle riots, collapse of the Doha Development Round, or other forms of backlash against globalization. Stable international cooperation can rest on the seemingly unstable foundation of domestic politics, both in theory and in the historical practice of 1815–1914. Global war, and not domestic backlash against globalization, brought this period to its end.

PART TWO

DOMESTIC POLITICS AND TRADE POLICY

TWO

Conceptualizing and Measuring Trade Policy

States cooperate in order to achieve certain goals better than they could without cooperation. Because the problems of noncooperation make cooperation a more attractive option, my study begins with the main features of an autonomous trade policy. I review four major dimensions along which trade policy may vary. Each dimension has received substantial attention in the existing literature, and each is interesting for some purposes. I am interested mostly in cross-national variation because cooperation involves two or more countries that may differ from one another. This stands in contrast to earlier work emphasizing variation in a single nation's tariffs from one good to another.

These first sections shows how various theories explain particular types of variation, clarifying which parts of it relate to the problem of variation in trade cooperation. Existing theories, especially in endogenous tariff theory (ETT), have provided an impressive explanation of variation in tariffs along *some* dimensions. For example, differences in industrial concentration or labor intensity explain variation in tariffs from one sector to the next. However, these variables do not explain international cooperation because they do not address *cross-national* variation in tariffs. However, clarifying the problem of variation in trade cooperation depends on explaining cross-national variation. The identities of countries, each with particular combinations of economic and political attributes ("grain-importing democracy"), shape cooperation.

The second half of this chapter builds on this analytical clarification by explicating different ways in which we can observe and measure trade policy. Because international cooperation depends on trade policy, this study requires a country-level measure that can capture cross-national variation in trade policy. Given the data available, openness (imports as a share of GDP) and the average tariff (tariff revenue divided by import volume) provide the best measures of trade policy, though each has limitations. I use both throughout this book, rejecting other possible measures for reasons of both theory and data limitations.

These two exercises, theoretical and empirical, set the stage for the remaining chapters of Part II. The goal is to understand what states do *before* they decide to cooperate. This status quo provides incentives or disincentives for cooperation. It also represents the reversion point if cooperation breaks down and thus the outcome that cooperating states wish to avoid. Part III shows that low-tariff countries are more likely to cooperate than high-tariff countries, but this begs the question of which countries fall into each category. The politics of the autonomous tariff must therefore be part of our explanation of cooperation.

Variation in Trade Policy and Cooperation

Chapter 1 argued that existing theories of cooperation have not emphasized variation, with many theories focusing instead on existence claims. In contrast, domestic-level theories of trade policy have given significant attention to variation in trade policy, but sometimes talk past each other. To make clear what this book does and does not address, this section reviews four kinds of variation in any single country's tariffs: variation by good, variation by a good's country of origin, variation by conditionality, and variation over time. In addition, tariffs vary cross-nationally; that is, from one country to the next.[1] This last category is the most important one here.

These same dimensions characterize international trade cooperation. Two states might cooperate on one good but not another, might cooperate with many states but not others, and might cease cooperating after having previously cooperated. States also vary in whether they are willing to cooperate at all; that is, whether their trade policies are autonomous (unilateral) or conditional. Each kind of variation suggests certain kinds of explanations, each with its own strengths and weaknesses.

Variation by Good

A glance at any country's tariff code reveals mind-boggling variation by good. Most countries impose different duties on wheat and iron, automobiles, and glassware. Indeed, countries vary the tariffs even on very similar products,

---

[1] I exclude a fifth form of variation in economic policy, variation across issue areas (see Keohane 1984; Milner 1997a) because I am looking only at trade cooperation. I also ignore the important question of why states use tariffs and not other policy instruments (see *inter alia* Mayer and Riezman 1987; Vousden 1990).

such as pickled herring in jars or barrels or different weights of architectural drafting paper (both found in the U.S. tariffs).

Most political scientists consider tariff variation by good within a general theory of trade policy. Krasner (1977) argues that American support for multinational corporations (MNCs) makes trade policy vary by good, as petroleum and tropical fruits have very different consequences for state power (see also A. Smith 1776: Book II, Chapter 2). Similarly, Marxists maintain that advanced capitalist states will differentiate their tariff by the level of processing, thereby forcing less developed countries into dependence on raw materials exports (Gallagher and Robinson 1953; I. Wallerstein 1974a, 1979, 1989).

Economists have made variation by good central to their analysis. ETT normally attributes variation by good to industry lobbying for protection (see Marks and McArthur 1990, 1993; Nelson 1988 for review). Following Mancur Olson's *Logic of Collective Action* (1965; see also Olson 1982), industries with few firms, or whose total sales are concentrated in a few firms, organize more easily and therefore obtain higher tariffs.[2] Lobbying for free trade, too, will be more successful if it rests on a geographically concentrated free trade lobby, such as the Manchester cotton industry in nineteenth-century Britain (Caves 1976; Gilligan 1997; Hansen 1990; Schonhardt-Bailey 1991b).

Building on these premises, research in ETT has developed an impressive list of hypotheses. Economic variables, such as average wages, capital intensity, elasticity of demand, industry growth rates, industry size, inequality of asset distribution, labor intensiveness, labor skill, market competitiveness, multinationalization, the number of capitalists, portfolio diversification, unionization, and value added per worker, affect each industry's success in obtaining protection (see *inter alia* Baldwin 1985; Basevi 1966; Brainerd and Verdier 1997; Caves 1976; Cheh 1974, 1976; Eicher and Osang 2002; Finger and Laird 1987; Goldberg and Maggi 1999; Grossman and Helpman 1994, 2002; Helleiner 1973, 1977; Hillman 1982; Laird and Yeats 1990; S. Magee 1971; Magee, Brock, and Young 1989; Marvel and Ray 1983, 1987; McKeown 1984, 1989, 1991; Mitra 1999; Nye 1991; Olarreaga and Soloaga

---

[2] Empirical studies have had difficulty confirming these hypotheses on concentration (for disconfirmations, see Anderson 1980; Baldwin 1985: 152–58; Cahan and Kaempfer 1992; Caves 1976; Godek 1985; Marvel and Ray 1983; McPherson 1972; Pincus 1975; Ray 1981a; Stigler 1971, 1974; but Olarreaga and Soloaga 1998). This probably reflects a misreading of contemporary models of public goods provision (Bergstrom, Blume, and Varian 1986; Cornes and Sandler 1986; Pahre 1999: Chapter 2; Warr 1983). Studies of industries' geographic concentration (i.e., Busch and Reinhardt 2000a; Mitra 1999; Pincus 1975; Schonhardt-Bailey 1991b) have had more empirical success, presumably because political institutions are organized geographically.

1998; Pincus 1975, 1977; Ray 1981a,b, 1987; Ray and Marvel 1984; Schattschneider 1935; Schonhardt-Bailey 1991a; Travis 1964; Vaccara 1960; Vousden 1990; M. Wallerstein 1987; Wellisz and Wilson 1986). These variables generally have good empirical support and must be considered by any study of trade policy variation by good.

Some studies have examined how these kinds of economic variables interact with more explicitly political concerns. For example, Gstöhl (2002) studied how variation in the decisions of several European countries to cooperate with projects of economic integration depended on balancing economic gains against the cost in political autonomy and other values. Gowa and Mansfield (1993, 2004) argue that economic variables such as scale economies may interact with military and security goals to account for variations in cooperation across goods. Hobson (1997) relates differences in states' fiscal systems to sectoral differences to account for variations between free trade and protection.

Offsetting pressure from consumers and upstream producers may also mute protectionist demands. However, Grossman and Helpman's (1994, 2002) "protection for sale" model of tariffs suggests that only the fact of organization, and not most measures of effort, should affect variation in tariffs from one good to the next (see Eicher and Osang 2002; Goldberg and Maggi 1999 for evaluations). Commodities higher in the processing chain receive higher levels of protection because opposition from diffuse consumers is muted (Finger and Laird 1987; Laird and Yeats 1990; Stern 1973). By a similar logic, protectionism is most common in sectors lacking strong international ties (Destler and Odell 1987; Milner 1988). Offsetting consumer pressure means also that producer lobbying for economically inefficient tariffs depends in part on economic efficiency; efficient interventions are politically easier than less efficient indirect interventions (Becker 1983, 1985; Donnenfeld and Weber 1985; Mayer and Li 1994; Rodrik 1986).[3]

For all their successes, studies of tariff variation by good neglect one important feature of most tariffs – they are set as part of legislation covering many goods at the same time. This legislation and the individual tariff lines within it necessarily reflect political compromises. These compromises fall outside ETT because the theory has generally neglected both the political process and politicians' objectives (Marks and McArthur 1990; Nelson

---

[3] Others argue that obfuscation leads to inefficient but difficult-to-understand forms of intervention in markets (S. Magee 1997; S. Magee et al. 1989). To my knowledge, neither claim has been tested empirically.

1988). If political compromises such as legislative logrolls affect outcomes, then tariff lines will be positively correlated across legislative districts (and thus also across goods), regardless of the economic structure of firms within each district. This violates the assumption of independence underlying the probit models common in the empirical literature. It may make better sense to look at the interests of the political leadership that produce a logroll. Studies might also benefit by focusing on cross-national or intertemporal variation in logrolls.

Just as it neglects tariff logrolling, ETT tends to give little attention to trade cooperation. ETT models generally explain a legal tariff that is rarely applicable because most goods from most countries enter under a "conventional tariff," so called because it is established by commercial conventions and treaties. Like tariff bills, these agreements package many tariff lines in a single compromise, whose reductions over time will therefore be highly correlated with each other. Again, looking at the political leaders who negotiate these treaties makes sense.

ETT has addressed conventional tariffs in an empirical tradition that sees reciprocity agreements mostly as an opportunity for import-competing industries to avoid having their tariffs reduced (Allen, Lewis, and Tower 1980; Baldwin 1976; Bale 1977; Cheh 1974, 1976; D. Clark 1980; Marvel and Ray 1983; McGillivray 1997, 2004; Olarreaga and Soloaga 1998; Ray 1987; Ray and Marvel 1984; Stone 1978). These lobbying efforts explain *exceptions* to negotiated liberalization, such as the exclusion of textiles or sugar from GATT rounds (see also analysis of GATT/WTO *disputes* in Busch and Reinhardt 2000b, 2001 or domestic administrative protection in Finger, Hall, and Nelson 1982; Takacs 1981, 1985). Similarly, C. Magee (2003) examines the distribution of Trade Adjustment Assistance (TAA), which has become part of U.S. treaty ratification packages in recent decades. However, these analysts cannot explain the liberalization in the first place or, more importantly, variation between cooperation and noncooperation. Still, this literature examining variation by good provides essential insight into the details of tariff lines once a treaty has been agreed to.

If the typical domestic-level theory were to explore commercial agreements, it would have to argue that consumers and exporters in two countries simultaneously demanded a treaty. This story is at odds with the explanation given for non-negotiated tariffs, which suggests that concentrated producer interests are able to achieve protection at the cost of diffuse consumers. Where concentrated consumers exist, such as steel consumers in the automobile industry, it is hard to see why they would lobby unsuccessfully for low tariffs but successfully for the reciprocal lowering of steel barriers. However, this focus on concentrated producers does explain a different kind of cooperation, the negotiation of voluntary export restraints (VERs). VERs provide rent to both import-competing producers and to foreign exporters who can charge a higher price for their now-restricted good. As a result, two governments may, solely as a result of producer lobbying, agree to a VER (Jones 1984).

One body of work has tried to explain commercial treaties in terms of domestic politics (Grossman and Helpman 1994, 2002; Moser, Hillman, and Long 1995; Pahre 1998; cf. Johnson 1965). At the micro level, Michael Gilligan (1997; cf. Kiyono, Okuno-Fujiwara and Ueda 1991) shows how multi-issue reciprocity induces concentrated exporters to lobby for treaties but not for unilateral tariff reductions or single-issue negotiations on market access. This work tends to shift attention away from the demands of producers and toward the politicians who supply these agreements. Unfortunately, this work has given primary attention to explaining the *existence* of trade agreements and has not yet explained variations between cooperation and noncooperation.

Cross-National Variation
We can better account for variations in cooperation by changing the level of analysis away from tariff variation by good. Reciprocal trade agreements occur between nations, not between industries. Understanding the incentives for these agreements therefore requires greater attention to **cross-national variation** in trade policy. Countries vary both in their initial tariff levels and in their willingness to sign trade treaties. These differences stem from domestic political differences along several dimensions.

First, domestic political institutions differ from one country to the next. Some countries have strong political parties, some have strong interest groups, and others are led by an autocrat who suppresses both parties and interest groups. Other political institutions determine the rules defining which actors can participate in politics and who has the most influence over policy (for examples of such studies, see Gourevitch 1986; Kindleberger 1951; McGillivray 2004; McGillivray and Smith 1997; Rosendorff 2006; Verdier 1994).

Not only the political institutions but also the economic interests of political actors vary across nation because some groups advocate protectionism, while others favor free trade. Using Heckscher-Ohlin-Stolper-Samuelson theories of the international economy, Ronald Rogowski's *Commerce and Coalitions* (1989) argues that a country's factor endowment determines how groups line up on trade policy.[4] When free-trade coalitions dominate, international cooperation will presumably be more likely.

Third, countries also differ in economic conditions. Cross-national differences in levels of development, size of the domestic market, and economic growth rates also affect tariff variation across countries (Conybeare 1984; Ray 1974), as do changes in the terms of trade, foreign exchange rates, unemployment rates, and inflation (Grossman and Helpman 1994, 2002; S. Magee et al. 1990: Chapter 13). Bilateral economic relations may also vary, and two countries may have complementary or competitive economic structures (see Zeng 2004).

Finally, politics takes place in disparate ideological contexts from one country to the next. In a classic article, Charles Kindleberger (1975) argues that the strength of Liberal ideologies in each country affects the success of protectionist demands. Ideology may also interact with material interests and party politics, such that party members may even act against their material interests (Schonhardt-Bailey 1998b, 2006).

These kinds of studies provide a good foundation for explaining variation in cooperation. Differences in political institutions, the relative influence of various groups, or economic conditions could easily explain why, say, Belgium cooperates with Germany but Sweden does not.

Even so, these studies of cross-national variation share some limitations with ETT's investigation of tariff variation by good. They tend not to examine explicitly how individual tariff observations may not be independent of one another. For example, trade cooperation poses a greater challenge because it conditions tariff reductions in two or more countries on one another. One might also ask whether foreign tariffs make home tariffs more or less likely or whether one country's liberalization could induce other countries to respond in kind (Pahre 1998). These kinds of reactions create collinearity between national observations.

Variation by a Good's Country of Origin

Cooperation may have another effect, in that a state may treat goods differently depending on their source. This variation **by a good's country of origin** (or "variation by target") provides a third dimension along which trade policies vary (see Leamer 1990 for an overview). For example, during

---

[4] Other assumptions about the international economy lead to a different understanding of cross-national variation. Using Ricardo-Viner-Cairns-Jones models that emphasize variation in factor mobility, Cassing et al. (1986) argue that cross-national differences in factor mobility produce differences in tariffs (see also Hiscox 2001, 2002; Mussa 1974, 1982).

the Cold War the United States treated goods from Eastern Europe and the Soviet Union differently from identical goods from Western Europe (Long 1989, 1996; Mastanduno 1988). In the early nineteenth century, many countries distinguished goods arriving by land from those coming by sea. This feature of the Russian tariff eventually became an important issue in its relations with Germany, just as France's system of coastal zones harmed British coal exports relative to Belgium's. Belgium too treated sea coal differently from land coal, thereby discriminating against Britain in favor of France (Ratcliffe 1978: 137).

Even ostensibly nondiscriminatory trade policies might be intentionally discriminatory. For example, the 1881 Austro-Hungarian tariff imposed a flat fee of 1 florin, 50 kreutzer per pig. This encouraged the importation of fatter pigs, intentionally discriminating against Serbia's leaner woodland-fed pigs (Palairet 1997: 303–04). Similarly, Belgian duties on woollen goods in 1841 were levied by weight, intentionally favoring lighter French woollens over the heavier but cheaper British product (Williams 1972: 185).

Cooperation often creates such discrimination. Preferential trading areas (PTAs), such as the EU or NAFTA, treat goods from within the area differently from goods from outside it (Bhagwati 1990; Hamilton and Whalley 1985; Mansfield and Milner 1997, 1999; Oye 1993). The EU has a particularly complex system of PTAs covering different goods from different countries signed at different times with different transition periods (Sapir 2000). Indeed, cooperation itself varies by target because a state may cooperate with one country but not another. Again, this could in principle explain why Germany cooperates with Belgium but not with Sweden, although, as it turns out, the reasons are to be found inside Sweden and not in Germany (see especially Chapter 9).

Imperial trade provides a different kind of cooperation, and most countries routinely discriminated by target in colonial trade.[5] For example, the Netherlands imposed double duties against non-Dutch goods entering the East Indies. These imperial systems lie behind the Generalized System of Preferences in the WTO, by which rich countries may treat developing country goods more favorably.

Studies of tariff variation by target usually emphasize general foreign policy considerations. Adversarial relationships such as the Cold War, alliances,

---

[5] Discrimination in trade might be based on the nationality of the carrying ship or on a good's country of origin. Many countries had strict navigation laws at the start of this period, making this a distinction without a difference, but liberalization of these laws complicated the interpretation of earlier treaty engagements. For a good discussion of these problems in British India and the Dutch East Indies, see Williams (1972: 309–27).

and particular foreign policy interests such as those in the British Common-wealth typically explain such variations. Relative gains theory has built on this claim, arguing that cooperation is more difficult in security affairs than in economic affairs and that cooperation is more difficult among two secu-rity rivals than among two allies (Gowa 1994; Gowa and Mansfield 2004; Grieco 1988, 1990; Lipson 1984; Long 1989; Pollins 1989; Snidal 1991). In principle, then, this literature could explain the variations in trade cooper-ation that we observe, because France would cooperate more with its allies.

Attractive as it seems, however, relative gains theory appears to be empir-ically false (see Morrow et al. 1999). I have argued elsewhere that a con-cern for relative gains does not explain variations in cooperation, but it may explain variations in the depth of cooperation (Pahre 1999: chapter 7). Allies cooperate more deeply, on more issues, than nonallies – but are no more likely to cooperate and may be less likely. Moreover, as argued above, differences in the domestic politics in a country's partners can also explain variation in cooperation by target. Chapters 10–12 will argue that foreign policy considerations do shape regime norms such as MFN and thus structure cooperation indirectly.

Variation by Conditionality

Just as tariffs may discriminate across targets, foreign trade policies may **vary by conditionality**, in that they may be either conditional or unilateral. A unilateral or autonomous tariff imposes duties chosen by the legislature or executive regardless of what other countries do. A conditional trade policy either promises home liberalization for foreign liberalization (positive reci-procity) or threatens new home barriers if foreign policy does not change (negative reciprocity). For example, when the United States discriminates against Japanese exports by negotiating VERs or threatens retaliation under the "Super 301" clause of the Trade Act of 1988, it does so as a form of leverage to change Japanese economic policy.

Milner and Yoffie (1989) provide the best extant domestic-level explana-tion of conditionality, tracing it to variation in firms' preferences. Firms that benefit from learning-by-doing and scale economies cannot jump foreign tariff walls because new investment would sacrifice both scale economies and learning effects. As a result, they will want reductions in foreign tariffs to be achieved through conditionality, which still provides some protection against third parties. Although the argument apparently explains substantial variations in industry demands in the contemporary United States, history shows that industries may favor reciprocity for other reasons. For example, Italian textile producers supported modest reductions in their own tariffs as part of reciprocal treaties that gained better export markets for Italian agriculture. Though they would face greater foreign competition at home, Italian textile firms expected that the income effects of liberalization would boost domestic demand by enough to offset this loss (Coppa 1971). Because Italian peasants produced much of their own clothing, anything that shifted rural labor into agricultural production would also increase factory sales (M. Clark 1996). Neither learning effects nor scale economies explain these preferences.

Michael Gilligan (1997: 68–69) provides an interesting example that would also seem to contradict Milner and Yoffie's claims. The National Association of Manufacturers was organized in 1894 in part to pressure the U.S. government to use reciprocity to expand exports. Its members were mostly small- to medium-sized producers who were competitive overseas and wished to tap into foreign markets. Very large producers, who presumably benefit most from scale and learning effects, usually did not seek reciprocity. In these respects, then, variation by conditionality would seem to depend on the same set of variables as variation in the tariff code by good – industries, sectors, and groups vary in terms of whether they seek a conditional trade policy. As argued above, these kinds of theories often provide powerful explanations of variation by good, but help us relatively little in explaining the cross-national variation underlying trade cooperation.

Variation Over Time
We have seen, then, four dimensions of variation: by good, by country, by target, and by conditionality. All four kinds of variations may themselves **vary over time**. Administrative decrees and new legislation change the tariffs, as do trade treaties, embargoes, boycotts, and trade wars. Such changes provide the major concern of tariff histories. Some political scientists, too, have tried to explain why some important policy happened at a particular time and not earlier, examining how changes in economic structure affect political interests and organization (i.e., Irwin 1989a,b, 1991, 1995; McLean and Bustani 1999; Schonhardt-Bailey 1991a,b, 1994, 1998a,b, 2006). Because changing economic conditions affect producers' incentives to lobby for tariffs, protection also varies with the business cycle (Cassing, McKeown, and Ochs 1986; Hillman 1982; Takacs 1981; Magee et al. 1989; McKeown 1983), levels of unemployment (Takacs 1981), surplus capacity (Cowhey and Long 1983; Takacs 1981), and surges in imports (Hillman 1982; Magee et al. 1989; Takacs 1981).

Another explanation of change over time comes from hegemonic stability theory (HST). HST predicts extensive cooperation when a single state leads the international political economy, but little or no cooperation without such a state. Some versions of this theory also expect extensive cooperation during a hegemon's decline or among several large states attempting to maintain the high levels of cooperation previously achieved by a leader (Keohane 1984; Pahre 1999; Snidal 1985b but McKeown 1983). Depending on the version, then, hegemonic decline might lead either to more or less cooperation.

These theories of intertemporal variation are poorly integrated with each other. Both business cycle and hegemonic stability theories expect cyclical alternation between cooperation and noncooperation, but for different reasons, and these cycles need not synchronize with each other. Attempts to link HST with the business cycle either rest on overly abstract generalizations (i.e., Gilpin 1981; Modelski 1978, 1982, 1987) or provide too historicist an account for rigorous theory building (i.e., I. Wallerstein 1974a,b, 1979, 1989). Neither business cycles nor hegemonic theory would predict the noncyclical pattern in cooperation that we observe: a series of three waves.

Some advocates of hegemonic theory have pointed to domestic politics as one promising way to account for variations in cooperation among non-hegemonic states (i.e., Brawley 1993). In this respect, the regime, cooperation, and hegemonic literatures agree: scholars must give greater attention to how domestic politics accounts even for systemic-level behavior, such as international cooperation.

The following chapters will show that the study of intertemporal variation also faces the challenge of changes occurring at different paces. Economic conditions change continually, and our datasets normally measure them annually. Political institutions tend to change only every generation or two in most of the countries examined in this book. Trade treaties are typically signed for seven or ten years. We will see that many of the more slowly changing variables work better for cross-national studies than for examining intertemporal variation in a single country, in part because the independent variables do not vary all that much intertemporally in a single country. Qualitative methods, because they are not tied down to annual data series, can often provide better intertemporal tests of hypotheses (see especially Chapters 9, 11, and 12).

Tariff Variations in General
For intertemporal variation, as for the others, internal political factors interact with international variables to produce trade policy. We may analyze this trade policy along several dimensions; I give the least attention to variation by good, which is treated well elsewhere. Cross-national variation and variation

over time are central to this book because they change the noncooperative outcome and thus the incentives to cooperate. I investigate discrimination by target in Part IV of this book, examining how nondiscriminatory rules (MFN) shape the incentives for cooperation. In short, I take for granted the best-understood form of variation in order to understand better how other kinds of variations affect trade cooperation.

Measures of Trade Policy

The previous section analyzed trade policy variations in the abstract. Variation by good, by country, by target, and over time can all be found in the literature, and each suggests a certain class of explanations.

I turn now to the concrete problem of measuring this policy, with an eye toward measuring cross-national and intertemporal changes. Though they do not make for thrilling narration, good measures play an essential role in characterizing trade policy accurately (see a similar discussion in Hobson 1997: Chapter 6). Without measures we must rely on the more limited judgments of contemporaries. The iron and steel tariffs of 1879 Germany for example, were about the same as France's historically low tariffs in the free-trade Cobden-Chevalier treaty of 1860 (Marsh 1999: 115), yet many histories describe the former as "protectionist" and the latter as "free trade." Good measures, valid across time and space, help us avoid condemning the one, while praising the other.

The centerpiece of trade policy is the tariff, a tax imposed on imports. Measuring tariffs seems a simple task: one might just look at a country's tariff code and calculate the average tariff.[6] Attractive as it sounds, this is exactly the wrong way to define a country's average tariff. For one thing, other forms of policy – such as import quotas, government procurement rules, trade-related investment measures (TRIMs), export subsidies, tradable import certificates (Gerschenkron 1943/1989: 68–70), veterinary regulations, and health and safety rules – also affect trade. The average tariff also excludes effective protection through navigation laws as well as protection through

---

[6] Many scholars use the average duty on dutiable imports (i.e., Lake 1988; Magee et al. 1989; Pincus 1975). This measure throws out substantial variation – all zero duties – and truncates the dependent variable. A similar measure uses the percentage of imports that pay any duty at all. This can be misleading. One pamphleter used this measure to argue that Baden had higher tariffs than Prussia in the 1820s because it taxed more articles; however, it taxed them at a much lower rate, in part to encourage smugglers to use Baden territory as a base (Price 1949: 187). Thus, these apparently higher tariffs reflected *lower* protection and *greater* openness.

port and tonnage duties.[7] Using tariff lines alone misses this nontariff protection.

Weighting provides a second serious problem. The seemingly sensible procedure is to calculate the average tariff by weighting each line item tariff by the proportion of imports entering under that tariff. If 10% of a country's imports are automobiles, and if these receive a 2.5% tariff, then this 2.5% would receive weighting of 0.10 in calculating an overall tariff. Unfortunately, this measure is unsatisfactory because the tariff itself plays a big role in determining the weighting.[8] For example, a prohibitive tariff receives no weight in this scheme because the good does not enter the country at all. Near-prohibitive tariffs are underweighted because very few of the goods enter.

Specific duties, which tax a good's quantity or weight, complicate annual measures further. For example, the *Zollverein* tariff levied a duty of 6 thalers per hundredweight on rough iron articles before 1862. If a good's price fluctuates over the year, it is hard to calculate the average specific duty as a percentage of the good's price. Predictable seasonal variation in prices causes another complication. High protection of, say, grain might allow substantial imports outside the home harvest season, thereby overweighting a politically less salient period of imports – though the purpose of the tariff was to provide high protection during the home harvest when domestic prices are at their lowest.

As another example, the Prussian tariffs of 1817–1818 reduced the number of wine classifications dramatically while switching to a system of specific duties (Hahn 1982: 39). Because a specific duty falls equally on cheap and expensive wines, this practice effectively discriminated against the cheap Nassau wines and in favor of French wines. This would affect the composition of wine imports and appear as a low *ad valorem* rate on the expensive wines that Prussians actually imported. The fact that the *ad valorem* rate on Nassau wines was about 100% would be hidden completely.

A second practical problem is the widespread use of official customs valuations instead of invoice valuations for calculating duties. This procedure was common in England (A. H. Imlah 1958), in the Dutch colonial trade

---

[7] Navigation laws included many indirect barriers. For example, classifying a city as a free port opened it to trade with foreigners, whereas other classifications might subject foreign ships to a duty or exclude them altogether. If transportation costs differ among the various ports, nominal duties will not capture these differences.
[8] Tariff reclassifications present additional complexity here. First, comparable trade statistics may not be available before and after the reclassification. Second, tariff changes may encourage importers to substitute across reclassified goods if they are partial substitutes.

(Williams 1972: 313–29), Latin America (Bulmer-Thomas 1994: 145–46; Williams 1972: 252–91), and elsewhere; the "American Selling Price" still used for some goods today is a remnant of this practice (Winham 1986). This official valuation system arose as an administrative remedy against importers reporting an unrealistically low invoice value; it also has the political advantage of increasing the effective level of protection. For our purposes, it introduces significant measurement error. Any list of duties will mischaracterize the actual tax rate, and calculations will depend on whether import statistics are kept in market or administrative valuations (see A. H. Imlah 1958 for full discussion).

If we cannot measure duties directly, a closely related operationalization measures them indirectly by calculating customs revenue as a percentage of import value (Nye 1991), a measure I call the *average tariff.*[9] Unfortunately, the weighting problem remains. With no tariff, tariff revenue is zero, so the measure correctly indicates free trade. However, tariff revenue would also be zero with a prohibitive tariff because no goods will enter the country. Near-prohibitive tariffs, with low tariff revenue, will be similarly indistinguishable from near-zero duties. Austria before the 1860s presents a good example of this problem at work (see the data in Chapters 3–5). Like the direct measure, this indirect measure too excludes quotas and other nontariff protection because they generate no revenue. For such reasons, Douglas Irwin (1993: 146) argues, "The rate of tariff revenue is an inadequate and potentially misleading indicator of whether a country's commercial policy tends toward free trade or protection."

With both of these measures, highly protective tariffs receive too little weight. A better measure would capture imports that never occur. Import value provides a start at identifying these goods. Low import value would suggest that some imports are missing, just as high import value would tend to indicate that tariffs and quotas do not block a country's imports significantly.

This measure works well intertemporally, capturing increases and decreases in a country's willingness to import. However, it has flaws for cross-national comparisons. A large country will naturally import more

---

[9] Like others, this measure uses nominal and not effective protection (for an introduction to the problem, see Basevi 1966, Stern 1973). Effective tariffs consider that the duty on a good differs from the duty on inputs, so that protection on value added differs from the nominal statutory rate. This measure may be difficult to use in a multi-commodity world because it is a relative measure, which must be compared to some base good (Ruffin 1969). Fortunately, we can avoid these complications because many studies have found that the nominal and effective rates of tariff are highly correlated (Caves 1976; Cheh 1974; Finger and DeRosa 1979; Helleiner 1977; Lavergne 1983: Chapter 4).

than a small country. In addition, a country with many neighbors such as Switzerland will import more than an isolated Australia or New Zealand. We must compare import value to some baseline to see whether a country imports more or less than we would otherwise expect.

Two baselines present themselves. One baseline is a country's GDP. Using this gives us a country's opennesss, defined as its import value as a percentage of GDP.[10] Although this measure captures the political choice to protect one's markets from imports, it is also affected by a country's marginal propensity to import, its distance from other countries, and perhaps its size (see O'Rourke and Williamson 1999: 29–32 for critical discussion). For example, less diversified small countries usually import more as a share of their GDP.

Second, we might use gravity models of bilateral trade to provide a baseline prediction of a country's imports, using the residuals from our estimates as a measure of how open or closed a country is. Gravity models estimate two countries' bilateral trade as a positive function of the logarithms of GDP and a negative function of the square of the distance between them. Though it is an application of Newton's gravity equations that lacks a solid grounding in economic theory, this model predicts bilateral trade better than any alternative (Deardorff 1984). Yet, although an attractive measure, these gravity residuals would be affected by the same kind of nonpolicy factors that affect openness, such as marginal import propensities. Because this measure makes no particular improvement on openness, at a significant cost in simplicity and ease of interpretation, I avoid using gravity residuals (but see Pahre 2001b).

For general trade policy, then, I confront the choice between average tariffs or openness.[11] The task would be easier if average tariffs and openness measured the same thing. If both were good measures of the underlying variable (tariff protection), then average tariffs and openness would be highly and negatively correlated with each other. Either would be a good substitute for the other, and average tariffs would probably be better because it is connected more directly to policy choices.[12]

---

[10] Some studies use (imports plus exports)/GDP. This measures a country's overall exposure to the world economy, but obscures the political issues. Increased imports are politically costly to politicians, whereas increased exports are politically beneficial; lumping them together does not capture the political trade-offs across the interests of different groups.

[11] Note also that the openness measure must lie between zero and 1, whereas the average tariff is only bound below (by zero). Average tariffs rarely range above 150%, whereas openness rarely exceeds 30%.

[12] These measures are calculated from GNP, GDP, NNP, and import and customs revenue data in Mitchell (1975 *et seq.*), supplemented by Cortés Conde and Hunt (1985), Imlah (1958), Lévy-Leboyer and Bourguignon (1990), and Palairet (1979).

Table 2.1. *Average tariffs and openness*

	N	Years	Mean openness	Mean average tariff	Correlation
Brazil	14	1900–1913	16.4	39.6	−0.558
Denmark	23	1902–1913	31.1	7.6	−0.505
Finland	31	1883–1913	2.6	11.7	−0.068
France	46	1868–1913	15.3	7.4	−0.070
Germany	34	1880–1913	19.5	7.6	−0.956
Italy	52	1862–1913	10.9	10.9	−0.347
	46	1868–1913	11.0	11.4	−0.458
Norway	39	1875–1913	23.4	11.4	−0.479
Spain	12	1902–1913	9.7	14.3	−0.801
Sweden	53	1861–1913	19.7	10.7	−0.487
	46	1868–1913	20.8	10.4	−0.205
United Kingdom	84	1830–1913	24.5	12.4	−0.886
	46	1868–1913	27.3	5.3	0.191
United States	99	1815–1913	5.5	24.3	0.360
		1868–1913	5.5	27.4	0.413

Unfortunately, this correlation varies significantly by country. Table 2.1 presents the correlation between openness and tariffs in every country for which I could find sufficient data. It is important to look at each country separately, working with the historiography, because countries with low protection, those with high protection, and countries moving from high protection to low protection (or vice versa) will produce data that behave differently.

In addition to the correlation for each country's full time series, I also show the correlation over the period 1868–1913. This is an important period for the statistical tests in this book because of data availability – if data exist for a country in this century, they generally cover this period. For this reason, the choice of appropriate measures must rest in part on this period, even if a longer time series is available for some countries.

The two measures capture largely the same thing in Germany and Spain. In the United Kingdom, they are very highly negatively correlated over the course of the century, but positively correlated at its end (1868–1913). Chapter 4 argues that this latter relationship reflects the logic of a revenue tariff, which is consistent with the conventional account of UK trade policy. France and Finland show essentially no relationship between the two measures, whereas Brazil, Denmark, Italy, Norway, and Sweden show a modest negative correlation. For most countries, then, the relationship is what we would expect.

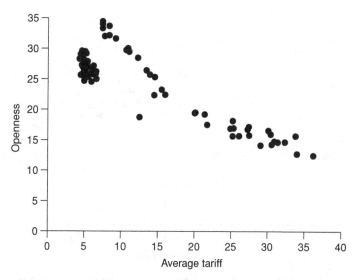

Figure 2.1. Correlation Between British Average Tariffs and Openness.

Visual inspection of the data can reveal further patterns. Figures 2.1–2.10 show that only Germany, Spain, and the United Kingdom exhibit a clean downward-sloping relationship between the two measures. France exhibits a flat inverse-U relationship. In such a case, openness is low at both high average tariff and low average tariff levels, suggesting that near-prohibitive

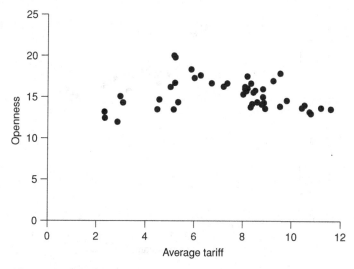

Figure 2.2. Correlation Between French Average Tariffs and Openness.

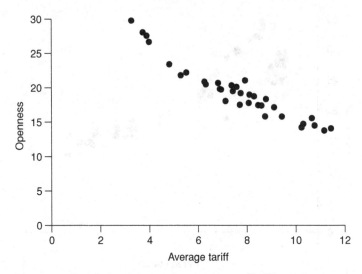

Figure 2.3. Correlation Between German Average Tariffs and Openness.

tariffs are a factor in the low-tariff region. When this occurs, openness is a much better measure than average tariffs. The pattern in Brazil and the four Nordic countries is not at all clear. Italy shows essentially no overall relationship, though a clump of points in the upper-left suffice to give it a negative correlation coefficient.

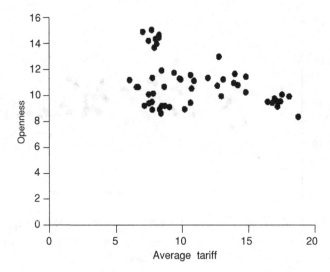

Figure 2.4. Correlation Between Italian Average Tariffs and Openness.

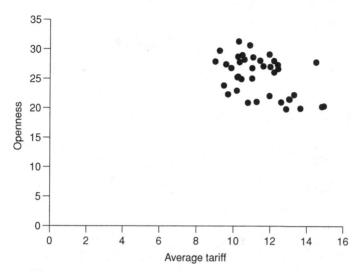

Figure 2.5. Correlation Between Norwegian Average Tariffs and Openness.

These data suggest that these two operationalizations measure different things for many countries, though these things are frequently related in the way we would expect. As argued earlier, each seems on theoretical grounds to be a reasonable if imperfect way to operationalize the concept of protection.

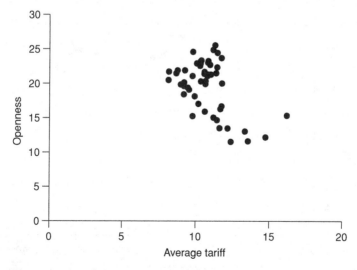

Figure 2.6. Correlation Between Swedish Average Tariffs and Openness.

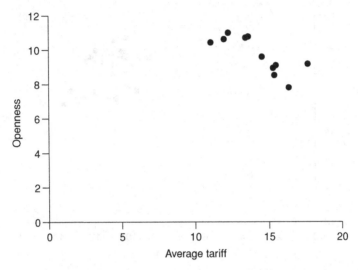

Figure 2.7. Correlation Between Spanish Average Tariffs and Openness.

Which, then, is a better measure of a country's trade policy? The average tariff measure works well when there is a clear downward-sloping relationship between the two measures. In contrast, openness is definitely a better measure if there is an inverse-U relationship between average tariffs and openness. Such a relationship implies that important near-prohibitive tariffs or nontariff barriers are not being captured by the average tariff measure

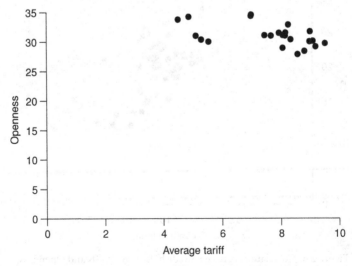

Figure 2.8. Correlation Between Danish Average Tariffs and Openness.

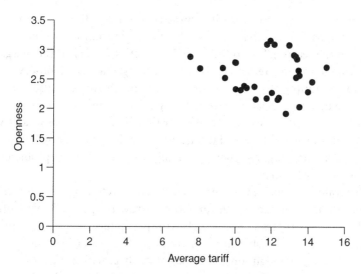

Figure 2.9. Correlation Between Finnish Average Tariffs and Openness.

when protection is high and openness is low. When average tariffs are a poor measure, then either high or low average tariffs will be associated with low degrees of openness. The average tariff measure represents the only alternative when GDP data are not available. For countries without high or prohibitive tariffs – such as Belgium, the Netherlands, and Switzerland – average tariffs should serve us well.

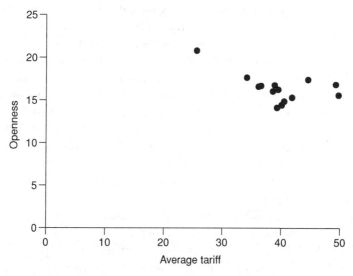

Figure 2.10. Correlation Between Brazilian Average Tariffs and Openness.

The two measures also have different strengths depending on the purpose of the analysis. For intertemporal study of a single country, openness provides a good measure. Economic variables affecting it, such as the marginal propensity to import, remain essentially unchanged across all observations for a single country, reducing measurement error. Openness is also not subject to the inverse-U relationships that might lead to incorrect inferences if we look at a country's average tariffs over time. Cross-nationally, however, these economic variables – and not trade policy decisions – might account for the variation that we observe, making openness a more problematic measure for these purposes.

I generally use both measures when possible, referring to these issues as appropriate. Though useful for more narrow purposes, I reject other possible measures of trade policy, such as the percentage of dutiable imports, average duties on dutiable imports, average effective tariffs, and gravity model residuals. Though some of these – notably gravity model residuals – would be attractive, the relative paucity of nineteenth-century bilateral trade data means that this measure is not yet feasible. In contrast, openness data are generally available. Moreover, openness data capture the political "cost" of imports to political leaders, thus also resonating well with the theory developed in coming chapters.

Overview of Trade Policies

The pattern of openness and tariffs for the 1815–1913 period provides the subject matter for the next three chapters, the data that we need to explain. The conventional wisdom expects steady liberalization until the depression of 1873–1896 and then a (partial) return to protection. The standard explanation for the liberalization is the ideology of free trade (see especially Kindleberger 1975), whereas domestic politics explain the shift away from free trade (see Gourevitch 1986 for a cross-national study). It is not obvious how to reconcile the two halves of this argument, though Polanyi's (1944) notion of marketization and backlash provides a possible foundation (see also O'Rourke and Williamson 1999; Rodrik 1997). As trade increases, societies seek to protect themselves from some of the instabilities and social costs of competitive markets. Tariff increases slow down the growth of trade without eliminating it.

This account accords with some of the evidence but not all of it. Figures 2.11–2.16 provide some illustrations of the changes for those countries for which I have data. These are mostly the countries of developing Europe, plus Russia. Data are available only for the largest American countries.

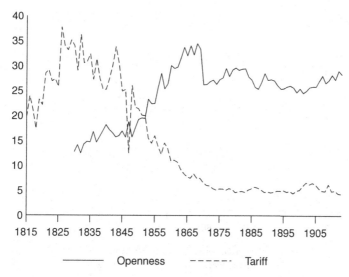

Figure 2.11. Openness and Average Tariffs in Britain, 1815–1913.

Figure 2.11 shows that Britain lowered tariffs steadily through the century, ultimately reaching about 5% of the value of imports from the 1870s onward. This represents a major decrease from earlier policy, with tariffs in the 20–60% range. Openness reached a plateau at mid-century, perhaps dropping off a bit after the boom of the 1860s. These data are broadly consistent with the conventional view, which has long seen the United Kingdom as an exception to the wave of protectionism in the late nineteenth century.

France, Germany, and Italy follow the conventional story, which was, after all, developed with these large economies in mind (see Figure 2.12). French tariffs increased under the Third Republic from the low levels of the Second Empire. French openness increased to a moderately high though more variable level in the 15–20% range. The low levels of openness at the start of the series are consistent with the finding above that there is no relationship between openness and the average tariffs because France used many prohibitions or near-prohibitive tariffs that generated little revenue and therefore do not appear in the average tariff measure. Italy had modest levels of openness in much of the period, in the 10–15% range from about 1890. Italy increased its tariffs in the late 1880s from low levels that were comparable to those of Britain and Scandinavia. Toward the end of the period, both French and Italian tariffs leveled off and then began to decline again, especially in Italy. In short, the conventional account would seem to describe France and Italy well.

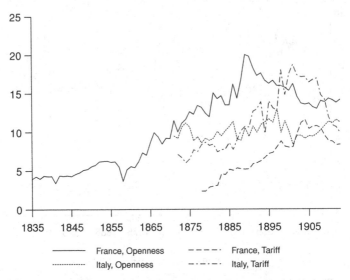

Figure 2.12. Openness and Average Tariffs in France and Italy, 1835–1913.

German openness (see Figure 2.17) declines precipitously from a high level in the early 1880s down to about 15%. However, it recovered somewhat in the following decades, returning to near 20%. The renewed liberalization from roughly 1895 to 1913 is often forgotten, and many scholars identify the Bülow tariff of 1902, which took full effect in 1906, as renewed protection. This interpretation is not supported by these data, but the clean, downward-sloping relationship between average tariffs and openness shown in Figure 2.3 means that both measures give us a consistent story of German policy. The common misinterpretation of policy from 1895–1913 stems from the fact that the potentially protectionist Bülow tariffs were accompanied by various tariff-reducing treaties, so that it neither raised the conventional tariffs nor reduced Germany's openness.

In contrast to the major continental powers, Scandinavia does not fit the standard account very well, largely because these countries tended to have open economies from early in the period. Figure 2.13 shows that Norwegian and Swedish tariffs remained fairly low for a half-century. Scandinavian tariffs were higher than Britain's, a little over 10% of the value of imports, and somewhat more variable as well. Openness increased steadily, most notably in Denmark and Norway. Swedish openness seems to have plateaued or even dropped off a little at century's end, though its tariffs also declined slightly in this period.

Even more than Scandinavia, Belgium and the Netherlands had such low tariffs to begin with that their liberalizations are hardly noticeable (see

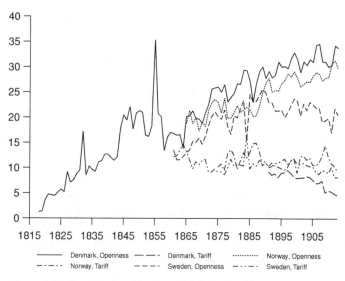

Figure 2.13. Openness and Average Tariffs in Scandinavia, 1815–1913.

Figure 2.14). Like the United Kingdom and Scandinavia, they also do not participate in the European move to protection from the 1870s.

Iberia shows no obvious pattern. It is possible to find an increase in Spanish tariffs in 1876–1896 if one looks for it in Figure 2.15, but an observer ignorant of these dates would probably not notice anything. Portuguese tariffs are lower after 1896, after having been volatile for several decades.

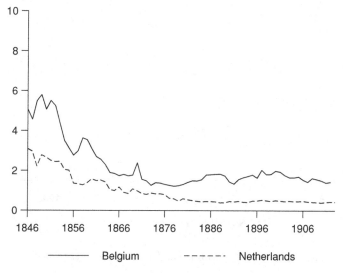

Figure 2.14. Average Tariffs in the Low Countries, 1846–1913.

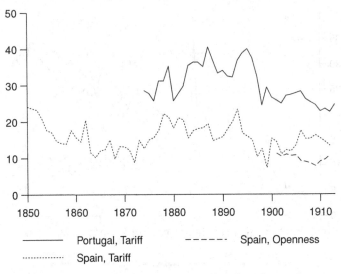

Figure 2.15. Openness and Average Tariffs in Iberia, 1850–1913.

These data loosely fit the conventional narrative, aside from the renewed liberalization after 1896 that resembles Germany.

In eastern Europe (see Fig. 2.16), only Austria-Hungary follows the standard account and only after a decade-long delay. Despite the increase during the Great Depression, its tariffs remain at low levels. Unfortunately, openness

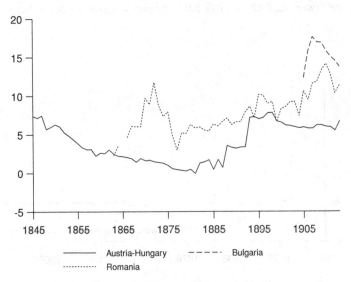

Figure 2.16. Average Tariffs in Southeastern Europe, 1845–1913.

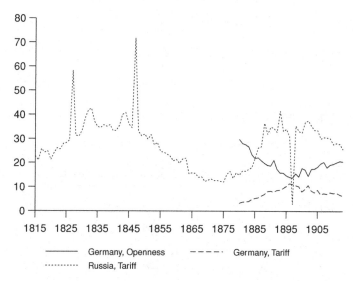

Figure 2.17. Openness and Average Tariffs in Germany and Russia, 1815–1913.

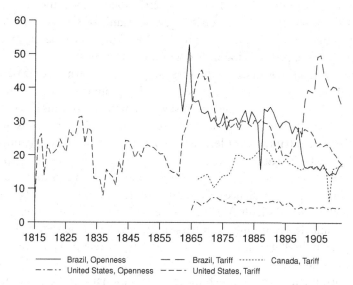

Figure 2.18. Openness and Average Tariffs in Brazil, Canada, and the United States, 1815–1913.

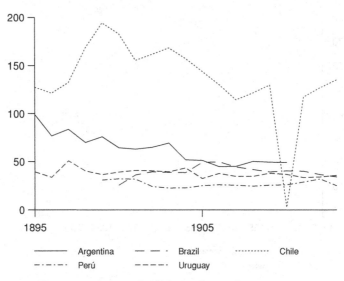

Figure 2.19. Average Tariffs in South America, 1895–1913.

data are not available so the changes in the effects of Austrian prohibitions cannot be observed. Russia (see Fig. 2.17) follows the same pattern as Austria-Hungary, but at higher tariff levels. Romania sees a steady increase in tariffs after reaching a low in the mid-1870s, though tariff levels remain modest. Bulgaria provides too little data for discussion.

The Americas show no sign of the allegedly general pattern. (see Figs. 2.18–2.19). Of course, U.S., Canadian, and Argentine grain exports were largely responsible for the price changes against which many Europeans reacted, so it is not surprising that trade policy would differ in the Western Hemisphere.

All these countries were at least as open as the largest trading countries of today, the United States and Japan, whose openness levels remain in the teens. Tariff levels were a little higher than industrialized countries' tariffs today, though the prevalence of nontariff barriers since the 1970s makes direct comparison difficult. Many countries see an increase in protection in the 1870s and 1880s, though countries on the European periphery did not participate in this pattern. The Western Hemisphere retained relatively high tariffs throughout.

In short, the data reveal much more cross-national variation than most accounts have recognized. Important as the large continental countries are, the low countries and Scandinavia join the United Kingdom as exceptions that are every bit as numerous as the countries that follow the alleged rule. In addition, the Americas do not follow the European pattern at all.

Summary

This chapter has reviewed how trade policy may vary by good, by target, cross-nationally, and intertemporally. Each type of variation is well represented in the literature on political economy, though variation by good has been the most prominent. This book focuses instead on cross-national and intertemporal variations, for these types of variations are better suited for the study of why some nations cooperate more than others, and at some times more than others.

This form of variation requires a measure appropriate for the task. I have argued for two measures, the average tariff and openness. Although the average tariff is seemingly a more direct measure, openness may be a better measure, especially for highly protective countries. Sometimes the two measures are related to each other in ways we would expect. In other cases they are not related or even related in the wrong way. For example, prohibitive systems in Austria-Hungary and Russia distort the average tariff data here. I use both measures throughout this study depending on data availability and theoretical appropriateness.

Being explicit about the measures, along with using a global perspective, also shows that the conventional account – liberalization in the 1860s followed by protectionism in the 1880s – describes only a few continental European countries well. Even Germany fits that narrative imperfectly. In Italy, France, and some other countries, the tariff changes are more dramatic than the changes in openness. This finding suggests that tariffs may have been capturing revenue from trade without changing openness much. Revenue concerns also affect the British data, whose modest average tariffs were imposed only on goods without domestic competition, and therefore had revenue, not protective effects (see Hobson 1997).[13]

These revenue concerns provide the focus of Chapter 4. Before that, however, Chapter 3 examines the politics of protection in general. This study of autonomous tariffs provides an essential foundation for the other chapters of this book.

---

[13] Some protection of substitutes resulted because tariffs on French wines probably helped support the price of British beer.

THREE

A Political-Support Theory of Trade Policy

"The elected National Assembly stands in a metaphysical relation, but the elected President in a personal relation, to the nation."
– Karl Marx (1852/1963: 33)

This chapter lays the foundation for the theoretical model used throughout this book, the theory of political support. Work in the political-support tradition has long been a common minority approach in economics, but for some reason has never caught on in political science.

We can consider the choice of model on theoretical, historical, or pragmatic grounds. Some models are theoretically attractive, perhaps because they are parsimonious or because they link up well with approaches to related topics. Marxism, rational-choice, and other similarly broad approaches to political economy share these advantages. At the other end of a spectrum of generalizability, some historical features compel us to a particular kind of model. One would not model the Hundred Years War with Weberian bureaucracies nor the Cold War through feudal patron-client relations in Washington (though this latter option is more tempting). Finally, pragmatic considerations might point in one direction or another.

The choice of the model developed here reflects such theoretical, historical, and pragmatic concerns. It would be shocking if all these considerations clearly favored one particular model. Let me argue more modestly that the theory of political support meets each concern reasonably well.

Explaining trade cooperation among 50 countries over the course of a century clearly requires a theory flexible enough to say something about countries of varying size, trade patterns, and political institutions. This chapter's political-support model of trade policy assumes that a state seeks political support from all social groups and that these groups grant support in pursuit of their own material interests. This theory is vague enough to model all states, making it a good pragmatic choice.

The theory is also theoretically attractive. It focuses attention on the motives of a central decision maker in each country. In this respect, it lends itself to synthesis with Realism and other state-centered theories that have dominated the study of international relations. At the same time, the theory looks at how this actor responds to domestic political pressures, letting us incorporate domestic-level concerns into the theory. By bringing together variables at both levels, it resembles Robert Putnam's (1988) theory of two-level games. Though not a two-level game in Putnam's sense, it can easily be combined with such theories, as I do in Chapter 9.

Though chosen for these theoretical reasons, the theory does not run roughshod over history. The political-support model captures well one important feature of nineteenth-century politics: the process of integrating new groups into the political system. It can also capture a wide range of domestic political systems. Though an enormous simplification, political support is far from a vacuous concept. Indeed, it compares well with other broad theories, such as interest group pluralism, class analysis, or the Realist assumption that states are unitary rational power maximizers.

This chapter develops the theory and a handful of hypotheses derived from it. After setting up the central parts of the model, I discuss its fit with nineteenth-century political economy. I focus discussion on the "integrative thesis" found in the historiographies of many countries. The theory of political support maps well into the executive-centered politics of developing democracies, semi-democracies, and autocracies in this century.

After this excursus I use political-support theory to derive ten comparative statics hypotheses about how trade policy will change in response to exogenous events, both economic and political. World price changes (terms of trade), declining transportation costs, country size, and domestic institutional changes help explain tariff variations in this theory, as in others (see Table 3.11). The theory also predicts that countries with high tariffs will have more volatile tariffs (Corollary 3.1). Because this volatility prediction clearly distinguishes political-support theory from other theories, I give it substantial attention. Several kinds of tests give this volatility hypothesis significant empirical support. Though underrecognized, tariff volatility also provides an important motive for trade cooperation, independent of tariff levels.

Two themes run through this chapter: compensation and backlash. Politicians generally compensate those harmed by exogenous change by moving policy in a direction favoring them. Backlash is a variant of this process by which increasing international openness produces political forces that work against this openness (see Rodrik 1997). Both processes work to reduce change, as any new action produces an opposite, but less than equal, reaction. They also lead to suboptimal outcomes, as any gain from freer trade leads to compensatory protection. Trade cooperation can remedy this suboptimality.

I provide illustrative evidence for these hypotheses throughout this chapter, along with quantitative tests where appropriate data are available. Though the illustrations come from a range of countries and periods, I make a point of including continental European policies in the Great Depression of 1873–1896. Applied to this period, my hypotheses largely follow the conventional wisdom (i.e., Kindleberger 1951) and do so for reasons consistent with this conventional wisdom. As we saw in Chapter 2, this account generally fits the major continental economies but not countries on the European periphery or in the Americas. The reason for this cross-national difference is simple – these countries produced different goods. Wheat importers and wheat exporters *should* respond differently to a large change in world wheat prices. These empirical referents are worth keeping in mind as I make more counterintuitive claims later, claims that nonetheless follow logically from these conventional claims.

A Theory of Political Support

Political-support models assume that a single policymaker in each country seeks to maximize "political support," such as votes and campaign contributions (Peltzman 1976; Stigler 1971; applied to trade by Hillman 1982; Long and Vousden 1991; Moser, Hillman, and Long 1995). In this way, a political-support model focuses on the decisions of the executive, whether a prime minister maximizing his party's seats in the legislature, a president seeking the support of public opinion, or a dictator trying to maintain backing for his position among many different groups. By assuming that a unitary support-maximizer chooses policy, I abstract from these differences while capturing the central problem that all these leaders face. Outside the field of economics, this resonates most closely with the tradition focusing on state autonomy (i.e., Evans, Rueschemeyer, and Skocpol 1985; Krasner 1977; Nordlinger 1981; Skocpol 1979; see Hobson 1997 and Chapter 7 for review).

Though drawn from economic studies of politics, the theory of political support represents a minority tradition in ETT, which has usually used one of three narratives to motivate its models of political economy. In an adding-machine narrative, each interest group demands some policy, and these demands are aggregated to determine policy (i.e., Pincus 1975, 1977). Stronger groups get more; weaker groups get less.

In a coalitional theory, groups form alliances to make policy (i.e., Riker 1962; in trade, Rogowksi 1989 *inter alia*). Those in the winning group obtain the policies they want, though they may have to compromise with one another. Those on the losing side get nothing. Being powerful usually makes a group a more attractive coalition partner, but some coalitions of the small may turn even large groups into losers (see Tarar 2005 for an example). In a variety of the coalitional theory applied mostly to American politics, two politicians or parties simply compete against each other for voters, with the winner implementing a promised policy (see especially Magee et al. 1989).

In the theory of political support, an individual politician – not groups – makes policy. He seeks votes and other political support from as many groups as possible. In looking to all groups for support, this theory echoes the adding-machine model, but differs from the winners-and-losers feature of a coalitional theory. Whereas in adding-machine theory, gaining wealth makes a group more powerful, in political-support theory wealth *reduces* a group's influence. As a group gains wealth, its marginal utility of wealth declines, so it "lobbies less hard" for further policy changes; equivalently, marginal support from each group becomes less valuable to the political leader as he obtains more and more of it.

Thus, the theory of political support sees politics as a matter of balancing interests against each other. If one grows strong, a politician will give a morsel to a weaker group that will value this tidbit more highly at the margin. Similarly, political-support theory emphasizes policy that compensates those harmed by exogenous change, drawing off benefits from winners to losers. Trade Adjustment Assistance in the United States today provides an excellent example of the kinds of policy that political-support theory expects, for it compensates workers and businesses harmed by trade liberalization.

In contrast to coalitional theories of politics, political-support theory leaves out the selection of leaders by coalitions of parties, elections, or other processes (see especially Bueno de Mesquita et al. 2003). This is a serious limitation. Still, leaving out selection processes brings benefits of analytical simplicity that are particularly important when studying the interaction of many political systems simultaneously, as here. The leader does not seek to obtain more votes or other support than her competitors, but rather as much support as possible. The political-support and coalitional (electoral) theories do not differ too much, because maximizing support will also tend to outsupport a rival politician. The major advantage of the theory of political support is its analytical simplicity. We need only model a single player's optimization problem instead of multiple *domestic* players, who would also have to take the reactions of other countries into account.

In the trade context, a politician must maximize political support from groups that disagree on the central question of free trade or protection. Existing research has generally examined the political conflict between producer and consumer interests (Grossman and Helpman 1994; Hillman 1982; Moser, Hillman, and Long 1995), though a few have extended these theories to include lobbying by foreign producers (i.e., Das 1990; Fischer 1992). Many such models pit producers against social welfare (i.e., Grossman and Helpman 1994, 2002). As it turns out, empirical studies have found that social welfare plays an important substantive role in tariffs (see especially Goldberg and Maggi 1999), a fact that political-support theory captures indirectly by giving positive weight to the income of all groups of producers.

My model assumes that the central conflict lies between different groups of domestic producers. Consumer interests in lower prices affect producer income, but I do not model them separately from their producer interest.[1] For simplicity, I assume that each individual either gains or loses from foreign trade.[2] I call these groups "exporters" and "import-competers," respectively. Divisions could be as simple as free-trade agriculture and protectionist capital in the antebellum United States (as in Rogowski 1989). There might also be complex sectoral-based patterns that do not follow class or factor lines. In Bavaria, for example, one part of the economy (salt mining, breweries, tobacco, and agriculture) demanded protective tariffs, whereas merchants, banks, and handicrafts generally wanted free trade (J. Schmidt 1973: Chapter 1). These groups can be classified as exporters and import-competers, but the underlying reasons for these interests lie outside the model.

To maximize political support, policymakers redistribute income from exporters to import-competers (or vice versa) until the import-competers' marginal gratitude exceeds the exporters' marginal resentment. When the marginal support from each group is equal, we have found the equilibrium policy. In subsequent analysis, I look at how this equilibrium might be disturbed by economic or political change and at how politicians choose a new equilibrium policy in response. The model in this chapter does not consider the revenue consequences of tariffs explicitly (see especially Hobson 1997), but I do consider these issues at length in Chapter 4.

I use a simple model of the economy. Exporters receive a price for a basket of their export goods, p_E, and import-competers receive a price for their goods, p_I. Income for these two groups (Y_E, Y_I) is a function of relative prices,

---

[1] Only consumers wholly dependent on nondiscretionary government spending, such as modern-day retired people living on pensions, lack producer interests.

[2] This assumption means that I cannot explain interindustry variation in trade policy because it lumps all import-competing industries together in one group and all exporting industries into another. See Chapter 2.

that is, the prices received as producers and paid as consumers. We can define relative prices as $p \equiv p_I / p_E$. Thus defined, exporter income decreases in p (so $\partial Y_E / \partial p < 0$), and import-competer incomes increases in p (so $\partial Y_I / \partial p > 0$).[3] This reduced-form approach sets aside production functions, demand, and other "economic" variables to focus on the political problem.[4] National income is then a sum of the income of both groups ($Y = Y_E + Y_I$) and therefore also a function of prices, so that $Y = Y_E (P) + Y_I (P)$.

Each group provides political support from its assets, and politicians can receive support from either or both groups.[5] My reduced-form equations do not explicitly model each interest group's decision problem. I assume that lobby formation is exogenous and has already occurred (see Eicher and Osang 2002; Grossman and Helpman 1994, 2002; Mitra 1999). Instead, I use as inputs a simplified version of results that models of interest group behavior produce as outputs (for models of this, see Austen-Smith 1981; Becker 1983; Wellisz and Wilson 1986). I also ignore political parties, elections, and similar forms of political competition (see especially Magee et al. 1989). This keeps the model simple, and more complex models generally yield similar reduced-form equations; moreover, many nineteenth-century polities lacked elections in any case. By using reduced-form equations for lobbyists' decisions, the focus remains squarely on the policymaker's connected choices at the international and domestic levels.

Groups give support either as a reward for past service or an inducement for better performance in the future. The greater a group's income, the more political support (M) it provides, so that $M = M(Y_E, Y_I)$, with $\partial M / \partial Y_E > 0$, $\partial M / \partial Y_I > 0$. Political support from any one group is subject to diminishing returns. We can think of these diminishing returns as reflecting the fact that the most valued supporters sign up first, so that the first units of support received are more valuable to the politician than later units. This pattern of diminishing returns also has some interesting implications. It means that integrating historically excluded groups can, at the margin, yield more political support than by providing yet another favor for historically dominant groups. Such integration was an essential part of nineteenth-century political development, and it continues to be important in many countries today.

---

[3] At some point, further changes in price will cease to have further effects on income, so $\partial Y_E / \partial p = 0$ and $\partial Y_I / \partial p = 0$ for sufficiently low (high) p; I therefore limit analysis to the interior of these thresholds. I also assume complete information, so that everyone knows where these thresholds are, among other information. Incomplete-information models in this area are rare, but see Bac and Raff (1997).

[4] For economic models incorporating such concerns, see Grossman and Helpman (1994, 2002), Moser et al. (1995), Long and Vousden (1991), and Vousden (1990), among others.

[5] This assumption contrasts with the specialization theorems in Magee et al. (1989), but is empirically more accurate (see Austen-Smith 1991).

These assumptions yield the following basic model:

$$
\begin{aligned}
&p \equiv p_I/p_E & &Y = Y_E(p) + Y_I(p) \\
&Y_E(p), Y_I(p) & &\partial Y_E/\partial p < 0, \partial Y_I/\partial p > 0 \\
&M = M(Y_E, Y_I) & &\partial M/\partial Y_E > 0, \partial M/\partial Y_I > 0 \\
& & &\partial^2 M/\partial Y_E^2 < 0, \partial^2 M/\partial^2 Y_I^2 < 0
\end{aligned}
\tag{3.1}
$$

Equations (3.1) describe a political maximization problem in which politicians balance support from one group against support from another in an environment in which not everyone can be fully satisfied simultaneously. Politicians face trade-offs between supporting one group's policy and supporting another, and they balance these trade-offs.

It is easy to find examples of this balancing reasoning in nineteenth-century politics. In the late 1820s, French Minister of Commerce Baron St. Cricq (cited in Levasseur 1892: 23–24fn) believed, "Since the Restoration, the tariff legislation has always sought to consolidate, with the prospect of a common protection, interests which have often been opposed and are always distinct – those of agriculture and those of industry and commerce." By implication, neither group would be completely satisfied, and politicians would have to strike a balance between them.

We find similar rhetoric, in a more colorful form, in Germany. Chancellor Prinz Bernhard von Bülow always advocated protection for both manufacturing and agriculture, explaining in his memoirs (cited in Gerschenkron 1943/1989: 60; see also Ashley 1926: 275) that

A ship without sufficient ballast in her hold, with masts too high and a rigging too heavy is bound to capsize. Agriculture is and remains the ballast. Industry and trade are the masts and the sails. Without them the ship cannot move forward. But without ballast she will turn turtle.

Several classic biographies make a similar argument for Sir Robert Peel, who sought to balance aristocratic survival, working-class welfare, and the needs of economic growth (i.e., Gash 1972; Kitson Clark 1951).

This balancing of contending interests produces an equilibrium tariff in which the marginal support from import-competers equals the marginal support from exporters. Equilibrium occurs at $(\partial M/\partial Y_E)(\partial Y_E/\partial p) + (\partial M/\partial Y_I)(\partial Y_I/\partial p) = 0$. This does not normally describe the same equilibrium as the income-maximizing case. If policymakers maximized national income $(Y = Y_E + Y_I)$, the equilibrium would be at $\partial Y_E/\partial p + \partial Y_I/\partial p = 0$; because it produces a different outcome, political maximization reduces national income, at least for a small country that does not affect world prices. I address the large country case later in this chapter.

The equilibrium relative price level balances the interests of both groups, because the joint maximization of both Y_E and Y_I yields a price more (respectively less) than the price that would maximize Y_E (or Y_I) alone. This provides our first hypothesis:

Hypothesis 3.1: The balancing hypothesis. The domestic price for protected goods is always less than the autarky price would be (cf. Hillman 1982; Peltzman 1975).

In other words, import-competers do not receive their maximum demand. The same is true for exporters, because further lowering of relative prices would raise Y_E above the support equilibrium level. This hypothesis is common to other models of political support.

The balancing hypothesis rules out policies that close the market to foreign producers, granting home producers a monopoly. Phrased differently, import prohibitions and domestic monopolies must result from factors other than political-support maximization. Except for the many corn laws in Europe, which prohibited grain imports below a certain price, most nineteenth-century import prohibitions were found only in autocracies, such as Russia, Restoration France and Spain, and Austria before 1848 (see Bairoch 1993: Chapter 2 for review). Pure prohibitions deny import goods to the domestic market entirely, so impure prohibitions that allow for exceptions are more common.

Because neither group receives its maximum demand, policy comes from the politician's balancing of contending interests against one another. Exogenous changes also lead to balancing. Anything that makes a group worse off will lead a politician to compensate that group. Because the equilibrium depends on balancing one group against another, however, the politician cannot fully compensate the harmed group, for that would impose the exogenous harm squarely on whomever pays the compensation, whether directly or indirectly. Instead, the politician compensates groups partially, reducing the harm to any one group by spreading it around (cf. Lamborn's 1983 account of revenue extraction in general). This implies the following:

Hypothesis 3.2: The partial compensation hypothesis. Compensation is always partial in that no group receives a policy that fully compensates it for disadvantageous exogenous changes.

This result is common in models of endogenous protection (i.e., Hillman 1982; Magee et al. 1989).

Without being labeled as such, the partial compensation hypothesis is also found frequently in the historiography. For example, it exactly captures Mommsen's (1995: 107) summary of the German tariff of 1879, which "mitigated the effects of overseas competition on agricultural markets but could not nullify them altogether." In particular, German grain imports continued to climb despite protection, from 1.2 million tons a year in 1885–1889 to 1.3 million in 1880–1884 to more than 1.5 million tons a year in 1890–1894 (Weitowitz 1978: 27). The marriage of iron and rye did not close Germany to grain imports nor even reduce its exposure, but merely slowed the rate of import growth (see Figure 2.17). Moreover, even these notorious grain tariffs were suspended when prices were sufficiently high, as in the near-famine of the winter of 1891–1892 (Dawson 1904: 99–100). This action follows naturally from the theory here, but it is not clear how it follows from others.

Although the equilibrium rests on balancing, the height of any particular tariff depends on the politician's relative valuation of protectionist and free-trade interests. Though I normally work with the general form $M = M(Y_I, Y_E)$, specific forms of this model such as the Cobb-Douglas $M = (Y_I)^\alpha (Y_E)^\beta$ would make explicit that politicians might value political support from different groups differently (i.e., $\alpha \gtrless \beta$). This functional form would capture the position of politicians who look first to a particular coalition. For example, Otto von Bismarck clearly valued political support from the Junkers much more than he valued an equivalent unit of political support from labor. This fact would appear as a parameter (α, β) in the model.[6] We can imagine bizarre values of these parameters – perhaps the Tsarina Alexandra cared only for Rasputin's support – but these are not found among the successful politicians who rise to the peak of a political system.

This feature of the model also lets it incorporate changing political or institutional conditions into the theory. Any institutional change affects a politician's valuation of political support from domestic groups. If any exogenous change increases the valuation (β) of export interests $(\partial M / \partial Y_E)$, the equilibrium price level $(p \equiv p_I / p_E)$ goes down. In contrast, anything that increases the valuation of import-competers (α) leads politicians to raise the equilibrium price level.[7] At least for interior solutions of the model,

Hypothesis 3.3: The group influence hypothesis. Any increase in the marginal valuation of a group will change equilibrium prices in its favor.

---

[6] Specifically, for import-competing Junkers and export-sector labor, $M = M(Y_I, Y_E)$, the value of M' for, say, $Y_I = 10$ and $Y_E = 5$ would be greater than M'' for $Y_I = 5$ and $Y_E = 10$.

[7] Proof. Rearranging, $(\partial M / \partial Y_E) = -(\partial M / \partial Y_I)(\partial Y_I / \partial p)/(\partial Y_E / \partial p)$. Increasing the marginal value of exporters $(\partial M / \partial Y_E)$ requires an increase in $-(\partial Y_I / \partial p)/(\partial Y_E / \partial p)$ for constant $(\partial M / \partial Y_I)$. This means raising $\partial Y_I / \partial p$ by lowering ∂Y_I, and lowering $|\partial Y_E / \partial p|$ by raising ∂Y_E, under the assumption of diminishing marginal returns to price changes (see also Chapter 7). Both of these changes entail lowering p.

Repeal of Germany's *Sozialistengesetz* (anti-Socialist law), for example, raised the marginal valuation of labor to national politicians, even those who opposed labor's demands. Because he weighted groups differently from his predecessor, Chancellor Leo von Caprivi was willing to make concessions to labor unions and the socialist party that Bismarck would never have made.

Analogously, the political mobilization of industry and the creation of trade associations helped raise the marginal valuation of capital in Tsarist Russia (Owen 1985). The Society for the Promotion of Russian Industry and Trade (*obshchestvo dlia sodeistviia russkoi promyshlennosti i torgovle*), founded in 1867, provided the major forum for the public discussion of Russian economic policy until the establishment of the Association of Industry and Trade in 1906. A few other organizations with limited constituencies emerged in the last decades of the tsarist period, including the South Russian Coal and Iron Association (1874), the Baku Petroleum Association (1884), the Russian Society of Sugar Producers (1887), and others. These organizations provided a backdrop of political support for Count Sergei Witte's trade policy and program of industrial development in the 1890s.

Although it does not predict how particular institutions affect trade policy, the model is logically consistent with the inductive analysis of political institutions and democracy that I develop in Chapter 5. In this way, the political-support assumption provides a framework in which I may examine institutional differences across countries in a more sensitive way than is possible in many abstract formal models. The group influence hypothesis is also sufficiently elastic to bring in ETT's analysis of how differences in interest group lobbying lead to variation in the tariff by good (see Chapter 2), though I do not do that here.

It is hardly counterintuitive to claim that increasing a group's influence would move policy in its favor. Again, such obvious claims at the root of the model add force to its less intuitive implications later on. This rather obvious claim also differs at a deeper level from some other, perhaps equally obvious, claims in the literature. For example, a growing number of scholars have suggested that democracy unambiguously makes lower tariffs more likely. However, Hypothesis 3.3 suggests otherwise. Extending the suffrage to a protectionist group such as Scandinavian farmers would increase the influence of those opposed to free trade. Although this democratization should lead to freer trade according to the growing orthodoxy, Hypothesis 3.3 makes the historically more reasonable claim that this kind of democratization will increase the strength of protectionist coalitions (for a similar view within a different theory of politics, see Rogowski 1989). Being explicit about even the "obvious" claims of a theory can help us make these kinds of analytical distinctions more precisely and so evaluate contending theories better.

The Integrative Thesis

Though I have argued for the model in theoretical and pragmatic terms, political-support theory is consistent with a historiographic interpretation of nineteenth-century tariffs that I call the "integrative thesis." This thesis maintains that the nineteenth-century state used the tariff to build political support among many social groups in a time of rapid change. Trade policy may sometimes have been a matter of ideological fervor, as it was for Richard Cobden in England, but it was more often a practical question that politicians addressed pragmatically. This kind of policymaking at the margin is captured well by the model.

Commercialization and industrialization produced greater political mobilization throughout Europe.[8] Nineteenth-century states therefore faced the challenge of moving from an *ancien régime* built on a narrow constituency to a modern democratic or authoritarian state based on popular support. Although the state could simply resist change, most governments tried to reconcile the new political groupings to the state. Making concessions that these groups desired – such as a wider franchise, higher social spending, or a favorable tariff – could serve this goal of reconciliation. Most elites found the tariff less threatening than these other reforms, for trade had long been an object of interest and not principle. Moreover, the tariff's role in government revenue was already a matter of political dispute among established groups (see Chapter 4; Hobson 1997).

As a result, tariffs become central to state-building in many European nation-states in the nineteenth century. Many governments used tariffs to integrate workers, peasants, and the petit bourgeoisie into the political system, giving every group in society some protection. Chambers of Commerce provided important "conveyer belts" of interest articulation in semi-democratic systems in Austria, France, and Germany, and they were always consulted before changing the tariff. Political goals then came to replace the revenue or mercantilist goals of previous trade policy.

The historians' integration thesis has its parallel in an older political science literature on a state's "penetration" into its own territory (LaPalombara

---

[8] Classical Marxists and some orthodox economic histories emphasize industrialization, capital accumulation, and class consciousness as causes of this mobilization. Neo-Smithian Marxists and many non-Marxists – including neoclassical political economists – argue that commerce and marketization can produce social transformations regardless of the mode of production. I suspect that this latter group comes more nearly to the truth.

1971; Rokkan 1975 *inter alia*). The Industrial Revolution made it easier for the state to deliver goods and services, coerce rebellions, and build legitimacy. It also made it easier for subjects to participate politically in both legitimate and illegitimate ways (Weiner 1971). Tariffs and other economic policies resulted from this process of penetration and participation.

We find this integrative thesis in the historiography of many countries. Michael Stephen Smith (1980: especially Chapter 5) argues that protection brought industry and agriculture together behind the Third Republic, helping thwart challenges to the regime. The failures of protectionist ideologues in the French Third Republic are also consistent with this pragmatic view.

The politics of unified Italy also illustrates the integrative thesis. Many historians see protectionism as having reconciled the North and South to Piedmontese rule. It helped create a *national* ruling class, a "permanent" alliance of interests and values, or a "historic bloc" in Gramsci's terms that dominated until after World War II (M. Clark 1996: 94–95). In the two decades before World War I, Giovanni Giolitti achieved notable success in using protectionism, industrial subsidies, and public works "to purchase the support of the isolated and divergent groups in society" (Coppa 1971: 5; see also M. Clark 1996: 136–40).

This integrative thesis probably finds its fullest expression in German historiography on the Wilhelmine Reich. This empire, many argue, rested on "organized capitalism" (*organisierter Kapitalismus*) in which the state and major economic groups regulated both politics and the market. From 1878, protectionism married heavy industry and eastern agriculture under the happy ministry of the state. Chancellor von Bülow extended this family in the 1902 tariff, based on an alliance "of all interests defending the state" (*Sammlung der staatserhaltenden Interessen*), successfully integrating Germany's various regions into the state.

In Germany as in France, the political-support approach captures well the central features of "Bonapartism" (Gall 1976; Gollwitzer 1952; Marx 1852/1963). Bonapartists appealed directly to the diverse interests of the population as a whole for political support, outside both modern parties and traditional interest mediation, such as chambers of commerce. Even after Bismarck, many scholars describe Wilhelmine Germany in similar terms, as a "Bonapartist dictatorial regime" (Wehler 1974 but Mommsen 1995: Chapter 1).[9]

---

[9] At the same time, it must be admitted that the theory of political support could be subject to Lothar Gall's (1976) critique of "Bonapartism" for being too flexible, mixing together Napoleon III, Disraeli, Schwarzenberg and Cavour, while doing substantial violence to the historical details.

The integrative thesis also finds resonance outside Europe. Latin America not only needed to adapt to modernization but also to build new states and even new societies. In *Los grandes problemas nacionales* (1909), the eminent Mexican sociologist Andrés Molina Enríquez argued that Mexican history had made great strides in *integración*, the process of forming an organic entity, since independence. Though it was not yet a homogeneous father-land (*patria*), he believed that President Porfirio Díaz had made especially great progress toward this integration, "without precedent in the history of humanity." He pointed to friendship (*amificación*) as Díaz's primary tool, granting benefits to particular groups in exchange for loyalty (Krauze 1997: 216). Tariffs represented one weapon in the armory of the Porfiriato.

In both Europe and Latin America, *amificación* in the form of patronage helped integrate locally oriented populations into a new national polity. Newly independent states faced the challenge of integrating these groups into the new political system (Clogg 1992: Chapter 3; Jelavich 1983: Chapter 4). In a patronage system, a politician distributes the outputs of government in exchange for political support. For example, the reign of Prince Ferdinand in Bulgaria from 1896 until World War I saw strong executives rely on patronage (*partisanstvo*) to stay in power. Such patronage led to a system of "oligarchic parliamentarism" in Latin America and the Balkans (Mouzelis 1986), though most tended to have liberal constitutions on paper.

To the extent that it unifies these accounts, the integrative thesis rests on a stronger historical foundation than coalitional analysis, the more common approach in political science (i.e., Gourevitch 1986; Riker 1962; Rogowski 1989). In coalitional analysis, domestic politics is largely distributive, with parties or groups trying to assemble a winning coalition to distribute income away from a rival coalition. This means that politicians do not balance interests against one another, as I assume, but side with one interest or the other, with the winner taking all. In coalitional analysis, each group's influence over trade policy depends on its power or, for simplicity, on its size. If exogenous events make exporting groups more powerful, for example, then they are more likely to obtain a trade policy in their interest.[10]

The core puzzle for a coalitional argument is why politicians compensate the losers who are excluded from their coalition. Such compensation is ubiquitous in trade policy, as two famous examples illustrate. French Emperor

[10] Notice that this claim is also found in the theory of political support if (unmodeled) processes cause a leader to change the weighting parameters for different groups (Hypothesis 3.3). However, economic change leads to endogenous compensation in the theory of political support.

Napoléon III hoped to obtain ratification of the 1860 Cobden-Chevalier treaty by combining it with long desired aid for reforestation, drainage, railroads, and canals, which he announced one week before the treaty. He also gave loans of 40 million francs to industrial groups who stood to lose from the treaty to help them adjust to its effects (Dunham 1930: 143–60).

British agriculture also received compensation in 1846, even as it lost the battle over repeal of the Corn Laws. Peel made changes in the distribution of several expenses between the localities and the central government (such as highways, prisons, poor-law medical officers, and teachers), provided public loans for the improvement of agriculture, reduced duties on corn inputs such as seeds and maize (for manure production), and abolished the law of settlement (Crosby 1976: 150; Hueckel 1981: 194; Irwin 1989a). These reforms seem to have cushioned agriculture from the otherwise harmful effects of trade liberalization and may help explain why English agriculture did not go into crisis in the 1840s and 1850s after the liberalization of corn imports.

Both of these cases are puzzling for the coalitional thesis because groups who lost on trade policy won on other issues at the same time. Of course, fairness requires that I note puzzles posed by the integrative thesis as well. First, my examples are forms of nontariff compensation for losses in tariff policy, a feature that lies outside the model in which tariffs provide the sole policy instrument. Although this weakness simply reflects the compensatory benefits of having a simple model, the various cases in which compensation did not occur raise more questions. For example, we might have expected the Tories to use protection to integrate Chartists into Victorian England in the 1840s. This did not happen. As a second example, surely the collapsing Ottoman Empire needed an integrative coalition in this century, yet it retained fairly low general tariffs until Kemal Atatürk. Odder still for the integrative thesis, in Norway, free trade – not protection – brought most sectors together against Swedish rule. These cases simply lie outside the potential scope of the integrative thesis.

The integrative thesis also downplays the inevitable exclusion of some groups from the state-led protectionist coalition. For example, agricultural labor in southern Italy was never really integrated into the kingdom, helping produce massive emigration to the Americas (O'Rourke and Williamson 1999). In Latin America and the Balkans, the bulk of the lower classes were either excluded through legal forms, such as property or educational qualifications, or local potentates controlled lower class votes through fraud, coercion, or other manipulation (Mouzelis 1986). While México began integrating groups in the Porfiriato, many Latin American countries had to await the populist period of the 1930s to see politicians build such integrative coalitions.

Like coalitional analysis, the theory of political support faces many anomalies because of its very breadth. To some extent, each captures the weaknesses of the other because the integrative thesis emphasizes the supply side of politics, whereas coalitional arguments address the demand side. The integrative thesis looks at how a policymaker uses trade policy to reward the members of different groups, focusing on the supply of tariff protection. Coalitional arguments assume that groups make demands for tariffs, and the winners determine the trade policy outcome.

We should not pose a false choice between integrative and coalitional approaches because, after all, both the demand and supply sides affect the outcome. Still, in this book I choose to bracket the demand side, including it only incidentally as a set of parameters, the valuation of each group. Hypothesis 3.3 and the analysis in Chapter 5 point toward a synthesis of the two approaches.

Political Support and the Tariff

The first part of this chapter used the political-support assumption to model politicians' incentives to change relative prices. As we have seen in the integrative thesis, tariffs are a particularly important policy instrument used to this end. This section moves explicitly to tariffs.

Tariffs make domestic relative prices ($p_d \equiv p_{dI}/p_{dE}$) diverge from world relative prices ($p_w \equiv p_{wI}/p_{wE}$). I assume for now that world prices are exogenous, relaxing this assumption when I examine country size later in this chapter. With an *ad valorem* tariff (t) on the import-competing goods, $p_d = p_w(1 + t)$. Now $Y_I(p_d)$, $\partial Y_I/\partial p_d > 0$, and $Y_E(p_d)$, $\partial Y_E/\partial p_d < 0$. The logic of political support remains the same, taking the form $M = M[Y_E(p_d), Y_I(p_d)]$. These assumptions yield the following model:

$$p_d \equiv p_{dI}/p_{dE} \qquad p_w \equiv p_{wI}/p_{wE} \qquad p_d = p_w(1 + t)$$
$$Y_I(p_d), Y_E(p_d) \qquad \partial Y_I/\partial p_d > 0, \partial Y_E/\partial p_d < 0 \qquad (3.2)$$
$$M = M[Y_E(p_d), Y(p_d)]$$

Because $\partial p_d/\partial t = p_w$, the political-support maximizing tariff still occurs where $(\partial M/\partial Y_E)(\partial Y_E/\partial p_d) + (\partial M/\partial Y_I)(\partial Y_I/\partial p_d) = 0$. This describes the equilibrium *unilateral tariff*. Because any trade policy can be converted into its tariff equivalent, this model can capture export subsidies, quotas, and other trade policy instruments. Unfortunately, it cannot explain the choice between such instruments, though the theory of political support extends easily to this problem (Cassing and Hillman 1985; Kaempfer et al. 1989; Levinsohn 1989). The choice of instruments depends on a fuller modeling of the distributional consequences of each (see also Rosendorff 1996; Vousden 1990).

This model also cannot capture the trade-offs between trade policy and nontrade policies, such as competition policy, intellectual property rights, investment rules, or research and development subsidies; the WTO charter reflects a growing concern with such instruments under the rubric of trade-related intellectual property (TRIPs) and trade-related investment measures (TRIMs). This leaves the model vulnerable to Daniel Verdier's (1994: Chapter 1) criticism of endogenous tariff theory, that firms seek particularist benefits without reference to issue area – making this theory incomplete because it does not consider firms' ability to trade off lobbying across issues. Although Verdier's point is persuasive in theory, it is very difficult to operationalize two different policy issues in a comparable way. McGillivray (2004) has examined both tariffs and industrial policy together, using stock market valuations to measure how individual firms benefit from policy intervention, whereas Rogowski and Kayser (2002) have tried to measure deviations from the law of one price to attain similar ends. These authors acknowledge the difficulties of their solutions, and in any case the necessary data would be lacking for the nineteenth century. As a result, I set these issues aside.

Though it is determined unilaterally, external factors such as changes in world prices clearly affect tariffs in this model. I am particularly interested in dt/dp_w, or how tariffs respond to changes in world prices. To see this, we totally differentiate equation (3.2), $\partial M/\partial t = 0$, which is itself a function of t and p_w. Using subscripts for the derivatives for convenience, the total derivative of this first-order condition is $M_{tt}t_{p_w} + M_{tp_w} = 0$, which rearranges to $t_{p_w} = -M_{tp_w}/M_{tt}$. Because the denominator is negative by assumption, the sign of dt/dp_w depends on $M_{tp_w} = M_{Y_E Y_E}(Y_{Ep_w})^2 + M_{Y_E}Y_{Ep_w p_w} + M_{Y_I Y_I}$ $(Y_{Ip_w})^2 + M_{Y_I}Y_{Ip_w p_w}$. A sufficient condition for $M_{tp_w} < 0$ is that both $Y_{Ep_w p_w} < 0$ and $Y_{Ip_w p_w} < 0$. I have already assumed these conditions above by limiting analysis to interior solutions – that is, by excluding the extremes at which changes in price have no further effect on incomes. One substantive implication of this assumption is that all statements following include the implicit qualification that they do not apply to those prohibitive systems that exist in some countries at the start of the century.

According to this analysis, if world prices increase, the policymaker will reduce tariffs (because $dt/dp_w < 0$). Increasing p_w disturbs the prior equilibrium, increasing import-competers' income and decreasing the income of exporters. The politician can gain political support by reducing the harm to exporters through skimming some of this windfall gain away from import-competers. The reverse is also true, of course: if the price of their products on world markets (p_w) falls, import-competers will receive compensatory protection. In other words:

Hypothesis 3.4: The declining prices hypothesis. Decreasing world prices (i.e., increasing terms of trade) lead to increased protection, and increasing world prices (decreasing terms of trade) lead to decreased protection.

This hypothesis captures the well-known tendency for industries in recession, and not those benefitting from price increases, to receive protection (cf. Hillman 1982; Magee et al. 1989: 18). The hypothesis also predicts a relationship between the business cycle and the tariffs, with protection increasing in the trough and decreasing in the peak (cf. McKeown 1984). It should be noted, however, that the comparative static approach here neglects some dynamic possibilities, such as industry "collapse," that circumscribe the claim here (i.e., Brainerd and Verdier 1997; Cassing and Hillman 1985).

A few have argued the reverse of Hypothesis 3.4. Frieden and Rogowski (1996: 35–6) maintain that "pressure for increased participation in the world economy will rise when a country's terms of trade *improve*; when terms of trade *decline*, pressure for less exposure to global economic trends will increase." Daniel Verdier (1994: 59; cf. Odell 2000) argues that the business cycle only affects the tariffs in countries characterized by pressure politics and not in systems dominated by either the executive or by party politics. Bulmer-Thomas (1994: 33–34) argues that revenue considerations could also lead to contrary results, because Latin American states facing a severe revenue constraint would change tariffs in response to external prices. Increased export earnings would reduce fiscal pressure and lead to lower tariffs. This book presents ample evidence against these views and in support of the conventional claim and Hypothesis 3.4.

Despite these dissenting voices, Hypothesis 3.4 echoes most of the political economy literature. One good example of this hypothesis at work is Latin America in the last quarter of the century. Falling import prices led to a rise in protection as specific duties were left unchanged in Brazil, México, and Uruguay (Bulmer-Thomas 1994: 141). Other states used unchanged official values for imports, with the same effect in practice.

The declining price hypothesis rests on the balancing logic of a political-support model. Politicians respond to change by balancing the added support they receive from those who benefit against the support they might gain

Table 3.1. *Terms of trade and protection in France and the United Kingdom*

| | United Kingdom | | France | |
	Tariff	Openness	Tariff	Openness
Constant	527.‡‡‡	−172.	−155.3‡‡	−250.‡‡‡‡
	(116.)	(156.)	(68.7)	(64.)
Net terms of trade	.20†††	−.094††	.094†††	−.064†††
	(.047)	(.040)	(.029)	(.024)
Year	−.29‡‡‡	.11	.081‡‡	.14‡‡‡‡
	(.062)	(.08)	(.036)	(.034)
rho	.84‡‡‡	.91‡‡‡	.82‡‡‡‡	.88‡‡‡‡
	(.049)	(.044)	(.059)	(.051)
N	98	83	45	88
F	26.2	3.24	8.98	15.03
Adj. R^2	.34	.05	.26	.24
Durbin-Watson original	.32	.27	.40	.38
transformed	2.57	2.30	2.22	2.21

$^{\dagger}\ p < .10$, *one-tailed*　　　　　　　　　　$^{\ddagger}\ p < .10$, *two-tailed*
$^{\dagger\dagger}\ p < .05$, *one-tailed*　　　　　　　　　$^{\ddagger\ddagger}\ p < .05$, *two-tailed*
$^{\dagger\dagger\dagger}\ p < .01$, *one-tailed*　　　　　　　　$^{\ddagger\ddagger\ddagger}\ p < .01$, *two-tailed*
$^{\dagger\dagger\dagger\dagger}\ p < .001$, *one-tailed*　　　　　　　$^{\ddagger\ddagger\ddagger\ddagger}\ p < .001$, *two-tailed*

by redistributing income toward those otherwise harmed. When improving terms of trade harm import-competers, politicians use tariffs to redirect some of exporters' gains toward the import-competing sector.

Table 3.1 shows the results of a test of the declining price hypothesis for the United Kingdom and France. This presents a necessarily rough test, reflecting both data limitations and the partial nature of the theory so far. I use a Cochrane-Orcutt (1949) regression to correct for serial correlation of the residuals. This procedure assumes that the variables on both sides of the equation at time t depend on their values at t-1, and beginning with the autocorrelation in the error terms, it seeks iteratively to estimate the auto-correlation of the other variables until this estimate converges reasonably. This estimation technique therefore assumes that we do indeed have a time series with autocorrelation, but makes the bare minimum of assumptions about the nature of the serial dependence or the structure of the error terms.

Here as elsewhere I use the minimum of control variables to keep the statistical models as close as possible to the formal model. Adding only some control variables can make omitted variable bias worse rather than

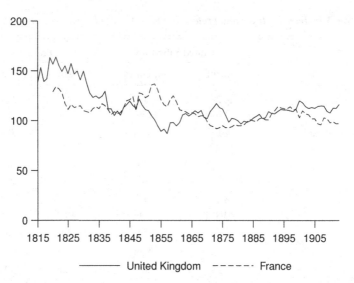

Figure 3.1. Terms of Trade for France and the United Kingdom, 1815–1913.

better, so it is better to keep control variables to a minimum (Clarke 2005). I make one exception because Part IV shows that there are theoretically explicable trends in trade policy over time. For the time being, using YEAR as a control variable will catch those trends for later explanation.

The test strongly supports the declining price hypothesis. We can reject the null hypothesis at the $p < .001$ level for Britain, and the $p < .01$ level for France. A similar test with openness as the dependent variable also supports the hypothesis at the $p < .05$ and $p < .001$ levels, respectively. The time series nature of the data is evident in both the serial correlation of the residuals, captured in rho, and the control variable YEAR.

In addition to statistical significance, the terms of trade have a substantively large effect on British tariffs. A 20-point increase in the terms of trade will raise protection by 4 percentage points. This represents a significant amount for a country with average tariffs of about 15% in this century. Indeed, the major movements in the terms of trade, shown in Figure 3.1, had very important effects on the tariff. The decline in the net terms of trade from 164 in 1819 to 87 in 1857 more than suffices to account for the entire reduction of the British tariff from 23% to 12% over those years, controlling for the secular decline in the tariff over this century.[11]

---

[11] The analysis so far does not control for possible endogeneity, in that a large country's lower tariffs should hurt its terms of trade. See later and Irwin (1988) for analysis of the British case.

The terms of trade have an even larger effect on French tariffs, doubtless because the range of the dependent variable is much larger in a more protectionist country. Improving the terms of trade by one standard deviation raises average tariffs by about 10 points. Changing the terms of trade by its entire domain from 92 to 137 (1885 = 100) yields about a 40-point change in average tariffs.

Although long time series for the terms of trade are lacking for other countries, evidence for particular price series also supports the declining price hypothesis. The most important such series is of grain prices from the 1870s to 1890s. Given the importance of agriculture to these economies, it is hardly surprising that grain prices had substantial effects on European protection. For example, Italy saw wheat prices fall from 331 lire per ton in 1878–1880 to 245 lire in 1883 and 228 lire in 1885 as a result of competition from cheap American grain and the lire's return to gold convertibility in 1883 (M. Clark 1996: 18–19). These price changes led northern agriculturalists, who competed against American wheat, to demand protection. The tariff rose to 3 lire a quintal in 1887, 5 lire in 1888, and 7 and then 7.5 lire in 1894 (Coppa 1971: 63).

Germany saw the same pattern in response to the fall of world agricultural prices in the late 1870s and early 1880s. The famous marriage of iron and rye dates to 1879, in the early phase of the price fall. As prices finally recovered in 1891, tariffs could be reduced once again (Barkin 1970; Dawson 1904; Gerschenkron 1943/1989; Gourevitch 1977; Rogowski 1989: Chapter 2; Weitowitz 1978: Chapter 2). Caprivi took advantage of the new environment to lower grain tariffs in a series of treaties with Germany's neighbors, as I discuss in greater detail later.

Important as those tariffs were, the logic of partial compensation (Hypothesis 3.2) continues to apply. Tariff increases compensate import-competers for less than the full price drop. Rolf Weitowitz (1978: 4) notes this effect in Germany, where "despite the tariff increases of 1885 and 1887 the fall of agricultural prices [in Germany] did not cease, though they did fall more slowly at home than abroad."[12] Exporters therefore enjoyed some of the benefits of lower global prices, whereas import-competers were cushioned from part of the costs.

In short, the declining price hypothesis receives substantial empirical support from British tariffs over the century, French tariffs over the last four decades of the century, and grain-importing tariffs from the late 1870s to

---

[12] "Trotz der Zollerhöhungen 1885 und 1887 wurde der Verfall der Agrarpreise nicht aufgehalten, obwohl diese langsamer fielen als im Ausland."

the early 1890s. This hypothesis is hardly unique here, and it plays a role in many other theories of political economy. Although its ubiquitous nature may give us confidence in its validity, additional hypotheses are necessary to show that the theory of political support performs better than plausible rivals. The next four sections provide these hypotheses, looking at specific duties, market power, the effects of transportation costs, and changes in tariff volatility.

Specific and *ad valorem* Duties

ETT includes a literature that examines the political motives for choosing among tariffs, import quotas, voluntary export restraints, and other instruments of protection (i.e., Cassing and Hillman 1985; Kaempfer, McClure and Willett 1989; Levinsohn 1989; Rosendorff 1996; Vousden 1990). To my knowledge, it has not yet examined the choice between specific and *ad valorem* tariffs, a choice that was more important in 1815–1913 than it is today. However, the theory of political support and its declining prices hypothesis (Hypothesis 3.4) extend easily to this question. When world prices for a good decline, a support-maximizing politician might raise tariffs through new legislation or by administrative decree. Either choice imposes some administrative costs. Self-adjusting tariffs would eliminate these costs and provide smoother price changes.

Specific duties serve this purpose admirably because they are indeed self-adjusting as a percent of value. The cost of a specific duty as a percentage of a good's value will vary with the good's price. A duty of 10 shillings a bushel of wheat weighs four times more heavily when the price of wheat is 20s/bushel than when it is 80s. As a result, a specific duty becomes more protective during deflation and less protective as prices increase.

In contrast, an *ad valorem* duty does not change as a percentage of the price of a good, though it does vary in absolute terms.[13] A 25% tariff on light trucks requires three times the payment on a truck valued at $15,000 as on a truck valued at $5,000. This increase with price works in a direction directly contrary to the declining price hypothesis. As a result, Hypothesis 3.4 implies that we should observe states using specific duties instead of *ad valorem* duties, at least for autonomous tariffs.

---

[13] Many countries used *ad valorem* duties on "official" prices that were fixed for long periods of time. These are effectively specific duties because they do not vary with changes in the market price.

We see this reasoning in French debates over a new tariff in 1878. Testimony from the Chambers of Commerce was virtually unanimous in wanting to substitute specific duties for *ad valorem* duties. They argued that specific duties would give greater protection if the price of foreign imports declined. These arguments swayed the commission, which converted many of the old tariffs to specific duties (M. S. Smith 1980: Chapter 4).

Foreigners might demand *ad valorem* duties in a treaty so as to avoid these effects. Romanian policy reflected these concerns in 1885, when protectionists successfully obtained a return to specific duties in the autonomous tariff, but retained *ad valorem* duties for countries with whom Romania had a tariff treaty (Antonescu 1915: 78–79).

Casual empiricism yields results consistent with this hypothesis. Specific duties were commonplace in Europe at the start of our century, when most countries had autonomous tariffs. For example, the reformed Prussian tariffs of 1818 and 1821 used mostly specific duties, as did the Austrian tariffs as they replaced the former prohibitive system in the first decades of this century. When Romania received tariff autonomy from the Ottomans, it moved to a system of specific duties in its 1874 tariff law (Antonescu 1915: 39).

In contrast, by century's end, many (perhaps most) European countries had moved to *ad valorem* tariffs. This change accompanied the increase in trade cooperation over this period. This greater use of *ad valorem* tariffs had the effect of binding tariffs contractually, taking away the flexibility of the previous specific duties. This contractual binding also had the politically unattractive feature of *increasing* the domestic price of goods still further when the international price was already high, an effect that could have discouraged the use of tariffs and made liberalization easier.

The political logic of the declining price hypothesis differs from an alternative explanation of specific duties relying on administrative capacity. Specific duties, which levy tariffs on goods by weight, do not require customs officials to determine the value of goods crossing a frontier. This means that specific duties require less capacity to administer than *ad valorem* rates. They would be attractive to states with low administrative capacity, especially the newer states of southeastern Europe and Latin America.

Both political-support and administrative capacity arguments predict that specific duties will be common at the start of our period and will become decreasingly prevalent with time. I cannot easily distinguish between the two arguments. Even if data were available, determining the relative importance of specific and *ad valorem* duties in a given country's tariffs raises all the questions of tariff weighting discussed in Chapter 2. For this reason, the choice between these two arguments must rest on their other observable implications.

Market Power and the Tariff

The analysis so far has assumed that each country does not affect the world price for the goods that it imports. If, in contrast, country A is large by the standards of traditional trade theory, then A's tariffs will lower the world price for the goods it imports. Using the notation of this chapter, this implies that $\partial p_w / \partial t_A < 0$.

Having this market power does not change the basic logic of the preceding sections. However, it does shift the equilibrium slightly, to $[(\partial M/\partial Y_E)(\partial Y_E/\partial p_d) + (\partial M/\partial Y_I)(\partial Y_I/\partial p_d)](1 + t_A + \partial p_w/\partial t_A) = 0$. This requires a higher t_A than in the equilibrium with exogenous world prices. This implies that:

Hypothesis 3.5: Large states and tariffs. Large states will have higher autonomous tariffs than small states.

A large state's market power is economically beneficial because it improves the nation's terms of trade. Even so, this market power is politically harmful. By reducing world prices for its imports, a large state hurts its own import-competers. To compensate, policymakers redistribute income to import-competers through tariffs.

O'Rourke and Williamson (1999: 85–86) find indirect evidence of this causal mechanism for Britain in the 1840s. They argue that a loss of market power drove repeal of the Corn Laws, as capitalists found themselves, and not foreigners, paying more of the costs of protecting landlords.

This hypothesis also accords with Germany's experience with grain tariffs in the 1870s and 1880s. Some policymakers apparently did not understand the logic of an optimal tariff when they noted that German tariffs had had only a limited effect on grain imports because world prices had continued to fall (Weitowitz 1978: 34). One reason why world prices fell was doubtless this very increase in the German price, which suppressed global demand somewhat. Germany's ability to improve its terms of trade hurt its import-competers.

Though the causal mechanism differs, my claim that small states choose lower tariffs than large countries also accords with small state theory (Kadar 1970; Katzenstein 1985; Mjøset 1986; 1987; Robinson, 1960; M. Schmidt 1981; Schwartz 1994). This literature argues that small states must rely more

Table 3.2. *Openness for large and small countries in Europe*

	N	Years	Mean
Denmark	96	1818–1913	20.5
	53	1861–1913	26.8
France	89	1825–1913	11.2
	53	1861–1913	14.8
Germany	34	1880–1913	19.5
Italy	53	1861–1913	10.9
Norway	49	1863–1913	24.3
Spain	12	1902–1913	9.8
Sweden	53	1861–1913	19.7
United Kingdom	84	1830–1913	24.5
	53	1861–1913	27.9
Average large		1861–1913	18.3
Average small		1861–1913	20.2

heavily on international markets for various reasons, and therefore they choose lower tariffs. The claim is well supported in the literature on the contemporary period (Katzenstein 1985), as well as the interwar period (Simmons 1994).[14] Paul Bairoch (1993: 25–29) argues, using a variety of qualitative evidence, that the same was true before 1914.

To extend this evidence into the nineteenth century, I conducted several tests of Hypothesis 3.5, reported in Tables 3.2–3.4. Table 3.2 shows the level of openness for those countries for which data are available. Tables 3.3 and 3.4 show the data on average tariffs, both over the entire data series and during a shorter period in which data are available for all countries. I also distinguish between developed countries (north and west of Austria-Hungary, inclusive) and less developed countries in the last table.

The evidence is always consistent with the hypothesis, though the difference between large and small states is not great. Table 3.2 shows that small states were slightly more open than large states in 1861–1913. Table 3.3 shows that large states also had somewhat higher average tariffs, though the length of the data series varies widely by country. Table 3.4 looks only at 1885–1913 for all countries and separates developed from undeveloped countries. Again, large states have higher tariffs than small states – though

[14] Though the predictions for the autonomous tariff agree, Chapter 8 shows that small state theory and political-support theory make opposite predictions for cooperation.

90   Politics and Trade Cooperation in the Nineteenth Century

Table 3.3. *Average tariffs in large and small countries in Europe*

	N	Years	Mean
Austria-Hungary	69	1845–1913	3.9
Belgium	67	1846–1912	2.3
Finland	31	1883–1913	11.7
France	46	1868–1913	7.4
Germany	34	1880–1913	7.6
Italy	52	1862–1913	10.9
Netherlands	68	1846–1913	1.0
Norway	39	1875–1913	11.4
Portugal	39	1875–1913	30.3
Romania	50	1864–1913	7.8
Russia	99	1815–1913	27.6
Spain	63	1851–1913	15.8
Sweden	53	1861–1913	10.7
Switzerland	29	1885–1913	4.2
United Kingdom	99	1815–1913	14.6
Average large			12.0
Average small			10.6

almost all of this difference in the population stems from the low tariffs of small developed countries compared to large developed countries. Although the evidence is consistent with the hypothesis, apparently a country's level of development has a larger substantive effect than does country size.

One reason for the relatively small effect of size is that even small countries may have some market power and may affect the price of goods on world markets for some goods. For example, one study of the antebellum United States suggests that, though it was then a small country, its optimal tariff was about 35–40% (James 1981, but Harley 1982). Although the United States may have been exceptional because of its dominant position as a raw cotton supplier, other small countries also dominated markets for some goods. Exports of livestock, for example, were highly concentrated in southeastern Europe until refrigeration opened up the transatlantic market for meat.

Though its effect may be modest, country size does seem to have an independent effect on tariffs exactly as Hypothesis 3.5 would predict. Because their market power can change world prices, large states have to impose higher tariffs to gain the same political advantage as smaller states can achieve with lower tariffs. This fact will affect the willingness of each country to cooperate with others, as I show in Chapter 8.

Table 3.4. *Average tariffs in Europe, 1885–1913*

	N	Dates	Mean
Austria-Hungary	29	1885–1913	5.4
Belgium	28	1885–1912	1.7
Bulgaria	9	1905–1913	15.4
Denmark	23	1891–1913	7.6
Finland	29	1885–1913	12.0
France	29	1885–1913	9.0
Germany	29	1885–1913	8.2
Italy	29	1885–1913	12.5
Netherlands	29	1885–1913	0.5
Norway	29	1885–1913	11.4
Portugal	28	1885–1912	30.2
Romania	29	1885–1913	9.1
Russia	29	1885–1913	30.9
Spain	28	1885–1912	15.3
Sweden	29	1885–1913	10.4
Switzerland	29	1885–1913	4.2
United Kingdom	29	1885–1913	5.2
Average large			11.9
large developed			8.1
Average small			10.7
small developed			6.0

Transportation Costs and the Tariff

In addition to analyzing the effects of market power, the theory of political support can also examine how tariffs respond to economic variables such as transportation costs. This question is important because the nineteenth century saw rapidly declining transportation costs (O'Rourke and Williamson 1999: Chapter 3). The century began with a wave of canal building. Railroads and steamships followed, along with advances in refrigeration that made possible long-distance trade in perishables. Development of road and rail networks was also essential for the economies of Romania (Antonescu 1915: Chapter 1), Spain (Vicens Vives with Nadal Oller 1969: Chapter 14), and Sweden (Heckscher 1954: Chapter 6), among many other countries. Generalizing considerably, these costs declined most rapidly in the 1820s–1830s (canals and railroads) and 1870s (steamships and refrigeration).

Contemporaries often recognized the ways in which tariffs and transportation costs could substitute for one another. For example, the protectionists of East Prussia, the Conservatives, and the Center Party opposed plans to build a Dortmund-Ems branch of the Mittelland canal in Germany in 1894 (Barkin 1970: 215–7). Konrad Freiherr von Wangenheim of the Farmers' League (*Bund der Landwirte*) argued, "So long as we are not able to have a tariff unregulated by treaties . . . so long will nothing be left for us but to decide against extensions of the canal" (cited in Barkin 1970: 216). The canal was defeated again in 1899, though it was known to be Kaiser Wilhelm's pet project – a remarkable breach of deference by a supposedly conservative, royalist movement.

The economic theory of trade analyzes transportation costs in the same way as an *ad valorem* tariff: high transportation costs drive a wedge between the world price and the domestic price of a good. We can use this divergence to analyze how exogenous changes in transportation costs affect trade policy.

Like tariffs, transportation costs make domestic relative prices ($p_d \equiv p_{dI}/p_{dE}$) diverge from world relative prices ($p_w \equiv p_{wI}/p_{wE}$). For simplicity, I assume that transportation costs (c) are proportional to the price of a good; thus $p_d = p_w(1 + c)$. This assumption obviously excludes variation between bulky low-price goods such as wheat and easy-to-transport high-price items such as jewelry, but it captures most shipping problems well. An *ad valorem* tariff might be applied to the invoice value of a good either f.o.b. (i.e., before transportation costs) or c.i.f. (including such costs).[15] It is mathematically easier to assume the former, so that with both transportation costs and the tariff, $p_d = p_w(1 + c + t)$. For now I ignore the effects of transportation costs on the price that exporters earn in foreign markets, reserving this issue for the two-country model. The logic of political support remains the same as before, yielding the following model:

$$p_d \equiv p_{dI}/p_{dE} \qquad p_w \equiv p_{wI}/p_{wE} \qquad p_d = p_w(1 + c + t)$$
$$Y_I(p_d), Y_E(p_d) \qquad \partial Y_I/\partial p_d > 0, \partial Y_E/\partial p_d < 0 \qquad (3.4)$$
$$M = M[Y_E(p_d), Y_I(p_d)]$$

The political-support maximizing tariff occurs where $(\partial M/\partial Y_E)$ $(\partial Y_E/\partial t) + (\partial M/\partial Y_I)(\partial Y_I/\partial t) = 0$. To find the effects of transportation costs (c) on the tariff (t), i.e., dt/dc, we conduct an analysis that exactly parallels that of Hypothesis 3.4 above, with c playing the role of p_w. This yields the result that dt/dc < 0 in the interior solutions here. This negative sign on the derivative implies

Hypothesis 3.6: Transportation costs. Declining transportation costs leads to higher tariffs, whereas increasing transportation costs leads to lower tariffs.

---

[15] For a straightforward review of the various measurement issues here, see Moneta (1959).

The logic is the same as for the partial compensation hypothesis (Hypothesis 3.2). Lower transportation costs hurt import-competers – and help exporters – so the government compensates import-competers out of some of the exporters' gains. The hypothesis would also expect protection in response to any reduction in transaction costs, of which tariffs and transportation are just two examples. Internationalization of production at the current time, for example, should be associated with a protectionist backlash.

The extension of major railroads in the Balkans provides an illustration of this hypothesis at work. The Vienna-Thessaloniki and Vienna-Istanbul lines, built after 1883, exposed Hungarian agriculture to competition from regions beyond neighboring Serbia (von Bülow 1902: 2). The result was increasing protection, both in the form of tariffs and in tighter veterinary regulations of livestock imports.

Railroad development had a similar effect in the Balkans, opening parts of Bulgaria and Romania to competiton from manufactured goods. Indeed, the political consequences of this process puzzled observers. Cornelius Antonescu (1915: 40) criticized Romanian policy for having supported railroad and port improvements, while reintroducing transit duties on the goods using the railroads and removing preferences for the major ports of Galatia and Braila. Of course, transportation improvements opened more local products to international competition, and the logic of compensation demanded a political response reducing this competition. Far from being puzzling, this policy package makes sense in terms of Hypothesis 3.6.

This transportation costs hypothesis accounts for global as well as regional changes. It explains very well Europe's response to the dramatic reduction in transportation costs for New World and Russian grain in the 1870s. With railroads opening the grain heartlands, steamships continuing to lower ocean shipping costs, and the start of refrigerated transportation, low-cost agricultural goods from afar rapidly flooded the European market. Country after country responded with tariffs, beginning with Austria's so-called autonomous tariff of 1878. More notorious acts followed, including Germany's marriage of iron and rye in 1879 and eventually France's Méline tariff of 1892. The result seemed paradoxical to Émile Levasseur (1892: 49):

We see men stretching out over the earth railroad lines, multiplying the number of their steam-ships, increasing in short the facility of the exchange of commodities by the reduction of the duration and price of transportation, and at the same time arresting these very commodities at their frontiers by a protective tariff; it is thus that we see every day the invention of means to produce commodities at a cheaper price, and at the same time a forced increase of the cost of living by protective systems.

Of course, the political-support theory here predicts exactly this response. In this I agree with subsequent historians, who have argued that these countries "were reacting to a common international problem – the sustained decline in primary product prices as new transport systems opened up the world's cheapest sources of supply from the 1870s" (Trebilcock 1981: 83; see also Bairoch 1989: 55–58; O'Rourke and Williamson 1999: 35–36). This is exactly the prediction of Hypothesis 3.6.

The hypothesis may also help explain a more mixed pattern of protection in the 1820s and 1830s, contemporaneous with such improvements as inland canals, clipper ships, and railroads. Many countries raised their tariffs in the 1820s and 1830s, coinciding with this smaller transportation boom. France raised its tariffs in 1822 and 1826, the Netherlands in 1822, Sicily in 1823 and 1827, and the United States in 1824 and 1828. Others exhibit a more mixed pattern. Austria raised its tariff in 1824, though it lowered it again in 1836. Sweden raised its tariff in 1823, lowered it in 1826, and raised it again in 1831. Though lowering internal tariffs, the trend in the *Zollverein* was toward higher external tariffs from the 1830s on. Only Russia is a clear exception to this hypothesis, lowering tariffs in the 1830s.[16] Britain too seems exceptional at first, but I have explained this elsewhere (Pahre 1999).

In each country, these moves to protection reflected protectionist demands from industries facing an increase in imports, notably from Britain (see Williams 1972). Britain's industrial revolution and declining transportation costs both seem plausible explanations, and of course these causes would have especially strong effects when working together. Whatever the exact mix of causes, declining transportation costs certainly provide part of the explanation for Europe's little-noticed move to protection in the 1820s and 1830s – coinciding, as we will see, with a wave of trade treaties in the 1830s in Germany.

This argument turns out to be quite important for our understanding of the nineteenth century. O'Rourke and Williamson (1999: 29) argue that "*all* the commodity market integration in the Atlantic economy after the 1860s was due to the fall in transport costs between markets, and *none* was due to more liberal trade policy." If correct, O'Rourke and Williamson's claim suggests that trade policy is of little substantive importance. However, their analysis is incomplete because they do not model policy

---

[16] A further complication is that these countries would have been reacting to one another's tariffs by liberalizing (see Hypothesis 7.1). Having a few anomalies is therefore not surprising theoretically.

endogenously. As we will see, the theory in this book suggests the following steps: (1) lower transport costs lead to endogenous protection; (2) protection offsets some of the economic gains of trade from lower transport costs; (3) states often negotiate reciprocal trade treaties lowering tariffs; and (4) these treaties undo some of the protection in the first step, recapturing the economic gains of lower transport costs. In this way, O'Rourke and Williamson could be entirely correct about the overall correlation between transportation costs and commodity market integration but they would still miss the essential political mechanisms intervening between this cause and effect. In this case, treaties play an essential counterfactual role, and policy makes a difference.

My position is closer, then, to Jean Sylvain Weiller (1971), who argues that commercial policies do not usually lead an economy in new directions, but return it to a long-run structural pattern after that pattern has been disrupted. Backlash and compensation are central processes in political economy. Their political importance is often great, and their effect on the economy needs to be understood within a model capable of asking counterfactual questions such as the one here.

Tariff Volatility

Not only the level of the tariff but its variability also depends on political support maximization. With *ad valorem* tariffs, the effect on domestic prices of a given change in p_w is magnified as t increases because $p_d = (1 + t)p_w$. The effect on domestic incomes of p_w is also magnified as t increases, so that for a given disturbance of a prior equilibrium a larger policy change is necessary to balance the political support of the various groups. As a result,[17]

Corollary 3.1: Tariff volatility. High tariffs are more volatile than low tariffs.

This tariff volatility result suggests that protectionist countries would design volatile forms of high protection. The many corn laws of Europe provide a good example. Britain's 1815 laws, the most well known, originally prohibited the import of "corn" ("wheat" in the United States) when the

---

[17] I label this a corollary because, though it follows easily from the partial derivatives of the equilibrium condition, taking the total derivatives (and thus taking all effects into account) yields messy and thus ambiguous results without making a very large number of auxiliary assumptions. Thus, it best fits the classification and standard of falsification for corollaries in Table 1.1. To my mind, it is best to acknowledge the looser derivation and see if it matches the empirics.

domestic price was below 80s. Around this price, effective protection could fluctuate violently. Modifications of the laws later introduced a sliding scale of prohibitions and duties around a series of price points, but the essential volatility remained (Prest 1996).[18] The laws had such strong effects that bankers in the City of London complained about the volatility of the foreign exchange markets that resulted from the corn trade (Howe 1997: 15).

For similar reasons, expensive imports also dampen tariff volatility, whereas cheap imports increase volatility. Paralleling Corollary 3.1, then:

Corollary 3.2: Price volatility. As the world price of an imported good increases, tariffs imposed on that good will be less volatile; as the world price of an imported good decreases, tariff volatility will increase. (Equivalently, worsening terms of trade reduce tariff volatility, and improving terms of trade increase tariff volatility.)

To the best of my knowledge, this volatility result does not follow from other types of endogenous tariff theory models. A theory based on winner-takes-all politics would have to argue that a strongly protectionist coalition, such as Bismarck's marriage of iron and rye, would be more unstable than a more liberal coalition.[19] It is hard to see why this would be true.

Because they depend on political reactions to the market, these predictions about volatility differ from those of economic theories. Economists rightly point out that greater trade allows consumers to smooth their consumption by substituting among tradable goods. This continual substitution leads to more volatile trade, investment, and output in individual countries (Razin and Rose 1994). On economic grounds, then, high levels of openness should be more volatile than low levels of openness. Corollary 3.1 predicts exactly the reverse by introducing politics within a theory of political support. Because it contrasts with these other theories, testing the volatility hypothesis helps distinguish political-support theory from others.

I can test these volatility hypotheses by looking at whether we observe the tariff volatility that the model predicts. Corollary 3.1 predicts that countries with higher tariffs will have more volatile tariffs than those with lower tariffs.

---

[18] Notice incidentally that the level of protection changes here in a direction consistent with the declining-price hypothesis (Hypothesis 3.4).

[19] Rogowski's (1987) argument would suggest a spurious relationship, in that trade dependence leads both to lower tariffs and to electoral systems using proportional representation, and these political systems dampen policy volatility. W. Mayer (1981) would suggest that low voting costs lead to greater volatility, whereas high voting costs reinforce the status quo. Messerlin (1996) suggests a different causal direction, arguing that unstable political institutions in France lead to protectionism because an inflexible bureaucracy takes over from elected politicians and favors higher tariffs.

Table 3.5. *Average tariffs and volatility*

	N	Years	Mean	St. Dev.	Volatility
Argentina	16	1895–1910	63.1	3.89	0.062
Austria-Hungary	69	1845–1913	3.9	0.29	0.075
Belgium	67	1846–1912	2.2	0.15	0.066
Brazil	19	1895–1913	39.6	1.61	0.041
Bulgaria	9	1903–1913	15.4	0.56	0.037
Canada	47	1866–1913	16.6	0.46	0.028
Chile	19	1895–1913	136.4	9.13	0.067
Denmark	23	1891–1913	7.6	0.31	0.042
France	46	1868–1913	7.4	0.36	0.049
Germany	34	1880–1913	7.6	0.37	0.049
Italy	52	1862–1913	10.9	0.52	0.048
Netherlands	68	1846–1913	1.0	0.089	0.092
Norway	39	1875–1913	11.4	0.25	0.021
Perú	19	1895–1913	26.9	0.87	0.033
Portugal	39	1875–1913	30.3	0.84	0.028
Romania	50	1864–1913	7.8	0.38	0.048
Russia	99	1815–1913	27.6	1.02	0.037
Spain	63	1851–1913	15.8	0.47	0.030
Sweden	53	1861–1913	10.7	0.21	0.019
Switzerland	29	1885–1913	4.2	0.12	0.029
United Kingdom	99	1815–1913	14.6	1.08	0.074
United States	99	1815–1913	24.3	0.75	0.031
Uruguay	19	1895–1913	38.0	0.99	0.026

I can test this against both tariffs and openness. Because openness is inversely related to tariffs, Corollary 3.1 predicts that the coefficient of variation for openness is *negatively* related to the mean.

At least some data are available for 15 European countries for some part of 1815–1913 (see Tables 3.5–3.6). Because volatility may vary across all these countries by decade for exogenous reasons, I also test the hypothesis against a smaller set of countries over the same period (1891–1913 for tariffs, 1880–1913 for openness). This second test eliminates any volatility that may be found in all countries in some period, such as the depression of the late 1870s, but for which data are available only for some countries.

To test the hypothesis, I first calculate the coefficient of variation for each country's average tariff or openness. (This is simply the standard deviation divided by the mean.) Then I regress the coefficient of variation against the mean. The result relates variability to average levels of the variable across countries. Though there are very few observations for each

Table 3.6. *Openness and its volatility*

	N	Years	Mean	St. Dev.	Volatility
Brazil	53	1861–1913	27.8	8.3	.30
Denmark	96	1818–1913	20.5	9.2	.45
France	89	1825–1913	11.2	4.9	.44
Germany	34	1880–1913	19.5	4.0	.21
Italy	53	1861–1913	10.9	1.8	.17
Norway	49	1865–1913	24.3	3.8	.16
Spain	12	1901–1912	9.8	1.1	.11
Sweden	53	1861–1913	19.7	3.7	.19
United Kingdom	84	1830–1913	24.5	5.6	.23
United States	49	1865–1913	5.5	.95	.17

test, regression is a servicable technique for the hypothesis-testing exercise here; I do not include any control variables so as to retain scarce degrees of freedom.

Although each coefficient of variation (volatility) is negatively related to its own mean by definition, there is no a priori reason why volatility must decrease as the means increase across countries; a reasonable null hypothesis is that the standard deviations increase proportionally to the means, leaving volatility unchanged. The fact that I make predictions in two directions (positive for the tariff, negative for openness) raises the evidentiary bar if spurious relationships between volatility and means are a problem.

The resulting regressions are shown in Tables 3.7 and 3.8 (standard errors in parentheses). For Europe, all four estimates are correctly signed, and three are statistically significant at conventional levels. The coefficient for the average tariff in the Americas is also correctly signed and statistically significant.

As a different kind of test, I also looked to see if each country's volatility varied with its tariffs over time. This captures the expectation that tariff volatility should decrease (increase) as a country's tariffs decrease (increase) over time. Table 3.9 shows the results, using a five-year moving average for both volatility and the average tariff. The prediction is correctly signed and statistically significant for 7 of the 12 countries. It is correctly signed but not significant for the remaining five countries. We may state this claim as an additional result, combining Corollary 3.1 with the empirical generalization that European tariffs decline over time:

Result 3.1. Tariff volatility decreases as tariffs decrease over time in Europe.

Table 3.7. *The volatility hypothesis in Europe*

	Predict	Average tariff		Openness	
		Entire series	Same years	Entire series	Same years
Constant		.40[‡‡‡‡]	.12[‡‡‡]	2.2[‡‡‡]	.22[‡‡]
		(.094)	(.030)	(.82)	(.063)
Mean tariff	+	−.0070	.0041[††]		
		(.0066)	(.0022)		
Mean openness	−			−.098[††]	−.0046[†]
				(.048)	(.0028)
N		15	14	8	7
Years		Varies	1891–1913	Varies	1880–1913
F		1.11	3.60	4.10	2.71
Adj. R^2		.01	.17	.31	.22

Column one countries are Belgium, Bulgaria, Denmark, France, Germany/Prussia, Italy, Netherlands, Norway, Portugal, Romania, Russia, Spain, Sweden, Switzerland, and United Kingdom; column two are the same excluding Bulgaria. Column three countries are Denmark, France, Germany/
Prussia, Italy, Norway, Spain, Sweden, and United Kingdom; column four are the same excluding
Spain.

[†] *p < .10, one-tailed test*   [‡] *p < .10, two-tailed test*
[††] *p < .05, one-tailed test*   [‡‡] *p < .05, two-tailed test*
[†††] *p < .01, one-tailed test*   [‡‡‡] *p < .05, two-tailed test*
[††††] *p < .001, one-tailed test*   [‡‡‡‡] *p < .001, two-tailed test*

Table 3.8. *Tariff volatility in the Americas,
1895–1913*

	Average tariff
Constant	.023[‡‡‡]
	(.0056)
Average tariff	.00035[†††]
	.00009
N	7
F	15.6
Adj. R^2	.71

[†] *p < .10, one-tailed test*   [‡] *p < .10, two-tailed test*
[††] *p < .05, one-tailed test*   [‡‡] *p < .05, two-tailed test*
[†††] *p < .01, one-tailed test*   [‡‡‡] *p < .05, two-tailed test*
[††††] *p < .001, one-tailed test*   [‡‡‡‡] *p < .001, two-tailed test*

Table 3.9. Tariff volatility over time in Europe

	Austria	Belgium	France	Germany	Italy	Neth.	Norway	Portugal	Romania	Russia	Spain	UK
Constant	.020	−.23	.72	.77	.72	−.016	−3.1	−17.3†	1.1	−11.0†	4.3†	.14
	(.19)	(.20)	(1.2)	(1.20)	(1.5)	(.076)	(2.7)	(8.2)	(1.4)	(6.4)	(2.5)	(.84)
Moving avg. tariff	1.00†	.34††††	.062	.11	.13	.24†††	.48††	.80†††	.15	.70†††	.033	.23†††
	(.52)	(.090)	(.14)	(.14)	(.12)	(.078)	(.23)	(.30)	(.15)	(.21)	(.16)	(.047)
rho	.73	.69††††	.74††††	.58††††	.79††††	.71††††	.65††††	.52†††	.80†††	.75†††	.66††††	.068††††
	(.086)	(.086)	(.11)	(.15)	(.092)	(.089)	(.14)	(.16)	(.085)	(.069)	(.10)	(.076)
N	64	62	41	29	47	63	34	17	43	94	58	94
F	.03	14.6	.18	.63	1.09	9.24	4.26	7.16	.94	10.64	.04	23.63
Adj R²	−.016	.18	−.021	−.013	.0019	.12	.12	.28	−.00	.94	−.017	.20
Durbin-Watson	.55	.56	.51	.83	.45	.60	.74	.76	.35	.54	.70	.66
D-W (trans)	1.82	1.25	.99	1.74	1.91	1.32	1.51	1.71	2.19	1.81	1.96	1.90

Cochrane-Orcutt regressions, using five-year moving averages centered on each year for the average tariffs and the standard deviation of the average tariffs.

† $p < .10$, one-tailed test
†† $p < .05$, one-tailed test
††† $p < .01$, one-tailed test
†††† $p < .001$, one-tailed test

‡ $p < .10$, two-tailed test
‡‡ $p < .05$, two-tailed test
‡‡‡ $p < .05$, two-tailed test
‡‡‡‡ $p < .001$, two-tailed test

Again, I use the term "result" for a claim that combines a deductive hypothesis with an inductive generalization or "finding."

Though the hypotheses are confirmed, tariff and openness levels have only modest substantive effects on volatility. Both tariffs and openness measure about 5–25% for most countries in most of this period. A significant change from 10 to 20% would raise volatility by only .04 for either variable. Most of the coefficients of variation are less than .20 (see Tables 3.5 and 3.6). As a matter of hypothesis testing the theory passes, but it seems not to have identified a substantively important effect in the cross-national test. However, the coefficients in the intertemporal single-country tests are two orders of magnitude larger. For the evolution of a single country's trade policy over time, the substantive effect is large. This suggests that cross-national volatility is affected by some unidentified variable, but the hypotheses here have an important substantive effect on intertemporal variation.

Small state theory suggests a third possible test of the hypothesis. This literature argues that the central concern of small states is that their high trade dependence and high specialization make them especially subject to the volatility of the world market (Marcy 1960). We would expect small country openness to reflect this volatility, which might also appear in policy responses such as average tariffs. In contrast, the theory of political support predicts that small states will have less volatile average tariffs and openness because they have lower effective tariffs. We can classify my claims as "results" that synthesize empirical findings about country size with my deductions about volatility:

Result 3.2. Small countries have less volatile tariffs than large countries.

Predictions about volatility therefore help distinguish the theory of political support from small state theory, though both predict low tariffs for small nations.

Table 3.10 presents the evidence on volatility for countries small and large. The average coefficient of variation for small country tariffs was .143, whereas large countries had an average coefficient of .200. In other words, large country tariffs are half again as volatile as small country tariffs. Openness shows a similar pattern, though the difference is less notable – small countries have a coefficient of variation of .110, large countries .134. This finding distinguishes the theory here (Hypotheses 3.5 and 3.7) from small state theory, though both agree with the observable relationship found in Hypothesis 3.5.

In short, the theory of political support passes all three tests of tariff volatility. Though tariff volatility is not intrinsically interesting in a study

Table 3.10. *Country size and tariff volatility*

Country	Coefficients of variation	
	Tariff, 1891–1913	Openness, 1880–1913
Belgium	.113	N.A.
Denmark	.199	.088
Finland	.135	.131
Netherlands	.074	N.A.
Norway	.114	.122
Portugal	.186	N.A.
Romania	.214	N.A.
Spain	.229	N.A.
Sweden	.102	.098
Switzerland	.065	N.A.
France	.116	.108
Germany	.173	.207
Italy	.348	.167
Russia	.229	N.A.
United Kingdom	.136	.054
Average small	.143	.110
Average large	.200	.134

of trade cooperation, it does provide an opportunity to distinguish the theory of political support from others. By addressing a topic neglected by earlier theorizing, the theory also demonstrates the ability to predict "new facts," an important standard for progressive theorizing in the philosophy of science (Lakatos 1970). Other theories seem not to have addressed volatility at all.

Conclusion

This chapter has argued that a theory of political support provides a good account of trade policymaking in a single country. Although couched at a high level of abstraction, the theory captures the central features of nineteenth-century politics. States seeking support from increasingly mobilized publics, and not popular groups forming coalitions to choose their head of government, dominated the political scene. A simple model shows that this search for political support meant that tariffs increased with declining world prices for imports, domestic political influence of import-competers, market power, country size, and falling transportation costs. The basic rule in Part III is that high tariffs make cooperation more difficult, so all of these factors will tend to make cooperation less likely (see especially Chapter 8).

Some of these hypotheses follow from other theories, but none of these alternatives predicts them all. Hypotheses on tariff volatility, not found elsewhere, help distinguish this theory from others. Suppressing this volatility provides a major motivation for trade cooperation, as we see in Part III.

The theory of political support always risks being so broad as to be empty of empirical content. At one level, it represents a guide. Much as interest group pluralism and class analysis point to some kinds of actors within certain kinds of relationships, so too does political-support theory. The theory of political support is more obviously political, treating the state as an autonomous actor and not just the result of social pressures or conflicts. On another level, political support is simply a parsimonious assumption much like power maximization in Realist theory or exploitation in Marxism. Its parsimony makes possible the study of many countries over a century. As I have argued with reference to the integrative thesis, the theory of political support also has the advantage of being grounded in historiographic controversies. This should give it greater empirical plausibility than many of its rivals (contrast the debate over Realism in Elman, Elman, and Schroeder 1995).

Looking at the our period, the hypotheses emphasize the role of low grain prices after 1815 and in the 1870s as a cause of agricultural tariffs in Europe. Transportation improvements also encouraged compensatory tariffs in the 1820s. Tariff volatility was high at the start of the period, but tended to decline as tariffs generally went down as a result of the treaties that we examine in Part III. Throughout the period, there are significant differences between the major continental countries and both the European periphery and the Americas, because these groups of countries had different profiles of exports and imports and therefore faced different import/export price ratios. In addition, larger countries tended to have higher tariffs than smaller countries. Such differences reflect the hypotheses of political-support theory, summarized in Table 3.11.

Though I have used the theory for nineteenth-century trade policy, it extends easily to the modern political economy. After all, the originators of the theory were economists studying the United States in the 1970s and 1980s. In addition to the effects of specific economic and political conditions on policy, the theory highlights the general processes of compensation. Politicians compensate groups for the harm from exogenous

Table 3.11. *Summary of hypotheses and results*

Hypothesis 3.1: The balancing hypothesis. The domestic price for protected goods is always less than the autarky price would be (cf. Hillman 1982; Peltzman 1975).

Hypothesis 3.2: The partial compensation hypothesis. Compensation is always partial in that no group receives a policy that compensates it fully for disadvantageous exogenous changes.

Hypothesis 3.3: The group influence hypothesis. Any increase in the marginal valuation of a group will change equilibrium prices in its favor.

Hypothesis 3.4: The declining prices hypothesis. Decreasing world prices (i.e., increasing terms of trade) lead to increased protection, and increasing world prices (decreasing terms of trade) lead to decreased protection.

Hypothesis 3.5: Large states and tariffs. Large states will have higher autonomous tariffs than small states.

Hypothesis 3.6: Transportation costs. Declining transportation costs leads to higher tariffs, whereas increasing transportation costs leads to lower tariffs.

Corollary 3.1: Tariff volatility. High tariffs are more volatile than low tariffs.

Corollary 3.2: Price volatility. As the world price of an imported good increases, tariffs imposed on that good will be less volatile; as the world price of an imported good decreases, tariff volatility will increase. (Equivalently, worsening terms of trade reduce tariff volatility, and improving terms of trade increase tariff volatility.)

Result 3.1. Tariff volatility decreases as tariffs decrease over time in Europe.

Result 3.2. Small countries have less volatile tariffs than large countries.

---

changes, paying for this compensation out of the windfall gains to those who benefit.

The result looks like backlash against an increasingly open, global economy in both the nineteenth century and today. Yet compensation is always partial. Backlash may slow, but will not stop or reverse today's globalization. It may also be constrained by trade cooperation, as I show in Part III.

FOUR

State Capacity, Fiscal Concerns, and the Tariff

"Although the 'free traders' might have been expected to press for the reduction of tariffs, their enthusiasm was tempered by the knowledge that government revenue had to be raised somehow, and one obvious alternative to the tariff – a tax on land – was abhorrent to the powerful *latifundistas*."
— Victor Bulmer-Thomas (1994: 140)

The political-support theory in Chapter 3 emphasized how trade policy responds to exogenous change, partially compensating those groups that are harmed. Though it examined some cross-national variation in trade policy, the focus was on intertemporal patterns, especially on economic variables such as the terms of trade.

This chapter and the next examine cross-national differences in political institutions that help explain further variations in the autonomous tariffs of each country. This chapter focuses on the administrative problems of revenue collection, whereas Chapter 5 examines the effects of democracy. The aftermath of the Napoleonic Wars, which produced both fiscal crises and partial democratization as taxpayers demanded greater representation, provides background conditions for the changes that I discuss.

The question of tax collection is important because scholars frequently argue that a state's need for tariff revenue precludes trade liberalization that the government would otherwise pursue. For example, Percy Ashley (1926: 27) argues that Austria could not negotiate tariff reductions with the German *Zollverein* until its finances were in better order, especially after the expensive lost war of 1859 (see also Matis 1973). The weak extractive capabilities of the German Empire led Bismarck to seek greater dependence on tariff revenue, which may have made Germany naturally more protectionist than Britain and others (Ashley 1926: 43, 120–23; D'Lugo and Rogowski 1993; Hardach 1967: 80–123; but see Webb 1982). Tariff and administrative reform came earlier in Hesse-Darmstadt than in neighboring Electoral Hesse or Nassau because of the more parlous state of its finances after the Napoleonic Wars (Hahn 1982: Chapter 2). Italy legislated higher tariffs and renounced treaties in 1878 to end chronic budget deficits (M. S. Smith 1980: 144–48). Difficulties in developing new forms of taxation apparently limited the ability of Latin American states to lower tariffs or negotiate tariff treaties (Bulmer-Thomas 1994; Williams 1972: Chapter 4).

As a result, many scholars argue that nineteenth-century liberalization depended on the development of new revenue instruments in Western Europe. When a government's fisc depended on customs revenue, it could lower tariffs only after developing other sources of revenue, such as an income tax (see *inter alia* Ashley 1926: 27–28; H. Grossman and Han 1993; Hobson 1997; Howe 1997; Imlah 1958: 146–55; Marsh 1999; Nye 1990; Stein 1984). These claims easily fit into the neoclassical theory of the state, which sees most policy as driven by the state's efforts to maximize revenue (i.e., North 1981).

These claims characterize a few countries well, but the full story is more complex. The first element of this complexity is the fact that nontariff sources of revenue, such as an income tax, also have distributional consequences. These distributional effects create winners and losers at home. Another distributional effect is the allocation of state revenue needs among citizens, as Harvey (1938: 7) notes,

Fiscal needs were often used to justify tariffs which were in reality protective, but it is possible that in many cases the ministers were really sincere in their statements that the foreigner would pay the tax. The tendency to resort to tariffs was stronger where financial difficulties were marked by depreciated currencies as in Russia, Italy, and Austria-Hungary. These were regularly debtor countries, and consequently their finance ministers were concerned with the foreign exchange situation and sought to improve it by cutting down imports through the tariff.

Similar considerations doubtless influence the high-tariff policies of many heavily indebted developing countries today. The challenge, addressed throughout this chapter, is to distinguish protective tariffs from revenue tariffs, given the data available.

A second factor making the revenue problem complex is that political-support maximization interacts with revenue concerns. If global trade increases, a government may raise tariffs slightly to capture additional revenue. This policy change also takes some of the gains to export interests from greater trade and redistributes them to import-competers, an effect distinct from the first, revenue-maximizing effect.

A third element is that, for historical reasons, states vary in terms of their institutional capacity across different means of revenue collection. Some are well equipped to collect tariffs, others land or income taxes, and still others may find excise taxes or state monopolies of tobacco and sugar easier to collect. John Hobson (1997) has gone furthest in developing a theoretical analysis of how these differences affect trade policy. In addition to institutional legacy, he rightly emphasizes the political coalitions that support particular fiscal systems. This argument points to state structure as a cause of trade policy instead of the distributional considerations that are central to the theory of political support. Hobson and I agree that differences in state fiscal structure can shape trade policy in important ways, and we agree that these differences have generally declined over time. We differ in details – how prevalent this factor is, and for how long, in the nineteenth century.

To determine the importance of revenue constraints, this chapter argues that we must distinguish between truly exogenous fiscal constraints and an endogenous choice to use tariffs instead of other available tax instruments. Only the exogenous constraints limit policy choices. After investigating the observable implications of exogenous and endogenous fiscal arguments, I conclude that exogenous revenue considerations strongly constrained only a few European states, such as Switzerland, Norway, and Sweden. A few others, notably the United Kingdom, made political choices that constrained subsequent governments. More often, apparent revenue constraints stemmed from political decisions to protect industry or to take advantage of increasing global trade by taxing it. These kinds of "endogenous revenue concerns" may encourage liberalization because they preclude liberalization that politicians might otherwise pursue.

Exogenous revenue concerns serve as a constraint on political-support maximization and thus point to a limitation of the theory in Chapter 3. In contrast, endogenous concerns fit easily into the theory of political support. Classifying each country's constraint as exogenous or endogenous matters for the overall argument because I connect these revenue constraints to international cooperation in Chapter 8. Revenue needs kept only a few states from cooperating with others. In some cases, exogenous revenue concerns constrained a country's ability to cooperate only until the 1860s; after reforms of the revenue instruments, these countries became more likely to cooperate. Examples include Austria-Hungary, Canada, Scandinavia, and the United States. For the rest of the world, endogenous revenue needs encouraged liberalization and actually made cooperation more likely.

The reason why each country fell into one category or the other lies outside the theory of political support. For this reason, this chapter yields inductive "findings" that describe which countries belong in each classification (see Table 4.6 for a summary). However, the consequences of these differences fit easily into the theory of political support and will be important throughout the rest of the book.

The Nature of the Revenue Constraint

Revenue needs might stem from several causes. Most simply, a government might rely on tariff revenue because of low state capacity. It may lack the staff to collect technically complex forms of taxes, or its administration may not yet have penetrated all of the territory nominally under its control. Such governments find tariffs attractive, for trade taxes can be collected in relatively few ports of entry.

Low state capacity may also affect the form of trade protection. Customs officials charged with imposing *ad valorem* duties must value imports properly because importers have an incentive to undervalue their goods. Specific duties present a less administratively challenging alternative, and many nineteenth-century states favored them for this reason (see Chapter 3). However, specific duties provide mixed protection for goods that vary in quality. For example, a specific duty levied on iron by weight will pose a much smaller obstacle to imports of high-quality iron than low-quality iron of equal weight (Cobden Club 1875: 117–18). A government might address this problem by differentiating specific duties by the different grades or values of a good, but this raises technical questions that again require significant administrative capacity.

Other administrative and technical problems might also exert an important influence on trade policy. For example, the Duchy of Baden had a long border relative to its area. Rather than trying to fight smuggling along such long frontiers, the duchy made the tariff lower than smugglers' estimated evasion costs. The many customs enclaves and exclaves in Germany presented similar administrative problems, because customs officials needed to control all points of entry. To make duty collection easier, two states could swap enclaves, or swap them for customs purposes, but retain sovereignty. This problem of enclaves led to the *Zollanschlüße* (tariff accessions) of 1818–1833, by which foreign enclaves acceded to the Prussian tariff system by treaty (Price 1949: Chapter 6). Because Prussia consisted of two major parts, traditional Brandenburg-Prussia and the Rhenish West Prussia, as well as various exclaves of its own inside other German states, the number of neighbors – and thus potential partners – was very large. These revenue problems loomed larger after 1815 because of the disruption in boundaries and heavy government debt stemming from the Napoleonic Wars. Finally, a government might face a severe revenue constraint because it wishes to spend money on new programs. Investment in roads and railroads, communication networks, and other public works played an important part in economic development policy in the nineteenth century. In Italy, ministers Agostino Magliani and Bernardino Grimaldi argued for tariff increases in 1887 to pay for public work projects and reduction of the land tax (Coppa 1971: 50–61).

These considerations have force for many historical periods. However, one may reasonably doubt whether they apply well to most of Europe in the nineteenth century. Austria provides an example. While Austria's finances may have needed reform at mid-century, tariffs were hardly the problem – Austria depended on tariffs for only about 5% of all government revenues, and its protective system used mostly import prohibitions that did not directly generate income. Its revenue relied instead on the salt and tobacco monopolies and on excise and land taxes (Henderson 1939/1984: 196–202; Matis 1973, 1984). These sources of income were irrelevant for trade policy, except that salt and tobacco were normally exempted from the provisions of trade treaties.

Less developed states in Europe had a similar array of revenue sources. Serbian prince Miloš Obrenović (r. 1815–30) had not only tariffs and indirect taxes on trade but also a head tax and a land tax at his disposal, as well as the revenue from several state monopolies (Lampe and Jackson 1982: 120–25). In the 1880s, his successors had royalties from, or monopolies of, tobacco, matches, alcohol, and salt, as well as consumption taxes (trošarine) on tobacco and local sweetmeats (Palairet 1979: 727–28). Even Montenegro, which had almost no domestic sources of revenue, did not need the tariff – it obtained sufficient revenue from Russia as a subsidy.

Newly independent Latin American states developed taxation resources more quickly than one might suppose, and "their states' tax-raising capacities were already comparable to those of the industrial centre" (Mouzelis 1986: 12; but Cardoso and Faletto 1979: 30–36). Argentina's per capita government revenue in 1913 exceeded Britain's and Germany's, though not France's; Chile's and Greece's levels exceeded Germany's and Sweden's. Indeed, the Chilean state was strong enough to appropriate half the gross profits of the foreign-owned nitrate industry through export taxes (Cariola and Sunkel 1985: 155). Many American states had multiple revenue sources, such as taxes on external trade (mainly import duties), taxes on mining (the *quinto*), the *alcabala* (a kind of sales tax), royal monopolies, a share of ecclesiastical tithes, Indian tribute (a poll tax), and the sale of public offices to *peninsulares* (Bulmer-Thomas 1994: 27).

We may also doubt whether revenue needs really explain the protective system found in many countries. Import prohibitions were common, notably in Austria and Russia, but these bring in no revenue. High tariffs also served as poor revenue generators. Reformers eagerly pointed out that lowering tariffs would increase a state's revenue by encouraging greater imports – as did James Deacon Hume, former Secretary to the Board of Trade in Great Britain, who gave evidence before the 1839 Committee on the Import Duties that "the prosperity of the revenue is greatly impeded by the protective system" (cited in Schonhardt-Bailey 1997: 45). Econometric evidence suggests that Hume and other political economists making this claim at mid-century were correct (Irwin 1989b). One goal of the *Zollverein* was to raise revenue by encouraging greater trade through lower tariffs and internal improvements (Henderson 1939/1984; cf. Dumke 1978). A trend toward tariff liberalization arose in some Latin American countries in part because of a similar awareness that a tariff cut could increase revenue if the import price elasticity was greater than 1 (Bulmer-Thomas 1994: 141). Reforms in Brazil in 1853 and Chile in 1864 reflect this trend by lowering tariffs on consumer goods; the average tariff fell to 20% in Colombia in the 1860s.

Of course, other forms of taxation might also spur a growth in trade, often in unintended ways. For example, taxes demanded in money might force subsistence farmers to sell produce on the market, as did Serbia's increased head tax in coin under Obrenović. This tax pushed peasants into selling hogs abroad, especially to the Habsburg Empire (Lampe and Jackson 1982: 113–14). Similarly, the conversion of the Ottoman tithe into a lower tribute from Bulgaria to the Porte encouraged both commerce and trade (Palairet 1997: Chapters 6–7).

We should not forget that revenue concerns were also a distributional issue. Latin American states lacked administrative capacity because the landowners who controlled most governments did not want either land or income taxes (Bulmer-Thomas 1994: 96, 140). In a dramatic illustration of these political challenges, when the Congress of the Central American Federation decided in 1838 to turn over control of the customs revenue to the federal government, the entire union disintegrated. Nicaragua, Costa Rica, and Honduras seceded in turn, each under local pressure from landowners (Perez-Brignoli 1989: 73).

Similar conflicts divided industrial Austria from agricultural Hungary. For example, the Austrian parliament blocked the coffee and petroleum tariffs of the 1878 tariff bill, labeling them tribute to Hungary, which refused to pay direct taxes to the joint offices in Vienna (von Bazant 1894: 38). In a different kind of distributional battle, the smaller German states were offended when the Prussian tariff of 1818 imposed duties on goods destined for customs enclaves. The Saxons saw this as a case of Prussia strengthening its own fisc through indirect taxes payable by the citizens of other states (Hartung 1923: 447–54). These issues became central to development of the *Zollverein* (see Chapter 11).

As they grew stronger through the century, the Socialist parties saw clearly the distributional consequences of revenue instruments. In country after country they demanded an end to indirect taxes of all kinds, to be replaced with a progressive income tax (see Hobson 1997). Of course, Conservatives fought back, often defending the tariff against an income tax. Mythology would have Socialist labor thwarted by the upper classes, but the peasantry provided opposition in some countries. Palairet (1979) shows that the fiscal burdens on Serbian peasants relative to their incomes actually declined markedly by 1914, with increased government income provided mainly by the nonfarm sector, including the working class. Socialist rhetoric against these taxes claimed a common interest with the farmers that has misled the historiography.

These examples show how claims about revenue constraints often covered real debates over distributive issues. These underlying battles often led to claims that revenue needs constrained actions in a given situation, but the revenue argument cannot really explain the trade policy outcomes. Clearly, apparent revenue considerations may stem endogenously from political decisions about protection. Having decided to protect industry for political reasons, a government can rely more heavily on tariff revenue than before, and perhaps even cut other taxes. This action may constrain future choices.[1]

A state might also choose to rely more heavily on tariff revenue for purely fiscal reasons. If international trade grows several times more quickly than GDP, it presents a nearly irresistible source of new revenue. For example, the expansion of foreign trade in the early years of Third Republic France almost doubled revenues from import duties, without raising their level (M. S. Smith 1980: 145). When a state raises tariffs as a choice among fiscal instruments, revenue concerns do not present an exogenous constraint.

---

[1] Though phrased differently, the issues raised in this paragraph parallel Hobson's (1997) "mode of taxation," his fundamental unit of analysis, and the concomitant "social relations of taxation."

Distributional battles over tariffs between exporters and import-competers lurked behind many supposed debates over revenue.

These issues should make us suspicious about the revenue argument on its own terms. Still, ample anecdotal evidence suggests that revenue concerns may limit trade liberalization in some countries at some times. The following sections evaluate these claims empirically. I examine two different kinds of data to see whether they suggest that each country faced exogenous or endogenous revenue considerations. These data are sometimes inconclusive, and I supplement my analysis with the historiography.

The Intertemporal Role of the Revenue Constraint

One way to evaluate the revenue argument is to look at the intertemporal pattern of governments' reliance on tariffs for revenue. Because governments developed new fiscal instruments throughout the century, and because they presumably did not lose any such instruments, tariff revenue dependence should hold constant or decrease over time if revenue constraints are exogenous.[2] If tariff revenue dependence is low or if it increases with time, that reliance on tariff revenue reflects a political choice and not limited state capacity.

To examine a state's dependence on tariff revenue, I use a measure of tariff revenue dependence equal to the percentage share of customs revenue in total central government expenditures. Figure 4.1 shows changing tariff reliance for the three European states that depended most on tariff revenue. Switzerland faced by far the most severe revenue constraint. Nearly all the federal government's revenue came from tariffs until the 1860s, when the percentage of revenue from tariffs dropped to a mere 80%. This level far exceeds any other European country's tariff dependence in this century. Cantonal control over tariffs and tolls, transport, and labor mobility weighed against any change in this system, though all but the wheat duty were low and imposed solely for revenue purposes (Hobson 1997: Chapter 5; Imlah 1966: 11–13, 100–103).

Both halves of Sweden-Norway also relied heavily on customs revenue. This reliance declined modestly with time, but remained comparatively high – the tariff supplied about 40% of all government resources in the last quarter of the nineteenth century.

---

[2] Note, however, that Hobson (1997) argues that the military revolution of the 1870s increased the demand for revenue, and this increased demand might provide exogenous pressure for tariff revenue.

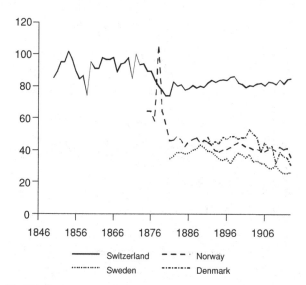

Figure 4.1. Tariff Reliance in Denmark, Norway, Sweden, and Switzerland, 1846–1913.

Figures 4.2–4.4 reveal very different trends in the rest of Europe. Belgium and the Netherlands relied on the tariff for only about 10% of government revenue, with no noteworthy trends evident. Russia, not known for its administrative capacity, also relied on the tariff for only 10–15% of all

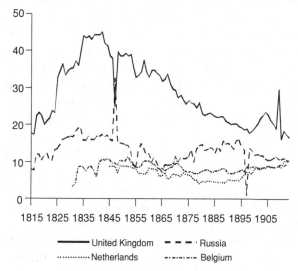

Figure 4.2. Tariff Reliance in the Low Countries, Russia, and the United Kingdom, 1815–1913.

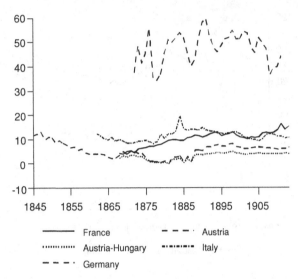

Figure 4.3. Tariff Reliance in Austria(-Hungary), France, Germany, and Italy, 1845–1913.

goverment revenue. These countries did not face a strong revenue constraint, nor did this constraint loosen over time (for a contending view of Russia, see Hobson 1997: Chapter 3).

The United Kingdom depended more heavily on tariff revenue than Russia and the Low Countries did. However, this reflected a political choice. Postwar governments repealed the wartime income tax in 1819, and no prime minister dared reimpose it for almost 30 years. As a result, the share of customs duties in the public fisc more than doubled from 1815 to 1840, forcing Robert Peel to reintroduce the income tax as part of his policy of tariff and fiscal reform in the 1840s. Still, Britain's revenue tariffs provided a comparatively high 20% of government revenue at century's end (for recent overviews see Hobson 1997: Chapter 4; Howe 1999; Marsh 1999).

Political choices are also evident in Figure 4.3, which shows tariff revenue dependence for Austria-Hungary, France, and Italy. Though they had many other fiscal instruments available, France and Italy increased their reliance on tariff revenue in the 1880s and 1890s. The Third Republic (1871–1940) steadily increased France's tariff revenue dependence to still modest levels of 10–15%. When revenue concerns were indeed important, as when the Third Republic had to pay reparations in 1871 (see Laughlin and Willis 1903), governments imposed revenue duties and not protectionist duties. For example, Prime Minister Louis-Adolphe Thiers had no trouble introducing duties on sugar, coffee, tea, cocoa, and pepper – which generally lacked domestic competition – but failed in his efforts to impose protective duties on manufactures and semi-processed goods (Ashley 1926: 307–10). Although he achieved duties of 5% on cotton and 2.5% on other fibers, none of these duties were to take effect without a corresponding surcharge on manufactured goods. However, these surcharges were impossible to impose because they would violate existing treaty obligations. In short, Thiers' protective legislation had no effect on actual tariffs, whereas his revenue tariffs did – a fact that casts doubt on many claims about the Third Republic's inherent protectionism.

Italy's tariff reliance increased slightly in the 1880s, though it apparently occurred in advance of the political decisions of 1887 and 1894 to increase the tariff. Like France, these tariffs reflected political demands for protection and not any exogenous fiscal constraint. In addition, trade represented an attractive source of revenue because it was growing more rapidly than GDP. Trade taxes could also provide revenue for many needed infrastructure projects and patronage spending in the south.

In contrast to France and Italy, Austria never made much use of the tariff. Its slight decline through 1865 would be consistent with the conventional claim of exogenous constraint. Even so, subsequent demands for a protective tariff in Austria (von Bazant 1894; Matis 1973) would also be consistent with endogenous revenue considerations. I decide between these two interpretations in the next section.

Because the revenue argument attributes higher tariffs to a lack of alternative fiscal instruments, we would expect it to apply most strongly to the weaker state structures in the periphery and semi-periphery. The data shown in Figure 4.4 do not support this claim. Bulgaria, Romania, and Spain all relied on tariffs for a low and steady share of government revenue. Both Bulgaria and Spain increased their dependence on tariff revenue over time, perhaps to take advantage of rising trade volumes. For Romania, a break came in the Paris Treaty of 1858, when the tariff became less a revenue instrument and more a means of development policy (Antonescu 1915: 5–6). At this point, the tariff was unambiguously a matter of income redistribution. Only the case of Portugal appears consistent with the revenue argument.

Revenue constraints played a more important role in the newer states of the Americas than in either the old or new states of Europe. Figures 4.5 and 4.6 show very high levels of revenue dependence by European standards. The U.S. federal government, like that in Switzerland, depended on tariffs for more than three-fourths of its revenue at the start of the century. O'Halloran (1994: 47–50) argues that revenue concerns were critical until about 1832 (see also Goldstein 1993; Hobson 1994: Chapter 5; Pincus 1977). Although

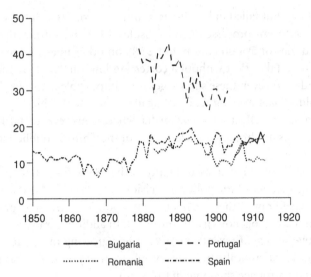

Figure 4.4. Tariff Reliance in Bulgaria, Portugal, Romania, and Spain, 1850–1913.

the central government developed new fiscal instruments in the Civil War, it still depended on tariffs for almost half of all revenue for the next 50 years. Canada lacked any such trauma, and its tariff reliance fluctuated between one-half and two-thirds of all revenue.

Data are lacking for many other New World countries, but the historiography paints a similar picture for most. Victor Bulmer-Thomas (1994:

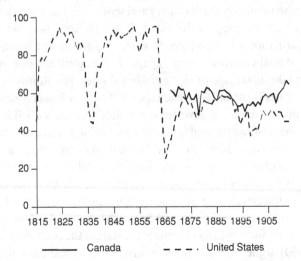

Figure 4.5. Tariff Reliance in the United States and Canada, 1815–1913.

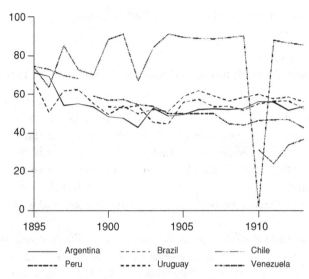

Figure 4.6. Tariff Reliance in Latin America, 1895–1913.

32–33) argues that after Latin American states lost the option of foreign borrowing in the 1820s, tariffs were determined largely by revenue concerns.[3] Taxes on land were politically impossible, and other nontrade taxes were both unpopular and easy to evade. We must also remember that export-oriented landowners dominated many Latin American countries, presenting the apparent paradox of open economies that nonetheless relied heavily on tariffs for government revenue. This is presumably an endogenous revenue constraint more than a protective one. Given this context, then, even this apparent constraint could be seen as a political choice.

In summary, the intertemporal evidence supports the endogenous revenue argument only for Norway, Portugal, Sweden, and Switzerland in Europe. In the other cases, revenue considerations limited the scope of action only after a political choice to rely on tariffs had already been made. This effect characterized Britain after repealing the income tax in 1819 and probably describes most of Latin America. Other countries made a political choice to take advantage of the rapid increase in trade in late century, raising tariffs modestly in part for revenue purposes. Austria-Hungary, Bulgaria, France, Italy, and Spain probably fit this category, but none relied on tariffs for more than 15% of their revenue. Many countries, such as Belgium, the

---

[3] In Argentina, the federal government only became dependent on tariff revenue in 1862, when it wrested control from the state of Buenos Aires (Cortés Condo 1985: 33).

Netherlands, Romania, and Russia, used tariffs for only a modest and steady level of revenue.

Openness, Tariff Revenue Dependence, and Average Tariffs

The preceding section considered the plausibility of the revenue argument intertemporally. This section investigates the causal claims underlying the revenue argument by looking at the relationship among tariff reliance, openness, and the average tariff in each country. The analysis distinguishes between (1) the conventional claim that revenue needs serve as an exogenous constraint on trade policy and (2) a more political claim that reliance on tariff revenue reflects a choice, making revenue needs endogenous to the political system.

The conventional wisdom predicts that average tariffs vary positively with the tariff as a share of government revenue because states tax imports more heavily when tariff revenue is important for the fisc. However, the causal arrow might point in either direction: the government may choose high tariffs because it depends heavily on tariff revenue, or it may rely heavily on tariff revenue simply because it collects a lot of revenue from the tariffs that it chooses for other reasons. This means that a positive relationship would be consistent with either exogenous or endogenous fiscal considerations.

To distinguish exogenous and endogenous revenue arguments, it helps to consider their other implications. First, if revenue considerations are exogenous, we would expect a negative relationship between tariffs and openness because, after all, the lack of alternative fiscal instruments supposedly makes a difference for trade policy outcomes. A positive relationship suggests optimal taxation instead, in which the state relies more heavily on tariff revenue as trade increases. The state will also keep these tariffs modest so as not to kill the golden goose.

The difference depends on the existence of alternative revenue sources. Where alternatives exist, governments shift in and out of relying on tariffs. Otherwise, they are stuck with the tariff. A clear example is the Chilean revenue structure. With the nitrate boom, Chile could extract income through export duties and use it to lower other taxes. The government ended the sales tax in 1884, *los derechos de imposición* in 1888, and devolved many taxes to the municipalities after 1891 (Cariola and Sunkel 1985).

A third relationship, between tariff revenue dependence and openness, also distinguishes the two arguments. If reliance on tariff revenue constrains state choice, then increasing reliance will be negatively correlated with openness. Because the state must rely so heavily on tariff revenue, its high tariffs

Table 4.1. *Expected correlations among revenue, openness, and tariffs*

	Tariff-Revenue	Tariff-Openness	Revenue-Openness
Exogenous constraint	Positive	Negative	Negative
Endogenous revenue	Positive	Positive	Positive
Potentially spurious	Positive	Negative	N.A.

will push openness down. In contrast, endogenous revenue considerations will lead to a positive relationship in which growing openness allows a state to rely more heavily on abundant tariff revenue.

Although these are theoretical relationships, empirical relationships are confounded by potentially spurious correlations because of the way that I must operationalize these concepts. I operationalize revenue considerations as the percentage share of customs revenue in total government revenue, and average tariffs as the percentage share of customs revenue in import value. This means that, when I correlate revenue concerns and average tariffs, a spurious positive relationship is possible because customs revenue appears on both sides. The same thing occurs with openness (imports as a percentage of GDP) and average tariffs (customs revenue as a percentage of imports), potentially yielding a spurious negative correlation. When GDP data are unavailable, I use import value in lieu of openness; this means that this spurious correlation will not be a problem.[4]

We should draw no substantive implications when an observed correlation agrees with an expected spurious correlation. The problem of spuriousness is especially important for exogenous revenue constraints. These exogenous constraints yield, on theoretical grounds, results identical to a potentially spurious relationship in two of these relationships. Only the revenue-openness relationship allows us to distinguish exogenous constraints from a spurious relationship. In contrast, we should draw a very strong inference on those uncommon occasions when the observed correlation differs from the possibly spurious relationship. Observing a positive correlation between tariffs and openness provides a stark contrast with the conventional wisdom and with the possibly spurious correlation, strongly suggesting that a state relies endogenously on tariff revenue.

Table 4.1 summarizes the expectations of each argument. It highlights the fact that it is difficult to distinguish an exogenous revenue constraint from a

---

[4] A different spurious correlation *is* a problem because import volumes are strongly increasing with time and will therefore correlate with any variable experiencing a secular trend of its own.

spurious correlation. This difficulty may explain why the revenue constraint argument plays a largely unquestioned role in the historiography – it is difficult to find quantitative evidence that might contradict it. Moreover, politicians have a political incentive to claim revenue motives no matter what the truth may be. This political motive then biases any historiography that depends on primary sources for claims about motivations. Given this, any nonpositive correlation in the third column is sufficiently striking that I classify the period as having endogenous revenue considerations. This would reflect changes in revenue constraints over time that I have been unable to uncover in a broad review of many countries.

In what follows I review the data for each country. My analysis is sometimes confounded by small or difficult-to-interpret patterns in the data. Again, the historiography informs the analysis, and I often break the data into historical periods around major political or institutional change. When the evidence is not clear, I classify a country as having had endogenous revenue concerns. This does not mean that I count ambiguous cases as support for the theory, but merely classify ambiguous cases in a certain way so as to retain a larger domain of applicability for the theory of political support. If this decision is a bad one, then I will be including inappropriate cases in the later analysis, making it less likely that the evidence will support the hypotheses drawn from the theory.

Exogenous revenue constraints seem to describe some countries well. Table 4.2 shows the relationship among openness, revenue dependence, and tariffs in ten countries. Because Norwegian data are available for a long period, I can distinguish between the periods of constitutional monarchy (1814–84), parliamentary government within the Swedish Union (1885–1905), and independent Norway from 1905. Regardless of the political institutions, Norway provides an excellent illustration of an exogenous revenue constraint. Norway shows a clear trade-off between openness and the average tariff (see also Figures 2.5 and 2.13). Revenue concerns played a consistently positive role in tariff considerations, though the substantive significance of these concerns naturally varied. Given the intertemporal pattern analyzed in the previous section, Norway clearly faced an exogenous revenue constraint.

Denmark and Spain both seem to face exogenous revenue constraints. However, in both countries the weakest relationship – the relationship between revenue dependence and openness – is theoretically the most important. In Spain this relationship is essentially zero. Because the intertemporal evidence (Figure 4.4) failed to uncover any exogenous restraint, we should classify Spain as having endogenous revenue considerations. In

Table 4.2. *Tariff revenue constraints when openness data are available*

	Tariff-Revenue	Tariff-Openness	Revenue-Openness
Brazil, 1900–1913	+.259	−.558	−.076
Denmark, 1891–1913	+.867	−.505	−.326
France, 1871–1913	+.893	−.070	+.248
Germany, 1880–1911	+.212	−.958	−.077
Italy, 1862–1876	−.486	−.533	−.004
Italy, 1877–1913	+.490	−.742	−.137
Norway, 1874–1884	+.284	−.800	−.461
Norway, 1885–1905	+.513	−.743	−.413
Norway, 1906–1913	+.438	−.689	−.163
Spain, 1902–1913	+.698	−.721	−.067
Sweden, 1861–1885	+.424	−.696	−.061
Sweden, 1886–1913	+.722	+.391	+.793
UK, 1830–1846	−.273	−.790	+.684
UK, 1847–1885	+.854	−.765	−.408
UK, 1886–1913	−.485	+.717	−.171
U.S., 1851–1861	−.293	–	–
U.S., 1865–1913	−.138	+.360	+.581

contrast, the Danish intertemporal pattern would also support a finding of an exogenous revenue constraint.

Latin American countries often show a relationship between tariffs and revenue dependence consistent with an exogenous revenue constraint. Tables 4.2 and 4.3 show that the tariffs depended positively on revenue dependence, and revenue dependence generally inhibited imports. Uruguay stands out as having endogenous revenue considerations. However, the negative correlations between revenue and imports (openness) are so weak for Argentina, Brazil, and Chile that we should not rule out the possibility of an endogenous revenue constraint, politically chosen. Using a different data series, McGreevey (1985: 36–38) finds no systematic relationship in Colombia either. It should probably be counted among this group. All these states saw a modest decline in tariffs at century's end that seems not to have harmed revenue, which is consistent with a move to more fiscally optimal tariffs.

It is interesting that the countries exhibiting an apparently exogenous constraint under this procedure overlap substantially with the group of countries highly dependent on tariff revenue analyzed in the previous section. Denmark, Norway, and Spain stand out in Europe as having an apparently exogenous revenue constraint despite having relatively low dependence on tariff revenue, and Switzerland may belong in this group though data are lacking. Peru and Venezuela, and by implication most of South and Central America, also depended heavily on tariff revenue, which served as an exogenous constraint. In contrast, Argentina, Brazil, Chile, and especially Uruguay may not have been severely constrained despite an apparently high reliance on tariff revenue. These Southern Cone countries follow the European pattern more than the inter-American one.

Other European countries display a more ambiguous pattern. Table 4.2 presents the corresponding data for Sweden before and after the introduction of parliamentary rule in 1885. Under the constitutional monarchy, the relationship between these variables in Sweden follows the exogenous constraint argument – though the predicted negative correlation between revenue dependence and openness is trivially small. This is consistent with the intertemporal evidence above (see also Figures 2.6 and 2.12). After 1885, however, successive governments appear to have seen increasing trade as a source of revenue worth nurturing. Sweden is interesting because the switch to parliamentary government occurred through minority political maneuvers on the tariff issue (Lewin 1988: 33–52). With higher tariffs reflecting a minority group, it is not surprising that trade policy was politicized enough to make revenue concerns disappear.

Except for Switzerland and Sweden-Norway, the only European country that relied heavily on customs revenue for a significant period was the United Kingdom (see Hobson 1997: Chapter 4). After abolishing the wartime income tax, England was forced to seek taxation elsewhere. As a result, the share of customs duties in the public fisc more than doubled from 1815 to 1840. Reliance on tariff revenue declined thereafter, but remained high in comparative terms, at about 20%.

Like Sweden, Britain exhibits a pattern that changes by institutional period, demarcated by repeal of the Corn Laws in 1846 and the Third Reform Act of 1885 (see also Figures 2.1 and 2.11). The historiography would suggest distributional conflicts in the early period (perhaps to 1846), when landowners forced reliance on protection to avoid the income tax. Britain then saw a revenue tariff after the Reform Act of 1885. In this last period, important tariffs were imposed on demand-inelastic goods without significant domestic production, such as sugar, coffee, and tea.[5] This fact adds force to the revenue claim and makes political explanations less

---

[5] These duties did have domestic supporters in the form of colonial landowners resident in England and the banks that financed them, as long as colonial preferences remained.

persuasive – though the decision to use a revenue tariff was itself a political choice, one not made in some earlier periods.

In contrast to Britain, France, Germany, and Italy exhibit a much more obviously politicized relationship among revenue, openness, and the tariff (see Table 4.2; see also Figures 2.3 and 2.17). The French Third Republic (1870–1940; here only 1870–1913) shows a relationship among tariff revenue dependence, openness, and the tariff that is clearly consistent with protectionism (see also Figures 2.2 and 2.12). This conclusion easily fits the historiography.

The German data could support almost any interpretation. The data coincide with the period of agricultural protection in Germany stemming from the marriage of iron and rye. At the same time, the German imperial government depended heavily on tariffs for its revenue (see Figure 4.3), supplemented by matricular contributions from the empire's constituent states (Hallerberg 1996). This made liberalization more difficult for the central state and also served the distributional goals of the dominant Junker class. The issue came to a head when the government wanted to increase military spending, especially for the navy, but neither Socialists nor the Center would support tariffs to that end. Given these battles, and the lack of any evident intertemporal constraint, I classify Germany as having endogenous revenue considerations. This conclusion differs significantly from Hobson's (1997: Chapter 2) analysis because of the different kinds of evidence we use, and resolving these differences is a task for a study focusing more narrowly on Germany.

In contrast to France and Germany, the data for Italy do not support a leading interpretation in the historiography. According to Coppa (1971), Italian governments of the Right came to consider tariffs as a source of revenue to help balance the budget, though higher industrial tariffs in 1878 were intended to be protective. However, the data here provide no evidence for this interpretation. I have broken the data in 1876, when the Left replaced the Right as the dominant party in government (see M. Clark 1996: Chapter 2). Before 1876, tariff increases are strongly associated with declining revenue, which suggests distributive tariffs chosen without reference to their fiscal consequences. After 1876, the first two correlations could be spurious, whereas the third is so small that endogenous revenue considerations are likely. This claim accords well with the facts of several important tariff increases. When Italian elites chose to raise tariffs in 1887 and 1894, they cited revenue needs as a major consideration. After all, fiscal reforms had recently reduced the price of salt and cut the land tax by two-tenths. However, the more important motive was protectionist, joining the general

Table 4.3. *Tariff revenue constraints for countries lacking openness data*

	Tariff-Revenue	Tariff-Imports	Revenue-Imports
Argentina, 1898–1913	+.582	−.808	−.139
Austria, 1849–1867	+.956	−.798	−.681
Austria-Hungary, 1868–1913	+.901	+.611	+.462
Belgium, 1849–1913	+.721	−.593	−.147
Bulgaria, 1905–1913	+.326	−.233	+.763
Canada, 1877–1913	−.004	−.357	+.291
Chile, 1895–1913	+.674	−.612	−.035
Netherlands, 1846–1913	+.426	−.642	+.318
Peru, 1899–1913	+.400	−.470	−.892
Portugal, 1884–1913	+.443	−.671	−.489
Romania, 1884–1913	−.348	+.406	+.065
Russia, 1815–1913	−.135	+.460	−.265
Spain, 1851–1913	+.324	−.355	+.612
Switzerland, 1885–1913	+.699	−.135	+.363
Uruguay, 1895–1913	+.043	−.643	+.247
Venezuela, 1906–1913	+.900	−.834	−.689

Because GNP (openness) is not available in these cases, I use import values instead.

European move toward protectionism (see Chapter 3). These tariffs reflected a political choice to reduce salt and land tax revenue, using tariffs to tax growing trade volumes and to protect Italian agriculture. We should code Italy as having an endogenous revenue constraint.

For other countries, analysis becomes more difficult as GNP (GDP) data are unavailable. Table 4.3 shows data for countries without GNP data. I must therefore use import volume in lieu of openness, but this measure is not very satisfactory because it increases over time for everyone. The data for the Netherlands suggest endogenous revenue concerns, in which the state takes advantage of increasing trade values to raise government revenue. The pattern in Belgium is consistent with an exogenous constraint, though the correlation betwen revenue dependence and import volume is weak. This is somewhat surprising, given its low tariff reliance (see Figure 4.2). Russia is clearly protective, like Italy before 1877, for high tariffs not only reduced import volume but also harmed the public fisc.

In Austria-Hungary, the 1866 *Ausgleich* (which took effect in 1867) makes a clean break in trade policy. Before 1867, revenue considerations did raise tariffs and reduce imports. Hungary would not grant direct taxes, so the empire took its revenue from Hungary indirectly through tariffs (Katzenstein 1976: Chapter 4). Thereafter, Austria-Hungary chose to tax rising imports without having an overtly protective effect. Indeed, maximizing revenue played an important political role in the Dual Monarchy because the central administration distributed tariff revenue in a manner advantageous to Hungary. As a result, Hungary favored revenue tariffs out of self-interest, whereas many Austrians saw this revenue as a way to buy Hungarian support for the union (see Eddie 1972, 1977; Huertas 1977; Hunt 1974; Matis 1973: 41–5 for overviews). This meant that revenue concerns were endogenous to the need for revenue, which itself stemmed from domestic distributional conflicts.

The revenue constraint appears to be exogenous in Portugal, a finding that is consistent with the intertemporal analysis above. In contrast, revenue concerns appear to be endogenous in Bulgaria, Spain, and Switzerland. This represents a surprise for Switzerland, where the federal government's fiscal instruments were extremely limited (see Hobson 1997: Chapter 5). Tariffs were low in any case as the fiscal demands on the central government were also low.

In contrast, this finding accords well with Bulgaria's need for revenue for internal improvements, especially during the Stambolovshtina period from 1887 to 1894 (Crampton 1997: Chapter 5). Bulgaria raised the general tariff from 8 to 14% in the 1890s, in part to pay for development projects (Crampton 1997: Chapter 6). The Konstantin Stoilov administration used this revenue to develop the harbors at Varna and Burgas, to make land grants for factory building, to subsidize road and railroad construction, to provide preferential railroad rates on state lines, and to grant other concessions designed to encourage business. Spain, another late developer with a reputation for protectionism, may also be seen as generating revenue for industrialization projects. Finally, the data reveal either a spurious relationship or an endogenous revenue constraint in Romania. I tentatively classify Bulgaria, Romania, and Spain as having endogenous revenue concerns. Given their weak states, the results for southeastern Europe may be surprising. It seems that development needs and not low state capacity best explain the relationship among openness, revenue needs, and tariffs in these countries.

Tables 4.2 and 4.3 also show the data for the three continental-sized nations in the Western Hemisphere: Brazil, Canada, and the United States. Brazil apparently faced an exogenous constraint, whereas the limited data suggest that Canada may have been characterized by endogenous revenue considerations in this period. This presumably reflects the "national policy" designed to encourage industrial development (Caves 1976; Dunlop 1946; Irwin 1996), especially development independent of the United States.

Table 4.4. *Summary of constraints by country*

Country	Type of Constraint
Argentina	Endogenous?
Austria-Hungary	Exogenous to 1866, endogenous from 1867
Belgium	Exogenous??
Brazil	Endogenous?
Bulgaria	Endogenous
Canada	Exogenous to 1866, endogenous from 1867
Chile	Endogenous?
Denmark	Exogenous?
France	Endogenous
Germany	Endogenous?
Italy	Endogenous from 1877
Netherlands	Endogenous??
Norway	Exogenous
Portugal	Exogenous
Romania	Exogenous
Russia	Endogenous?
Spain	Endogenous
Sweden	Exogenous to 1885, endogenous from 1886
Switzerland	Exogenous
United Kingdom	Endogenous, 1815–1846 and 1886–1913
United States	Exogenous to 1865, endogenous from 1866
Uruguay	Endogenous

Protective tariffs that did not sever the country from trade and that maximized tariff revenue for investment in industry would suit this policy well. The United States after the Civil War presents a rather puzzling case. The historiography describes this as a period of high protection under the Republicans, and both the revenue-openness and revenue-tariff relationships are consistent with this claim. At the same time, the positive relationship between openness and the average tariff suggests a concern for revenue, presumably for internal improvements.

As we have seen, the correlations in this section generally reveal a more ambiguous pattern than the intertemporal analysis of the preceding section. The summaries in Table 4.4 should therefore be viewed as tentative. Again, I have not made theoretical predictions about where we will find each country, but have only claimed that these are two broad categories in which these countries will fall. These classifications will be useful in Chapter 8, providing a form of cross-national variation in autonomous tariff levels that then helps explain variation in cooperation. I also use these findings in Chapter 5 as control variables when examining the effects of democratic institutions on the autonomous tariff.

The specific results differ from some existing claims. The analysis is consistent with the conventional wisdom on Britain, in which high dependence on five revenue tariffs (spirits, sugar, tea, tobacco, and wine) made trade treaties difficult (Howe 1997: 113–4; Marsh 1999: Chapter 1). Unlike some scholars, however, I do not generalize the British pattern to other countries. We may summarize this chapter's main findings as follows:

Finding 4.1: In Europe, exogenous revenue constraints characterize only Denmark, Norway, Portugal, Sweden to 1885, and Switzerland.

Finding 4.2: Endogenous revenue constraints characterize Austria from 1867, France, Germany, Italy from 1877, and perhaps Bulgaria and Romania.

Finding 4.3: The limited data available support the claims of exogenous revenue constraints throughout Latin America, except in the more developed Southern Cone (Argentina, Brazil, Chile, and Uruguay).

Finding 4.4: High exogenous revenue dependence in North America apparently give way to endogenous considerations after the American Civil War (1861–1865) and Canadian Confederation (1866).

Other countries have weak data or ambiguous patterns in the data, or they vary by period. These cases include Belgium, the Netherlands, and Russia. I code the Netherlands and Russia as possibly endogenous by my default rule, but Belgium is very difficult to classify.

Several additional features of this history warrant mention. There seems to be a trend for states to move from exogenous to endogenous revenue constraints as the century progresses and they develop more fiscal instruments. This move has the indirect effect of politicizing the tariff because revenue needs alone no longer drive policy. Related to this, federalism seems to be related to exogenous constraints early in the century (cf. Hobson 1997: Chapter 5), but this relationship too declines with time. Third, major wars can spark important changes in fiscal institutions, as in Austria-Hungary, Italy, and the United States. The effect of wars is particularly interesting as it coincides with the second wave of trade treaties, traditionally attributed to the Cobden-Chevalier treaty. Global wars clearly damage trade relations, as did World War I, but these local wars sparked changes that sometimes encouraged trade cooperation by reducing the reliance on tariffs for revenue.

A Quantitative Test of Revenue Dependence

Though this chapter on revenue may seem distinct from Chapter 3's model of tariffs, their logic overlaps. For example, the balancing logic of the political-support theory helps explain the role of endogenous fiscal concerns in tariffs discussed above. As openness increases, the government raises tariffs to shift some gains away from the export sector toward the import-competing sector. This causal direction, in which increasing openness leads to an increased use of tariffs for revenue, characterizes many European states. This means that many states *choose* to rely on tariff revenue, though other fiscal resources were doubtless available. France and Italy in the 1880s and Austria(-Hungary) in the 1890s provide noteworthy examples. In each case, greater dependence on tariff revenue followed a political choice to provide greater protection for industry. Apparently, revenue constraints play a different role in nineteenth-century trade policy than many scholars believe.

This section combines the analysis of revenue dependence in this chapter with the hypotheses on terms of trade from Chapter 3. Hypothesis 3.4 (the declining price hypothesis) predicts that a country's tariffs will vary with its terms of trade. Revenue dependence should have a significant independent effect on tariffs. We can test both of these claims together.

Data are available only for the United Kingdom and France. Table 4.6 shows a test of this hypothesis, using the average tariff and openness in Great Britain and France. As elsewhere, I controlled for YEAR as a way to capture certain century-long trends identified later in this book. I again used Cochrane-Orcutt regression to correct for serial correlation of the residuals. I used the tariff revenue constraint for both Britain and France, and a dummy revenue variable for Britain equal to 1 in 1815–1846 and 1886–1913. The tariff revenue constraint should be positively associated with the average tariff for spurious reasons. However, it is informative when tested against openness. I expect Britain's exogenous revenue constraint to reduce openness, whereas France's endogenous considerations will be associated with *greater* openness – a difference in predicted signs reflected in the +/– label in the second column.

The tests strongly confirm the hypotheses for both countries, for both the average tariff and openness. The variables also seem substantively important. Lowering revenue dependence by one percentage point reduces British or French tariffs by about one-half of a percentage point. Revenue dependence has about the same substantive effect on French openness, though the effect on British openness is only one-fifth as large. This marks an interesting contrast to Nye's (1991: 463) finding, based on a very different analysis,

Table 4.5. *Terms of trade and the average tariffs in the United Kingdom and France*

	Predict	UK		France	
		Tariff	Openness	Tariff	Openness
Constant		302.‡‡‡	−152.	−6.1‡‡	153.‡
		(64.)	(132.)	(.2.2)	(88.)
Net terms of trade	+/−	.18††††	−.082††	.088††††	−.14†††
		(.038)	(.039)	(.021)	(.047)
Revenue constraint	+/−	.49††††	−.092†	.47††††	.52†††
		(.073)	(.059)	(.070)	(.19)
Revenue dummy (UK)	+/−	4.4††††	−1.9†		
		(1.2)	(1.1)		
Year		−.17‡‡‡‡	.10		−.068
		(.032)	(.070)		(.047)
rho		.65‡‡‡‡	.89‡‡‡‡	.82‡‡‡‡	.62‡‡‡‡
		(.076)	(.049)	(.057)	(.12)
N		98	83	45	45
F		77.0	3.99	35.49	5.05
Adj. R^2		.76	.13	.61	.22
Durbin-Watson original		.87	.36	.50	1.00
transformed		2.17	2.16	1.94	1.90

Theory predicts a positive effect of variables on the tariffs, a negative effect on openness; because of its endogenous revenue constraint, French openness should be postively associated with revenue. Dummy = 1 in 1815–1846 and 1886–1913.

†† $p < .05$, *one-tailed*   ‡‡ $p < .05$, *two-tailed*
††† $p < .01$, *one-tailed*   ‡‡‡ $p < .01$, *two-tailed*
†††† $p < .001$, *one-tailed*

that revenue concerns were important for explaining Britain's trade policy but not for France's. These differences between Britain and France appear as different signs on the openness coefficients in Table 4.5, each consistent with the analysis of exogenous (UK) or endogenous (France) revenue constraints.

In short, the evidence is consistent with claims of this chapter and the preceding one (Hypothesis 3.4 and the revenue findings). Britain presents an interesting case, because many scholars argue that it was exceptional, being unexpectedly reliant on free trade. The evidence here suggests that *intertemporal* changes in Britain's tariffs are consistent with a reasonable model of trade policy. Of course, Britain's tariffs level may be low *cross-nationally*, which may show up in future tests (see especially Chapters 5 and 8). The intertemporal model is also consistent with the French evidence, though revenue dependence has a substantively small effect on French policy.

Table 4.6. *Findings on revenue constraints*

Finding 4.1. In Europe, exogenous revenue constraints characterize only Denmark, Norway, Portugal, Sweden to 1885, and Switzerland.

Finding 4.2. Endogenous revenue constraints characterize Austria from 1867, France, Germany, Italy from 1877, and perhaps Bulgaria and Romania.

Finding 4.3. The limited data available support the claims of exogenous revenue constraints throughout Latin America, except in the more developed Southern Cone (Argentina, Brazil, Chile, and Uruguay).

Finding 4.4. High exogenous revenue dependence in North America apparently give way to endogenous considerations after the American Civil War (1861–1865) and Canadian Confederation (1866).

Conclusions

This chapter has examined the effects of fiscal needs on trade policy both intertemporally and cross-nationally. Endogenous concerns, which directly reflect the logic of political support, characterize most European countries. Exogenous constraints, which serve as a constraint on political-support maximization, are found in the European periphery and much of the Americas. Table 4.6 summarizes these findings. Again, these are inductive generalizations that simply classify countries by their revenue constraint for reasons external to the theory. However, Chapter 8 shows that the classification here affects each country's likelihood to cooperate with others, with exogenous revenue constraints making cooperation less likely.

This historical analysis sometimes yields the expected results, but may also produce surprises. The allegedly revenue tariffs of "Liberal Italy" after 1877 seem to have been as protective in effect as tariffs in neighbors Austria-Hungary and France, for example. It is also striking that exogenous revenue constraints seem to be important only in the northern periphery of Europe and the less developed new states of the Americas. Being weak in the international system may not constrain a state, but being weak relative to one's society does.

The methods used here should apply directly to developing countries today, many of which still rely heavily on tariff revenue. The World Bank and IMF recognize that tariffs may be a reasonable source of revenue for developing countries, if their protective effects are small. Hobson (1997) implicitly disagrees, arguing forcefully that development of the income tax has been essential for developed country liberalization after 1945. The approach here would highlight instead how variations in state structures conditions the effect of revenue concerns on liberalization. Analyzing the correlation coefficients between revenue dependence, openness, and average tariff provides a simple first cut for evaluating the consequences of particular revenue tariffs.

It may be true that some developing countries rely so heavily on tariff revenue that it keeps them from liberalizing in the WTO. In other cases reliance on tariffs reflects a political choice that does not exogenously constrain cooperation.

This interplay between revenue constraints and political choices is also conditioned by democracy, both in the nineteenth century and today. For this reason, before moving to cooperation, I examine the effects of democratization on trade policy. As is well known from the British case – dating back to the Magna Carta – fiscal crises often lead groups to demand "democratic" control over their taxes. The same pressures appear in the nineteenth century, as in Hesse-Darmstadt, where the fiscal crises resulting from the Napoleonic Wars forced Grand Duke Ludwig I to accept constitutional government in 1820 (Hahn 1982: 28–35). Such changes in both fiscal systems and democracy, first sparked in many cases by the Napoleonic Wars, ultimately helped produce trade liberalization and cooperation in German states and many other countries.

FIVE

Political Institutions and Tariffs

'

"Above all, we should not fail to recognize that the widening and strengthening of constitutionalism everywhere on the Continent in the second half of the century had the unavoidable effect of placing powerful pressure on the governments' commercial policy, pressure that was unconcerned with the international division of labor and markets and that signified national egoism in international affairs."[1]
  – Johann von Bazant (1894: 14–15)

Trade policymaking touches on many different aspects of politics. Chapter 3's theory of political support emphasized the distributional side of policy – protection benefits some and harms others. Politicians balance these interests when setting the tariff.

Chapter 4 examined an administrative side of politics, the problem of revenue collection. I argued that exogenous revenue constraints had modest effects on tariff-making in the population of countries. More important were endogenous, politically chosen revenue needs that logically preceded the political choice to rely on tariffs instead of other revenue sources. So defined, these revenue needs may be seen in many countries, and even more often in the rhetoric of politicians. They reflect distributional concerns connected to the theory of political support.

This chapter turns to a third aspect of domestic politics, the question of political institutions. Politicians seek political support in a wide range of institutional contexts. Although this book focuses primarily on politicians'

[1] "Es darf überhaupt nicht verkannt werden, daß mit der Verbereitung und Erstarkung des Konstitutionalismus auf dem Kontinente allenthalben in der zweiten Hälfte dieses Jahrhunderts und infolge des unvermeidlichen Druckes auf die Regierungen jene Handelspolitik an Macht und Geltung gewann, welche unbekümmert um die Lehrmeinung von der internationalen Teilung der Arbeit und des Marktes den nationalen Egoismus im internationalen Verkehr bedeutet."

willingness to supply protection, some changes to the demand side will affect these calculations. Changes in electoral institutions, for example, will affect the relative strength of the various groups in a country. By making one group stronger or weaker, the changes will affect each politician's marginal valuation of political support from that group (Hypothesis 3.3, the group influence hypothesis). Through this effect on groups' political value, institutional changes will affect trade policy.

The causal mechanisms behind such changes are familiar to endogenous tariff theory and other domestic-level explanations of trade policy. Observing changes in political power is difficult but not impossible, as a growing body of work on the nineteenth century shows (i.e., Irwin 1989a, b; McKeown 1983; McLean 1998, 2001; Schonhardt-Bailey 1991a, b, 1994, 1998a, b, 2001, 2006). However, these studies necessarily limit their attention to a single country and at most a few parliamentary votes. Using this method is not practical for understanding the broad sweep of an international treaty network over a century nor can it examine the effects of changes in one country on another country.

This chapter necessarily paints more broadly, looking at cross-national differences and differences in institutions over time. My point of reference is the recent claim that dictatorships produce more protectionist policies than democracies or, equivalently, that democracy and free trade go together (Frieden and Rogowski 1996; Mansfield et al. 2000, 2002a, b; Morrow et al. 1998, 1999; Mueller 1999; Rosendorff 2006 but Dai 2002; Remmer 1998). These studies have mostly focused on the period since 1945, which is unusual in many relevant respects (see Chapter 1). As we will see, different results obtain in the nineteenth century. The varied relationships between democracy and the autonomous tariff in this chapter differ from the unambiguously positive relationship between democracy and trade cooperation that we see in Chapter 8, a pattern that highlights the importance of distinguishing noncooperative from cooperative outcomes.

The nineteenth century provides an excellent subject for examining these questions. It saw dramatic changes in political institutions, which were sparked in many cases by the turmoil of the French Revolution and the Napoleonic Wars, and the legacies faced by Restoration regimes (Crouzet 1964). It began with a conservative reaction against Bonapartism. The Restoration regimes and the settlement at Vienna enshrined the status quo, attempting to turn back the clock on the social events of the previous two decades. Even in England, reaction carried the day for five or six years. Elsewhere, the restoration regimes were not seriously challenged until the revolutions of 1830 (for an overview, see Church 1983). The revolutions of 1830 and 1848 led to more democratic change, as did the wars of national unification in Germany and Italy from 1854 to 1870.

This history provides much greater intertemporal change in institutions over a greater proportion of the international system than does the period since 1945. In contrast, the post-1945 period provides mostly cross-national variation between the developed and less developed worlds. This cross-national variation raises problems of spurious relationships in this latter period.

Although the recent literature has argued that democracy strengthens consumer and social welfare interests, the nineteenth century shows that democracy can also empower protectionist groups. We should not expect any simple relationship between democracy and liberalization of the autonomous tariff. In short, democracy can strengthen either side in the distributional battles over tariffs.

Democracy and the Tariff

Two schools, which we may call "institutional" and "distributive," dominate thinking about trade policy. The first sees institutions as producing certain outcomes regardless of setting. According to this view, autocracy leads to protectionism and war, democracy to free trade and peace (Mansfield et al. 2000, 2002a, b; Mueller 1999; Russett 1993; cf. Waltz 1967). Within democracies, larger constituencies, more broadly based parties, a more participatory franchise, longer terms in office, and more stable partisan loyalties all weight decisions more in favor of aggregate welfare (Frieden and Rogowski 1996: 35). This line of argument assumes that the rules of the political game produce the same results, regardless of the identity or the goals of the players. It is reflected in a large tradition in ETT, which models the trade-offs between producer interests and consumer interests (or general welfare), so that increasing democracy naturally leads to freer trade as consumers are better represented.

Edward Mansfield, Helen Milner, and Peter Rosendorff (MMR) have become the leading advocates of this position in political science. They claim that democracies have lower unilateral tariffs and that they are also more likely to sign liberalizing trade agreements with one another. (I examine the unilateral tariff here and trade agreements in Chapter 7.) However, they look solely at PTAs in the period since World War II. Democracies in this period are overwhelmingly rich, developed countries, either European or lands of European settlement, sharing important political alliances (NATO) and other ties (EEC/EU, NAFTA). In these countries democracy rests on a population of historically unprecedented educational levels, that is, human capital. Trade is intrasectoral and even intrafirm, reducing political conflicts of interest and raising the incentives for cooperation. It is suggestive that, outside this set of countries, Karen Remmer (1998) has found that democracy in the Southern Cone is associated with trade liberalization only in the absence of various control variables; when these controls are included, any independent effect of democracy disappears.

In the nineteenth century, democracy enfranchised English workers, French and Norwegian farmers, and Serbian and Romanian peasants. Some of these groups gained from trade, whereas others did not. For example, democratization of the French Third Republic is certainly not associated with tariff liberalization (M. S. Smith 1980),[2] nor is the introduction of parliamentarism in Sweden in 1885 (Lewin 1988). One would not really associate the greater constitutionalism of post-*Ausgleich* Austria-Hungary with a commitment to free trade either (see Chapter 9). Against this background, the MMR hypothesis would receive striking confirmation if it were consistent with the nineteenth-century data, especially because it has generally not controlled for how the partisan makeup of governments might affect trade policy (contrast Hobson 1997; Simmons 1994).

The alternative, distributive school sees the effects of institutions as contingent. Expanding the democratic franchise strengthens labor and peasants. If these masses favor free trade, then this support leads to greater openness; if they support protection, then tariffs go up. Because countries vary in factor endowment (Rogowski 1989) and in details of political institutions, we might expect the effect of democracy to vary by country (for a study of such contingent effects, see McGillivray 1997, 2004). This perspective is reflected in the assumptions of the model in Chapter 3, in which contending producer groups, rather than protectionists and consumers, square off over trade policy.

A concrete example may illustrate the importance of these conflicts among producers even in two countries with similar institutions. Bulgaria and Romania designed constitutions that were formally similar in many ways;

---

[2] Interestingly, Frédéric Bastiat presented data in his "Democratie et libre échange" (1862) that related universal suffrage and more open trade policies in France (Gerschenkron 1943/1989: 65–6). Of course, he could not have predicted the tariff politics of the Third Republic in the coming decades.

both were modeled on Belgian precedents (Black 1943; Crampton 1997). Yet they had very different effects. Romanian institutions empowered the landed aristocracy in a patron-client political system, and this aristocracy had significant export interests. Bulgarian institutions favored Christian elites, which meant the bourgeoisie of the mountain towns and not the often Muslim landlords of the lowland plains. These towns included many traders and craftsmen and some proto-industrial firms; some had export interests, whereas others competed with imports. This means that we should expect more liberal policy in Romania than in Bulgaria despite the institutional similarities. Though not many data are available for Bulgaria, Figure 2.15 shows that the evidence is consistent with this prediction. It is also true that tariff revenue dependence was much greater in Bulgaria than in Romania (see Figure 4.4). The evidence in Chapter 4 also suggested that the Bulgarian tariff was subject to an endogenous revenue constraint and the Romanian tariff was chosen for distributional reasons. Romanian latifundists long cultivated relations with their Austrian export market, whereas Bulgarian government was dominated by a developmental coalition pursuing some forms of import substitution. In short, democratization had different effects on adjacent countries, because the interests of newly enfranchised groups differed at a similar level of development.

Our tests must allow for the possibility, then, that the same institution may have different effects even in apparently similar neighboring countries. For this reason I present single-country regressions, as well as pooled regressions by region. The theory of political support says that these institutions should matter, but it does not predict the direction (Hypothesis 3.3, the group influence hypothesis). I turn to this quantitative study in the next section.

An Inductive Study of Democracy and the Autonomous Tariff

Because the theory does not predict the direction of effects, I use a largely inductive approach to evaluate these contending claims about the effects of institutions on trade policy. I look first at the effects of POLITY III variables on average tariffs. This widely used dataset has four variables relevant to this task: autocracy, democracy, participation, and political competition. Unfortunately, all four are highly correlated with each other, making it infeasible to test for their independent effects. Like others, I therefore use a single variable, "net democracy," defined as the POLITY democracy score less the POLITY autocracy score. Though lacking any real theoretical justification, this definition follows common practice in the study of international relations. Although there are clearly measurement errors in the database,[3] these are the best cross-national data on institutions that we have for this century. POLITY's unidimensional treatment of democracy is useful for the kind of quantitative investigation in this chapter, but we should keep these significant reservations in mind (Munck and Verkuilen 2002).

These data treat democracy not only as unidimensional but as a continuous variable. This differs from practice in a part of the democratic peace literature, which uses a dichotomous variable for democracy. Dichotomization suits some theoretical arguments about democracy well – either a country has democratic norms of dispute resolution or it does not; either it has institutional constraints on the executive or it does not. However, the effect of democratization on the relative power of interest groups is likely to be continuous. Expanding working-class suffrage, for example, should increase labor's influence over trade policy anywhere within a range from zero to full democracy, without any threshold effects.

I explore more qualitative and multidimensional operationalizations in Chapters 8 and 9, when looking at the effects of democracy on trade cooperation. In those chapters, the dependent variable is cooperation, for which I have data over the entire period. In this chapter, there are so few regime changes in periods for which we have tariff data that any results are suspect. For some countries that follow, it is possible to include a dummy variable for regime changes, and I make note of this where relevant.

The nineteenth century also provides ample intertemporal variation in democracy. It differs from the post-1945 world, in which the advanced industrial countries have been long-term stable democracies lacking in variation. Tests for the effects of democracy in the post-1945 world are therefore cross-national and correlated with other variables by which industrial countries differ from others, including wealth, political stability, geographical location, and alliance membership (among others). In contrast, the tests here look for the effects of democratization in a single country over time. Later I use pooled regressions to search for cross-national effects as well. Future

---

[3] Some POLITY codings in this century are mysterious to me. Let me take just two. POLITY codes of a major liberalization in England in 1837, midway between two important changes, the First Reform Act (1832) and the first election of an opposition party (1841). Sweden is coded as no-data in 1906–1913, a period of Liberal-led constitutional change. The codebooks do not illuminate these codings; see Chapter 11 for additional discussion of Sweden. I also suspect that the data collection partakes of significant hindsight. It would be tempting to classify Belgium or the Netherlands as more democratic than Imperial Germany, Spain, or Bulgaria because we know how these countries' histories turned out in the twentieth century. Contemporaries often had different views; see Mark Twain's *Innocents Abroad* (1869/1966) or *A Tramp Abroad* (1880/1977) for excellent observations without access to hindsight.

research would do well to look at both intertemporal and cross-national effects over a long time to resolve some of the differences here.

Drawing from the analysis in Chapter 4, I control for the revenue constraint in all countries. Revenue dependence should be positively associated with the average tariffs in all countries, though the relationship may be spurious for reasons discussed in Chapter 4. I have included revenue dependence here because it also has a nonspurious negative effect on openness and because including it reduces the standard errors on all the other variables in the average tariff regressions. More theoretically interesting are dummy variables for a revenue constraint for a limited period in some countries. These are included based on the country analyses in Chapter 4, summarized in Table 4.4.

I use both the average tariff and openness as the dependent variable. Not surprisingly, I obtain a lower level of statistical significance and goodness-of-fit for openness, which depends more strongly on unobserved economic variables than does the average tariff. Where available, I include each country's GDP (or GNP or NNP, as available) as a control variable in the average tariff equations. I do not include GDP in the openness equations because openness is defined as a function of GDP (imports as a percentage of GDP).

Virtually all regressions exhibited substantial serial correlation, which I controlled by using Cochrane-Orcutt regression. Where I did not report transformed Durbin-Watson statistics in the tables, the regression is OLS. When the Durbin-Watson diagnostic yielded ambiguous results, I used a Cochrane-Orcutt regression anyway, for comparability with the other cases.

Again, I included YEAR as a control variable, serving as a proxy for century-long trends analyzed in Parts III and IV. YEAR is positively associated with the tariff for most large countries, but has no obvious unidirectional effect on small countries. Chapter 11 argues that "clustering" trade negotiations in a few years leads to higher tariffs than do nonclustered negotiations. Because clustering was led by the larger countries later in the century, that chapter would expect a positive association between YEAR and the tariff for large countries and perhaps others.

For consistency and to avoid the appearance of data manipulation, I include these control variables for all countries, even when they are irrelevant and worsen the fit of the equation for a particular country. Yet, even when insignificant themselves, they do generally improve the other estimates and generally raise the summary statistics F and adjusted R^2. When conducting an exercise such as this for 20 countries, it is desirable to make the equations

Table 5.1. *Institutions and the average tariffs in large European countries*

	Predict	Austria	France	Germany	Italy	Russia	U.K.
Constant		−139.‡‡‡‡	−206.	−514.	−562.‡‡‡‡	−39.	−3.0
		(38.)	(123.)	(465.)	(114.)	(126.)	(240.)
GDP			−.00017†††	−.00020	−.00066‡‡‡‡		−.0039
			(.000051)	(.00017)	(.00015)		(.0039)
Revenue	+	.50††††	.55††††	.076††	−.040	2.1††††	.46††††
		(.064)	(.094)	(.040)	(.15)	(1.6)	(.083)
Revenue dummy	+	.74†			2.3††		7.3††††
		(.57)			(1.2)		(2.2)
Democracy		−.044	.043	−.040	−2.1‡‡‡‡	.47	.60‡‡
		(.18)	(.064)	(.19)	(.41)	(1.4)	(.29)
Year		.075††††	.11‡	.28	.30††††	.023	.00088
		(.020)	(.066)	(.25)	(.061)	(.064)	(.13)
rho		.80††††	.86††††	.82††††	.36†††	.70††††	.83††††
		(.064)	(.080)	(.088)	(.13)	(.072)	(.047)
N		68	38	31	51	97	83
F		22.05	14.59	1.07	24.66	54.10	22.00
Adj. R^2		.56	.60	.01	.70	.62	.56
Durbin-Watson		.83	.67	1.24	1.53	.65	.62
D-W transformed		2.02	1.50	2.22	2.12	2.39	2.31

Revenue dummy for Austria-Hungary equals 1 in 1815–1866; dummy for UK equals 1 in 1815–1846 and 1886–1913; dummy for Italy equals 1 in 1877–1913. We should expect no relationship between revenue considerations and the tariff in Italy before 1877. See Chapter 4. † $p < .10$, *one-tailed;* †† $p < .05$, *one-tailed;* ††† $p < .01$, *one-tailed;* †††† $p < .001$, *one-tailed;* ‡ $p < .10$, *two-tailed;* ‡‡ $p < .05$, *two-tailed;* ‡‡‡ $p < .01$, *two-tailed;* ‡‡‡‡ $p < .001$, *two-tailed*

as comparable as possible and not to add or subtract control variables from one regression to the next.

There are a very small number of observations for some countries, so we really cannot have much confidence in any inferences, especially when we add the Cochrane-Orcutt control for positive serial correlation. I have included these countries anyway to facilitate comparisons and to provide information about how each country may differ from the others, information that disappears when I pool countries later. After all, it is easier for skeptical readers to ignore some regressions than for curious readers to reconstruct regressions that I do not present.

The results are reported in Tables 5.1 through 5.4. The equations are a poor fit for about half the countries. The fit is usually poorest for countries for whom few observations are available, and is therefore not worrisome in itself. Only the equations for Germany and Canada obtain poor fits despite having a moderate number of observations.

Table 5.2. *Institutions and the average tariffs in smaller European countries*

	Predict	Belgium	Bulgaria	Denmark	Netherlands	Norway	Portugal	Romania	Spain	Sweden
Constant		37.	1000.	-60.	48.‡‡‡	-116.	-455.	-356.	193.	-486††††
		(30.)	(568.)	(126.)	(7.5)	(199.)	(731.)	(135.)	(1039.)	(139)
GDP				-.0031‡‡		-.0052‡			-.16	-.0031††††
				(.0013)		(.0027)			(2.1)	(.00075)
Revenue	+	.26††††	.84††	.088†††	.18††††	.044††	.29†	.30††††	.88††	.099†
		(.040)	(.42)	(.024)	(.017)	(.023)	(.17)	(.13)	(.30)	(.062)
Revenue dummy	+									2.7††††
										(.71)
Democracy		-.045‡			-.051	.20	-4.5‡	1.1		
		(.024)			(.047)	(.21)	(2.4)	(.86)		
Year		-.020	-.52	.036	-.026‡‡‡	.069	.24	.19‡‡	-.10	.26‡‡‡
		(.016)	(.30)	(.067)	(.0040)	(.11)	(.38)	(.069)	(.55)	(.073)
rho		.90‡‡‡			.84††††	.55††††	.68††††	.31	.61‡‡	-.48‡‡
		(.040)			(.046)	(.14)	(.15)	(.18)	(.22)	(.16)
N		66	9	23	67		24	29	11	32
F		15.00	2.05	92.72	44.64		2.40	16.02	3.07	16.21
Adj. R^2		.39	.21	.93	.68		.15	.62	.38	.66
Durbin-Watson		.67	1.73	1.78	.23		.66	1.39	1.05	2.86
D-W transformed		2.27			2.37		1.75	1.96	1.90	2.02

Sweden's revenue dummy equals 1 in 1815–1885. † $p < .10$, *one-tailed;* †† $p < .05$, *one-tailed;* ††† $p < .01$, *one-tailed;* †††† $p < .001$, *one-tailed;* ‡ $p < .05$, *two-tailed;* ‡‡ $p < .01$, *two-tailed;* ‡‡‡ $p < .001$, *two-tailed*

Table 5.3. *Institutions and the average tariffs in the Americas*

	Predict	Argentina	Brazil	Canada	Perú	Uruguay	U.S. (1)	U.S. (2)
Constant		5069.‡‡‡	1214.	46.	-1759.‡	44.	585.	160.
		(758.)	(1208.)	(211.)	(951.)	(840.)	(393.)	(172.)
GDP			-2.9				-.056	
			(1.7)				(.22)	
Revenue	+	.44†	.67††	.048	.90††††	.11	.089	.10††
		(.26)	(.12)	(.10)	(.40)	(.24)	(.095)	(.057)
Revenue dummy	?						-6.1‡‡	-10.‡‡‡
							(2.8)	(3.7)
Democracy				.085		-1.2	-.28	-2.2
				(.45)		(1.2)	(1.2)	(1.4)
Year		-2.6‡‡‡	-.63	-.017	.91‡	-.0072	-.28	-.062
		(.40)	(.64)	(.11)	(.49)	(.44)	(.21)	(.092)
rho			.60‡‡‡	.72‡‡‡	.44‡	-.35	.79‡‡‡	.78‡‡‡
			(.04)	(.099)	(.24)	(.23)	(.087)	(.059)
N		16	13	46	14	18	48	98
F		37.7	23.63	.08	2.55	3.63	6.34	3.03
Adj. R²		.83	.85	-.065	.19	.32	.36	.08
Durbin-Watson		2.21	1.32	.54	1.23	2.61	.72	.69
D-W transformed		N.A.	2.46	2.36	1.56	2.16	1.85	1.88

U.S. revenue dummy equals 1 in 1815–1865. † $p < .10$, *one-tailed*; †† $p < .05$, *one-tailed*; ††† $p < .01$, *one-tailed*; †††† $p < .001$, *one-tailed*; ‡ $p < .10$, *two-tailed*; ‡‡ $p < .05$, *two-tailed*; ‡‡‡ $p < .01$, *two-tailed*; ‡‡‡‡ $p < .001$, *two-tailed*

The revenue constraint is strongly associated with the average tariff, except in Italy and some Latin American countries. Again, this relationship could easily be spurious, so it is not informative by itself. When a dummy revenue constraint is appropriate for certain periods in some countries (see Chapter 4), it has a statistically significant effect everywhere.

This revenue dummy effect is in the predicted positive direction for all countries except the United States. The negative effect in the United States means that tariffs were unexpectedly low in 1815–1865 or, equivalently, that they were unexpectedly high in 1865–1913. This latter fact has not gone unnoticed in the literature on the United States (Goldstein 1993; Lake 1988; Rhodes 1993) and should come as no surprise here. The analysis in Chapter 4 would expect a positively signed dummy variable both for 1815–1865 (exogenous constraint) and 1865–1913 (endogenous constraint), but is agnostic as to which effect is greater. For this reason, I have used a two-tailed test of its significance here.

For several countries, the revenue dummy variable coincides with changes of political regime, complicating inference. For example, the Austrian revenue dummy equals 1 in 1815–1866, that is, before the *Ausgleich* took effect in 1867. We may interpret the positive sign on this dummy variable as indicating either that Austria faced an exogenous revenue constraint in 1815–1866 or that the greater level of democracy in Austria in 1867–1914 lowered the tariff by three-fourths of a percentage point. Sweden poses a similar problem, with tariffs almost 3 points higher before the introduction of parliamentary government. Either interpretation of these cases would be consistent with the theory here, and statistics cannot resolve the issue of causation.

I can distinguish the institutional and revenue claims only when the data let me. The only country with a sufficiently long data series, lack of variation in the nature of the revenue constraint (see Chapter 4), and an observable qualitative change is Belgium. It had an electoral reform take place in 1892 that expanded the suffrage. (For whatever reason, this reform does not affect Belgium's net democracy score in POLITY, which remains at 6.) Table 5.4 shows the effect on the tariff. Because I have not made theoretical predictions about the effects of democracy on the tariff, I use two-tailed tests. Neither net democracy nor the electoral reform has any statistically significant effect in Belgium. However, if I were to take the neo-Cobdenite literature as the hypothesis to be tested, I would have used a one-tailed test of significance under which both variables would cross the $p < .10$ threshhold that I use throughout this book: net democracy at the .053 level, electoral reform at .075. However, the latter coefficient is wrongly signed for the institutionalists' claim, because expanding the suffrage *raises* the tariff in Belgium after 1892. Moreover, the electoral reform outweighs the POLITY

Table 5.4. *Electoral reform and the tariff in Belgium*

	Predict	Belgium
Constant		31.6
		(20.31)
Revenue	+	.29[††††]
		(.034)
Democracy		−.030
		(.018)
Electoral reform, 1892		.27
		(.18)
Year		−.017
		(.011)
rho		.88[††††]
		(.026)
N		64
F		23.33
Adj. R^2		.59
Durbin-Watson		.62
D-W transformed		2.31

[†] $p < .10$, *one-tailed;* [††] $p < .05$, *one-tailed;* [†††] $p < .01$, *one-tailed;* [††††] $p < .001$, *one-tailed;* [‡] $p < .10$, *two-tailed;* [‡‡] $p < .05$, *two-tailed;* [‡‡‡] $p < .01$, *two-tailed;* [‡‡‡‡] $p < .001$, *two-tailed*

democracy variable substantively, with an effect equal to 9 points of net democracy (almost half the entire range, and three-fourths of the Belgian range from −5 to 7). Democratization can clearly strengthen protectionists more than free traders.

Having looked at the average tariff, one can now turn to openness. The openness tests reported in Table 5.5 show somewhat weaker results than the average tariff equations. The revenue variable is rightly signed and statistically significant for about half of the countries, and is never wrongly signed and significant. Revenue dummy variables are statistically significant for three of four countries. Most weak results occur in country regressions, with a small number of observations, such as Brazil or Denmark.

In contrast to the average tariff regressions, democracy never has a statistically significant effect on openness. I suspect that this reflects the more indirect nature of the openness measure (see Chapter 2). In many of the tests so far in this book, the standard errors are greater when we use openness instead of the average tariff, suggesting that it is associated with greater measurement error.

Table 5.5. *Tariffs, revenue, democracy, and openness*

	Predict	Brazil	Denmark	France	Germany	Italy	Norway	Sweden	UK	U.S.
Constant		−31.	109.	213.‡‡‡	144.	−183.‡‡‡	−416.‡‡‡	1.7	−66.	129.‡‡‡
		(283.)	(335.)	(69.)	(111.)	(45.)	(107.)	(126.)	(104.)	(22.)
Average tariff	−	.011	−1.6††	−1.5††††	−1.5††††	−.37††††	−.63††††	−1.3††††	−.37†††	−.080††††
		(.12)	(.75)	(.14)	(.17)	(.062)	(.14)	(.16)	(.076)	(.023)
Revenue	varies	−.049	.19	1.0††††	.17††	.25††	−.015	.49††††	.083	.082
		(.13)	(.11)	(.13)	(.045)	(.075)	(.020)	(.10)	(.066)	(.14)
Revenue dummy	−			−.98†				−.12	−.82	−4.05†††
				(.60)				(1.0)	(1.04)	(.62)
Democracy		.026	−.039	−.31	−.26	−.15	.022		−.078	.015
		(.15)	(.17)	(.54)	(.19)	(.27)	(.17)		(.20)	(.19)
Year				−.10††	.088	−.10	.24†††	.0090	.050	−.066†††
				(.038)	(.058)	(.024)	(.056)	(.064)	(.056)	(.011)
rho		.20	109.	.20‡	.51‡‡‡	.23	.37‡‡	.31‡	.86‡‡‡	.57‡‡‡
		(.16)	(335.)	(.12)	(.10)	(.14)	(.15)	(.17)	(.054)	(.064)
N		13	22	36	31	51	38	32	83	48
F		.06	2.43	47.49	30.01	35.48	37.06	23.61	8.85	28.03
Adj. R^2		−.31	.17	.87	.79	.73	.80	.75	3.2	.74
Durbin-Watson		1.46	1.39	1.25	1.35	1.74	1.48	1.60	.69	1.17
D-W transformed		1.69	1.39	1.92	2.24	2.07	1.80	1.95	2.06	2.12

The analysis in Chapter 4 expects the revenue constraint to increase openness in France in 1871–1891, Germany, Italy, and Sweden after 1885; to reduce openness in Denmark and Norway.

Revenue dummy equals 1 for France in 1871–1891, Sweden in 1815–1885, United Kingdom in 1815–1846 and 1886–1913, and United States in 1815–1865.

† $p < .10$, *one-tailed;* †† $p < .05$, *one-tailed;* ††† $p < .01$, *one-tailed;* †††† $p < .001$, *one-tailed;* ‡ $p < .05$, *two-tailed;* ‡‡ $p < .01$, *two-tailed;* ‡‡‡ $p < .001$, *two-tailed*

Behind all the details, one clear implication emerges. The tests show that the institutional view of democracy is wrong when we look at individual countries over time. Net democracy has no effect on the average tariff for 10 of the 14 countries, and no statistically significant effect on openness anywhere. In contrast to twentieth-century evidence that finds a positive association between democracy and liberalization, democracy is associated with protectionism in Britain. However, democracy is associated with liberalization in Italy and Portugal. The substantive effect of this variable is mixed: strong in Italy and Portugal and intermediate in Britain. Belgium is puzzling, because the continuous net democracy variable is associated with tariff reductions, whereas an increase in the franchise in 1892 raised the tariff as much as a change of 9 points in the 21-point net democracy scale.

This pattern is closest to the kind of contingent effects that the distributional school would expect. In predominantly rural societies, increasing democracy gives the vote to farmers, peasants, and agricultural workers. These people have export interests in countries such as Italy and Portugal, and should favor free trade. The countryside should be more protectionist in Britain, which may account for the different result there – despite the free-trade interests of the urban working class. Both the free-trade working class and the protectionist lower classes in the countryside were also strengthened by democratization.

Lack of data precludes extensive use of the terms of trade (Hypothesis 3.4, declining prices hypothesis) as a variable in these equations. Because data on the terms of trade are available only for Britain and France, I run a separate test for these countries. Table 5.6 shows the results, testing for the effects of democracy, while controlling for GDP, revenue dependence, and the terms of trade, again using a Cochrane-Orcutt regression to control for serial correlation. As in the simpler tests above, democracy is associated with higher tariffs in Britain (using a two-tailed test because the contingent-effects theory does not predict the sign on the coefficient). Democracy also raises the tariff in France. Revenue dependence has a consistently positive effect on tariffs, though this may be spurious (see chapter 4).

In summary, this section has found that the relationship between democracy and trade policy seems to be limited. Of the 14 countries examined, we can identify a statistically significant relationship in at most 5. Democracy lowers the tariff in Italy and Portugal, raises it in Britain and perhaps France, and has mixed effects in Belgium. One limitation of these findings is that intertemporal change in democracy is infrequent in a single country, so that important effects of democracy may have been overlooked. Cross-national

Table 5.6. Trade policy in Britain and France

	Predict	UK Tariff	UK Openness	France Tariff	France Openness
Constant		544.[‡‡‡]	−185.	−144.[‡‡]	205.[‡‡]
		(180.)	(133.)	(64.)	(88.)
GDP		.0022		−.00013[‡‡]	
		(.0032)		(.000048)	
Revenue dependence	+/0	.47[††††]	−.096	.55[††††]	.43[‡‡]
		(.081)	(.059)	(.088)	(.18)
Revenue dummy	+/−	5.0[††††]	−1.8[†]	N.A.	
		(1.1)	(1.1)		
Terms of trade	+/−	.11[††]	−.077[††]	.094[†††]	−.16[††††]
		(.053)	(.040)	(.026)	(.047)
Democracy	?	.45[‡]	−.25	.22[‡‡]	−.15
		(.27)	(.22)	(.086)	(.16)
Year		−.31	.12[‡]	.073[‡‡]	−.09[‡]
		(.097)	(.071)	(.035)	(.047)
rho		.63[‡‡‡‡]	.88[††††]	.65[‡‡]	.64[††††]
		(.084)	(.048)	(.098)	(.10)
N		83	83	38	38
F		47.90	3.48	22.41	4.62
Adj. R²		.77	.13	.74	.28
Durbin-Watson		.93	.44	1.51	1.40
D-W transformed		2.14	2.14	1.89	1.59

First prediction is for the tariff and second is for openness (high tariffs imply low openness and vice versa).
UK revenue dummy equals 1 in 1815–1846 and 1886–1913.
[†] $p < .10$, one-tailed; [††] $p < .05$, one-tailed; [†††] $p < .01$, one-tailed; [††††] $p < .001$, one-tailed; [‡] $p < .10$, two-tailed; [‡‡] $p < .05$, two-tailed; [‡‡‡] $p < .01$, two-tailed; [‡‡‡‡] $p < .001$, two-tailed

tests may better identify these effects and may also find inductively the qualitative change we saw in Belgium. The next section addresses these possiblities.

Regional Patterns in the Tariff

One weakness of the previous section is that the small number of observations for some countries makes the individual-country regressions of dubious value. To obtain more observations for each regression, we can combine several countries into a series of regional regressions.

My basic rule of thumb was to use natural regions, such as Latin America (five countries with data), the Mediterranean (again, five countries), or northern Europe. Classifying Austria-Hungary and Germany requires some comment. At the start of this period, the eastern half of Prussia cannot be characterized as part of the industrial West. However, data are available only after German unification, when the center of economic gravity lay well to the west. Austria-Hungary is difficult to classify because the smaller but more populous half of the country lay north of the Alps, and the other half south or east of them. Yet, its economic center of gravity certainly lay to the north, for Bohemia was as industrialized as any region on the continent. In contrast, Hungary was an agricultural exporter, whereas Croatia-Slavonia (and later Bosnia-Herzegovina) had levels of development comparable to the rest of the Balkans. I classify both tentatively as part of northern Europe, but also count Austria-Hungary, Germany, and Russia as a separate region within the north ("Holy Alliance").

There are various ways to address the problems of combining time-series data from several countries (see Stimson 1985 for overview). With only 15 to 20 observations for each Latin American country, I found that an OLS regression provided a good fit when we simply controlled for year and added three country dummy variables (Argentina, Brazil, and Chile). The same shortage of observations for Mediterranean countries made a dummy variable approach natural. This approach implies that the dummy variables will pick up variations attributed to some untheorized variables associated with each country, such as history or ideology; referring to the historiography and to previous chapters in this book can help with this problem. Although more complicated cross-sectional pooled time-series analysis would be possible for the longer time series of Britain, France, and a few others (see Beck and Katz 1995 for critiques), I prefer to keep a simpler model that is more directly comparable to the Latin American and Mediterranean regressions. Most of these other techniques also require that time series be equal in length for all countries, which would require me to throw away a lot of data here.

The results are reported in Tables 5.7 and 5.8. Revenue concerns have familiar effects. The revenue constraint is strongly associated with higher tariffs in all these regions, but this relationship could be spurious. Only when we turn to trade treaties in Chapter 8 can we distinguish possible relationships.

The most interesting findings concern the effects of democracy. In Latin America and Scandinavia, democracy has no statistically significant effect on the tariff. This corresponds to the single-country findings.

Elsewhere matters become more complex. In general, democracy *raises* the tariff in the core of Europe, but *lowers* the tariff in the Mediterranean. However, the Mediterranean results depend heavily on Italy. When I exclude

Table 5.7. *Average tariff by region: the core*

	Predict	Britain-France	Northwest1	Holy Alliance	Northwest2	All North
Constant		159.	171.[‡‡‡‡]	35.	338.[‡‡‡‡]	122.[‡‡‡‡]
		(111.)	(47.)	(39.)	(104.)	(32.)
GDP		−.000079			.000050	
		(.000058)			(.000034)	
Revenue	+	.61[††††]	.55[††††]	1.2[††††]	.30[††††]	.48[††††]
		(.059)	(.028)	(.12)	(.038)	(.036)
Democracy		.50[‡‡‡]	.29[††††]	1.2[‡‡‡‡]	.32[‡‡‡]	.16[††††]
		(.18)	(.048)	(.35)	(.12)	(.058)
Terms of trade*	+	.79[††]				
		(.037)				
United Kingdom		−12.[‡‡‡‡]	−3.7[‡‡‡‡]		−4.4[‡‡‡‡]	−6.1[‡‡‡‡]
		(2.0)	(.56)		(1.1)	(.98)
France		4.6[‡‡‡‡]				
		(.31)				
Netherlands		2.4[‡‡‡‡]				−3.6[‡‡‡‡]
		(.47)				(.63)
Belgium						−4.4[‡‡‡‡]
						(.73)
Germany				−54.[‡‡‡‡]	−9.0[‡‡‡‡]	−18.[‡‡‡‡]
				(5.6)	(1.7)	(1.8)
Russia				19.[‡‡‡‡]		19.[‡‡‡‡]
				(1.8)		(.73)
Year		−.088	−.093[‡‡‡‡]	−.017	−.18[‡‡‡]	−.063[‡‡‡‡]
		(.060)	(.025)	(.020)	(.055)	(.017)
rho		.87[‡‡‡‡]	.76[‡‡‡‡]	N.A.	.85[‡‡‡‡]	.45[‡‡‡‡]
		(.034)	(.035)		(.035)	(.039)
N		120	257	199	152	531
F		51.60	358.62	171.17	31.90	203.21
Adj. R^2		.72	.89	.81	.55	.81
Durbin-Watson		.67	1.04	1.83	.54	1.23
D-W transformed		2.41	2.58	N.A.	2.74	2.21

Regressions are Cochrane-Orcutt if rho and transformed Durbin-Watson are reported; OLS otherwise.
Northwest1 is Belgium, France, Netherlands, and UK.
Northwest2 is Northwest1 plus Germany.
Holy Alliance is Austria-Hungary, Germany, and Russia.
North is all countries north of the Alps, including Austria-Hungary. Not shown for reasons of space are the estimated coefficients on dummy variables for Denmark (−16.), Norway (−12.), and Sweden (−8.0), all significant at the $p < .001$ level.
[†] $p < .10$, *one-tailed;* [††] $p < .05$, *one-tailed;* [†††] $p < .01$, *one-tailed;* [††††] $p < .001$, *one-tailed;* [‡] $p < .10$, *two-tailed;* [‡‡] $p < .05$, *two-tailed;* [‡‡‡] $p < .01$, *two-tailed;* [‡‡‡‡] $p < .001$, *two-tailed*

Italy, the democracy variable narrowly misses statistical significance. Again, if I were testing the deductive theories in the literature as my own, a one-tailed test would have found a significant result here.

The results of a pooled regression against openness is shown in Table 5.9. Because of the greater number of observations, I can distinguish between the

Table 5.8. *Average tariff by region: the peripheries*

	Predict	Latin America	Mediterranean five	Mediterranean four	Scandinavia
Constant		2545.‡‡‡‡	−308.‡‡‡‡	−84.	−30.
		(705.)	(53.)	(127.)	(100.)
GDP					−.0014
					(.00092)
Revenue	+	1.1††††	.40††††	.29†††	.034
		(9.15)	(.082)	(.10)	(.022)
Democracy		.76	−1.7‡‡‡‡	−.73	.078
		(1.3)	(.23)	(.45)	(.12)
Country dummy 1		28.‡‡‡‡	8.0‡‡‡‡	−3.8‡	2.3‡‡‡‡
		(4.7)	(1.1)	(2.3)	(.59)
Country dummy 2		12.‡	18.‡‡‡‡	15.‡‡‡‡	3.6‡‡‡‡
		(6.7)	(1.90)	(3.0)	(.93)
Country dummy 3		72.‡‡‡‡	25.‡‡‡‡	11.	
		(6.9)	(2.8)	(6.9)	
Year		−1.4‡‡‡‡	.16‡‡‡‡	.047	.021
		(.37)	(.027)	(.065)	(.053)
N		83	152	100	75
F		119.0	179.3	117.	6.98
Adj. R^2		.90	.88	.88	.33
Durbin-Watson		1.82	2.05	2.06	1.88

Latin American countries are Argentina, Brazil, Chile, Perú, and Uruguay. Country dummies are Argentina, Brazil, and Chile.
Mediterranean Five countries are Bulgaria, Italy, Portugal, Romania, and Spain. Country dummies are Italy, Portugal, and Spain. For Mediterranean Four, drop Italy and substitute Romania as dummy.
Scandinavia is Denmark, Norway, and Sweden. Country dummies are Norway and Sweden.
† $p < .10$, *one-tailed;* †† $p < .05$, *one-tailed;* ††† $p < .01$, *one-tailed;* †††† $p < .001$, *one-tailed;* ‡ $p < .10$, *two-tailed;* ‡‡ $p < .05$, *two-tailed;* ‡‡‡ $p < .01$, *two-tailed;* ‡‡‡‡ $p < .001$, *two-tailed*

usual revenue constraint and those countries (and periods) with endogenous revenue considerations. As was true in the pooled tariff regressions, the results here are much stronger and clearly consistent with the analysis of revenue considerations in Chapter 4. Because of the likely spurious relationship between revenue dependence and the average tariff, I used a dummy variable for countries and periods that I expected would have different patterns of revenue dependence than the others. I can use a different, preferable strategy for openness.

In summary, then,

Finding 5.1: Democracy raises the tariff in northwest Europe, lowers the tariff in the Mediterranean, and has no effect elsewhere.

These findings are especially interesting because they emerge from what is effectively a cross-national test of democracy's effects. In Latin America,

Table 5.9. *Openness in northern Europe*

	Predict	Openness
Constant		−53.
		(44.)
Exogenous revenue	−	−.15[tttt]
		(.035)
Endogenous revenue	+	.24[ttt]
		(.092)
Democracy		.18[‡‡‡]
		(.062)
Denmark		10.[‡‡‡‡]
		(1.1)
France		−16.[‡‡‡‡]
		(1.4)
Germany		−14.[‡‡‡‡]
		(4.3)
Norway		3.3[‡‡‡‡]
		(.75)
Year		.043[‡‡‡]
		(.023)
rho		.52[‡‡‡‡]
		(.056)
N		229
F		95.79
Adj. R^2		.77
Durbin-Watson		1.04
D-W transformed		2.36

Countries are Denmark, France, Germany, Norway-Sweden, and the United Kingdom. Endogenous revenue variable equals the revenue constraint for France and Germany and zero otherwise. [t] *p* < .10, *one-tailed;* [tt] *p* < .05, *one-tailed;* [ttt] *p* < .01, *one-tailed;* [tttt] *p* < .001, *one-tailed;* [‡] *p* < .10, *two-tailed;* [‡‡] *p* < .05, *two-tailed;* [‡‡‡] *p* < .01, *two-tailed;* [‡‡‡‡] *p* < .001, *two-tailed*

for example, only Uruguay exhibits intertemporal variation in democracy in the period for which tariff data are available; this means that the test is overwhelmingly cross-national.

An explanation of these varying effects by region probably requires a distributional model. Thanks to Rogowski's *Commerce and Cleavages,* much of the field is used to thinking about political coalitions on trade in terms of the Heckscher-Ohlin-Stolper-Samuelson model (HOSS), in which the main players are factors of production (labor, capital, and land). This model is misleading here. Ricardo-Viner-Cairns-Jones (RVCJ) models, in which labor moves between sectors employing fixed capital (Mussa 1974; see Hiscox 2001, 2002 for tests), seem a better fit. In these RVCJ models, labor tends to share the interests of capital in the sector in which it is employed (see S. Magee 1971). For example, the rural proletariat in the United Kingdom and many other northern countries would share the protectionist interests of the landed interests.

This means that democratization empowered not only urban workers with an interest in free trade but also agricultural workers, farmers, and peasants, with varying degrees of land ownership and interests in protection. For example, the interest of the "little people" in trade policy is not clear in Scandinavia and the Southern Cone.[4] Scandinavia and the Southern Cone of Latin America both had economies based on primary product exports, with some significant industrial development in some regions and cities. Agriculture was not internationally competitive in either Norway or Sweden, whereas Denmark was competitive in animal products but not grains after about 1875. Argentina and some of its neighbors had large grain and beef exports, with significant mining sectors. Norway and Sweden lacked grain and beef exports, but shared the mining interests. Some Scandinavian farmers owned significant forests that they worked in during winter, whereas they might become rural or village proletariat in the summer. Such people have both export and import-competing interests at different times of the year.[5]

Peasants had similarly mixed interests in Romania, though this changed over time. As the market opened, goods produced by the rural population during their free time were threatened by cheaper Austro-Hungarian manufactured goods. Domestic industrial products were largely driven from the market by foreign goods, and almost the entire textiles industry was destroyed (Antonescu 1915: 66–67). Over time, then, a peasantry with mixed agricultural export and crafts import-competing interests came to rely on its export earnings.

My finding that democracy matters more cross-nationally than intertemporally has significant implications for the historiography. As I noted in Chapter 1, tariff histories almost always focus on trade policymaking in a single country. This research design excludes cross-national differences by definition. Yet it appears here that cross-national differences in institutions are much more important correlates of trade policy than are changes in a single country's institutions over time. Concretely, this finding suggests that a study comparing Britain and Prussia in the 1830s would likely be

---

[4] Notice, incidentally, that Rogowski (1989) finds the Scandinavian countries hard to classify in terms of relative factor abundance.

[5] For models that can encompass such effects, see W. Mayer (1984) and Mussa (1982).

more fruitful than studying Britain before and after the Reform Act of 1832. Unfortunately, the latter kind of study dominates the historiography.

Finally, the dummy variables reveal that some countries have consistently higher or lower tariffs than their regional peers even when we control for other variables. Britain's tariffs are lower than expected, France's tariffs higher than expected. Neither of these would surprise historians. It is more unexpected to see that Dutch tariffs are a little higher than the baseline, but we must recall that they are being compared to Belgian tariffs. The Netherlands were less likely to sign tariff treaties than Belgium because of a difficult legislature with ratification authority, and this probably kept their tariffs a little higher than their neighbors to the south (see Chapter 9).

More surprising, perhaps, is that German tariffs are 9 points lower than the Belgium-France-Netherlands baseline in the final column of Table 5.5. I suspect that this finding reflects the fact that these data present a very incomplete picture of Wilhelmine politics, which combined free-trade city-states in the north, democratic and urbanized states in the southwest, a moderately open, peasant-dominated state in Bavaria, and a highly autocratic Prussian state with a privileged role in the federation (and a dominant position in the coding decisions of POLITY). As a result, the data capture the pressures for protection in the German federation but do not capture the countervailing pressures for freer trade, and these appear in the dummy variable.

Norway and Sweden have higher tariffs than Denmark, which was known for its free-trade policies in this period. Italy, Portugal, and especially Spain have higher tariffs than Bulgaria and Romania. This probably reflects legacies of foreign intervention in Bulgaria and Romania, when they were autonomous parts of the Ottoman Empire with a reserved political position for Russia. These foreigners would put downward pressure on tariffs, because Ottoman or Russian exporters would benefit from liberalization of Bulgaria and Romania. Tariffs are substantially higher in Argentina, Brazil, and Uruguay than in Chile and Peru. No explanation for this finding suggests itself.

Country dummies are theoretically unsatisfying, but may suggest further research questions. There seems to be a western Mediterranean core of higher protection countries comprising France, Italy, and the Iberian peninsula. These countries share a "Latin" political culture and various elements of economic structure and political history. These commonalities, including a currency union at one point, are unmeasured here, but provide plausible candidates for further investigation.

The estimates also provide some intertemporal information. Average tariffs go down over time in Latin America and northern Europe. Tariffs seem to increase over time in the Mediterranean, but Italy is largely responsible for this finding. The previous section showed also that tariffs went up in Austria-Hungary. In summary:

Finding 5.2: Austria and Italy exhibit increasing tariffs over time, even after controlling for other variables; tariffs decline over time in Latin America and northern Europe.

It is tempting to attribute these trends to transportation costs, which are difficult to measure but presumably decline throughout this period. Agricultural exporters such as Italy and Hungary would be especially hard-hit by declining transatlantic transportation costs and therefore be most likely to raise tariffs in response. However, the contrary results for northern Europe and Latin America do not lend themselves to any such interpretation.

In summary, northern Europe has a lower base tariff and a downward trend in the tariff, but increasing democratization tends to raise this tariff. The Mediterranean has a higher base tariff, but it declines with democratization. Latin America has a high tariff with a downward trend and no clear effect of democratization. Regional differences show that we cannot claim that democracy has any simple, universal effect on the autonomous tariff.

Conclusions

This chapter has used the differences between the distributional and institutional approaches as a point of reference, and its findings support the distributive approach at the core of the theory of political support. Institutions such as democracy do not have uniform effects on trade policy; these effects are mediated by the constellation of interests in each country. Though I have not presented the data because the results are overwhelmingly negative, differences between federations and centralized states also do not seem to affect tariffs in any systematic way. This contrasts with the analysis in Hobson (1997), a difference that can be reconciled with closer attention to the relations between different units of government in Chapter 9.

The chapter has also surveyed the trade policies of the world in 1815–1913, using the variables from all the chapters in Part II when available. Quantitative tests confirm the deductive hypotheses of the theory and provide some inductive generalizations about behavior when the theory was agnostic about effects. These inductive findings revealed some regional patterns in the politics of trade policy. Northern Europe, the Mediterranean, and Latin America make three natural regions with different base tariffs and effects of democratization. The Scandinavian and Balkan peripheries

Table 5.10. *Findings about democracy and the tariff*

Finding 5.1: Democracy raises the tariff in northwest Europe, lowers the tariff in the Mediterranean, and has no effect elsewhere.

Finding 5.2: Austria and Italy exhibit increasing tariffs over time, even after controlling for other variables; tariffs decline over time in Latin America and northern Europe.

---

sometimes warrant separate treatment. These are summarized in Table 5.10, and are used as control variables in Part III as appropriate.

The evidence here poses particular challenges for those who argue for an unconditional relationship between democracy and freer trade. One reasonable response would be that nineteenth-century democracy differs significantly from post-1945 democracy, which is true. This negative objection could be made into a positive research agenda if the literature were to explore greater institutional variation among democracies (as in Pahre 2006; Tarar 2005; Tsebelis 2002). A richer conceptualization of "democracy" may well reconcile the MMR analysis with the evidence here.

Such a synthesis would be particularly desirable because, as this chapter shows, institutions generally do have significant effects. Though the data are not as good as we would like, presumably the major institutional changes of 1848–1867 in Austria-Hungary, Canada, France, Germany, Italy, and the United States provided the foundations for changes in trade policy and thus for the second wave of trade treaties.

In Part III, we will see how the resulting autonomous tariff affected the likelihood of cooperation for these countries. I will also argue that democracy has much less ambiguous effects on trade cooperation than on autonomous trade policy. This makes the overall relationship between democracy and cooperation much more complicated than the existing literature has realized.

PART THREE

POLITICAL SUPPORT AND TRADE COOPERATION

SIX

The Trade Agreements Database

"There is, unfortunately, a kind of alchemy about figures which transforms the most dubious materials into something pure and precious; hence the price of working with historical statistics is eternal vigilance."
– Thomas Carlyle (cited in Landes 1998: 196fn)

Having examined autonomous trade policies in Part II, I now turn to cooperation, the central focus of this book. Part III examines the conditions that make a country more or less likely to engage in cooperation than other countries or that make it more or less willing to cooperate over time. The focus is on cross-national differences between countries, building on the country-level and intertemporal analyses of Part II.

Studying cooperation requires both a definition and an operationalization of the term. This chapter provides first a definition of cooperation and then discusses the Trade Agreements Database (TAD) that I use to operationalize cooperation. Many of the decisions here reflect the fact that cooperation is a dichotomous concept, not a continuous one, and that I wish to explain both cross-national and intertemporal variation in cooperation. These theoretical issues point toward count variables for each country in the trading system.

I next define several variables derived from TAD that I use throughout the rest of the book. Foremost among these are the number of treaties that a country initiates each year and the number of treaties that each country has in effect at a given moment. Both are country-level variables, measuring some ways in which countries differ from each other or in which a single country varies over time.

These choices are all motivated by an interest in what makes *countries* cooperate and what makes some countries cooperate more than others. Certain political institutions or economic conditions that a country faces will facilitate cooperation, whereas others will not. Policy analysts will want to understand such factors when thinking about their country's policy. As we saw for revenue concerns in Chapter 4 and for democracy in Chapter 5, the effects of these variables may vary by country. Individual countries and cross-national variation between them lie at the center of my concerns.

I do not attempt to explain each act of cooperation, which would imply using each treaty as an observation. In this I differ from the literature on international conflict, which generally uses each war or other conflict as an observation. Countries routinely engage in many acts of cooperation simultaneously, but do not routinely engage in several wars at the same time. This makes it easy for me to study how a highly cooperative country differs from a medium or low cooperator, because I can count simultaneous cooperative acts. Looking at individual treaties may (or may not) prove to be an interesting subject for future research. The data requirements would also be very high for such a project, because one needs every variable of interest for both sides of every treaty; in contrast, looking at each country's treaty counts only requires data for one country at a time.

Forms of Trade Cooperation

The field of international relations has largely agreed on a common definition of cooperation: it occurs when "actors adjust their behavior to the actual or anticipated preferences of others, through a process of policy coordination" (Keohane 1984: 51–52). In other words, cooperation requires that states make a conscious choice to change their behavior.

This definition implies a dichotomous definition of cooperation, in that states either choose to adjust their behavior or do not. Although this definition does not rule out continuous dimensions such as the depth of cooperation or the number of issues covered, the core notion of cooperation itself is dichotomous. Whether two states cooperate a lot or a little is a continuous variable distinct from (non)cooperation itself.

Most studies of cooperation have examined at most a few cases, in which the author can easily demonstrate that some behavior meets this definition. For example, each contributor to *Double-Edged Diplomacy* (Evans et al. 1993) paired one case of cooperation against one case of noncooperation. A few more scholars have looked at economic cooperation between a larger number of actors, using bilateral trade as a measure of cooperation (i.e., Gowa and Mansfield 1993; Mansfield 1994; Mansfield and Bronson 1997; Mansfield et al. 2000). Unfortunately, bilateral trade is a continuous variable that does not capture the dichotomous nature of the definition. Still, bilateral trade levels are interesting for many other purposes and may be a good measure of the *depth* of cooperation.

To capture the dichotomous choice between cooperation and noncooperation, this book uses a new compilation of trade cooperation, the TAD.[1] This database seeks to include all agreements by which two states agree to lower trade barriers between them.[2] The Austro-Prussian treaty of 1853 provides a typical example. It eliminated most import prohibitions on both sides and put certain raw materials and semi-manufactured goods on the duty-free list. The two states also gave each other preferential duties on various manufactured goods (Henderson 1939/1984: 213–28). By focusing on such agreements, my operationalization of cooperation captures the conscious choice of mutual policy adjustment that is central to the definition of cooperation.

Because of its reciprocal tariff concessions, the typical nineteenth-century treaty differed from its typical eighteenth-century counterpart. In the eighteenth century commercial treaties sought permission for British merchants to engage in commerce and protection for their persons and property in foreign lands. They provided a legal foundation for commerce, but not reciprocal reductions in duties. Britain's Methuen treaty with Portugal foreshadowed the future, as did the Vergennes-Eden treaty with France in 1786 (I. Wallerstein 1989: 86–91; Williams 1972: 143), as both treaties lowered many duties on a reciprocal basis. In contrast, many "unequal treaties" with peripheral states in the nineteenth century resembled the older pattern of protecting persons and property engaged in commerce.

To provide an idea of what the TAD looks like, Table 6.1 lists those treaties signed in 1888, which was an unexceptional year for trade cooperation.[3] These 15 treaties include intra-European, intra-American, and interregional agreements – even one trans-Pacific treaty establishing MFN relations between Japan and México. In contrast to the clustering years that I examine in Chapter 11, no pattern of cooperating countries emerges

---

[1] The original research design for TAD was developed with Gerald Schneider of the Universität Konstanz with the post-1945 period in mind. I have made some changes in this design for the nineteenth century, for which he is blameless. The data in TAD are available from the author and at the Web site, https://netfiles.uiuc.edu/pahre/www/agreeable.html.

[2] This lowering of barriers might effectively raise barriers against third parties, a question that is central to Part IV. For reasons developed in the next chapter, my theory predicts that states will never sign an agreement raising tariffs between them. I am happy to report that I have never found such a treaty.

[3] This year was exceptional in one respect, for it was the "year of the three kaisers" (*Dreikaiserjahr*) in Germany. For what it is worth, this dynastic instability probably suppressed German treaty initiation.

Table 6.1. *Treaties signed in 1888*

Date signed	Countries	Title	Summary	Duration
2/26/1888	Italy-Spain	Treaty of commerce and navigation	Reciprocal MFN, except for state monopolies or during war. Listed tariff concessions and elimination of transit duties. National treatment in shipping except for coasting trade and territorial fishing.	Denounced by Spain on 1/26/1891.
2/29/1888	Italy-Switzerland	Convention on commerce	Reciprocal MFN treatment on all import, export, and transit matters.	In force from 3/1/1888. New treaties signed in 1889 and 1892.
11/23/1888	Austria-Hungary-Switzerland	Treaty of commerce	Reciprocal MFN treatment in trade excluding border districts and customs unions, with listed tariff concessions. Freedom of navigation.	In force to 2/1/1892, and thereafter unless denounced. New treaty in 1891.
11/27/1888	Austria-Hungary-Liechtenstein	Additional convention	Additional terms to earlier customs union.	Lasted through World War I.
1/12/1888	El Salvador-Germany	Convention on commerce	Renewal of 1870 treaty.	Ten years and thereafter unless denounced.
3/8/1888	Guatemala-México	Convention on commerce	Freedom of commerce except for wheat.	Five years and thereafter unless denounced. Never ratified.

Date	Parties	Type of agreement	Description	Duration/Status
5/9–11/1888	Italy-Nicaragua	Exchange of notes	Extends the 1868 treaty until a new treaty is signed.	Six months, starting 9/22/1888.
6/20/1888	Germany-Guatemala	Protocol to treaty of 1887	Adhesion of Luxemburg and interpretation of MFN provisions.	Same as 1887 treaty.
6/22/1888	Ecuador-Switzerland	Treaty of amity, commerce, and navigation	Reciprocal MFN treatment.	In force to 7/13/1899, and thereafter unless denounced.
7/2/1888	Germany-Honduras	Protocol to treaty of 1887	Adhesion of Luxemburg to 1887 treaty and modifications to MFN.	Same as 1887 treaty.
7/10/1888	Ecuador-México	Treaty of amity, commerce, and navigation	Reciprocal MFN treatment.	Ten years and thereafter unless denounced.
7/18/1888	Bolivia-Brazil	Treaty of amity, commerce, and navigation	Reciprocal MFN treatment.	Five years and thereafter unless denounced.
11/27/1888	Britain-México	Treaty of friendship, commerce, and navigation	Reciprocal MFN in all commercial and navigational matters. Includes most British colonies.	México denounced on 12/22/1925, but did not terminate it until 6/30/1928.
11/30/1888	Japan-México	Treaty of friendship and commerce	Reciprocal MFN customs treatment.	Indefinite until denounced. Replaced by treaty of 10/8/1924.
12/14/1888–1/21/1889	Italy-Nicaragua	Exchange of notes	Extends 1868 treaty to 3/22/1890 during international negotiations for a transoceanic canal through Nicaragua.	In force to 3/22/1890.

from this list. The table illustrates the variety of subject matters found. Many treaties provide for mutual MFN status, but this list includes a customs union, some navigation and fishing provisions, and a treaty linked to the proposed Nicaraguan canal.

The list also illustrates the multitude of legal forms in which such cooperation can occur. The countries of Europe and the Americas used a wide range of formal instruments to cooperate in tariffs, which I summarize in Table 6.2. Not surprisingly, the main types are conventions and treaties. Several other instruments could modify, renew, or extend these treaties and conventions or maintain existing cooperation provisionally during renegotiations.

Because this book examines the politics of trade cooperation, I do not wish to exclude any of these many forms of cooperation. Each represents a conscious choice to adjust a country's policy, conditional on the activities of another. For this reason, I coded any treaty, exchange of letters, or other understanding as a trade agreement as long as the states made mutual tariff concessions or granted each other mutual MFN status. This definition of trade cooperation includes both those temporary agreements made while negotiating a treaty and treaties observed without legally being in effect. The legal form of the agreement, although important for international law, does not seem to affect the political problems surrounding these treaties.

Including all these different legal forms is not without its problems. For one, less formal kinds of cooperation may be substantively different from more formal agreements (Lipson 1991). Second, the choice of instruments affects the permanence of concessions. Permanence is central to treaty duration, which provides a significant question in itself (Koremenos 2001).

A more subtle difficulty concerns the difference between temporary and "final" agreements. An example should make these problems clear. Many protectionists viewed provisional treaty extensions in the late 1870s – which I code as trade cooperation – as a form of *noncooperation*. Joseph Neuwirth (cited in von Bazant 1894: 34), a leader of the protectionist deputies in the Austrian parliament, argued that these provisional arrangements indicated the end of trade cooperation: "In a word: only the aversion, or if I may say, the horror against the workings of trade treaty system can explain why in Europe at this moment – and we cannot of course foretell the future – the treaty system is only seen in the form of provisional agreements."[4] As a result,

---

[4] "Mit einem Worte: nur die Aversion, oder wenn ich sagen soll, die Scheu gegen das Vertragssystem und seine Wirkungen kann es erklären, daß in Europa, wenigstens in diesem Augenblicke [1878] – und die Zukunft kann man ja nicht vorhersehen – das Vertragssystem nur als Provisorium bekannt ist."

Table 6.2. *Types of trade agreements*

Formal title	Uses in this period
Convention on Commerce (and Navigation)	Common instrument for long-term agreements, but also used for temporary extensions while negotiating a convention or treaty.
Treaty of Commerce (and Navigation)	Common, though less common than conventions.
Treaty of Amity/Friendship and Commerce (and Navigation) (and Establishment)	Common for newly independent states or a first treaty between a pair of states.
Declaration on Commercial Relations	Common during renegotiations, especially for Italy; used very rarely for mutual grant of MFN without making specific tariff concessions.
Extension of Treaty (or Convention)	Typically short-term extensions of six months to three years while negotiating renewal or a new treaty (convention).
Protocol on Extension of Commercial Treaty	Often used during renegotiations, especially by Italy.
Exchange of Notes on Commercial Relations	Unusual; when used, normally grants reciprocal MFN without making additional tariff concessions; sometimes used to extend an earlier convention or treaty, especially during negotiations.
Commercial Arrangement	Unusual; typically grants MFN provisionally while negotiating over details.
Provisional commercial arrangement	Unusual; sometimes an extension of an earlier treaty or convention with modifications, sometimes a temporary agreement concerning specific goods.
Commercial Agreement	Rare; typically covers trade in specific goods, sometimes used to extend earlier treaties indefinitely, rarely clarifies the position of a colony with respect to existing treaties.
Declaration Concerning Treaty (or Convention) (or Provisional Agreement)	Less common instrument used to extend previous arrangements during negotiations; also occasionally used to modify or clarify terms of previous treaties.
Treaty of Peace (etc.)	Rare but often important.
Tariff Agreement	Rare; all cases involve Ottoman Empire.
Commercial Accord	Rare.
Customs Union	Rare except in Germany before unification.
Customs Treaty	Rare.
Modus vivendi; Exchange of Notes on *modus vivendi*	Rare; most examples involve Spain or Brazil.
Agreement on Commercial Relations	Only example is Canada-France, 1893.
Treaty of Reciprocity	Rare.
Provisional Convention	Rare.
Provisional Commercial Arrangment	Rare.
Additional Convention to Treaty (or Convention)	Unusual choice of instruments to modify tariff reductions or add MFN provisions to an earlier treaty.

he believed that the provisional nature of these agreements signaled the end of the trade treaty system, a development that he welcomed.

If correct, this view suggests that we should distinguish fixed treaties from temporary agreements. However, we know with hindsight that these temporary agreements of the 1870s became "permanently" renewed treaties. In a word, these provisional agreements were a mere interlude in the working of the trade treaty system and did not reflect an unwillingness to renew treaties. For this reason I have not distinguished them from more permanent treaties and conventions.[5]

Not only the legal form of cooperation but also the substance of these treaties and conventions requires decisions about what to include. One type of agreement deserves special note here, namely, those MFN treaties that did not explicitly make line-item tariff concessions. I have included these treaties because they imply concessions on tariff lines – by granting each other MFN today, states may need to change their tariff codes.[6] In a system of many interlocking trade agreements, such as the environment in which most MFN treaties were reached, line-item concessions are inevitable even if a simple MFN treaty does not provide for them. For example, Britain explicitly recognized in 1886 that a simple MFN treaty with Spain would entail duty reductions in practice (Marsh 1999: 164).

These treaties also guaranteed future concessions, should tariff reductions be given to a third party. They also locked in concessions, with the result that "denouncing a single trade treaty would not fundamentally endanger the tariff, as long as other treaties with the same tariff remained in force"[7] (Weitowitz 1978: 71). Still, these treaties were typically less important than treaties making line-item concessions, a distinction I explore in Chapter 11.

Although preferring to be inclusive, I have excluded four categories of treaties. First, I do not include shipping treaties, by which I mean those agreements concerning navigation and shipping matters alone. This category includes treaties limited to the navigation of particular provinces or rivers or to transit duties through them, such as treaties on trade in Poland or along the Danube. Some of these treaties, such as the capitalization of the Scheldt or the Danish Sound dues, were major international undertakings

---

[5] Notice that I would have included these agreements no matter what the subsequent history; I have used hindsight to decide not to create two categories in the database.

[6] Several countries, notably France, Spain, and the United States, tried dual-column tariffs in which the MFN minimum rates were set down by the legislature and were not negotiable. In practice, each negotiated small changes in the minimum.

[7] "Durch die Kündigung eines Handelsvertrages würden die Zollsätze nicht grundsätzlich gefährdet, solange andere Verträge mit den gleichen Tarifen in Kraft blieben."

with important effects on trade, but they did not entail reciprocal trade concessions. However, if one state makes tariff concessions in exchange for navigational concessions, I have included the treaty.

I also exclude shipping treaties that grant MFN treatment in customs duties only if the goods are transported in national ships. These treaties aim primarily to provide MFN treatment in navigation laws, not in import and export duties, and they would best be classified as navigation treaties. Moreover, the fact that MFN status is limited to national ships means that the considerations above would tend not to apply. Cooperation in navigation would provide a worthy subject, going back well before 1815–1913, but is best left to another project.

Third, I have excluded treaties granting reciprocal rights of establishment. Although it was doubtless important for trade that foreigners have the right to establish business operations without prejudice, it seems very difficult to measure the effects of such rights. For the same reason, I exclude treaties granting the citizens of each signatory national treatment, that is, the right to be regulated in the same way abroad as locals engaged in the same activity. In addition, many of these treaties are notoriously unequal, giving Europeans rights in China and elsewhere without reciprocity.

Finally, I have excluded Europe's unequal treaties with Africa and Asia (for summary, see Williams 1972: 292–342). For this purpose, Asia is defined as states other than Russia east of the Ottoman Empire and west of Japan. Japan is included because its initially unequal treaties, such as Perry's treaty, gave way to more reciprocal forms of cooperation. Still, some care is necessary in interpreting Japanese "cooperation" before the 1890s.

After much consideration, I have included Ottoman Turkey's allegedly unequal capitulations.[8] The substantive effects of Turkey's treaties were small, such as a reduction in the Ottoman tariff from 8 to 7%. Such a minor change is unlikely to be coerced. In addition, the Ottoman government had long favored the interests of Christian traders within the Empire for domestic political reasons, and these capitulations are understandable as political concessions to Muslims who wished to compete with the Christians for commerce. Moreover, the boilerplate provisions for reciprocal freedom of commerce found in unequal treaties were presumably meaningless for,

---

[8] I have also included the unequal Austro-Serbian treaty of 1881, which made Serbia a virtual economic satellite of Austria. This treaty significantly limited Serbian sovereignty, requiring it to adopt Austro-Hungarian veterinary regulations and to ban cattle imports from Bulgaria, Romania, and Turkey. Even so, Serbia received important concessions not received by others, many under the guise of special treatment for "border traffic" in the Kraina.

say, Siamese ships unable to travel to England. Yet these provisions could be valuable for many Ottoman subjects – especially Armenians, Greeks, Jews, and other ethnic groups with extensive mercantile ties to the outside world. Thus, these treaties were not so unequal after all.

Even without the unequal treaties, the list of countries in TAD is wider than those typically found in the study of international relations, such as the Correlates of War (COW), POLITY, or Militarized Interstate Dispute (MID) databases. The states in TAD include minor countries such as Liechtenstein, Luxemburg, and Monaco, as well as the smaller German and Italian states prior to unification, and Texas from 1838 to 1848. Latin American republics that negotiated treaties with England or France before receiving formal recognition are included, as are the self-governing Dominions of the British empire and Balkan nations that were formally autonomous parts of the Ottoman Empire. Moldavia and Wallachia are treated as independent until forming a customs union in 1847; this does not agree with their constitutional history but will do for our purposes. I also include Norway for some purposes because it had tariff autonomy even under Swedish rule. Hungary, which had nearly as much autonomy as Norway after the 1866 *Ausgleich* (see Szijártó 1994), did not sign separate treaties but did keep separate statistics. Yet, Hungary also had an autonomous tariff until 1850, so it sometimes requires separate treatment (see Chapter 9).

The question of effective autonomy, as well as the ability to negotiate tariff conventions with outsiders, was often unclear for Europe's newer countries. Most countries in the Balkans began the century under Ottoman rule and ended with full independence. However, they had stages of autonomy or sovereignty with the payment of tribute along this path. It is hard to tell both when they have tariff autonomy so that they can establish new tariffs and when they have the ability to raise the tariff in violation of agreements signed by the Porte that had previously bound them.

For example, the principalities of Moldavia and Wallachia raised the import tariff from 3 to 5% in 1845, and then to 7.5% in 1866, in violation of European treaties with the Ottoman Empire *if those treaties continued to bind Romania* (Antonescu 1915: Chapter 2). This latter question remained unclear, and European states had a political interest in recognizing Romanian autonomy that conflicted with their economic interest in lower foreign tariffs. Austria in particular preferred not to complain too much even when these stirrings of Romanian autonomy harmed Austrian economic interests.

Complicating matters, these states sometimes sought direct negotiations with outsiders as a way of establishing a claim of sovereignty. As we might expect, this was true of Romanian negotiations with Austria in 1868–1871. According to Antonescu (1915: 34), Romanian Foreign Minister

Vasile Boerescu "made it a condition that any treaty [with Austria] would be reached directly between the two powers without any involvement by the Porte, because it was important for Romania to establish a precedent of autonomy through this trade convention."[9] We see similar demands in Latin America. In 1822, the Republic of Gran Colombia offered commerce, free residence, and full reciprocity to all countries that would recognize it; México and Argentina made similar offers in the 1820s (Williams 1972: 257–58).

Autonomous units within the state represent one form of nonstate cooperation. International organizations, some of which had the ability to negotiate tariff treaties, are another form. The German *Zollverein* provides the most important example of such an organization. However, Prussia almost always negotiated on the *Zollverein*'s behalf, so I count these treaties as if they were Prussian.[10] When they existed, the German Tax Union (*Steuerverein*) and the North German Confederation also had the power to negotiate commercial treaties on behalf of their members and are briefly treated as separate states.[11] I treat the Peru-Ecuador Confederation and Gran Colombia (modern Colombia, Venezuela, and Ecuador) in the same way as the German customs unions.

With these definitions, TAD encompasses more than one thousand trade treaties signed around the world from 1815 to 1913. These data allow not only a comparative study of foreign economic policy but also a regional or even global perspective on the trade treaty regime.

Sources for TAD

The main sources for TAD are government documents and similar compilations (Calvo 1862; Cardoso de Oliveira 1912; First International American Conference 1889–1890; Hertslet 1875-; Macgregor 1846; Ministerio degli Affari Esteri 1865–1899; *Recueil des Traités et Conventions* 1858–; Triepel, 1900–1945; U.S. Department of State 1890; U.S. Tariff Commission 1940; Vial Solar 1903). These sources are usually comprehensive for the countries and periods covered.

---

[9] "Er [Boerescu] machte aber zur Bedingung, daß der Vertrag direkt zwischen den beiden Mächten ohne irgend eine Einmischung der Pforte geschlossen werde, denn es sei für Rumänien wichtig, durch diese Handelskonvention einen Akt der Autonomie zu statuieren."

[10] Voting members of the *Zollverein* had to ratify any treaty the Prussians signed. I discuss this important power in Chapter 9.

[11] The Middle German Customs Union and Thuringian Customs Union also had this power, but did not sign any treaties. Agreements signed by the Bavaria-Württemberg Customs Union are assigned to both Bavaria and Württemberg, who acted jointly.

Because all treaties require two signatories, even a one-sided official source provides a lot of information about other countries. Other indirect information comes from the fact that many treaties refer to previous treaties, both expired and not. As a result, the data available are excellent for the major trading countries of Europe and good for other European countries.

The secondary literature occasionally lists treaties not in these other sources. This literature has been essential for compiling *Zollverein* treaties (i.e., Henderson 1939/1984; Price 1949). Outside Germany, secondary sources have provided some treaty data for southeastern Europe, Scandinavia, and South America. The secondary sources have been most useful for data on countries that no longer existed in 1914, such as the Texas treaties or the agreements of 1835 and 1847 between Moldavia and Wallachia.

Finally, information on a few treaties has come from personal communications. Marc Flandreau, David Lazer, and Daniel Verdier have each provided information about some treaties that they have found in the course of their own researches on this century.

Having worked with these data for some years now,[12] I think the dataset is reasonably complete. Consulting new sources occasionally yields information about a previously excluded treaty or two, but the numbers are always small. I suspect that a few nonratified treaties did not make it into the database. This may affect the findings of Chapter 9 but not other chapters, because nonratified treaties are otherwise excluded.

The major limitation of the database is the lack of end dates for many Latin American treaties. This means that data on the number of treaties in effect at a given moment in Latin America are suspect. Fortunately, Latin American treaty initiation data are as good as Europe's. These two variables are discussed at greater length in the next section.

Measures of Trade Treaties

Simply listing treaties in a database is only the first step to studying trade cooperation. Understanding the politics of trade cooperation requires further concepts, which I label the "annual treaty initiation" and "annual treaties in effect" variables for each country. In other words, the database has variables for Denmark such as DENINIT and DENSUM, with one observation per year from 1815 to 1913, for Denmark's annual treaty initiation and annual treaties in effect; and so on for other countries. These concepts

---

[12] The first publication using these data is Pahre (1998); in addition to his independent research, David Lazer had access to an early version, reflected in his dissertation and in Lazer (1999).

Table 6.3. *Annual variables in the trade agreements database*

Variable	Distinguished	Example
Treaty initiation (sum) TARGI	By country	Argentina signs a treaty with Germany.
Zollverein treaty initiation (sum) ZBAVI	By country	Bavaria signs a *Zollverein* treaty with Hesse-Darmstadt.
MFN treaty initiation (sum) TCANMI	By country	Canada signs an MFN treaty with Italy.
Treaty in effect (yes/no) TDENJPN	By dyad	Denmark and Japan have a treaty in effect.
Treaties in effect (sum) TECUSUM	By country	Ecuador has five treaties in effect.
Zollverein treaties in effect (sum) ZFRKSUM	By country	Frankfurt has two treaties in effect in the *Zollverein*.

Each year is an observation, with $1815 = 1$ and $1913 = 99$.
The variable names are not used in the text but are included as illustrations of variables found in the Stata files available from the author.

distinguish one country from another, making possible transnational comparisons such as whether democracy or other national-level features make a country more likely to cooperate with other countries. These variables are summarized in Table 6.3.

Treaty Initiation

Treaty initiation is simply the date on which two nations signed an agreement, not the date on which the agreement took effect. This definition captures a government's decision to negotiate agreements, regardless of whether legislatures or monarchs subsequently ratify these agreements. Ratification and whether the treaties ever took effect are important for other questions (see Chapter 9), but do not affect the treaty initiation data.

Annual treaty initiation simply adds up the number of treaties that a country signed in a given year. A few exchanges of notes on commercial policy have created difficulties for coding initiation dates. Although most exchanges of notes occur close in time, they may still straddle the December 31/January 1 divide between years, as does the Italy-Nicaragua example in Table 6.1. Because the substantive negotiations obviously precede the first note, I use the earlier date in such cases.

This variable is the central dependent variable for this part of the study, for it captures the decision to cooperate or not. In addition, this variable actually varies substantially from one year to the next. This feature makes

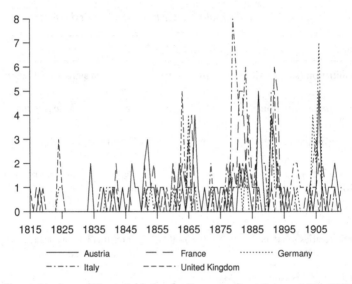

Figure 6.1. Annual Treaty Initiation for European Great Powers, 1815–1913.

it a good measure of cooperation when independent variables such as the average tariff or revenue considerations also change each year.

As an illustration of what these data look like, Figure 6.1 shows the treaty initiation data for European great powers other than Russia, which was not an active cooperator. Most countries have low levels of initiation most of the time. Later in the century this initiation increases and is often clustered in a few years, with periods of few treaties in between (see Chapter 12). The highest spikes in the second half of the period belong to Austria-Hungary, Germany, and Italy – though the secondary literature emphasizes Britain and France. Even at this first cut, then, we see the need for a substantial adjustment of how we view international cooperation in the nineteenth century.

Treaties in Effect

Treaties in effect counts the number of treaties that a country has in effect at a given moment. A trade agreement counts as being in effect in a given year if it was in effect for at least six months. I also counted it as being in effect if the parties agreed to honor a former treaty provisionally while negotiating a new one. In a few cases, countries honored expired treaties without any formal agreement to that effect.[13] This practice characterized Anglo-French

---

[13] An important modern analogue is the SALT II treaty, which the Reagan Administration honored for six years without signing.

trade relations for several decades before World War I. I have included this tacit cooperation because the two states meet the definition of cooperation. This variable provides a crude estimate of how much a country cooperates with others. Because it is an unweighted average, it assigns no value to whether a country cooperates with its major trading partners, its regional neighbors, the great powers, or other states of unequal importance.

It is unlikely that a more sophisticated variable would qualitatively change our analysis. Table 6.4 shows the number of years in which a treaty was in effect for most European dyads. As one might expect, large states have treaties in effect for longer periods of time with other large states, and small states cooperate longer with large states than with small. (Compare the large-large upper-left quadrant with the small-small quadrant in the lower right and the mixed upper-right quadrant.) France is the only exception, cooperating longer with small states than with large. Aside from this exception, any treaties-in-effect variable that gave greater weight to large states or to major trading partners would yield rank-order results generally similar to the unweighted count that I use here. For this reason, I use the simpler unweighted count.

I sometimes break this total down by categories. For example, including the minor German and Italian states before unification has a significant effect on the number of Prussian treaties before 1870 and a minor effect on Austrian treaty counts. To take this effect into account, I calculate cooperation both with and without these minor states when comparing Prussia or Austria to other countries (see especially Chapter 9). I also calculate separate totals for European and Western Hemisphere treaties to examine the spread of the regime from Europe to Latin America. The European totals are also more accurate because there is greater measurement error in the Latin American data.

The treaties-in-effect data present several problems. First, the sources often do not list the expiration dates for a treaty. I normally assumed that a treaty had the same length as comparable treaties signed by those states at roughly the same time. This assumption and occasional judgment calls introduce significant measurement error into the database.

Second, many treaties provided that they would stay in effect from year to year unless denounced by one state or the other. I always assume that a treaty remains in effect if a subsequent treaty between the same two parties makes mention of the earlier treaty. In many cases, countries renegotiated such a treaty over several years, typically exchanging notes to the effect that the earlier treaty remains in effect during negotiations. Even in the absence of such an exchange of notes, I assume that an expired treaty remained in

Table 6.4. Number of years with treaty in effect, European dyads, 1815–1913

	Austria	France	Italy	Prussia	United Kingdom	Belgium	Denmark	Netherlands	Portugal	Spain	Sweden
Austria	–	48	44	49	75	32	27	10	2	21	42
France		–	35	53	54	60	0	56	47	49	49
Italy			–	64	42	30	10	10	7	36	10
Prussia				–	58	61	10	65	15	15	8
United Kingdom					–	43	0	0	72	12	21
Belgium						–	0	5	29	25	5
Denmark							–	0	0	21	0
Netherlands								–	39	25	5
Portugal									–	13	12
Spain										–	13
Sweden											–

effect over any modest period of two or three years. Sometimes the secondary literature describes longer renegotiation periods.

Some treaties lasted decades without being denounced or renegotiated. For example, the Belgian-Nicaraguan Treaty of Friendship, Commerce, and Navigation of May 18, 1858, was denounced by Nicaragua 76 years later on April 5, 1934. Although this treaty is the longest lasting example that I could find, many others also lasted decades.

To make matters worse, countries often found themselves disagreeing about whether a treaty was still in effect between them. In 1916, France denounced an 1856 treaty that Honduras then claimed to have already denounced in 1876. German-American trade treaties provide a more substantively important example. The United States maintained until World War I that the 1828 treaty with Prussia applied only to that state, whereas Berlin maintained that it applied to all the members of the German Empire (Fisk 1903).[14] However, the United States honored the Prussian treaty as if it applied to all Germany.

I have coded all such cases as well as possible, with help from the secondary literatures that I have consulted. Because the Prussian-American treaty was observed through World War I, I have it as being in effect *de facto* if not *de jure*. I deem the Franco-Honduran treaty as denounced because Honduras no longer believed itself bound by it in 1876; if France continued to observe it, then France was simply being exploited unilaterally. In the absence of information about duration, I assume that a treaty was in effect for ten years, beause this is the most common duration for all treaties. Still, some of the decline in treaties in the database after 1900 is probably more apparent than real, reflecting treaties that were being honored without appearing as such in the official treaty series. This problem is especially severe for the smaller Latin American countries, whose treaty counts should be treated only as approximations.

These limitations make the treaties-in-effect variable subject to more measurement error than treaty initiation. This variable also varies less from year to year than does treaty initiation, because treaties in effect one year tend to remain in effect the following year. Yet, this feature has an advantage in capturing a state's decision not to denounce a treaty even if economic conditions change (see Chapter 8). Because it is a less variable measure of cooperation, it is also easier to use in tests when an independent variable,

---

[14] The German position has its ironies, given Bismarck's insistence on the continued sovereignty of the "confederated governments" that made up the German *Reich* (see Mommsen 1995: Chapter 2).

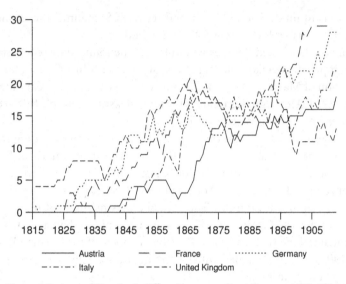

Figure 6.2. Annual Treaties in Effect: European Great Powers, 1815–1913.

such as country size, does not vary much over time. As these points suggest, it is often more useful cross-nationally than intertemporally.

Figure 6.2 shows the annual treaties in effect for the European great powers. These data give a very different picture than Figure 6.1, suggesting a steadily expanding network of cooperation. This visual continuity reflects the expansion of the network to include most countries by century's end. Britain's relative aloofness from the network in the last quarter-century is also visible; Austria-Hungary's seemingly low cooperation reflects a relative lack of treaties with the Western Hemisphere, whereas its level of cooperation with other European countries was very high (see Chapter 9). France and Germany appear as the leading cooperators at late century, a view consistent with some historiography (i.e., Lindberg 1983; Marsh 1999).

Conclusions

The TAD provides unprecedented coverage of trade cooperation for many countries over an extended period of time. Its systematic coverage not only lets us test a wide range of theories about international cooperation but also gives us new substantive knowledge of the international trade regime in the nineteenth century. This information yields several surprises, such as the important role that Austria-Hungary played after 1867 or the small role of Sweden and the Netherlands compared with Belgium or Bulgaria.

The research design in this book differs from the more typical approach in international relations in that I calculate the number of treaties for each country instead of coding each dyad, or pair of states, as either cooperating or not. It differs from research in international relations that looks at the dyad or a pair of states.[15] Quantitative research on war, for example, calculates the probability that a given dyad will be at war in a given year (i.e., Bueno de Mesquita and Lalman 1992; Huth 1996), research on alliances examines the likelihood that each dyad will have an alliance in effect, and research on deterrence looks at the interaction among challengers, defenders, and targets (i.e., Huth 1988; Lebow and Stein 1990). This conventional research design focuses on the ways that dyads differ from one another, such as the power relationships between any two states.

By calculating country-level data, my research design instead directs attention to how countries differ from one another. This cross-national focus fits easily with my theoretical emphasis on domestic politics, a dimension along which countries differ from one another (see Chapter 2). It also means that research points more toward domestic politics as an explanation for cooperation than to power relationships – that is, more comparative politics than international relations. The reader can judge whether this focus succeeds.

This research design also implies differences in statistical testing from that used in dyadic studies. Studies of war use probit or logit to estimate the effects of their variables on the probability that a dichotomous variable will be realized as war or peace. When using a count variable such as treaty initiation as a dependent variable, I naturally use Poisson regression instead. The strong serial correlation in the treaties-in-effect variable raises different issues, discussed in Chapter 8.

These different theoretical purposes also have implications for the independence of these observations from one another. Treaties-in-effect data for each country are naturally serially correlated and should not be treated as independent observations. Treaty initiation data are usually not correlated in this way (but see Chapter 11). Even so, both treaty initiation and treaties-in-effect data reflect some correlation between countries' observations, because two countries sign any bilateral treaty.

---

[15] I have compiled many dyadic-level data, such as whether each dyad has a treaty in effect in a given year, but I use only country-level data as a dependent variable in regressions. Future researchers can use these data for different theoretical purposes than I do.

A related question is whether one country's initiation or in-effect data are independent of other countries' data. Such relationships are common and provide the subjects covered in Part IV. Chapter 11 examines the groupings of many initiations into "clusters," whereas Chapter 12 studies the spread of cooperation from one country to another. Part III ignores these issues, aside from the fact that I prefer using country-level regressions (in which such nonindependence cannot occur) to pooled regressions. However, I report both, noting the possible problems as appropriate.[16]

Like any other data, these data were constructed with particular theoretical and substantive problems in mind. I continue to refer to these peculiarities when using the data in coming chapters.

---

[16] There are not, to my knowledge, off-the-shelf packages for analyzing these effects in Poisson models. Fortunately, both theory and evidence in Part IV show that these problems will often *not* be found, allowing us to ignore them.

SEVEN

Political Support and Trade Treaties

"In regard to commercial relations between States, freedom cannot be actuated unless other countries also consent to it. Thus, from the moment that all States in Europe, in fact all the States in the world raise tariff barriers around themselves it is necessary to find the means by which these be opened to our products of farm and factory."
     – Francesco Crispi (cited in Coppa 1971: 70)

Part II examined countries' autonomous trade policies. This chapter extends the political-support theory of tariffs to two countries. I consider first how each country affects the other's autonomous policy, that is, the effects of unilateral liberalization or protectionism on others.[1] Then I look to the possibilities of joint action, that is, cooperation.

Most previous theorists have not considered how one country's trade policy affects the policy choices of other countries (but see Coates and Ludema 2001; Ethier 2001; Krishna and Mitra 2005; Wonnacott and Wonnacott 2005). These effects are important. I find that any two countries' trade policies move in opposite directions unless a trade treaty is in effect between them. Each country's unilateral actions affect the other, which leads the second state to compensate domestic groups harmed by the first's policy. This compensation leads to policy change in the opposite direction. In short: liberalization begets protectionism, and protection induces liberalization.

The resulting outcome is both politically and economically inefficient. The potential gains give politicians an incentive to negotiate mutual tariff reductions, acting jointly instead of separately. The analysis here thus differs from those who have argued that joint action gives a state influence over

[1] For a welfare analysis of unilateral liberalization, which raises various problems of the second best, see Vousden (1990: Chapter 9).

177

foreign tariffs. Although agreeing with this claim, my theory goes further, showing that a failure to act jointly (i.e., unilateralism) actually makes foreign trade policy less effective, in that one country's unilateral changes will be partially counteracted by the response of other countries (contra Ethier 2001; Wonnacott and Wonnacott 2005; but see Coates and Ludema 2001; Krishna and Mitra 2005). Diffusion theories also expect that home liberalization would have positive effects abroad (i.e., Simmons and Elkins 2004), an effect not found here.

The normal form of joint action is a reciprocal trade agreement. Such an agreement will increase political support for both signatories because additional support from export and consumer interests will outweigh the support lost from import-competing interests. In addition, some groups that oppose unilateral liberalization may support reciprocal liberalization.

This political environment also affected the ideologies of trade policy. In response to this constellation of interests, many nineteenth-century politicians were "protectionist reciprocitarians," supporting both protectionism and reciprocal liberalization. This apparently contradictory policy follows naturally from the theory of political support. Previous scholars have preferred to see this combination of views as "inconsistent," overlooking the internal logic of this position.

The theory has two further implications. Tariff treaties bind tariffs against tariff changes that politicians would otherwise make. As a result, the hypotheses derived in Chapter 3 will not apply to a country that cooperates extensively. This gives a conventional tariff – one bound by convention or treaty – greater stability than an autonomous one. This finding is particularly important because, in the absence of treaties, international economic conditions and domestic institutional change will cause tariffs to go both up and down (see Chapters 3–5). Treaties lock in tariffs and immunize parties against exogenous change, at least to a point.

This chapter presents only qualitative evidence, mostly anecdotal, for its claims. Quantitative tests are problematic because it is difficult to extend the negative reaction claims of the two-country model to an n-country world. Country A's policy leads to an opposition reaction in B, but C reacts to both A and B, with effects in opposite directions but of unclear magnitude and thus having an unclear net effect. Country B will also react to country C's policy change, with effects that might overwhelm the effects of A's policy on B.[2] These kinds of effects are difficult to control for systematically in a quantitative test, but are relatively straightforward qualitatively. Chapters 8

---

[2] Notice that a hypothesis of positive reactions would not face this testing problem.

and 11 build on this chapter's hypotheses in ways that make the implications of this argument more amenable to quantitative testing.

Tariffs in Two Countries

This chapter builds on the model of political support in Chapter 3, extending it to two countries. The results of Chapter 3 stem from the interaction of external price changes and domestic political needs. When we examine two countries simultaneously, however, the tariff in one country is also of interest to exporters in the other country.

If we assume that international markets are not perfectly competitive, then there is some effect on exporters of restricted access to a given country's market. For example, exporters may not find new buyers costlessly. This means that higher foreign tariffs lower the income that home exporters receive for their exports. In this way, exporter income in A is also a function of tariffs (not prices)[3] in B. As a result, A and B face the following problem:

$$M_A = M_A[Y_{EA}(P_{dA}, t_B); Y_{IA}(P_{dA})] \qquad P_{dA} = (P_w)(1 + t_A)$$
$$M_B = M_B[Y_{EB}(P_{dB}, t_A); Y_{IB}(P_{dB})] \qquad P_{dB} = (1/P_w)(1 + t_B) \tag{7.1}$$

In equilibrium, $(\partial M_A/\partial Y_{EA})(\partial Y_{EA}/\partial p_{dA}) + (\partial M_A/\partial Y_{IA})(\partial Y_{IA}/\partial p_{dA}) = 0$ and $(\partial M_B/\partial Y_{EB})(\partial Y_{EB}/\partial p_{dB}) + (\partial M_B/\partial Y_{IB})(\partial Y_{IB}/\partial p_{dB}) = 0$.

To see how each country reacts to the policy of the other, I look at the problem from A's perspective (B's problem is symmetric). Totally differentiating the equilibrium condition $\partial M/\partial t_A = 0$ yields $(\partial^2 M/\partial t_A{}^2)dt_A + (\partial^2 M/\partial t_A \partial t_B)dt_B = 0$, which rearranges to $dt_A/dt_B = -(\partial^2 M/\partial t_A \partial t_B)/(\partial^2 M/\partial t_A{}^2)$. The denominator of the right-hand side is negative, so the sign of dt_A/dt_B depends on the sign of the numerator. I will assume that B's tariffs affect only A's exporters, not the import-competers, so $\partial^2 M/\partial t_A \partial t_B = (\partial M_A/\partial Y_{EA})(\partial^2 Y_{EA}/\partial p_{dA} \partial t_B) + (\partial^2 M_A/\partial Y_{EA}{}^2)(\partial Y_{EA}/\partial p_{dA})$. The second term is unambiguously negative, so the sign depends on the first term. As in Chapter 3, I will assume that price (and) tariff changes have diminishing marginal effects on incomes, so $(\partial M_A/\partial Y_{EA})(\partial^2 Y_{EA}/\partial p_{dA} \partial t_B) < 0$. This means that $dt_A/dt_B < 0$. In other words, any increase in B's tariffs will be met with a *decrease* in A's tariffs:

Hypothesis 7.1: The reaction hypothesis. Increasing protection in one country reduces protection in the other country and vice versa.

[3] I use B's tariffs, not B's prices, in the utility function of A's exporters. The effect of B's relative domestic prices on A's exports is not clear, depending as it does on where these exporters spend their income as well as the effects of price on demand for their product.

This result will surprise those who think in terms of tariff wars and automatically reciprocated tariff concessions, but the political logic is straightforward. Raising B's tariff hurts A's exporters, which disturbs the political equilibrium in A. In the initial equilibrium, the marginal political support from both domestic groups was equal. Now that A's exporters have less income, they give less support. Politicians in A can gain more support at the margin by lowering A's tariff until the increased political support from exporters equals the cost in lost political support from import-competers. Thus, A responds to B's protectionism by liberalizing. Country A responds to this disturbed equilibrium by redistributing some income back to exporters through tariff reductions.[4]

Although the question of such reactions rarely arises in adding-machine or coalitional theories of tariffs, the result that $dt_A/dt_B < 0$ stands in marked contrast to their implicit reasoning. By their logic, a reduction in B's tariffs should make A's exporters wealthier, and these resources should make the export interest more powerful than before. As exporters grow more powerful, they presumably demand tariff reductions, and they should be increasingly successful. This process is found explicitly in several works. For example, Coates and Ludema (2001) show that the beneficial effects of home liberalization on foreign interest groups may in the long run outweigh the short-term losses. Using the influential Grossman-Helpman "protection for sale" framework, Krishna and Mitra (2005) similarly maintain that home liberalization can lead foreign export industries to form lobbying groups and move foreign policy in a more liberal direction.

Though surprising, Hypothesis 7.1 enjoys broad empirical support. This negatively sloped reaction function lay behind the response of many countries to Britain's unilateral liberalization in the first half of the nineteenth century. Although most Liberals believed that Britain's example would be followed by other countries, they were soon disappointed. When Robert Peel introduced his motion to repeal the Corn Laws in 1846, he noted that "other countries have not followed our example [of liberalization], and have levied higher duties in some cases upon our goods" (cited in Schonhardt-Bailey 1997: 82). The causal mechanism is simple. British liberalization not only increased British imports but also spurred competitive sectors to export more, inciting protectionists abroad. As one example,

---

[4] With both consumers and two producer groups, it might be possible to obtain positive reaction functions because home liberalization (protection) would help (harm) two foreign groups, and with the right valuation the politician might have an incentive to treat these two natural allies differently, which might require liberalization (protection).

British iron exports in the 1820s threatened French manufacturers, who then successfully demanded increases in French iron tariffs (Ashley 1926: 276; see also M. S. Smith 1980). Such responses limited Britain's ability to lead Europe on the path to free trade, in contrast to arguments about hegemony (but Pahre 1999: Chapter 6) and the beliefs of most British political economists.

This illustrates how liberalization in one country can breed protectionism in others. The reverse also occurs, with liberalization in response to foreign protectionism. This second mechanism slowed the European descent to protectionism in the 1880s and 1890s. All the countries of Western Europe faced similar problems in the 1880s, especially a large increase in grain imports from outside Europe (see Gourevitch 1986). Some responded with protection, and others tried to keep their export markets open. Reactions to the protectionist states inhibited retaliation, just as Hypothesis 7.1 would suggest. For example, Chancellor Leo von Caprivi decided not to respond to Russian tariffs with a protective German tariff in the 1890s because retaliation would hurt German export industries even more than the Russian tariffs did. The best response to Russian protectionism, most of his government agreed, was a central European customs union that would effectively lower Prussian tariffs (Weitowitz 1978: 47–48, 56–59). As a result, protectionism spread unevenly, and some countries remained open.

This reaction hypothesis highlights the complexities of any system of interacting states. In the absence of trade treaties, we should not expect simple waves of free trade or protection rolling over a system. Instead, any protectionist action may lead to liberal reactions and vice versa. A snapshot of any system should capture polities moving in both directions. These complexities should also slow any process of trade policy diffusion and may help account for the mixed empirical results of diffusion models (i.e., Simmons and Elkins 2004) when applied to trade policy.

The implications of this hypothesis for a system of many states are therefore difficult to entangle. A lower British tariff will lead to French and German protection, but France's reaction to Germany's tariff will be greater liberalization. Germany's response to France will also be a lower tariff, in contrast to Germany's response to Britain. The net effect is theoretically unclear, making quantitative tests difficult. Extending this hypothesis in some other directions, as I do in Chapter 11, will yield hypotheses about the spread of cooperation that rest on Hypothesis 7.1 but are more amenable to quantitative testing. Reciprocal liberalization in this treaty network counteracts the negative reactions of the autonomous tariff found in Hypothesis 7.1.

Reaction Functions and the Historiography

The reaction hypothesis (Hypothesis 7.1) contradicts not only the implicit logic of interest group theories but also runs counter to most historians' expectations. Historians, following the claims made in their sources, typically argue that protectionism leads other states to respond in kind. For example, Eduard Bernstein, the leading revisionist social democrat in Germany, opposed protection in part because it increased international tensions (Fletcher 1983). Such arguments follow the thinking of Cobden and Bright in England, among others.

I have found it very difficult to uncover the causal reasoning behind this general belief – apparently it is so obvious to everybody else that it does not require explanation. However, Adam Smith (1776: 467, 468) recognized retaliation as a legitimate response for reasons of both revenge and pragmatism. The second motive is analyzed more easily, as it depends on a statesman's judgment as to whether such retaliation will induce the target to change its policy.

Historians have claimed to see these retaliatory pressures in Germany, among many other countries. Rolf Weitowitz (1978: Chapter 1) argues that Europe's agrarian states began to protect their markets from German industrial exports in the face of German agricultural tariffs. In this way, Bismarck's economic policy allegedly led to a "peaceful and quiet" ("friedlichen und stillen") tariff war with Austria-Hungary. Similarly, Weitowitz maintains that Austria's industrial tariff increases in the 1880s were partly a response to the German agricultural tariffs and import restrictions on cattle and meat. Somewhat less commonly, historians also maintain that liberalization induces other countries to follow suit. In short, the historiography expects positive reaction functions.

This expectation generally follows the claims of contemporary politicians. British policymakers provide a good example of this belief, for they expected that unilateral free trade would lead others to liberalize as well. James Deacon Hume (cited in Schonhardt-Bailey 1997: 54) testified that "I feel the strongest confidence that if we were to give up our protective system altogether, it would be impossible for other countries to retain theirs much longer."[5] Richard Cobden told his compatriots in 1846 that "if you

---

[5] The British eventually decided otherwise. Louis Mallet concluded in 1875, "The reforms which preceded and followed the Repeal of the Corn Laws, as well as that decisive measure itself, were made without any attempt to secure the co-operation of other countries. This may have been, at the time and under the circumstances, the best policy to pursue; but at all events, the hope that foreign nations would profit by our experience, and follow our example, was signally disappointed" (Cobden Club 1875: 5–6).

abolish the Corn Law honestly and adopt Free Trade in its simplicity, there will not be a tariff in Europe that will not be changed in less than five years to follow your example" (cited in Anderson and Tollison 1985: 203). The belief that British liberalization would lead to *Zollverein* liberalization was best expressed by John Bowring's report to Palmerston, *Report on the Prussian Commercial Union* (1840). Indeed, Bowring believed that the *Zollverein* could only *morally* justify tariffs if Britain had tariffs (J. Davis 1997: 44–47). As I noted above, these predictions proved to be wrong.

Although most people assume positive reactions, a few dissidents thought otherwise. In 1884, E. S. Cayley (quoted in Schonhardt-Bailey 1997:185) sarcastically repeated the conventional arguments:

Every year foreign countries are becoming more and more restrictive, and less inclined to receive the produce of British labour: notwithstanding that, for the last twenty years, the free trade theory has been constantly inducing Parliament to sacrifice more and more of its former protection to British labour, in the fallacious hope that, if we neglected the interests of our own industry, other nations would do the same by theirs.

To my knowledge, Arthur Balfour stands out among British prime ministers, criticizing "the Cobdenites for having failed to see that other countries would not follow Britain's free trade lead, but rather would seek to protect their own infant industries . . . " (Schonhardt-Bailey 1997: 54). These dissidents' claims are better supported by the evidence (Pahre 1998).

I can only speculate about the reasons why the model stands in opposition to so much conventional wisdom. What appears as retaliation may really reflect a problem of inference, a problem intensified in studies with entangling multiple causes examining only a small number of cases. In the late 1870s and 1880s, for example, most European countries faced similar problems of falling grain prices and rapidly increasing imports. These forces led everyone to protect agriculture, for reasons identified in Hypothesis 3.4 (the declining prices hypothesis). These common exogenous shocks meant that many states' tariff changes were positively correlated. As a result, it looked to both contemporaries and modern historians that everyone was responding to one another's protectionism. My hypothesized negative reactions are a second-order response that may be smaller in size than the declining prices effect.[6] Even so, not all countries grew more protectionist (see Chapter 2), and this mixed pattern follows naturally from my theory.

---

[6] The periods covered by trade and GNP data (often 1870–1914), the Great Depression (1873–1896), and the years of extensive cooperation (1860–1914) coincide. These facts make quantitative tests that can sort out these effects very difficult.

Second, we should recognize two kinds of "tariff wars." The reaction hypothesis rules out Type I tariff wars in which one country's unilateral tariff increases lead another country to raise its own tariff unilaterally. In a Type II tariff war, one country raises tariffs in violation of a trade treaty; the other country also denounces the tariff treaty and raises tariffs. As I show in Chapter 8, this second kind of tariff war follows naturally from the enforcement conditions of a trade treaty and will appear as tit-for-tat retaliation to many. Many tariff histories conflate these two types of tariff wars, which rest on very different causal logics.

By making these distinctions and deriving multiple hypotheses, political-support theory can account for both the evidence and improve on the conventional wisdom. For more than a century, economists have overwhelmingly favored a policy of free trade. They argue that free trade is optimal, regardless of the policies other nations choose. Politicians have not found these arguments persuasive. The traditional explanation is that politicians are too confined by political interests and constraints to do the economically rational thing. The model here shows that even an economic philosopher-king unconcerned with his own political position might hesitate before liberalizing unilaterally. In a world in which *foreign* politicians worry about political support, lowering his own tariffs would induce increases in foreign tariffs. Unilateral liberalization therefore has domestic welfare losses – to exporters – as well as gains.[7] In short, the model highlights the importance of being aware of other countries' unilateral reactions to changes in trade policy.

Reciprocal Tariff Liberalization

The reaction hypothesis (Hypothesis 7.1) suggests that the default reactions of each country to the tariff changes of another work to minimize change: liberalization breeds protection and vice versa. Even so, mutual tariff reductions can achieve political gains for both states because each country's unilateral tariffs (and reactions) impose externalities on others.

The results so far follow from the single-play Nash equilibrium, in which each player chooses her best response to the other's strategy. However, countries A and B might select their tariffs jointly or make simultaneous changes to their equilibrium tariffs. Neither A nor B will agree to any outcome unless

---

[7] There may be compensatory favorable effects of unilateral liberalization, highlighted by Coates and Ludema (2001), Ethier (2001), Krishna and Mitra (2005), Vousden (1990: Chapter 9), and Wonnacott and Wonnacott (2005).

both can guarantee themselves at least the same level of political support as in the Nash equilibrium.[8] To understand these conditions, I explore what changes in other variables must occur for A to be able to lower tariffs and yet retain constant utility.

Differentiating (7.2) totally, $dM_A|_{dp_w=0} = (\partial M_A/\partial Y_{EA})(\partial Y_{EA}/\partial p_{dA})$ $dp_{dA} + (\partial M_A/\partial Y_{EA})(\partial Y_{EA}/\partial t_A)dt_B + (\partial M_A/\partial Y_{IA})(\partial Y_{IA}/\partial p_{dA})dp_{dA}$. Where $dM_A = 0$, A's total political support remains unchanged. Thus, we can maintain or increase A's equilibrium level of political support $(\widehat{M}_A)$ for a given p_w under the following condition:

$$\left.\frac{dt_A}{dt_B}\right|_{M_A=\widehat{M}_A,dp_w=0} \geq \frac{-\frac{\partial M_A}{\partial Y_{EA}}\frac{\partial Y_{EA}}{\partial t_B}}{p_w\left(\frac{\partial M_A}{\partial Y_{EA}}\frac{\partial Y_{EA}}{\partial t_{dA}} + \frac{\partial M_A}{\partial Y_{IA}}\frac{\partial Y_{IA}}{\partial p_{dA}}\right)} \qquad (7.2)$$

The numerator is unambiguously positive, so $dt_A/dt_B \geq 0$ iff $(\partial M_A/\partial Y_{EA})$ $(\partial Y_{EA}/\partial t_A) + (\partial M_A/\partial Y_{IA})(\partial Y_{IA}/\partial t_A) \geq 0$. This condition holds whenever the reciprocitarian tariff is less than the unilateral tariff (that is, $t_A < \hat{t}_A$), for it implies that further increases in the tariff would increase A's political support. The same is true for $t_B < \hat{t}_B$. In this region, then, it is possible for these countries to agree on simultaneous tariff reductions ($dt_A < 0$ and $dt_B < 0$) that do not decrease M_A from its equilibrium level; the same is true for M_B.[9] Given these constraints, it is easy to find those regions where simultaneous tariff reductions raise the utility of both. In short,

Hypothesis 7.2: Liberalizing treaties. Two countries can always sign a reciprocity treaty reducing tariffs, but not one increasing tariffs.

---

[8] It is also necessary that the discounted benefits from cooperation be greater than the onetime benefits from cheating followed by the discounted utility from the noncooperative outcome (after the other country retaliates). I assume in this chapter that both countries place a sufficiently high value on future payoffs such that it is always rational for both to cooperate; this assumption is common for many game theoretical purposes (see for example Fudenberg and Maskin 1986; Kreps, Milgrom, Roberts, and Wilson 1982). Chapter 8 assumes Grim Trigger enforcement, by which any deviation from the cooperation equilibrium is punishment by permanent reversion to the single-play Nash equilibrium. In Chapter 8, states may not have sufficiently high discount factors to support cooperation, and this possibility drives many results.

[9] For positive tariffs, simultaneous tariff increases ($dt_A > 0$ and $dt_B > 0$) are ruled out because they would move both countries into the region where the denominator in (7.3) is negative. If we consider unilateral $\hat{t}_A < 0$ such that $t_A > \hat{t}_A$ would *raise* income, then a reciprocal reduction of the absolute value of negative tariffs is possible. An example would be a Euro-American agreement to limit wheat export subsidies. In short, reciprocal liberalization is possible, but reciprocal protection is not.

The reason for this is simple: tariffs impose political externalities on other countries, but no state considers these externalities when making trade policy unilaterally. Making trade policy jointly through a trade treaty allows states to take these externalities into account, leading to lower tariffs. In this way, these treaties allow the executive to take advantage of the economic gains from trade.[10]

Hypothesis 7.2 differs from the claims of many other theories in showing how it can be politically rational to pursue the economic gains from trade (cf. Becker 1985). Each country's concessions bequeath an economic gain to the other government: an economic gain with concrete beneficiaries and therefore also a political gain that unilateral tariff reductions alone cannot yield (cf. Gilligan 1997). This gain more than offsets the lost support from import-competers. These treaties allow the executive to take advantage of the economic gains from trade, skimming off some of these gains in the form of increased political support from exporters.

Under reciprocity, total political support increases whereas political support from import-competers decreases, imposing a political cost on the government. This cost is the reason they are called – contrary to economic rationality – "concessions." Austrian trade minister Johann Freiherr von Chlumecky explained the political logic in parliamentary debate in 1878, arguing that a treaty had advantages despite the victims it created on both sides: "for me, a treaty is worthwhile because of the advantages it brings by furthering trade and industry, advantages for which both sides must offer sacrifices in compensation" (cited in von Bazant 1894: 37).[11] Italian Prime Minister Giovanni Giolitti also recognized these sacrifices when he announced his policy of renewing Italy's trade treaties in 1903 (cited in Coppa 1970: 754, 757): "In these negotiations, we will above all aim to facilitate the exportation of agrarian products and to that end we are prepared to diminish the protection granted to industry, insofar as it does not endanger its existence."[12]

---

[10] The earliest formal statement of this logic that I have found is Johnson (1965); see also W. Mayer (1981). More recent models include Grossman and Helpman (1995); Moser, Hillman, and Long (1995), and Pahre (1991). Tasca (1938/1967) makes the point more informally. For a normative analysis in a complex n-country setting with customs unions and other distortions, see Turunen-Red and Woodland (1991) and Vousden (1990: Chapter 10).

[11] "mir ist der Vertrag wertvoll der Vorteile wegen, die dadurch dem Handel und der Industrie zugeführt werden, Vorteile, welche even in Kompensationen bestehen, welche man sich beiderseits für dargebrachte Opfer bietet."

[12] Notice that Giolitti's condition that cooperation not eliminate industry altogether reflects the logic of Hypothesis 3.1 (the nonmonopoly hypothesis).

Germans viewed the problem the same way in 1892, according to Dietzel (1903: 367):

It was clear that tariff treaties would be purchasable only at the price of certain sacrifices which our producers would have to make. In order to influence other nations to reduce permanently their tariffs on German manufactures, Germany must treat them in the same way.

This reasoning about trade-offs also seems to have been important for the most famous nineteenth-century treaty, the Cobden-Chevalier Treaty of 1860. A report from the Gironde sent to the French Bureau of External Trade in 1842 complained of the stagnation of French wine exports in the 1840s, recommending that important concessions by foreigners could only be obtained if France were willing to open its trade, particularly manufactured items, to other nations' imports in exchange. Although the report acknowledged that opening trade would cause difficulties for France's producers of textiles, iron, and steel, it argued that these losses must be balanced off against the gains to wines and other exports (Nye 1991: 469).

The reasons why joint action is necessary differ somewhat from the argument for reciprocal liberalization given by classical political economists. Because Britain was large enough to influence its terms of trade, Robert Torrens and J. S. Mill argued that liberalization would have to be reciprocal if it were to have welfare-improving effects for Britain. Torrens argued that "the advantages which the advocates of free trade had predicted could not be realized but on terms of perfect reciprocity," whereas Mill believed that "the only mode in which a country can save itself from being a loser by the duties imposed by other countries on its commodities" was "to impose corresponding duties on theirs" (both cited in Semmel 1970: 188). The theory here does not need to assume market power to explain reciprocity. Instead, I need assume only that home exporters are affected by foreign tariffs. Large countries provide one case of a general rule, as developed further in Chapter 8.

My causal mechanism also differs from one leading domestic-level explanation found in the literature. Eckart Kehr's (1965) famous thesis maintains that the principal problem of foreign policy for German conservatism at the turn of the century was the relation between agrarian and industrial states (England and Germany) and the relations between competing agrarian states (Russia and Germany). The marriage of iron and rye precluded favorable relations with either England or Russia. Because of a domestic alliance between two groups with different foreign enemies, Kehr argues,

Germany alienated more opponents than necessary (cf. Fry and Gilbert 1982; Gordon 1979; A. Mayer 1969).

Instead of looking at the particular foreign policy enemies (or allies) of domestic coalitions, the model here emphasizes the potential gains for a political leader who can play these coalitions off against each other enough to find the mutual gains from trade cooperation. Indeed, imperial Germany did exploit these gains and had treaties in effect with both Russia and the United Kingdom even during the period that Kehr examines. Though the British denounced their treaty for reasons of imperial policy, both sides continued to observe it until the war.

In short, this section has shown the basic existence result of this chapter: trade cooperation makes political sense. The model also shows how a state can rationally set a tariff and rationally negotiate this same tariff downward.

The implication is that trade agreements do what they are said to do: open markets. Indeed, it would be surprising if states continued to sign these treaties if they failed to do what they were intended to do. Ample quantitative evidence confirms that preferential trade agreements (PTAs) do indeed increase bilateral trade (Frankel and Wei 1998; Li 2000; Mansfield et al. 2000; Mansfield and Bronson 1997; Pollins 1989).

The strongest possible evidence against this hypothesis would be the group of "autonomous" tariffs passed by various European states in the late nineteenth century. These began with the Austro-Hungarian tariff of 1878, whose conclusion began a "period of storm and stress that was important for international commercial politics. Austria-Hungary had made the first breach in the nearly unassailable theory of free trade, and other states soon followed" (von Bazant 1894: 39).[13] Examples include the Romanian tariff of 1891 and France's Méline tariff of 1892. "Autonomous" tariffs were a favorite demand of protectionists, who did not wish their hard-fought tariff increases to be negotiated away in treaties. If these tariffs were in fact never negotiated downward, this would raise an important class of exceptions for Hypothesis 7.1.

Most of the historiography seems to take these claims of tariff autonomy seriously, except in Austria-Hungary. Yet, the facts are otherwise. Romania's ostensibly autonomous tariff of 1891 lasted only until 1893, when it signed a comprehensive treaty with Germany (Antonescu 1915: Chapters 15–16). France first negotiated concessions in the supposedly non-negotiable

---

[13] "Dann war aber auch dieser Abschluß einer Sturm- und drangsvollen Übergangsperiode von Bedeutung für die internationale Handelspolitik. Österreich-Ungarn hat die erste Bresche in die schier unüberwindliche Theorie des Freihandels gelegt und die anderen Staaten folgten bald nach." The choice of words "Sturm und Drang" makes literary illusions in German not found in English.

minimum Meline rates in treaties with Russia in 1893 and Switzerland in 1895. About 70 of 654 tariff lines in the tariff were negotiated downward in 1905–1907 in conventions with Russia, Romania, Switzerland, and Japan (Haight 1941: 69fn).

Only some very particular institutions make treaties impossible. The organic regulation of 1831 gave Romania the right to raise tariffs in its own interests with the prior approval of the Porte, but not to lower them; this provided no scope for trade negotiations with the outside world (Antonescu 1915: 2–3; Lampe and Jackson 1982: 90–99). Of course, this regulation was imposed on an autonomous Romania by an outside power, so it is not very anomalous for any theory that assumes that states control their own tariffs. Moreover, the Romanians regularly tried to overturn it, both for foreign policy reasons and for domestic political reasons familiar here.

The facts that treaties do liberalize markets and that supposedly non-negotiable tariffs were indeed negotiable support the theory here. These claims are not unique to this theory, so this chapter and the next develop additional hypotheses that distinguish the theory of political support from possible rivals.

Treaties and the Effects of Economic Change

When states sign a trade treaty they promise to keep their tariffs at a certain level. They give up some freedom of action that was central to my analysis of the tariff in Part II. This situation also runs counter to the two-country analysis earlier in this chapter. Reciprocal liberalization affects the validity of Hypothesis 7.1, which states that any two countries' tariffs will be negatively correlated in the absence of a trade treaty. A tariff agreement can counteract tariff increases stemming from terms of trade effects or from changes in the other country's level of protection. In particular:

Hypothesis 7.3: Treaty correlation. When two countries sign a tariff agreement, their tariffs will be positively correlated. (Thus, Hypothesis 7.1 does not apply.)

Because each country makes tariff concessions to the other, changes in tariffs will be positively correlated. The same positive correlation occurs when the treaty is no longer in effect, because both countries will reject the reciprocitarian tariff and return to their higher single-play Nash tariffs. These mutual increases in tariffs will also be positively correlated with one another.

Because of the mechanics of real trade treaties, I also expect a positive correlation in the period between the signing and denouncing of a treaty. Many treaties make tariff concessions over time, so signatories' tariffs will be positively correlated during the phase-in period. Even after the phase-in, the MFN clauses in these treaties require future reductions as the result of new treaties signed with third parties. As signatories negotiate these third-party treaties, these continual tariff reductions will ensure that the signatories' tariffs remain positively correlated.

If we think about a real-world international system, in which some countries have treaties in effect, while others do not, reactions may grow quite complex. States will react directly to, say, Germany's move to protection in 1879, but will also react indirectly by reacting to everyone else's reactions. Some reactions will counteract this change (Hypothesis 7.1), whereas others will not (Hypothesis 7.2). I find that the best way to isolate these effects is by looking at reactions to customs unions, as I do in Chapter 11. This approach at least holds constant the policies of all the countries in the customs union, because they must have the same tariff by definition.

Looking at any pair of countries, however, this section has argued that states' tariffs will be positively related at the time they sign a treaty, throughout the term of any treaty, and when they denounce a treaty. In contrast, their tariffs will be negatively correlated in the absence of a treaty (for an empirical examination of these hypotheses, see Pahre 1998). Cooperation dramatically changes how two states will react to one another.

Political Support and Trade Treaties

This section and the next use qualitative evidence to uncover the causal logic of the model at work in the world. At the theory's core lies two related propositions: first, that a treaty makes tariff cuts possible that would be politically impossible unilaterally, and second, that a treaty yields political support from exporters greater than the accompanying political support lost from import-competing groups.

Because governments can increase their political support through reciprocity treaties, politicians who sign a trade agreement should (*ceteris paribus*) have greater support than those who do not. In hypothesis form:

Hypothesis 7.4: Treaty support. Governments that sign reciprocity agreements receive more political support than those that do not.

Given the ability of such agreements to generate intense controversy, such a result may be surprising.[14] Because it is difficult to measure political support directly, I will test this claim indirectly.

---

[14] The result contrasts with Michael Gilligan's (1997: 25–33) analysis of lobbying and liberalization. He argues that political contributions from both exporters and protectionists

First let us consider the effects of democracy. One feature of democracy is that it increases the value that leaders attach to political support from their constituents. Therefore, democratic leaders will be more likely to value the political support from trade treaties than will leaders in other kinds of political systems:

Corollary 7.1: Democracy and treaties. Democracies are more likely to cooperate.

This claim differs from the findings in Chapter 5, in which democracy lowered the autonomous tariff in some countries but raised it in others (Finding 5.1). The difference reflects the fact that the politics of trade treaties is very different from the politics of an autonomous tariff. Treaties yield welfare and political gains within a country instead of being a more zero-sum distributive conflict. Though I have argued the claim nonformally, it also characterizes formal models such as Rosendorff's (2006).

These political gains from reciprocity make treaties useful for politicians trying to broaden their political base. Germany's Chancellor Caprivi provides an excellent example. Among other goals, he wanted to reintegrate labor into the Wilhelmine Reich, because Bismarck's *Sozialistengesetz* clearly had not stemmed the growth of trade unions or the proscribed Socialist Party. Lowering grain tariffs might regain worker loyalty by reducing the cost of living for the typical worker. Securing export markets would be good not only for capitalists but also for the workers that they employed. In the first Reichstag debates over his trade policy, Caprivi stressed this political function of commercial treaties: "We dare not give up the hope of winning even these people back"[15] (cited in Weitowitz 1978: 149; see also Barkin 1970: Chapters 2–3). In this way, the greater democratization of post-Bismarck imperial Germany facilitated trade liberalization.

With such concerns lying behind any trade policy, it will be true that

Corollary 7.2: Reciprocity and liberalization. Reciprocity makes possible tariff concessions that are impossible unilaterally.

This feature of reciprocity has been shown graphically since at least Johnson (1965; see also W. Mayer 1981).

England's Board of Trade analyzed Prussian trade policy in the 1860s in exactly these terms. Though tariff reductions would serve Prussian interests,

---

will rise in response to a policy of reciprocity, which implies that reciprocity will be more divisive than unilateral tariffs. I argue the reverse.

[15] "Wir dürfen die Hoffnung nicht aufgeben, auch diese Leute wieder zu gewinnen."

the Board recognized that reductions were politically impossible because of the special interests opposing them. In contrast, a treaty with France (signed in 1862) could provide political support sufficient to overcome this opposition. Prussia, the Board argued (cited in Davis 1997: 155)

> is still so much under the influence of class interests that nothing short of the reciprocal concession which it is in the power of France either to confer or to withhold could in my Lordships' opinion have induced them to agree even to the reductions which this treaty would effect.

These reciprocal concessions from France gave Prussia political benefits to offset the losses of its own concessions.

The fact that reciprocity treaties benefit specific export interests also makes them politically easier than unilateral liberalization. One interesting example is how the political logic of reciprocity helped divide Germany's marriage of iron and rye in the 1890s. The Central Federation of German Industrialists (*Centralverband Deutscher Industrieller*, CDI) issued a statement in February 1891 claiming that German industry did not want any tariff advantage in the negotiations with Austria-Hungary if it came at the expense of agriculture. The Union of German Iron and Steel Industrialists (*Verein Deutscher Eisen- und Stahlindustrieller*, VdESI) and other industrial interest groups supported this statement, though the brewers (*Deutscher Brauerbund*) and distillers (*Verein der Destillateure*) distanced themselves from it.[16] The agrarians optimistically believed that these statements demonstrated industry's fundamental opposition to tariff treaties, whereas industry meant to signal only that it had not yet been offered enough concessions to sell out its agrarian allies. After all, the CDI had warmly welcomed ("freundig begrüßt") Caprivi's trade policy. The CDI soon clarified its position in March 1891, stating that it would favor reductions in agricultural tariffs if the government found such reductions necessary to reach a tariff agreement with others (Weitowitz 1978: 24–25). This was not a high price for support because the government would have to offer something as a concession in any case, and agricultural tariffs were the natural choice in many negotiations. Just as Corollary 7.2 expects, Caprivi could appeal to this latent support from industry by using commercial treaties instead of unilateral liberalization.

The model also helps illuminate some otherwise puzzling historical events. The traditional indictment of Giolittian Italy stresses the

---

[16] These differences are explained by the fact that the food-processing industry uses agricultural goods as raw materials and sells to consumers, whose real incomes increase with any tariff liberalization.

government's support for northern industrialists and organized workers at the expense of southern agriculture, giving concessions to southern agriculture only when necessary to obtain support for the northern tariffs and subsidies he favored. Whatever its merits in explaining autonomous tariffs and subsidies, this interpretation cannot explain his commercial policy. The trade treaties of the 1880s and 1890s served southern interests almost exclusively. They successfully retained the rich Central European market for their agricultural exports to the three Central Powers, thanks to sacrifices made by Italian industrialists. Coppa (1971: 82) notes, "It is thus difficult to understand how these treaties can be interpreted as the work of industrial pressure groups or how they betray subservience to the plutocrats and proletariat of the North." Yet Giolitti's actions make perfect sense in political-support terms, for they used reciprocity to gain support from new groups through tariff reductions that would be politically impossible unilaterally.

This last example highlights not just the supply side advantages of reciprocity for politicians but one way in which treaties change interest groups' demands for protection. Although my model, like standard economic theory, treats each person as favoring either free trade or protection, some producers do have mixed interests (see W. Mayer 1981). This implies the following:

Corollary 7.3: Mixed interests and reciprocity. Some groups who oppose unilateral liberalization will favor reciprocal liberalization.[17]

For example, many Great Lakes farmers feared the free entry of Canadian wheat in the 1911 reciprocity treaty because Winnipeg prices were typically six to ten cents lower than those in Minneapolis. However, farmers did desire lower tariffs on manufactured goods that they consumed. Because of this support, an opponent of reciprocity such as Representative Charles August Lindbergh, Senior, of Minnesota could declare (cited in USTC 1920: 71):

If all the tariff laws between the two countries were to be repealed and all commodities produced in either admitted free to the other, it would be a very different question than that which confronts us . . . In that case, I would be enthusiastically for it. . . . We should, however, see that no important industrial necessity of our country is put out of relation with other industries. . . . The proposed agreement makes the farmers of the United States and Canada compete with each other on a free-trade basis, but protects the factories of each country against competition with the other; it puts one industry on a free-trade basis and the others on a protective-tariff basis.

[17] If I were to model the economy explicitly, this conclusion would follow more naturally from a Ricardo-Viner-Cairns-Jones specific-factor model than from a Stolper-Samuelson model. Factor portfolios can also produce mixed interests (see W. Mayer 1984).

In short, Minnesota farmers could tolerate competition from Canadian farmers if they could also reap the benefits of cheaper manufactured imports.

Important as these political externalities are, the historiography normally examines trade treaties as stemming from the same domestic pressures as regular tariff bills. For example, Michael Stephen Smith treats the political choice between trade treaties or lower unilateral tariffs as being no different than the choice between tariffs and quotas. As a result, he does not deem it curious that a large majority of French chambers of commerce in the 1870s supported trade treaties but also favored unilateral protectionism (M. S. Smith 1980: Chapter 1). Similarly, farmer groups in the center and south of France called for both higher tariffs and trade treaties (Smith 1980: 168). In these cases interest groups internalize some of the externalities of trade policy, considering the effects of each firm's maximum tariff demand on other firms (for theoretical treatment, see Kiyono et al. 1991). Politicians responded accordingly, using treaties to bring exporters gains that outweighed any losses to import-competers. The theory here makes a clear distinction between tariffs and trade treaties and shows how a support-maximizing politician might favor both.

Some of the best examples of Corollary 7.3 at work are those groups formed to lobby for commercial treaties. One Austrian example is the Central Organization for Protection of Agricultural and Forestry Interests in the Conclusion of Trade Treaties (*Zentralstelle zur Wahrung land- und forstwirtschaftlicher Interessen beim Abschluß von Handelsverträgen*), formed in 1898 (Matis 1973: 53). The Italian "Organization for the Safeguarding of Southern Interests in the Renewal of the Commercial Treaties" provides another example. It received a surprising ally in Piedmontese cotton manufacturers, who were willing to countenance a reduction in their own duties in order to help agriculture abroad. This position was not entirely selfless, of course, because the industrialists expected that increased agrarian incomes would raise the demand for their own products.

Germany also saw several otherwise protectionist sectors form groups to lobby for trade treaties. Light industries formed the *Bund der Industriellen* in 1895 as a counter to the protectionist CDI. Other organizations followed, including the Office for the Preparation of Commercial Treaties (1897), the Association for Commercial Treaties (1900), and the anti-agrarian Hansabund (1909). These groups did not favor unilateral liberalization, but did see benefits in export markets for which they were willing to give up some of their own protection.

The United States also had such groups. Export industries, such as manufacturers of iron and steel, agricultural machinery, processed grain, furniture, and locomotives, formed a National Reciprocity League in 1902. They were joined by the American Manufacturers Export Association in 1909, made up of producers of specialized goods that exported much of their production. The National Association of Manufacturers was organized in Ohio in 1894 in part to pressure the government to use reciprocity. Its members were mostly small- to medium-sized producers who were competitive overseas and wished to tap into foreign markets (Gilligan 1997: 68–69). This pressure for reciprocity contrasts with the protectionism of American business when faced with an autonomous tariff and illustrates how protectionists may favor reciprocal trade treaties but not unilateral tariff concessions.

Although the evidence in this section is merely illustrative, finding a similar political logic at work in several different countries adds to the plausibility of political-support theory. Only the United Kingdom seems to have been immune to the charms of reciprocity. One illustration will suffice. When Britain sought lower German iron tariffs in 1853, Prussia saw that it could exploit the political possibilities of a reciprocity treaty. English reductions on goods exported by southern Germany – such as silk and linen, games, paints and brushes, glasses, optical instruments, and sealing wax – could bring southern governments to support iron liberalization that they had previously opposed. When Prussia floated exactly this idea, a young William Gladstone at the Board of Trade simply eliminated all these tariffs (except for silk) unilaterally. This action pulled the rug out from Prussian policy, and England never received its iron reductions (Davis 1997: Chapter 4). Similar missed opportunities recurred from the 1880s on (Marsh 1999: Chapter 7). For now, Britain's exceptionalism is simply inexplicable, though I develop some possible explanations for this position in future chapters (see also Pahre 1999).

Protectionist Reciprocitarians

Perhaps the best qualitative evidence for the preceding view of tariff policy is a particular economic ideology that I infelicitously call "protectionist reciprocitarianism." Leading proponents include Leo von Caprivi and Bernhard von Bülow in Germany; Robert Gascoyne-Cecil (the third Marquess of Salisbury, thus often called Robert Salisbury), Arthur Balfour, and Joseph Chamberlain in Britain; and William McKinley, Theodore Roosevelt, and Robert Taft in the United States. Each supported both tariffs and reciprocal tariff reductions. Indeed, Benjamin Harrison's Secretary of State James G. Blaine argued that reciprocity was a logical extension of protectionism when a country needed larger markets for its protection: "The enactment of reciprocity...is the safeguard of protection. The defeat of reciprocity is the opportunity of free trade" (cited in Rhodes 1993: 31). President Roosevelt said in a message to Congress, "Reciprocity must be treated as the handmaiden of Protection" (cited in Bairoch 1993: 36).

The combination sounds odd to modern ears. Indeed, it has often gone unnoticed – or has been misunderstood – in contemporary theorizing. For example, Judith Goldstein (1993: 135–136) argues that the late nineteenth-century American policy of high tariffs and reciprocity simply reflected protectionist ideology, a claim that misses the reciprocitarian element of thinking at the time.

The theory in this chapter can help explain this important historical political position. It follows naturally from the treaty support hypothesis (Hypothesis 7.4) and its corollaries. Some groups will prefer reciprocity to unilateral tariffs, and unilateral tariffs to unilateral free trade (Corollary 7.3). Politicians with a political base in these sectors will share this preference ordering. Other politicians may come to share these preferences. These might be pragmatic free traders who realize that reciprocity makes possible liberalization that would be impossible unilaterally (Corollary 7.2). Pure office-seekers may also end up as protectionist reciprocitarians, recognizing that reciprocity agreements increase their political support (Hypothesis 7.4), even when unilateral protectionism is rational (cf. Chapter 3). Although these represent distinct motives, all can lead politicians to the same position, favoring both unilateral protectionism and reciprocal liberalization.

German Chancellor Leo Graf von Caprivi (1890–1894) provides a classic example of a protectionist reciprocitarian. He made commercial agreements a centerpiece of his economic policy though many of his supporters were protectionists (see Weitowitz 1978). On trade policy, his coalition relied on various liberals, social democrats, centrists, and even national liberals who favored trade treaties. This grouping represented a mix of free trade and traditionally protectionist groups.

Many politicians in supposedly Liberal Italy shared these views. One key decision maker, Luigi Luzzati, provides a good example. Though he wrote the less liberal tariffs of 1878 and 1887, Luzzati was also Giolitti's main treaty negotiator. He claimed to be a pragmatist on the tariff, favoring a tariff on grain for political reasons and not out of ideology (Coppa 1971: 31). Though foreigners criticized him as pro-tariff, Italian protectionists did not consider him one of their rank: "At crucial moments they found that he assumed a position midway between the extremes" (Coppa 1971: 54). His political pragmatism made him support both tariffs and tariff treaties, and he carried significant influence with Giolitti.

Though it is notoriously difficult to identify his core beliefs, Napoleon III may well belong in the category of protectionist reciprocitarian. He did not have any notable commitment either to free trade or protectionism, and he supported liberalization in the 1850s mostly as a way to increase working-class support. John Vincent Nye (1991: 468) argues that liberalization did not cause a major upheaval in French politics largely because "the essentially pragmatic, tariff-moderating agreement of 1860 was in line with the Emperor's desire for a less restricted trading structure, but represented no sudden ideological commitment to the benefits of free trade." France's other treaties in the 1860s followed this model.

Arthur Balfour also believed that free (or at least freer) trade was in the national interest, but could only be obtained through negotiation with foreign governments. Because England needed its own tariffs to threaten retaliation in negotiations, he proposed the selective imposition of retaliatory tariffs sufficient to force foreign concessions. He proposed "Freedom to negotiate" as a rallying cry. Aaron Friedberg (1988: 68) argues, "It was hardly an inspiring slogan. Raising tariffs in order to lower them had a certain awkward logic, but it was not a position likely to generate widespread public enthusiasm." Joseph Chamberlain thought these proposals timid and left the government to wage a campaign for tariff reform – by which he meant tariff increases, mostly through imperial preference – from the outside (Sykes 1979).

The same kinds of beliefs could be found in many smaller countries. In Bavaria, successive ministries faced a balancing act. The high ministerial bureaucracy (i.e., Gustav Schlör and Karl Freiherr von Schrenck von Notzing) tended toward a judicious liberalism ("tendierten einsichtigerweise zum Wirtschaftsliberalismus"), but anti-Prussian resentments and a generally favorable position toward Austria led them to temper this with protectionist words. However, the political, economic, and confessional structure of Bavaria also played a role because bankers, factory owners, and businessmen (and many of the state middle class) were liberal or later progressive, small Germans (*kleindeutsch*[18]), and in favor of free trade; whereas large estate owners, the old aristocracy, small farmers and the Catholic clergy were often Great Germans (*grossdeutsch*) and protectionists (J. Schmidt 1973: Chapter 1).

Recognizing the dangers of reciprocity, true protectionists in the 1880s and 1890s began to insist on an "autonomous" tariff that could not be

---

[18] Refers to programs of German unity that would exclude Austrian (and Swiss) land, in contrast to Greater German (grossdeutsch) proposals.

lowered through reciprocal treaties. For example, the French Society of Agriculturists demanded that all the treaties should be annulled before their expiration date of 1892 and that no other treaties should be negotiated so that France might have an autonomous tariff (Levasseur 1892). The first such autonomous tariff was the Austrian bill of 1878, though its ostensibly non-negotiable tariffs were in fact regularly negotiated downward.

Protectionists feared that this example of negotiable "autonomous" tariffs would be copied elsewhere, leaving them open to liberalization. To address this problem, several countries developed a double-tariff system (Fay 1927). Though first introduced in Spain in 1877, the most important double-tariff system was France's 1892 Méline tariff. This system established two different rates of duty. Countries that signed a reciprocity treaty with France or Spain (or later the United States) would receive the lower tariff; others would receive the higher tariff. The lower treaty tariff was meant to be non-negotiable.

As suggested above, one must be careful in interpreting the histories of "autonomous" tariff policies. Johann von Bazant (1894), with decades of experience as an Austrian trade official, argues that the "autonomous" Austrian tariff of 1878 was neither autonomous nor intended to be – the language of "tariff autonomy" was merely rhetorically attractive to protectionists. Michael Stephen Smith (1980) describes the minimum and maximum levels of France's Méline tariff as non-negotiable, but notes cases in which tariffs were in fact negotiated. Carolyn Rhodes (1993) insists that American "reciprocity" policy before 1934 rested on a non-negotiable autonomous tariff, but also mentions in passing that the United States had 40 bilateral trade treaties *in effect* before the Reciprocal Trade Agreements Act of 1934, many negotiated during our period.

Even protectionist "autonomous" tariffs, it seems, were subject to reduction through reciprocity. This evidence clearly support the claim of Hypothesis 7.2 that reciprocal treaties are always possible.

Sticky Trade Treaties

Preceding sections have argued that reciprocal trade treaties have political advantages in linking home liberalization to foreign tariff reductions. They have a second major advantage in that they are contractual. This makes them less flexible than autonomous tariffs, because changing a treaty-bound tariff violates a contract.

Chapter 3 showed that a country's tariff depends in part on external market conditions. According to the declining prices hypothesis (Hypothesis 3.4), declining prices for a country's imports will lead to higher tariffs on those imports. Hypothesis 3.5 predicts that higher tariffs will be more volatile than low tariffs, and Hypothesis 3.6 relates tariff volatility to the terms of trade. Because reciprocal liberalization affects the validity of these hypotheses, signing a trade treaty means that a country is no longer free to change its tariff unilaterally:

Hypothesis 7.5: Treaty stability. When two countries sign a tariff agreement, Hypotheses 3.4 through 3.6 do not hold up to some point.

A treaty commits both countries to some tariff level. Changing this tariff for whatever reason counts as "cheating" and would be punished. As a result, changing terms of trade will not change domestic tariffs bound by a tariff agreement. This only holds up to a point because a sufficiently large external change may reduce the (discounted) benefits from cooperation to a level below the incentive to break the agreement.[19] The Great Depression of 1929–1939, for example, saw such treaty denunciations. A dramatic difference between the way today's leader values political groups and the way his predecessor would, also lead a country to denounce a previous treaty, though this is less common than one might expect.

When not denounced, then, a trade treaty insulates countries against tariff fluctuations stemming from changes in terms of trade. This proved to be important for France and others in the 1880s as cheap foreign grain flooded European markets. As Daniel Verdier (1994: 103) notes, "The reason why slumps did not trigger protectionist legislation is that they occurred at times when the conventional tariff [set by treaties] was not up for renewal." Countries were constrained from changing their tariffs in response to external price developments.

Germany's Caprivi treaties provide another good example. Grain prices went down from about 1892 until 1894. Though this led agriculture to agitate for renewed tariffs, the treaties precluded any increase. The Junkers had to satisfy themselves with bringing down Caprivi's government, though this yielded them no policy advantages. Higher agricultural tariffs had to await passage of a new tariff in 1901–1902 (Ashley 1926: 84–87) and later renegotiation of the treaties.

This tariff-inhibiting effect accounts for the common concern found among contemporary statesmen for "stability." Policymakers regularly

---

[19] For models of how countries have developed institutions to deal with the temptation to break an agreement, see Bagwell and Staiger (1990), Milner and Rosendorff (1997, 2001), and Rosendorff (2005).

argued that tariff treaties would give trade relations greater security. Louis Mallet argues that treaties are better than unilateral action because they take into account the national conditions of signatories and because they bind tariffs for a certain number of years (Cobden Club 1875: 5–6). Similarly, Johann von Bazant (1894: 40) argued that although the 1878 Austro-Hungarian tariff of that year did not really harm German exports, "nevertheless it was always hoped that it would be possible to bestow greater stability and security on trade relations through a tariff treaty with Germany."[20]

Germany shared this concern. When presenting the treaties to the Reichstag, Caprivi argued, "the first requirement of every industry is stability, that it may know what are the conditions with which it has to deal" (cited in Dawson 1904: 107, 111). In particular,

The concluding of the treaties for a term of twelve years will bring about the stability in the customs duties earnestly desired by the business world, and the Government entertain the conviction that they will not only do away with the former dangerous fluctuations in the commercial relations of the Empire, but also tend to increase the volume of its trade and commerce.

Germany faced a new situation with the change in French policy in 1892. The ministry decided to take the lead in negotiating its own tariff treaties. One reason was its belief that "stability in the conditions of international exchanges was an indispensable condition to the prosperous development of domestic industry" (Dietzel 1903: 367).

This stability was also a major impetus for German negotiations with Sweden. Before 1906, German-Swedish relations were unregulated by treaty (though both sides had a single-line tariff so they effectively enjoyed MFN treatment). Although the German tariff rested on treaties with others, the Swedish tariff was largely unbound. This meant that German exports were subject to changing Swedish tariffs that could only be stabilized by treaty (Werner 1989: Chapters 2, 7).

Treaties also protected a country against a future protectionist government. For example, Adolphe Thiers could not make effective a July 1872 law raising tariffs because of opposition from states with which France had treaties of commerce (Levasseur 1892: 27–28). Indeed, this concern for stability may explain why most of the tariff wars in this century tended to follow not from high tariffs but from the denunciation of a previous trade

---

[20] "Nichtsdestoweniger wurde immer noch an der Hoffnung festgehalten, daß es möglich sein werde, durch einen Tarifvertrag mit Deutschland den Verkehrsbeziehungen eine größere Stabilität und Sicherheit zu verleihen."

agreement. Walter Bennett Harvey (1938: 244) explains, "It is the change in the tariff rather than the height of it that causes friction, because *it is the change that destroys markets.* Thus it comes about that there is no correlation between the injury done by a tariff and the feeling it engenders." The stability hypothesis and the tit-for-tat logic of punishment in a Prisoners' Dilemma easily explain this pattern (see also Conybeare 1987).

If we recall from Chapter 3 that high tariffs are also more volatile, this stability becomes particularly important. A country might wish to bind high foreign tariffs without receiving significant concessions, simply to prevent future tariff volatility. Even a treaty that simply froze existing tariffs in place would have significant advantages for future stability. This feature of tariff-binding treaties helped influence the coding rules for TAD, discussed in Chapter 6.

This stabilizing effect of the treaties had system-wide consequences. The trade treaty system in place during the Depression of 1873–1896 helped keep European markets open in the face of increasing protectionist demands. Falling grain prices and lower transportation costs put severe pressure on European agriculture; many industrial sectors also suffered from foreign competition (Gourevitch 1986). This led to tariff increases in many countries, but treaties bound others not to raise protection. Although the period saw modest increases in protection in France, openness merely fell back from its peak to the levels of the late 1860s and early 1870s (see Figure 3.5). Britain, Italy, and most smaller countries remained open, and only Germany saw a large drop in exposure to world trade (Figures 3.3–3.6).

The period 1860–1885 shows the importance of sequence. Had Bismarck's coalition of iron and rye taken place in the absence of important commercial treaties, we would have seen a massive return to protection in Germany. Instead, a treaty network, begun under more favorable economic conditions, inhibited protectionism when times turned bad.

Conclusion

This chapter has explored the political foundation of tariff treaties, showing how politicians who cannot lower tariffs unilaterally can nonetheless lower them through trade treaties. The theory also highlights the logic behind politicians who favored both protection and reciprocal liberalization. Table 7.1 summarizes these hypotheses and their corollaries.

Both of these points imply that we should move beyond a simple classification of political beliefs as "protectionist" or "liberal." Interest groups

Table 7.1. *Hypotheses and corollaries concerning trade cooperation*

Hypothesis 7.1: The reaction hypothesis. Increasing protection in one country reduces protection in the other country and vice versa.

Hypothesis 7.2: Liberalizing treaties. Two countries can always sign a reciprocity treaty reducing tariffs, but not one increasing tariffs.

Hypothesis 7.3: Treaty correlation. When two countries sign a tariff agreement, their tariffs will be positively correlated. (Thus, Hypothesis 7.1 does not apply.)

Hypothesis 7.4: Treaty support. Governments that sign reciprocity agreements receive more political support than those that do not.

Corollary 7.1: Democracy and treaties. Democratization makes treaties more likely.

Corollary 7.2: Reciprocity and liberalization. Reciprocity makes possible tariff concessions that are impossible unilaterally.

Corrolary 7.3: Mixed interests and reciprocity. Some groups who oppose unilateral liberalization will favor reciprocal liberalization.

Hypothesis 7.5: Treaty stability. When two countries sign a tariff agreement, Hypotheses 3.4 through 3.6 do not hold up to some point.

---

and politicians alike may have different views on unilateral policy than on conditional forms of trade policy such as cooperation.

Trade treaties give the international political economy greater stability. It is therefore not surprising that such stability is also an important goal of the GATT/WTO system. One frequently finds arguments that failure to begin a new round of negotiations, for example, would lead to instability in trade relations as market actors lost confidence in their expectations about future tariffs.

The model implies, like several other models, that negotiators will seek to increase exports, while limiting imports. This is a basic principle of GATT-speak (Bhagwati 1990). Harry Johnson (1965) believes that it characterizes much bargaining over customs unions. One concrete example from our century is the Canadian goal in the negotiations over the 1854 Reciprocity Treaty with the United States (Ankli 1971). Though individually rational, this goal is obviously collectively incoherent. Not all signatories to a treaty can simultaneously increase exports by more than imports; one country's exports are obviously another country's imports. This parallels the discussion of democracy in Chapter 5.

Important as the logic behind treaties is, this chapter has shown only existence, showing that trade treaties make political sense and that the causal logic behind treaties was familiar to nineteenth-century policymakers. I have not yet examined the conditions under which treaties are more or less likely. I turn to this task in the next chapter.

EIGHT

Variations in Trade Cooperation

"The Commission has come to the conclusion that the interest of our country is to make no more treaties, and to remain masters of her tariff."
– Jules Méline (cited in Levasseur 1892: 40fn)

Chapter 7 showed that tariff treaties are always politically rational. However, they are not inevitable. Countries sometimes fail to cooperate even when they would gain from it. This suggests that we need a more probabilistic model of cooperation, in which cooperation and noncooperation each occur some of the time. In such a model the main theoretical task is to determine the conditions that make cooperation more or less likely.

To see what makes tariff treaties more or less likely, this chapter examines the stability condition indicating whether or not a given treaty can be enforced. States will not cooperate when the long-term rewards of cooperation are less important than the short-term temptation to cheat. Then I examine the comparative statics of this equation to find the conditions that make states more likely to cooperate. Doing so lets me find out how changing economic conditions or political institutions make cooperation more or less likely.

The most important variable affecting this condition is the average tariff. Intuitively, there are two possibilities. Higher tariffs might make tariff treaties more likely because the gains from such a treaty are greater. This is the intuition found in most of the literature, which argues that increasing the rewards from cooperation makes cooperation more likely (see Baier and Bergstrand 2000; Keohane 1984; Milner 1997a: Chapter 2; Oye 1986). This also seems to be the intuition among policymakers. Many French politicians believed that the two-tiered Méline tariff of 1892 could use its high maximum levels to force other countries into making concessions if they were to receive the lower minimum tier tariffs. Alternatively, lower tariffs might make tariff

204

treaties more likely because the incentive to cheat is smaller. Moreover, with lower tariffs on both sides, any threats to return to the single-play reversion point are more credible because they are less costly to the sanctioner.

This chapter shows that low tariffs make cooperation more likely – that is, the second and less usual intuition is correct. Part II examined the factors that make this autonomous tariff low. Underlying the average tariff are both economic conditions such as the terms of trade and political conditions such as revenue needs or level of democracy. Combining the findings from Part II with the hypotheses of this chapter yields results about how both economic and domestic political variables affect international cooperation. Anything that makes the autonomous tariff low – such as worsening terms of trade or a lack of exogenous revenue constraints – makes cooperation more likely. As a result, cooperation begins in low-tariff countries when import prices are high and other economic conditions are politically favorable.

Democracy is an exception to this rule of thumb, making cooperation unambiguously more likely even though its effects on the autonomous tariff vary by country (see Chapter 5). This implies that trade cooperation will start with more democratic countries.

In short, states sign treaties when tariffs are driven down by world prices or domestic institutional change or if they are democratic. Then the tariffs stay low as long as they are bound, even if they would have gone back up as world prices continued to change. These processes are especially important for the Great Depression of 1873–1896, when the trade regime tempered European protectionism.

The Temptation to Defect

Cooperation places part of a country's fate in the hands of other countries, whose tariff reductions represent the main attraction of a trade treaty. Depending on another country's liberalization in this way may be problematic. Each state is harmed politically by the actions it takes unilaterally and gains only from the liberalization of others. Therefore, both sides in any agreement have an incentive to cheat.

As is well known, international agreements can be self-enforcing in repeated play, if both sides use conditional enforcement strategies such as tit-for-tat to punish cheating (Axelrod 1984; Fudenberg and Maskin 1986; Kreps et al. 1982; Taylor 1976/1987). From the standpoint of a government considering a reciprocity agreement, the relevant considerations include the government's own discount rate or the extent to which it values future benefits; the government's beliefs about the likelihood that the other country will cheat, and the government's beliefs about its ability to put together a domestic coalition capable of imposing punishment should the other nation cheat.

One must first understand why a country might defect from an agreement that it has signed. No one will sign a treaty with a country that is expected to violate the treaty, so such violations must be unanticipated.[1] For example, there might be unanticipated changes in parameters, such as domestic preferences, discount factors, or the underlying economy. Therefore,

Remark 3.1: Unanticipated defection. Defection occurs only in response to unanticipated changes in the parameters of the political support function.

This means that, to understand defection, we must think about unexpected changes, an issue that I address in Chapter 9's study of nonratification.

Somewhat paradoxically, states might expect some unanticipated changes even if they cannot predict them exactly. For example, Canadian opponents of the 1911 reciprocity treaty argued that political conditions in the United States were too unsettled for a reliable treaty partner, that Washington's interest in reciprocity was based on a heterogeneous coalition of Democrats and "regular" Republicans against "insurgent" Republicans. Any change in this unstable party alignment, some Canadians feared, would lead to repeal (USTC 1920: 82). Observing such fears, the U.S. Tariff Commission subsequently admitted that "[p]erhaps the most valid point" made by Canadian opponents of reciprocity was its uncertain duration (USTC 1920: 81):

The trade of Canada would be diverted from its present channels; European markets for Canadian produce would be neglected for the United States, and other countries would occupy Canada's markets overseas; the entire structure of Canada's business would be readjusted to reciprocity; if, then, after this process was completed, the arrangement should be terminated, Canada's commerce would be suddenly paralyzed.

The early abrogation of the 1854 Reciprocity Treaty, which both countries remembered, added weight to these concerns.

In principle, a country should be able to deter such cheating through punishment. Lord Salisbury argued in 1892 that "in this conflict of commercial treaties, to hold your own, you must be prepared, if need be, to

---

[1] The existence of violations is never unanticipated, and often affects the structure of cooperation (see Downs and Rocke 1995; Milner and Rosendorff 2001; Rosendorff 2006). Still, a country will not sign a treaty with another country if it expects *that country* to defect in the near future. Countries expect some violations, but are uncertain who the violators will be.

inflict upon the nations which injure you the penalty which is in your hands, that of refusing them access to your markets" (cited in Marsh 1999: 172). A good example is British retribution against Portugal earlier in the century. Negotiations on a new Anglo-Portuguese treaty after the Napoleonic Wars were suspended on the outbreak of revolution. After long debate, the Cortes voted to ignore the treaty of 1810 and reimpose the old 30% duty on British woollens. After cautious efforts to undo this duty, Britain decided to equalize duties on French and Portuguese wines in 1831. The Portuguese immediately retaliated by admitting the goods of all countries at 15% and repudiating the valuation clauses of the 1810 treaty. It also declared that the 1810 treaty would terminate on April 30, 1836 (Williams 1972: 151–55).

One obstacle to such enforcement strategies is that punishment comes at a cost to the enforcer as well as to the cheater. As a result, executives often shrink back from threatened retaliation. For example, the U.S. tariff of 1909 provided for penalty duties of 25% *ad valorem* on the dutiable products of all countries that unduly discriminated against the United States. Canada seemed guilty of such discrimination, for a recently concluded treaty with France granted that country concessions not enjoyed by the United States. However, President Taft deemed it wise to negotiate the matter with Canada before starting a tariff war, and this led – ironically enough – to the 1911 reciprocity treaty. Immediate punishment would have hurt U.S. interests unduly.

Concerns about defection and enforcement are, then, common. The theory here does not predict either denunciations or a country's willingness to punish. Like many other rational-choice theories, I analyze how states deter defections that, in equilibrium, will never occur. Remark 8.1 hints at the question of these defections, which nonetheless lie outside the model.

The Enforcement of Trade Treaties in Repeated Play

Once they have signed a tariff treaty, politicians must decide whether to observe it. In each round of a repeated-play game, they may defect from the agreement or continue to adhere to it. Considering this problem requires an evaluation of future payoffs. These future payoffs are worth less than today's payoffs, so A's payoffs in the next period are discounted by a discount factor $\delta_A < 1$, payoffs in the third period are discounted by δ_A^2, and so on. Any payoff that X receives forever is therefore valued the infinite sum $X + \delta_A X + \delta_A^2 X + \cdots = (1 - \delta_A)^{-1} X.$[2]

---

[2] Proof. The sum S of the series $(X + \delta_A X + \delta_A^2 X + \cdots)$ is also equal to the term $X + \delta_A S$. Solving $S = X + \delta_A S$ yields $S = (1 - \delta_A)^{-1} X$.

With discount factors δ_A, A's payoff from continued adherence to a treaty with tariffs is $U\{t_A, t_B\} = (1 - \delta_A)^{-1}M_A[Y_{1A}(p_{dA}(t_A), t_B); Y_{2A}(p_{dA}(t_A))]$. This long term is just the discounted value of the rewards of cooperation, received indefinitely. If A defects from the treaty today, returning to the single-play tariff t^*_A,[3] B will return to its single-play tariff t^*_B in subsequent rounds, yielding A the following payoff: $\delta_A M_A[Y_{1A}(p_{dA}(t^*_A), t_B); Y_{2A}(p_{dA}(t_A))] + (1 - \delta_A)^{-1}\delta_A M_A[Y_{1A}(p_{dA}(t^*_A), t^*_B); Y_{2A}(p_{dA}(t^*_A))]$. The first term captures a single incidence of unilateral defection, the second indefinite noncooperation.

We have, then, a situation in which country A must choose between two options based on the payoff associated with each. To figure out what A will do, we find a threshold – when the payoff is above the threshold, A cooperates, and when the payoff is below the threshold A does not cooperate. The basic inequality is that A will cooperate if and only if $(1 - \delta_A)^{-1}M_A[Y_{1A}(p_{dA}(t_A), t_B); Y_{2A}(p_{dA}(t_A))] > \delta_A M_A [Y_{1A}(p_{dA}(t^*_A), t_B); Y_{2A}(p_{dA}(t_A))] + (1 - \delta_A)^{-1}\delta_A M_A[Y_{1A}(p_{dA}(t^*_A), t^*_B); Y_{2A}(p_{dA}(t^*_A))]$.

This equation is not only messy but unwieldy because the interesting terms occur on both sides of the inequality. I therefore rearrange it so that the discount factor appears on one side and everything else on the other side. Having done this, I find that A will adhere to the treaty if and only if

$$\delta_A \geq \frac{M_A[Y_{1A}(p_{dA}(t^*_A), t_B); Y_{2A}(p_{dA}(t^*_A))] - M_A[Y_{1A}(p_{dA}(t_A), t_B); Y_{2A}(p_{dA}(t_A))]}{M_A[Y_{1A}(p_{dA}(t^*_A), t_B); Y_{2A}(p_{dA}(t^*_A))] - M_A[Y_{1A}(p_{dA}(t^*_A), t^*_B); Y_{2A}(p_{dA}(t^*_A))]}$$

(8.2)

The rest of this section examines the comparative statics of this equation, looking to see how it changes as prices and tariffs change. Again, formalization is essential to the argument, because it provides a language to keep track of all the different ways that a given tariff change (in t_A or t_B) affects prices, incomes of import-competers and exporters, and thus A's political support, under conditions of cooperation, defection, or retaliation.

Because the discount factor stands alone on the left-hand side of (8.2), it is trivially true that

Remark 8.2: Discount factors and cooperation. The more a state values the future (high discount factor), the more likely it is to cooperate; the less

---

[3] An alternative assumption would be that A defects by choosing the tariff $t^{**}_A > t^*_A$ that maximizes M_A when B's tariff is $t_B < t^*_B$, reverting to t^*_A when B retaliates with t^*_B. This assumption complicates the notation, but does not change the analysis with respect to changes in t^*_A. Though I have simply assumed Grim Trigger punishment here, it is interesting that most countries use much weaker punishment strategies in the modern trade treaty system, a puzzling pattern analyzed well by Ethier (2001).

it values the future (low discount factor), the less likely it is to cooperate. (Axelrod 1984; Taylor 1976/1987).

We cannot measure decision makers' valuation of the future directly. However, we may be able to observe the economy-wide valuation of the future as represented by the time value of money. Studies of economic behavior have been used to infer valuation of the future and the probability of nuclear war, for example (Russett and Slemrod 1993). To see if the time value of money could be used as an operationalization of discount factors to test Remark 8.2, I used annual data on interest rates in London and Paris.[4] Then I used a Poisson regression to see if variations in these interest rates were associated with annual treaty initiation (again controlling for year). We would expect a negative relationship between interest rates and cooperation, because high interest rates suggest a low valuation of the future. The causal relationship only makes sense in terms of cooperation theory, as international cooperation should not lead the market to raise interest rates – rather the reverse, as it would be associated with the anticipation of better economic conditions as countries received the gains from trade.

I do not report these regressions here but do summarize the results. London interest rates are almost never significant and are usually wrongly signed in any case. In contrast, Paris interest rates are rightly signed and statistically significant for 8 of 16 countries: Austria, Bulgaria, France, Germany, Greece, Italy, Spain, and Switzerland; they are insignificant for Belgium, Netherlands, Portugal, Romania, Russia, Serbia, Sweden, and the United Kingdom (one-tailed test). Normally this kind of mixed result would not deserve comment, but it is striking that Paris interest rates matter for the continental core of the trading system. Only Belgium among those countries associated with the continental network did not have a significant relationship between interest rates and cooperation, and only Greece is peripheral to the system (recall that Bulgaria is a high cooperator after independence). Those countries without a relationship between cooperation and Paris interest rates are all geographically peripheral, and most have close ties with the British economy.

This relationship is all the more striking because it does not seem to depend on a few years or a single period. Figure 8.1 shows the evolution of interest rates in Paris from 1820 to 1913. Although a slight downward trend is evident over the century, these interest rates jump around a lot. In

---

[4] The correlation coefficient between the two is .569, so clearly there were different valuations in the two locations and traders were unable to arbitrage all these differences away.

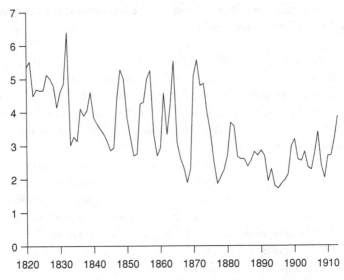

Figure 8.1. Interest Rates in the Paris Market, 1820–1913.

any five-or ten-year period, it seems that countries choose to initiate more cooperation when interest rates reach a temporary trough.

It would appear, then, that Paris interest rates are closely associated with cooperation for the continental countries that made up the core of the system. When these interest rates were high, people did not value the future highly and were less likely to cooperate; when they were low, decision makers were more eager to cooperate. For this "Paris Club" of countries, I use Paris interest rates as a variable in the regressions that follow. I also report regressions without this variable for comparison with the countries outside the Paris Club.

It remains mysterious why London interest rates, which were more important for the international economy, had no evident effect on cooperation anywhere. It is similarly obscure why states on the periphery of the continental network were unaffected.

We can explore the effects of more easily measured variables by looking at changes in the right-hand side of equation (8.2). To find out how the preagreement tariff levels affect the probability of a tariff treaty, I take the partial derivative of the right-hand side with respect to t^*_A, the autonomous tariff. Though Part II sought to explain variation in this autonomous tariff, I effectively treat it as exogenous in this part, investigating whether high- or low-tariff countries are more likely to cooperate. The denominator is always greater than zero, so the sign of the derivative depends on the sign of the following:

$$\{M_A[t^*_A, t_B] - M_A[t^*_A, t^*_B]\}(\delta M_A/\delta Y_{1A})(\delta Y_{1A}/\delta p_{dA})(\delta p_{dA}/dt^*_A)$$
$$+ \{M_A[t^*_A, t_B] - M_A[t_A, t_B]\}(\delta M_A/\delta Y_{2A})(\delta Y_{2A}/\delta p_{dA})(\delta p_{dA}/dt^*_A)$$

$$(8.3)$$

The term in (8.3) is positive if $M_A [t^*_A, t_B][(\delta M_A/\delta Y_{1A})(\delta Y_{1A}/\delta p_{dA})) + (\delta M_A/\delta Y_{2A})(\delta Y_{2A}/\delta p_{dA})] > M_A[t_A, t_B](\delta M_A/\delta Y_{2A})(\delta Y_{2A}/\delta p_{dA}) + M_A[t^*_A, t^*_B] (\delta M_A/\delta Y_{1A})(\delta Y_{1A}/\delta p_{dA})$. In the trade treaty equilibrium, a given price increase will yield a greater marginal increase in political support from import-competers than its marginal loss from exporters, so $|(\delta M_A/\delta Y_{1A})(\delta Y_{1A}/\delta p_{dA})| < |(\delta M_A/\delta Y_{2A})(\delta Y_{2A}/\delta p_{dA})|$. Because $(\delta M_A/\delta Y_{1A})(\delta Y_{1A}/\delta p_{dA}) < 0 < (\delta M_A/\delta Y_{2A})(\delta Y_{2A}/\delta p_{dA})$, (8.3) is greater than zero, the numerator of the derivative above is positive. This means that increases in the single-play tariff t^*_A increase the right-hand side of the stability condition, making cooperation less likely. This term yields the following hypothesis:

Hypothesis 8.1: *Tariffs and cooperation.* Tariff treaties are less likely to be stable for high-tariff countries than for low-tariff countries.

This sounds perfectly reasonable from one point of view, but it is worth noting that it means that countries are most likely to cooperate when the gains are smallest. In the WTO, for example, the states pushing hardest for the elimination of duties are the industrial countries for whom duties are already very low. Gains from trade in such cases are minor. In contrast, high-tariff countries may stay outside the regime entirely. This was true of Russia until the 1890s, for example (Ashley 1926: 69–70). In the post-1945 world, many high-tariff developing countries, such as México, remained outside the GATT/WTO until the 1980s or 1990s.

Testing this hypothesis presents some problems of endogeneity, because low tariffs should lead to more tariff treaties, which in turn should lower a country's tariff. As a simple initial test, I take a cross-section of countries before and after a wave of trade treaties. Low-tariff countries before a wave of negotiations should be more likely to sign treaties, whereas higher tariff countries will sign fewer treaties.

Extensive tariff data are available for two waves of treaties, the first in the 1860s and the second lasting from the late 1880s through the early 1890s. Figures 8.2 and 8.3 graph average tariffs in 1860 (or 1885) against the number of European treaties in effect ten years later. Using a ten-year delay washes away the year-to-year variations reflecting political events, economic cycles,

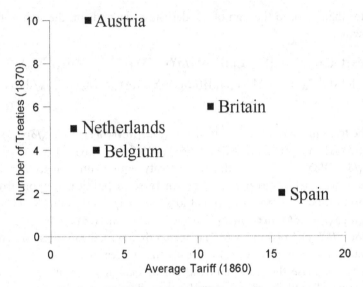

Figure 8.2. Tariffs in 1860 and Subsequent Cooperation.

or treaty renewal dates. Using the treaties-in-effect variable picks up all the treaty decisions of the decade, unlike annual treaty initiation. Because treaties normally last seven to ten years, a ten-year delay suffices to capture all the intervening treaty initiation decisions. Both figures show a visible, if weak, negative relationship between tariffs and the number of treaties.

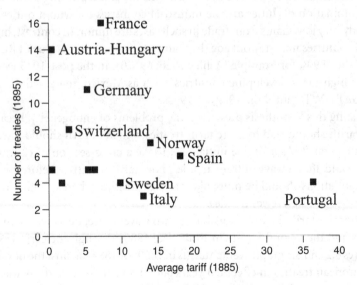

Figure 8.3. Tariffs in 1885 and Subsequent Cooperation.

Table 8.1. *Effects of the tariff on trade cooperation*

	Treaties, 1870	Treaties, 1895
Constant	7.2	8.3
	(1.9)	(1.6)
Tariffs, 1860	−.27	
	(.22)	
Tariffs, 1885		−.14
		(.12)
N	5	13
F	1.58	1.28
Adjusted R^2	.126	.023

Constants are significant at the .05 and .001 level, respectively. Tariffs are significant at the .15 level, one-tailed test.

Table 8.1 confirms these ocular regressions with a simple statistical test. Neither relationship approaches conventional levels of statistical significance (both are $p < .15$, one-tailed), but both are correctly signed. Because the number of observations in both cases is very low, the large standard errors are hardly a surprise. In addition, Table 8.1 shows the population, not a sample, of the countries and should be interpreted in that light. This evidence does confirm the causal sequence here, with tariffs preceding treaties. The reverse claim would be strongly rejected. This finding will be important later in this chapter.

Not only one's own policy but also foreigners' policies affect the likelihood of cooperation. A similar analysis is possible to see how foreign tariffs (t_B) affect the home likelihood of cooperation. Here the reverse intuition holds – larger gains from cooperation make treaties more likely:

Hypothesis 8.2: Foreign tariffs and home treaties. Tariff treaties are more likely to be stable when foreign tariffs begin high than when foreign tariffs begin low.[5]

High foreign tariffs raise the gains from a trade agreement to domestic exporters without affecting the costs at all. By the same logic, low foreign

---

[5] We must assume for simplicity that the cooperative tariff t_B is independent of the single-play tariff t^*_B. (If we relax this assumption, then the sign of the derivative depends on the sign of $[(\partial Y_{1A}/\partial t_B)(\partial t_B/\partial t_B^*) - \partial Y_{1A}/\partial t_B^*]$.) Proof follows easily from (8.2).

tariffs reduce the benefits of trade treaties without changing their domestic political costs. In a roundabout way, it confirms Adam Smith's (1776: Book iv. cap. 11) analysis that raising home tariffs might sometimes bring other countries to the bargaining table.

The logic of his hypothesis is illustrated by the American decision to turn away from its commercial isolation in the 1880s. U.S. agricultural exports declined by more than half between 1879 and 1885 in response to foreign tariffs stemming from the agricultural depression of the period. President Chester A. Arthur and his Secretary of State Frederick Theodore Frelinghuysen sought negotiations to lower agricultural trade barriers and reduce duties on exported manufactures and freer importation of goods in which U.S. investors held significant interests (Rhodes 1993: 23–25). Higher foreign tariffs, it seems, pressed the United States to cooperate.

Both Russia and Sweden were similarly pressed to join the treaty network in the 1890s. In part, their interest reflected higher foreign tariffs on agriculture; German grain tariffs hit Russian wheat exports, for example (see Ford 1902: 115–16). These countries also faced higher effective levels of protection because of foreign trade treaties, a topic that I examine in greater depth in Chapter 11.

This hypothesis suggests that foreign tariff increases may induce a country to initiate discussions leading to a treaty. For example, Romania increased its general tariff from 5% to 7.5% when Prince Carol (Karl) von Hohenzollern ascended the throne in 1866, and then it raised this level still further in 1875. Each of these increases led Austrians to pursue direct negotiations with Romania, regardless of the desires of the nominal suzerain, Turkey. These efforts finally culminated in an agreement in 1875 (Antonescu 1915: Chapters 2–4).

Increasing an export duty has similar effects on foreigners. It raises the price of imports and hurts export interests as well as any importers who use the goods. In either case, it increases the incentives for the politician to cooperate with foreigners to remove the export duty. Proposed Swedish export duties on iron had exactly this effect on Germany (Werner 1989).

Another extension of this hypothesis concerns the effect of British reforms on the trade policies of the Dominions. In the middle decades of the century, Britain gradually eliminated preferential treatment of colonial timber, sugar, and other goods. This loss of preference in the British market meant that the colonies faced an effective tariff increase in the UK market. The theory predicts that they would then be more likely to cooperate, presumably with third parties. The most important result of such incentives was Canada's

Reciprocity Treaty with the United States that was reached in 1854 (Howe 1997: 18).

The hypothesis also allows some predictions about which partners a country might approach first when seeking a new treaty. For example, the German *Zollverein* chose to negotiate with high-tariff France before negotiating with low-tariff England in 1861–1862. Though Britain sought negotiations with the *Zollverein*, Prussia asked it to wait until the *Zollverein* renewal in 1866. Yet, Prussia began negotiations with France right away because France's tariffs were higher and Prussia therefore had more to gain (Davis 1997: 150).

The claim that tariff levels affect the likelihood of cooperation has interesting implications for cooperation in Germany before unification in 1870. The conventional wisdom explains variations in German cooperation through political concerns and the struggle for influence between Prussia and Austria. The theory here emphasizes economics. It predicts that lower tariff countries will cooperate first. This means that Prussia, North Germany, and Baden would form the core of German economic cooperation, as proved to be the case. One of the several problems that they sought to address was the system of Restoration tariffs throughout Germany, which was disrupting trade networks that had grown up in the freer internal trade of Napoléon's Continental System. Though facing a similar environment in the 1820s, higher tariff countries, notably Austria and Bavaria, cooperated with greater difficulty. In this light Prussia's triumph appears inevitable for economic, not political, reasons (see also Chapters 9, 11, and 12).

Though I have set aside tariff variation by good in this book, the logic of this hypothesis should extend easily to the choice of goods within a treaty. And though I have modeled states as setting only a single tariff, the logic should extend to a model with multiple tariff lines. For the same reasons as in Hypothesis 8.1, a country's low tariff lines will be easier to cut than its higher lines. Higher duties may even be excluded from a trade treaty altogether. This implies the following:

Conjecture 8.1: Treaty variation by good. Tariff concessions are more likely on duties that are already low, whereas high-tariff goods are more likely to be excluded from a trade treaty.

The bargaining incentives identified here provide a regular obstacle in WTO talks. Both Japan and the EU wish to exclude highly protected agriculture from trade reductions, just as the United States wishes not to discuss antidumping procedures that protect a few sectors such as steel. In contrast, low-tariff sectors such as automobiles and computers have historically yielded relatively easy agreement. Similarly, in regional regimes such as the NAFTA or MERCOSUR, "sensitive industries" such as textiles, agriculture, and steel typically receive special treatment that keeps these duties higher for a longer time than the duties on other sectors.

The logic behind Hypothesis 8.2 creates tension in our predictions. Countries with low tariffs negotiate more readily, and they negotiate most readily over their lowest tariffs. Unfortunately, they wish to negotiate with exactly those high-tariff countries that are least likely to have an interest in treaties themselves. In the quantitative analyses that follow, this means that country-specific variables such as revenue constraints yield much stronger results than relational variables such as the terms of trade. Relational variables affect home and foreign countries in opposite directions, making cooperation both more and less likely. Country-specific variables have more easily observed effects.

Trade Treaties and Terms of Trade

Although well supported, Hypothesis 8.1 sounds simplistic, maintaining that countries whose tariffs are already low are more likely to lower them further through reciprocal treaties. The theory becomes less intuitive when we consider how certain countries end up with low tariffs. Recall that the terms of trade play an important role in determining the single-play tariff. A country with increasing terms of trade will turn protectionist, whereas a country with decreasing terms of trade will liberalize. Falling prices for imports lead to increasing terms of trade, but also harm import-competers, who receive compensatory protection. Conversely, rising prices for imports harm exporters so politicians will lower tariffs when the country's terms of trade decline. Combining Hypotheses 3.4 (declining prices hypothesis) and 8.1 (tariffs and cooperation), then, we have the following:

Hypothesis 8.3: *Treaties and the terms of trade.* Tariff treaties are more likely among countries with decreasing terms of trade than for countries with increasing terms of trade.[6]

This hypothesis captures one factor behind the wave of trade treaties in the 1890s. As grain prices increased again, European grain importers found their terms of trade decreasing. With reduced pressure for agricultural protection,

---

[6] Proof follows from the chain rule: the effect of the terms of trade on tariffs and then the effect of the tariffs on treaties.

these governments found trade treaties easier to negotiate. Germany began this wave with the Caprivi treaties, followed by Austria-Hungary's treaties with its Balkan hinterland (Ashley 1926: 64–65; see also Chapters 11 and 12). Declining food prices made the next group of treaties, with Serbia, Spain, and Romania, much more difficult (Ashley 1926: 68).

At century's end, Germany was a grain importer whose terms of trade had improved as grain prices fell. Conditions had been very different in the 1820s, when Prussia was a grain exporter facing lower grain prices abroad. International grain prices fell precipitously in peacetime, a price fall made worse by the English Corn Laws. This deterioration in its terms of trade harmed exporters, leading to a policy in the exporters' interest: freer trade and trade treaties. The *Zollverein* began among the grain exporters of the north, spreading last to the industrial and mercantile regions. In this way, changing terms of trade were probably an important factor in the first *Zollverein* wave of treaties.

In both periods, Prussia/Germany faced the same obstacle. The most attractive targets for its diplomacy, grain importers in the 1820s and grain exporters in the 1890s, were raising their tariffs and were therefore less likely to cooperate with it. It is hard to say what the net effect of all these changes on the overall treaty regime should be because it takes two countries to sign a treaty. I address the question again when I turn to the quantitative tests of the theory.

Revenue Concerns and Trade Treaties

Like economic conditions, political institutions also affected cooperation. Revenue concerns have two effects on trade treaty initiation. First, they affect the autonomous tariff. As Chapter 4 showed, exogenous revenue concerns raise tariffs, whereas endogenous revenue concerns lower them. By the logic of Hypothesis 8.1 (tariffs and cooperation), exogenous constraints make cooperation less likely, whereas endogenous considerations make cooperation more likely. Second, the increased trade from trade treaties provides an additional source of revenue. Any country that values revenue could be better off with at least a small reciprocal liberalization. Because increased trade can only come by lowering tariffs, however, the revenue per unit of trade must go down. There is a trade-off, then, between the lower revenue obtained from lower tariffs on a constant volume of trade and the potential revenue gains from an increase in trade. This trade-off affects countries with both exogenous and endogenous revenue constraints.

Whether this first effect outweighs the potential revenue gains is an empirical question. We can say, however, that exogenous and endogenous revenue constraints will have systematically different effects on the likelihood of trade treaties:

Result 8.1: Endogenous revenue and cooperation. An endogenous revenue constraint makes tariff treaties more likely.

Result 8.2: Exogenous revenue and cooperation. An exogenous revenue constraint makes tariff treaties less likely than does an endogenous revenue constraint and may or may not make tariff treaties less likely altogether.

Result 8.2 would capture the reasoning behind William Gladstone's statement, "I do not like bargaining away revenues for Treaties" (cited in Marsh 1999: 124).

I state these claims as "results" because they rely on synthesizing a formal result (Hypothesis 8.1) and an empirical generalization (the analysis of revenue constraints in Chapter 4). Falsifications would point to the hypothesis or to my reasoning connecting the hypothesis to the inductive finding, though we would not be able to tell which step in the overall reasoning is responsible (see Table 1.1).

For individual countries, I treat revenue concerns in a country-specific way following the analysis in Chapter 4, summarized in Table 4.4. I test these claims in the next section by using two revenue constraint variables. The first captures the potentially revenue-enhancing effect common to all states, whatever their revenue constraint, which makes cooperation more likely for all. The second variable, exogenous revenue constraint, is equal to 1 only for countries and periods with an exogenous restraint, and equal to zero otherwise. I expect a positive coefficient for the endogenous revenue constraint variable and a negative coefficient for the exogenous revenue constraint variable. The analysis does not predict whether the *net* effect of these two variables (i.e., coefficient one plus coefficient two, when applicable) will be positive or negative – that is an empirical question. Because it is an interesting substantive question, however, I use an F-test to find out whether it is significantly different from zero.

Quantitative Tests of the Hypotheses

This section tests the hypotheses of this chapter using the annual treaty initiation variable. This variable reflects the political decision to sign a treaty in a given year, reflecting current economic and political conditions. It is a count variable; for most countries in most periods, it is Poisson-distributed and should be analyzed with Poisson techniques.[7]

I have argued that some variables (revenue constraints, terms of trade, and sometimes democracy) affect a country's average tariff, thereby affecting trade cooperation indirectly, and treaty initiation directly. Because I include the average tariff on the right-hand side of these regressions, I am in effect testing only for the *direct* effects of these variables; the indirect effects were captured in the analysis of the average tariff in Chapters 4 and 5. As we will see, however, most of these variables do yield strong independent results on trade treaty initiation.

Two control variables deserve comment. I have included the control variable GDP in the single-country regressions, but I have not included it in the regional regressions because it is measured in different and incompatible units across countries. The variable YEAR was consistently insignificant in the country regressions. Because many of these regressions have very few observations, I have dropped YEAR in all single-country estimations to retain degrees of freedom. I have included it in regional regressions, however, where it was sometimes significant and degrees of freedom were not an issue. Again, YEAR provides one way to capture how the context for treaties changes over time, looking forward to the systemic-wide variables in Part IV.

As in Chapters 4 and 5, I wish to allow for the possibility that some variables have opposite effects in different countries. This is most important for revenue concerns, which might be exogenous or endogenous. Unlike Chapter 5, I expect democracy to have a similar positive effect on trade cooperation across countries. The single-country regressions allow me to test this claim without obscuring single-country exceptions within a regional regression. Unfortunately, many countries have very few observations – with degrees of freedom sometimes very low, especially after controlling for serial correlation. These low-n regressions should not be taken seriously on their own, but as aids in interpreting the regional regressions.

I begin with regressions that use the average tariff as a measure of protection, because this measure is available for a larger set of countries. Tables 8.2–8.4 show Poisson regressions for each country separately, whereas

---

[7] Chapter 11 analyzes exceptions in which the distribution of annual treaty initiation for MFN treaties is not Poisson-distributed, but even when this exception applies, the annual treaty initiation variable may still be Poisson-distributed. The annual treaty initiation variable exhibits some serial correlation for some countries in the latter decades of our century, for reasons also analyzed in Chapter 11. This violates the assumptions of Poisson regression when it occurs, justifying alternative methods. See Chapter 12.

Table 8.2. *Average tariffs and annual treaty initiation in large European countries*

	Predict	Austria	France (1)	France (2)	Italy	United Kingdom	Germany
Constant		.40	−5.20	3.7†	2.1	−4.1	.74
		(1.2)	(6.64)	(2.2)	(1.6)	(4.5)	(3.78)
GDP	0		−.00018††††	.00011	−.00020‡‡	−.0017‡	.000098
			(.000053)	(.000018)	(.00008)	(.0010)	(.000040)
Democracy		.13	.24	.0057	−.086	.55‡‡	.63‡‡
		(.21)	(.25)	(.033)	(.18)	(.23)	(.25)
Revenue	varies	.15†	.77†††		−.010	.10	.11†††
		(.11)	(.26)		(.050)	(.081)	(.046)
Revenue dummy	+	.20			2.2††††	.28	
		(.41)			(.46)	(.59)	
Average tariff	−	−.19††	−.73††		−.088†	−.098†	−.78††††
		(.11)	(.35)		(.043)	(.076)	(.23)
Terms of trade	−	.064	.064	−.039††		.0062	
		(.069)	(.069)	(.019)		(.0034)	
N		69	39	83	52	84	32
Pseudo R²		.02	.15	.06	.18	.10	.23
Log likelihood		−92.2	−55.7	−107.8	−80.9	−60.3	−37.6

Endogenous revenue constraint (+) for Austria, France, Germany, and Italy; exogenous revenue (−) for the UK.
Revenue dummies equal 1 in 1867–1913 for Austria, 1877–1913 for Italy, 1815–1846 and 1886–1913 for UK. See Table 4.4.

† p < .10 (one-tailed)
†† p < .05 (one-tailed)
††† p < .01 (one-tailed)
†††† p < .001 (one-tailed)

‡ p < .10 (two-tailed)
‡‡ p < .05 (two-tailed)
‡‡‡ p < .01 (two-tailed)
‡‡‡‡ p < .001 (two-tailed)

Table 8.3. *Average tariffs and annual treaty initiation in smaller European countries*

	Predict	Belgium	Bulgaria	Denmark	Netherlands	Portugal	Romania	Russia	Spain	Sweden
Constant		-2.9	8.3‡‡‡‡	27.‡‡	-4.5	-1.1	-11.2‡‡	2.5	-5.6‡‡‡‡	14.
		(4.7)	(2.4)	(11.)	(5.4)	(5.7)	(5.3)	(1.6)	(1.3)	(9.7)
GDP				-.0077						-.0016
				(.0039)						(.011)
Democracy	+	.35††			-.48	-1.3	-.16	.54†††		
		(.16)			(.74)	(1.5)	(.69)	(.19)		
Revenue	varies	-.68	-.77††††	.022	-.29	-.12	.37††	-.096	.32††††	-.17
		(.74)	(.26)	(.22)	(.82)	(.18)	(.15)	(.11)	(.077)	(.14)
Revenue dummy	+									1.3
										(1.2)
Average tariff	−	1.8‡‡	.19	-2.5†	1.0	-.15	.47‡‡	.068‡	.0097	-.69†
		(.75)	(.20)	(1.7)	(1.7)	(.17)	(.19)	(.039)	(.054)	(.52)
N		67	8	23	68	24	30	99	63	33
Pseudo R^2		.21	.48	.33	.18	.10	.25	.13	.19	.07
Log likelihood		-16.9	-9.4	-10.3	-10.8	-6.25	-24.93	-44.76	-55.6	-25.4

Revenue constraint is exogenous (−) for Belgium, Denmark, Portugal, and Sweden and endogenous (+) for Bulgaria, the Netherlands, Romania, Russia, and Spain. See Table 4.4.

Sweden's revenue dummy equals 1 in 1886–1913.

† $p < .10$ *(one-tailed)*
†† $p < .05$ *(one-tailed)*
††† $p < .01$ *(one-tailed)*
†††† $p < .001$ *(one-tailed)*

‡ $p < .10$ *(two-tailed)*
‡‡ $p < .05$ *(two-tailed)*
‡‡‡ $p < .01$ *(two-tailed)*
‡‡‡‡ $p < .001$ *(two-tailed)*

Table 8.4. Annual treaty initiation in Latin America

	Predict	Argentina	Brazil	Chile (1)	Chile (2)	Perú	Uruguay	All
Constant		.86	−8.0	−3.5	−.76†††	−3.3	−13.	223.‡‡‡
		(3.4)	(14.)	(3.4)	(.28)	(11.)	(1763.)	(.82.)
Democracy	+				.083		−6.1	−.20‡
					(.074)		(588.)	(.12)
Revenue	−	−.051	−.12††	−.0052	−.000015†		.069	.0068
		(.074)	(.059)	(.032)	(.000010)		(.074)	(.022)
Average tariff	−	.014	−.47	.017		−.23	−.24†	.010
		(.034)	(.49)	(.012)		(.44)	(.16)	(.0073)
N		16	14	19	84	15	19	83
Pseudo R^2		.02	.24	.06	.03	.05	.42	.15
Log likelihood		−11.6	−8.3	−18.4	−62.0	−3.5	−8.4	−54.3

I expect all countries, except possibly Uruguay, to have exogenous revenue constraints. See Table 4.4.

† $p < .10$ (one-tailed)
†† $p < .05$ (one-tailed)
††† $p < .01$ (one-tailed)
†††† $p < .001$ (one-tailed)

‡ $p < .10$ (two-tailed)
‡‡ $p < .05$ (two-tailed)
‡‡‡ $p < .01$ (two-tailed)
‡‡‡‡ $p < .001$ (two-tailed)

Table 8.5. Cooperation in the "Paris Club"

	Predict	Austria	Belgium	France	Germany	Greece	Italy	Spain
Constant		1.7	-5.5	4.7††	1.5	.27	.98	-1.9
		(1.1)	(5.4)	(2.2)	(3.7)	(1.2)	(1.7)	(1.8)
Interest rates	−	-.26††	.43	-.29††	-.75†	-.62††	.30‡	-1.1†††
		(.15)	(.41)	(.16)	(.58)	(.37)	(.16)	(.41)
GDP				.0000065	.000028		-.00020‡‡‡	
				(.000019)	(.000041)		(.000077)	
Democracy	+	.21	.37††	-.013	.63†††	-.00092	-.099	.017
		(.21)	(.17)	(.034)	(.25)	(.050)	(.18)	(.12)
Revenue	varies	.23††	-.51		.14†††		-.026	.27††
		(.12)	(.70)		(.052)		(.052)	(.15)
Revenue dummy	+	.062					2.7††††	
		(.43)					(.53)	
Terms of trade	−			-.038††				
				(.018)				
Average tariff	−	-.28††	1.6‡‡		-.91††††		-.08††	.011
		(.12)	(.72)		(.26)		(.045)	(.077)
N		69	67	83	32	84	52	56
Pseudo R^2		.03	.23	.08	.25	.06	.20	.26
Log likelihood		-90.8	-16.4	-105.9	-36.7	-43.0	-79.1	-47.8

All are Poisson regressions.

† $p < .10$ (one-tailed)
†† $p < .05$ (one-tailed)
††† $p < .01$ (one-tailed)
†††† $p < .001$ (one-tailed)

‡ $p < .10$ (two-tailed)
‡‡ $p < .05$ (two-tailed)
‡‡‡ $p < .01$ (two-tailed)
‡‡‡‡ $p < .001$ (two-tailed)

Table 8.6. *Annual treaty initiation in Latin America: democracy only*

	Predict	Bolivia	Colombia	Costa Rica	Ecuador	El Salvador	Guatemala	México	Venezuela
Constant		-.84††††	-.86††††	-.82††	-1.2††††	-.69††	-70.††††	-.51†	-2.1†
		(.18)	(.20)	(.32)	(.44)	(.28)	(.20)	(.29)	(1.3)
Democracy	+	.041	-.085††	-.096†	.10	.17	.13††	-.017	-.14
		(.055)	(.042)	(.057)	(.31)	(.15)	(.058)	(.047)	(.27)
N		86	67	76	84	70	72	85	84
Pseudo R^2		.00	.04	.03	.00	.01	.05	.00	.00
Log likelihood		-69.7	-56.4	-49.8	-56.2	-56.2	-56.3	-100.7	-50.0

† *p* < .10 *(one-tailed)*
†† *p* < .05 *(one-tailed)*
††† *p* < .01 *(one-tailed)*
†††† *p* < .001 *(one-tailed)*

‡ *p* < .10 *(two-tailed)*
‡‡ *p* < .05 *(two-tailed)*
‡‡‡ *p* < .01 *(two-tailed)*
‡‡‡‡ *p* < .001 *(two-tailed)*

Table 8.7. *The average tariffs and treaty initiation in Northern Europe*

	Predict	North	UK-France (1)	UK-France (2)	Scandinavia
Constant		44.‡‡‡	134.‡‡‡‡	76.‡‡‡‡	81.
		(14.)	(35.)	(24.)	(.94.)
Average tariff	−	−.13 ††††	−.13††		−.89††
		(.029)	(.082)		(.50)
Revenue constraint	+	.031†††	.12††		
		(.013)	(.082)		
Exogenous revenue	−	−.053††††	.033		−.24††
		(.010)	(.027)		(.14)
Democracy	+	.15††††	.68††††	.49††††	.19
		(.051)	(.22)	(.14)	(2.0)
Terms of trade	−		.028	−.037†††	
			(.024)	(.016)	
Belgium dummy		−3.2‡‡‡‡			
		(.49)			
Netherlands dummy		−2.7‡‡‡‡			
		(.77)			
Sweden dummy		2.4‡‡‡‡			
		(.73)			
UK dummy			−3.5‡‡‡‡		
			(1.0)		
Year		−.024‡‡‡	−.075‡‡‡‡	−.040‡‡‡	−.033
		(.0075)	(.020)	(.014)	(.046)
Revenue F-test		$\chi = 3.07$	N.A.		
		p = .08			
N		326	123		36
Pseudo R^2		.21	.18		.20
Log likelihood		−238.70	−118.36		−22.12

† $p < .10$ *(one-tailed)*
†† $p < .05$ *(one-tailed)*
††† $p < .01$ *(one-tailed)*
†††† $p < .001$ *(one-tailed)*

‡ $p < .10$ *(two-tailed)*
‡‡ $p < .05$ *(two-tailed)*
‡‡‡ $p < .01$ *(two-tailed)*
‡‡‡‡ $p < .001$ *(two-tailed)*

Tables 8.6–8.10 show pooled regressions for various regions.[8] Table 8.5 shows the regression for the Paris Club of European countries whose treaty initiation rates seem to depend on interest rates in the Paris market. I have

---

[8] Hungary and Norway pose potential problems within their dual monarchies, though only Norway has a sufficiently long data series for real analysis. Test regressions showed that Norwegian economic and political conditions did *not* affect Sweden-Norway's treaty initiation, though Sweden's did (at levels just shy of statistical significance). This is consistent with the Norwegian accusation that Swedish policy ignored Norwegian conditions.

Table 8.8. *Average tariffs and treaty initiation in the Mediterranean*

	Predict	Mediterranean
Constant		27.[‡‡]
		(13.)
Average tariff	−	.074[†††]
		(.027)
Revenue constraint	+	.066[††]
		(.038)
Democracy	+	.056
		(.053)
Portugal dummy		−6.2[‡‡‡‡]
		(1.1)
Romanian dummy		−.78[‡‡]
		(.32)
Spain dummy		−1.8[‡‡‡]
		(.62)
Year		−.015[‡‡]
		(.0069)
N		152
Pseudo R^2		.18
Log likelihood		−199.31

[†] $p < .10$ *(one-tailed)*   [‡] $p < .10$ *(two-tailed)*
[††] $p < .05$ *(one-tailed)*   [‡‡] $p < .05$ *(two-tailed)*
[†††] $p < .01$ *(one-tailed)*   [‡‡‡] $p < .01$ *(two-tailed)*
[††††] $p < .001$ *(one-tailed)* [‡‡‡‡] $p < .001$ *(two-tailed)*

two different data series for Chile and show the results for each. Because tariff data are available for a much shorter period than are democracy and the terms of trade data for France, I show the regressions both with and without the revenue and average tariff.

The central claim of this chapter is that high average tariffs make cooperation less likely; many of the other results work indirectly through this hypothesis. The hypothesis receives strong support from data from large European countries, but only mixed support from data from other countries. Specifically, the data support the hypothesis for Austria, France, Germany, Italy, and the United Kingdom, as well as Denmark and Sweden. The estimated coefficient is wrongly signed and significant for Belgium, Romania, and Russia and insignificant for Bulgaria, Netherlands, Portugal, and Spain. The hypothesis receives support only for Uruguay among the five Latin American countries.

Some of the weaker results – but not all – reflect large standard errors stemming from the fact that many of these smaller countries have very few observations. In the pooled regional regressions, the effect of average tariffs on treaty initiation is rightly signed and strongly significant for the regions of northern Europe. It is wrongly signed for Latin America and the Mediterranean and statistically significant for the Mediterranean. In short, the hypothesis performs well in the European core, less well elsewhere.

These results reflect the tension above between the claims that low home tariffs lead to greater cooperation (Hypothesis 8.1) and that high foreign tariffs lead to greater cooperation (Hypothesis 8.2). It seems clear that tariff developments in the European core dominate both home tariff initiation in that core and foreign initiation throughout the international system, a pattern that we explore more deeply in Part IV.

Revenue concerns exhibit a broadly similar pattern, performing better for large countries in the core than for small or peripheral countries. The variable is rightly signed but insignificant for most individual Latin American countries, where the shortage of observations is most serious. Oddly, given the single-country results, the variable is wrongly signed and insignificant in the pooled Latin American regression.[9]

Surprisingly, Britain's revenue constraint did not inhibit cooperation. This finding contrasts markedly with the historiography's claim that dependence on five revenue duties made the Treasury reluctant to abandon any one of these duties through commercial negotiation (see *inter alia* Howe 1997: 113–14).

Revenue concerns obtain better results in the regional regressions. Endogenous revenue concerns are always rightly signed (positive) in Europe, but wrongly signed and insignificant for Latin America's exogenous revenue concerns. I also included a separate variable in Europe for countries and periods with an exogenous revenue constraint, which we would expect to be negative. This always obtains rightly signed results, which are statistically significant in both Scandinavia and northern Europe as a whole.

In contrast, the revenue dummy variables did not perform very well in the individual country regressions. Only in Italy is it rightly signed and significant. In some cases, such as Sweden, a shortage of observations is doubtless to blame for the large standard errors; the *t*-ratio narrowly misses statistical significance. In Italy, the revenue dummy variable has a very strong positive effect, swamping the revenue variable itself. Once again, the infrequent

---

[9] I used the shorter Chilean series in the pooled regression because Chile would otherwise make up more than half of all observations (84/148).

change in each country's revenue constraint dummy over time doubtless explains these results.

Where possible, I also used an F-test to determine whether the absolute value of the exogenous revenue constraint is larger than the coefficient for endogenous revenue concerns, though the theory makes no prediction either way. Like the revenue dummy itself, this difference is significant only for Italy (at the $p < .001$ level).

Democracy is significant only for 4 of the 14 countries, yet when it is significant the effect is always in the right direction. This is true for Belgium, Germany, Russia, and the United Kingdom. However, it is more noticeable in countries with long time series (except the Netherlands), suggesting that its effects show up only in long periods that encompass dramatic changes. Unlike economic variables, which vary from one year to the next, structural political variables do not change very often. As a result, democracy does not have consistently strong effects over time in most individual countries.

Democracy has more noticeable effects in the regional regressions, where cross-national variations pick up the structural differences that are not evident in the short single-country time series. This resembles the pattern found in tests of the democracy variable in Chapter 5. Democracy is positively associated with treaty initiation in northern Europe and in the Mediterranean, whereas this relationship does not near statistical significance in Scandinavia. Once again, Latin America is exceptional. The relationship between democracy and Latin treaties is both wrongly signed and significant.

The final variable is the terms of trade. Britain and France are the only two countries for which long series of annual terms-of-trade data are available.[10] In both of the individual regressions and in the regression pooling them together, the coefficient is wrongly signed and not statistically significant. Yet if we look at France over a longer period, by dropping variables for which only 39 observations are available, the coefficient on the terms of trade is both rightly signed and statistically significant. Dropping the same variables for the pooled regression with Britain also yields rightly signed and statistically significant results.

This is a substantively important finding, because France's terms of trade did not vary much in the 39 years from 1873 to 1913 (see Figure 8.4). In contrast, the full period picks up the important changes in the French terms of trade in the 1860s. These changes are so strong that one could attribute

---

[10] I have also found some terms-of-trade data for Hungary (but not Austria). Unfortunately, the role of Hungary in the Austrian political economy and the nature of trade policymaking in Austria and Austria-Hungary make it difficult to know what effects we should expect (see Chapter 9). In test runs, these data had no consistent effect on tariffs or treaty initiation.

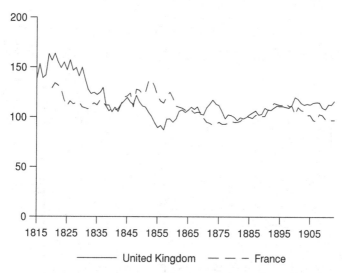

Figure 8.4. Terms of Trade in France and the United Kingdom.

the wave of French treaty initiations of the 1860s primarily to changes in the terms of trade (see also Nye 1991). Using the longer data series therefore picks up the most substantively interesting period and identifies patterns consistent with the theory.

The weak results for Britain and for the shorter period in France are not too surprising. The natural explanation is that the terms of trade necessarily cut both ways: when Britain's terms of trade decline, some other country's terms of trade must improve, with the opposite effect on the foreign country's willingness to sign treaties. This consideration does not apply to single-country variables, such as revenue dependence or democracy, for which I obtain much stronger empirical results.

Tables 8.9 and 8.10 repeat these exercises using openness, not the average tariff, as a measure of protection. Higher openness should make cooperation more likely, while other variables are the same as before. Again, the single-country regressions yield results that are somewhat mixed, but are generally consistent with the theory. The revenue predictions receive support from Denmark, France, and Germany but not Italy, Sweden, and the United Kingdom. The revenue dummy is also significantly greater than the revenue variable for Italy ($p < .001$), but not for other countries.

Democracy has the predicted positive effect at significant levels in Germany and the United Kingdom but not France and Italy. These are the same results as in the regressions with the average tariff as the measure of protection.

Table 8.9. Openness and annual treaty initiation

	Predict	Denmark	France	Germany	Italy	Sweden	United Kingdom
Constant		52.‡‡	−2.2	−8.9‡‡	.90	5.2	−5.1
		(23.)	(7.2)	(3.6)	(1.8)	(6.0)	(5.0)
GDP		.0013	−.00013‡‡	.000029	−.00025‡‡‡	−.00072	−.0015
		(.0019)	(.000052)	(.000039)	(.000089)	(.00079)	(.00097)
Democracy	+		.080	.33†	−.069		.53†††
			(.23)	(.20)	(.18)		(.22)
Revenue	varies	−.30††	.30††	.074†	−.093	−.14	.052
		(.14)	(.17)	(.047)	(.068)	(.15)	(.060)
Revenue dummy					2.0††††	.94	−.37
					(.43)	(1.2)	(.57)
Openness	+	−1.4†	.20†	.23††††	.20††	−.041	.073
		(.73)	(.14)	(.078)	(.12)	(.20)	(.057)
Terms of trade	−		−.0075				.0019
			(.051)				(.032)
N		23	39	32	52	33	84
Pseudo R^2		.50	.13	.16	.18	.035	.10
Log likelihood		−7.65	−56.81	−41.31	−81.51	−26.36	−60.35

Revenue considerations are endogenous (+) for France and Italy, but exogenous (−) otherwise; dummy is (+) for Italy in 1877–1913, Sweden in 1885–1913, and (−) for United Kingdom in 1815–1846 and 1885–1913.

† $p < .10$ (one-tailed)
†† $p < .05$ (one-tailed)
††† $p < .01$ (one-tailed)
†††† $p < .001$ (one-tailed)

‡ $p < .10$ (two-tailed)
‡‡ $p < .05$ (two-tailed)
‡‡‡ $p < .01$ (two-tailed)
‡‡‡‡ $p < .001$ (two-tailed)

Table 8.10. *Openness and annual treaty initiation in northern Europe*

	Predict	All	Less Scandinavia
Constant		57.‡‡‡‡	94.‡‡‡‡
		(16.)	(19.)
Democracy	+	.19††††	.32††††
		(.043)	(.074)
Revenue	−	−.042††††	−.045††††
		(.013)	(.014)
Endogenous revenue	+	.077††††	.11††††
		(.014)	(.016)
Openness	+	.053††	.082††††
		(.023)	(.025)
Year		−.032‡‡‡‡	−.052‡‡‡‡
		(.0089)	(.011)
Revenue + dummy		$p < .01$	$p < .001$
N		191	155
Pseudo R^2		.11	.14
Log likelihood		−202.37	−167.99

Endogenous revenue equals French or German revenue considerations.
† $p < .10$, *one-tailed;* †† $p < .05$, *one-tailed;* ††† $p < .01$, *one-tailed;* †††† $p < .001$, *one-tailed;* ‡ $p < .10$, *two-tailed;* ‡‡ $p < .05$, *two-tailed;* ‡‡‡ $p < .01$, *two-tailed;* ‡‡‡‡ $p < .001$, *two-tailed*

Openness has the predicted positive effect for France, Germany, and Italy; a wrongly signed coefficient for Denmark; and no significant effect for Sweden and the United Kingdom. The average tariff variable was rightly signed and significant for all these countries. As noted many times in this book, we expect openness as a measure of protection to be subject to much more measurement error and thus larger standard errors in any regression.

The regional regressions obtain very strong results in the direction predicted by the theory. Again, this suggests that some hypotheses are failing to receive more support because of short data series. It may also mean that cross-national effects are stronger than intertemporal effects in each country.

Two of the results in this section deserve further comment. The consistently *positive* effect of a tariff revenue constraint on trade cooperation should be surprising in light of the conventional wisdom. If a need for tariff revenue limits a country's freedom of action in trade policy, this finding is incomprehensible. In contrast, Chapter 4 argued that revenue considerations are typically *endogenous*. Signing trade treaties increases bilateral trade, making modest taxes or tariffs an attractive source of government revenue. Only for a few countries with exogenous constraints should the conventional expectations hold.

Another interesting result is the regularly positive effect of democracy on trade cooperation in Europe, which stands in contrast to the more mixed effect of democracy on tariffs and openness. These different effects help us distinguish between preference-based and structure-based theories of democracy and trade policy. Mansfield et al. (2000) develop a preference-based theory in which democratic polities both favor lower autonomous tariffs and are more likely to sign trade treaties. The evidence in this book supports the latter of these claims and calls the first into serious question.

Looking at all these results, it is clear that the hypotheses perform best when explaining treaty initiation by large countries and by northern Europe in general. These countries make up what world-systems theorists (i.e., I. Wallerstein 1974a,b, 1979) would call the "core" of the international political economy. It is good that the hypotheses explain the behavior of these states that are most important for the system. On the other hand, the evidence for the hypotheses is weakest in Latin America, the "periphery" of the system. The Mediterranean, which is described as the semi-periphery in this period, yields mixed results.

The natural inference from this pattern is that international structural conditions affect the pattern of trade cooperation. These conditions may even be more powerful determinants of cooperation than the single-country conditions for smaller countries. High tariffs may lower the incentive for Portugal to cooperate, but they raise the incentives for other countries to cooperate with Portugal. These foreigners doubtless have power resources, not modeled explicitly here, that enable them to force Portugal to the table. Chapters 11 and 12 model some of these systemic-level and coercive factors.

For the purposes of this chapter, these factors mean that the average tariff variable will be less likely to be significant for peripheral countries. Revenue concerns should be unaffected by this problem, and revenue constraints obtain more consistent results in the regressions.

Country Size

This mention of power highlights an important variable that has not appeared so far in this chapter: country size. Country size is subject to data limitations and thereby requires separate treatment. It requires cross-national comparisons using a single unit, but no common units are available for the nineteenth century. I present the theory in this section, along with some tests that get around the data problem.

The theoretical analysis depends on the necessary condition for cooperation. The necessary conditions for a trade treaty are that $\partial Y_{EA}/\partial t_B \neq 0$ and $\partial Y_{EB}/\partial t_A \neq 0$. These conditions require that changes in B's tariff affect A's exporters and that changes in A's tariff affect B's exporters. This section considers the implications of these necessary conditions from A's perspective; B's position is symmetric. If A is a small country, its market is less likely to be important for B's exporters than if it were large. These exporters might easily switch to third countries if A increases its tariff, implying that $\partial Y_{EA}/\partial t_B = 0$. In these cases, B will not sign trade treaties with A. In other words, being a small country makes large countries less likely to want to sign a treaty with you.

This claim is best interpreted probabilistically because of the absence of data on the elasticity of imports. A small state such as Luxemburg might be important for West Prussia but not for Russia, as Montenegro might be important for some Austrian industrial goods but not for the United Kingdom. If foreign exporters suffer any loss in finding new markets when the small country raises its tariff, the necessary condition is met. This suggests that

Hypothesis 8.4: Country size and treaties. Small states are less likely to sign trade treaties than large states.

This hypothesis stands in contrast to small state theory, which argues that trade dependence forces small states into more cooperative relations with the rest of the world (East 1973; G. Heckscher 1966; Katzenstein 1985; Marcy 1960; Mugomba 1979; M. Schmidt 1981; Vogel 1979). It also differs from models of cooperation to provide public goods (i.e., Pahre 1999: Chapter 7), in which small states gain much from a public good, while contributing little.

The reason for this difference does *not* stem directly from the attributes of small states. Instead, the small country's lack of effect on other countries' exporters may make them a less attractive bargaining partner. In this way, it picks up an effect that small state theory has overlooked, explaining the difference in prediction.

Testing this hypothesis explicitly is difficult because measures of country size such as GDP are not comparable across countries. Converting these different national accounts into a common metric would take us well beyond the bounds of this project.[11] However, the dummy variables found in the

---

[11] The easiest way to do this in the nineteenth century would be to use current exchange rates, which were relatively stable in the core if not in the periphery. Purchasing power parity is probably a more reliable method, but would be much more difficult to calculate, given

treaty initiation regressions earlier in this chapter are suggestive. Portugal, Romania, and Spain all signed trade treaties at a lower rate than Italy, which was by far the largest of the set.[12] Belgium and the Netherlands, despite being highly trade-dependent, signed fewer treaties than we would otherwise expect. Only Sweden among the small countries had a positively signed dummy variable. This may simply reflect the fact that the economic data series begin in 1881, about the same time that Sweden joined the trade treaty regime in earnest (see Chapter 9). Thus, the dummy variables are patterned as Hypothesis 8.4 would predict.

Data presented in an earlier chapter present a second way to test this hypothesis. Table 6.4 shows the number of years from 1815 to 1913 that each European dyad had a treaty in effect. The large states generally have treaties in effect more often, with more partners, than do the smaller countries. In addition, countries both large and small tend to sign treaties with large countries before signing them with smaller countries. This pattern is consistent with the theoretical claim that small countries cooperate less because of the reduced incentive for their partners, as opposed to the small countries' own preferences.

A third kind of test allows us to go much further back in time at the cost of losing all the control variables. To capture long-standing patterns of cooperation instead of annual treaty initiations, I use annual treaties-in-effect as the dependent variable. Table 8.11 shows the number of treaties in effect for most European countries every ten years from 1820 to 1910. For simplicity, I divide these countries into large and small. In any given year, the large states have more treaties in effect than the small countries. This evidence strongly confirms the hypothesis. Only one country in each group, Russia among the large and Belgium among the small, stands out from this general pattern. Geography provides an easy explanation for both of these exceptions, for reasons familiar to the historiography.

Apparently, the direct effects of country size on trade treaty negotiation outweigh contrary, indirect effects. According to Hypothesis 6.6, small countries will have lower tariffs than large countries. Hypothesis 8.4 would therefore imply that small countries will sign *more* trade treaties than large countries. This causal chain follows the reasoning of small state theory. The evidence of the previous section, along with the single-country regressions of

---

the spotty data on prices available. Either method would confirm the obvious: Britain and France are larger than Sweden or Spain.

[12] Bulgaria apparently signed treaties at the same rate as Italy, though with only eight observations one cannot have any confidence in this result.

Table 8.11. *Annual treaties in effect, selected dates*

	1820	1830	1840	1850	1860	1870	1880	1890	1900	1910
Austria	0	1	0	4	5	11	12	13	15	16
France	0	2	3	8	14	19	11	14	23	29
Italy	–	–	–	–	5	20	16	14	16	20
Prussia	0	4	5	4	11	10	11	13	20	26
Russia	0	0	0	1	1	2	2	1	3	7
United Kingdom	3	8	7	8	15	16	13	18	10	11
Belgium	–	–	3	4	8	13	6	9	9	11
Bulgaria	–	–	–	–	–	–	–	–	3	13
Denmark	0	2	1	0	1	2	1	1	3	6
Netherlands	0	5	5	1	4	5	4	3	7	9
Portugal	1	1	0	2	2	4	6	6	3	6
Romania	–	–	–	–	–	–	1	1	6	11
Serbia	–	–	–	–	–	–	–	–	3	7
Spain	0	0	0	0	0	2	2	3	6	8
Sweden	1	1	0	1	0	1	2	2	5	11

Chapter 3, suggests that each step of this argument is empirically correct – small countries do have lower tariffs, and countries with lower tariffs do sign more trade treaties. Even so, small size by itself directly inhibits cooperation. This direct effect apparently outweighs the other, indirect effect.

Testing the Treaty Stability Hypotheses

The preceding sections have argued that we should expect the number of treaties that a country signs to go up or down each year, reflecting various economic and political conditions. At the same time, the treaty stability hypothesis (Hypothesis 7.5) maintains that, whenever one country has signed a treaty with another, it will keep that treaty even as conditions change – up to a point. After all, one reason for signing treaties is to lock in policy changes and to provide greater stability in trade policy.

Testing this claim requires a different measure of trade cooperation: the annual number of treaties in effect. Like annual treaty initiation, this is also a count variable, but its properties are very different. The number of treaties signed each year need not exhibit any serial correlation; indeed, Chapter 11 shows that this variable is often Poisson-distributed. The annual number of treaties in effect, in contrast, depends very heavily on the number of treaties in effect the previous year – most treaties remain in effect for seven or ten years, if not indefinitely. Using this measure as a dependent variable therefore

Table 8.12. *Annual treaties in effect, larger European countries*

	Predict	Austria	UK	France	Germany	Italy	Russia
Constant		−102.[‡‡]	30.	−473.[‡‡]	57.	163.[‡]	−11.[‡‡]
		(.41.)	(95.)	(188.)	(383.)	(92.)	(4.4)
Lagged treaties	+	.79[††††]	.88[††††]	.67 [††††]	.42 [††]	.51[††††]	.77[††††]
		(.066)	(.071)	(.12)	(.20)	(.079)	(.063)
GNP			−.000043	.000026	.00019	.00027[‡‡]	
			(.0015)	(.00011)	(.00019)	(.00013)	
Democracy		.29[‡]	.086	−.20	.079	.49	.37[‡‡‡‡]
		(.17)	(.11)	(.21)	(.21)	(.36)	(.094)
Revenue		.32[‡‡‡]	.024	−53.	−.058	.026	.0090
		(.12)	(.043)	(.39)	(.047)	(.098)	(.020)
Average tariff		−.36[‡‡‡]	−.036	.19	.18	−.033	.0027
		(.15)	(.047)	(.46)	(.24)	(.11)	(.0066)
Terms of trade			−.022	.046			
			(.021)	(.085)			
Year		.056[‡‡]	−.014	.25[‡‡‡]	−.026	−.083	.0080[‡‡‡]
		(.022)	(.052)	(.10)	(.20)	(.050)	(.0025)
N		69	84	39	32	52	97
F		458.71	122.85	171.12	47.89	27.78	351.53
Adjusted R^2		.97	.91	.97	.91	.76	.95
Durbin-Watson		2.00	1.94	2.02	1.92	2.26	2.15

[†] $p < .10$ *(one-tailed)*   [‡] $p < .10$ *(two-tailed)*
[††] $p < .05$ *(one-tailed)*   [‡‡] $p < .05$ *(two-tailed)*
[†††] $p < .01$ *(one-tailed)*   [‡‡‡] $p < .01$ *(two-tailed)*
[††††] $p < .001$ *(one-tailed)*   [‡‡‡‡] $p < .001$ *(two-tailed)*

requires some controls. Two techniques for dealing with it are including a right-hand-side lag variable, or using first differences as a left-hand-side variable. These amount to nearly the same thing, and they have the effect of making the variable no longer a count variable. For example, the first difference variable can now take on negative values, and its distribution does not follow the Poisson distribution.

The treaty stability hypothesis suggests that all the economic and political variables that are associated with annual treaty initiation will *not* be related to the annual treaties-in-effect measure (up to a point). Because a few coefficients will be statistically significant by pure chance, the theory predicts that the number of significant coefficients will be no different than chance; the "up to a point" caveat might allow another significant coefficient occasionally. Tables 8.12–8.14 show the result of regressing the annual number of treaties in effect for each country against the same variables as in

Table 8.13. *Annual treaties in effect, smaller European countries*

	Predict	Bulgaria	Belgium	Netherlands	Norway	Portugal	Romania	Spain	Sweden
Constant		-455.	.39	-.91	-48.	130.	-75.	-82.‡‡‡	-162.‡‡‡
		(801.)	(19.)	(25.)	(.37.)	(115.)	(98.)		(56.)
Lagged treaties	+	.58†	.84‡‡‡‡	.66‡‡‡‡	.58‡‡‡‡	.56‡‡‡	.72‡‡‡‡	.67‡‡‡‡	.47‡‡‡
		(.33)	(.071)	(.084)	(.15)	(.18)	(.14)	(.095)	(.18)
GNP					.00096				.00058
					(.00061)				(.00062)
Democracy			-.0066	-.61‡‡‡	.00013	.36	-.29		
			(.086)	(.21)	(.053)	(.47)	(.49)		
Revenue		-.31	.46‡‡	.42‡‡‡	.011	.062	-.11	.031	-.11‡‡
		(.48)	(.20)	(.13)	(.0082)	(.037)	(.084)	(.041)	(.047)
Average tariff		.70	-.50	-1.5‡‡‡	-.081‡	-.019	.29	.0019	.043
		(.38)	(.42)	(.48)	(.046)	(.034)	(.12)	(.029)	(.086)
Year		.24	-.00089	.0039	.026	-.067	.039	.044‡‡‡	.088‡‡‡
		(.42)	(.010)	(.13)	(.020)	(.060)	(.052)	(.015)	(.030)
N		9	67	68	39	25	30	63	32
F		8.09	87.05	115.92	59.72	16.71	115.61	264.44	257.41
Adjusted R^2		.78	.87	.90	.90	.77	.95	.94	.98
Durbin-Watson		1.96	1.87	1.97	2.11	2.48	1.80	1.77	2.63

† $p < .10$ (one-tailed)
†† $p < .05$ (one-tailed)
††† $p < .01$ (one-tailed)
†††† $p < .001$ (one-tailed)

‡ $p < .10$ (two-tailed)
‡‡ $p < .05$ (two-tailed)
‡‡‡ $p < .01$ (two-tailed)
‡‡‡‡ $p < .001$ (two-tailed)

Table 8.14. *Annual treaties in effect, Latin American countries*

	Predict	Argentina		Brazil		Chile		Peru		Uruguay	
		Long	Short	Long	Short	Long	Short	Long	Short	Long	Short
Constant		−7.4	66.	15.	210.‡‡	−29.‡‡	−240.‡‡	2.1	82.	−12.	66.
		(23.)	(180.)	(9.7)	(71.)	(12.)	(81.)	(8.8)	(132.)	(7.7)	(40.)
Lagged treaties	+	.92††††	−.37	.83††††	−.24	.84††††	.30	.96††††	.46	.89††††	.67††††
		(.044)	(.31)	(.055)	(.26)	(.059)	(.28)	(.038)	(.48)	(.052)	(.15)
Democracy		−.0085		.14‡		−.037		.010		−.047	
		(.10)		(.077)		(.044)		(.043)		(.057)	
Revenue			−.057		.095‡‡		−.011		−.026		−.051‡‡
			(.035)		(.040)		(.010)		(.052)		(.021)
Average tariff			.015		.0027		.0073		.023		−.084‡‡‡
			(.035)		(.024)		(.0060)		(.051)		(.028)
Year		.0042	−.029	−.0071	−.11‡‡	.016‡‡	.13‡‡	−.0010	−.041	.0066	−.031
		(.012)	(.094)	(.0050)	(.037)	(.0064)	(.043)	(.0048)	(.068)	(.0041)	(.021)
N		82	16	90	14	96	19	89	15	84	19
F		279.8	.97	103.45	2.63	467.32	11.20	464.33	4.25	272.71	8.30
Adjusted R^2		.91	−.01	.78	.54	.94	.69	.94	.63	.91	.62
Durbin-Watson		2.26	1.89	1.72	2.16	1.97	2.09	2.22	2.02	1.58	1.66

† $p < .10$ (one-tailed)
†† $p < .05$ (one-tailed)
††† $p < .01$ (one-tailed)
†††† $p < .001$ (one-tailed)

‡ $p < .10$ (two-tailed)
‡‡ $p < .05$ (two-tailed)
‡‡‡ $p < .01$ (two-tailed)
‡‡‡‡ $p < .001$ (two-tailed)

the preceding section, with the lagged annual treaties as a control variable. Not surprisingly, the lagged annual number of treaties in effect is strongly and positively associated with the dependent variable in each equation. This association is so strong that these equations obtain summary statistics (adjusted R^2 and F) in the fantasy range. The other control variables, GDP and YEAR, are significant at about the same modest rate as we have seen throughout this book, in both directions.

The hypothesis receives strong support from large countries. Only 4 of the 20 coefficients are significant at the $p < .10$ level. Three of these appear in the regression for Austria-Hungary, in which all the variables were significant. This means that Austria-Hungary *did* denounce or let lapse treaties in response to exogenous economic events, perhaps reflecting the peculiar internal compromise found in that empire (see Chapter 9). Setting Austria-Hungary aside, only 1 of the 16 coefficients was statistically significant – just below what we would expect by chance.

For small European countries, 6 of the 21 coefficients are significant at the same level. This is more than we would expect by chance. Half of these six are found in the regression for the Netherlands, where all the variables are strongly statistically significant. All the effects are in the same direction we would expect if trying to predict treaty initiation, and none of these variables were significant in the treaty initiation estimations for the Netherlands (see Table 8.3). Clearly the Netherlands does not fit the theory, possibly for reasons that I discuss in Chapter 9.[13] Without the Netherlands, only 3 of the 18 coefficients are significant, only one more than we would expect by chance.

I obtain similar results for Latin America, with one country providing most anomalies. For each of five countries, I have one long data series that includes treaties and democracy, and a shorter series with revenue and the average tariff.

Skeptics might respond to these results by arguing that it is easy to predict the nonsignificance of variables. Levels of annual rainfall or religious observation, for example, are probably also not associated with the number of trade treaties in effect. The results in this sections appear much more striking when we recall that *these same variables* are indeed associated with trade treaty initiation. The theory predicts a systematic difference between treaty initiation and treaty nondenunciation, which is reflected in the treaties-in-effect variable. Moreover, even the failed predictions were highly patterned,

---

[13] In particular, strongly "divided government" in the Netherlands makes the assumptions of a pure political-support model less reasonable for examining that country.

for Austria-Hungary and the Netherlands account for most of the wrongly significant estimates. We see in Chapter 9 that Austria-Hungary and the Netherlands are in a small group of countries that stand out as having ratification problems, though the nature of the ratification problem differed significantly in the two. These ratification issues might make their treaty levels more sensitive to changing economic conditions.

Despite such issues, the treaty stability hypothesis is well supported. It captures a concern often noted in the qualitative literature, as by Peter Marsh (1999: 207): "The network also served the more modest function, valued among businessmen, of stabilising tariff rates, and it provided for periodic adaptation of those rates to changing economic and governmental demand when treaties expired and had to be renewed." This stability is also a major value of the WTO and its member states today. Predictability, no less than the value of tariffs themselves, is an important result of trade cooperation.

The quantitative evidence here shows that having treaties *does* insulate the international system from protectionist pressure. This stability effect coexists with earlier findings that economic conditions affect treaty initiation. The lesson for free traders is clear: sign many treaties when import prices are high, and make the terms long enough to outlast the next business cycle.

Possible Extensions

One of the strengths of the theory of political support is that it extends easily to other issue areas. For example, one might look at the indirect effects of monetary policy, capital movements, or labor migration on trade policy and thus on international trade cooperation. This section explores these connections in a speculative way, setting out these issues as questions for future research more than as settled findings.

Some of the historiography on the nineteenth century draws links between monetary policy and trade policy. The usual claim is that the depression of 1873–1896 reduced the price of many goods, whose producers then demanded protection. However, the depression also reduced the price of goods that people consumed. Lower prices on imports should lead to demands for protection, whereas lower prices for exports should lead exporters to demand relief in the form of *lower* protection on imports. As a result, we should see no clear net effect between deflation per se and either tariffs or cooperation. Of course, if the deflation were much more dramatic on the import side than on the export side – as was true for Europe's grain imports in the depression – then protection should result.

Table 8.15. *Migration and the tariff: simple correlations*

	Average tariff	Openness
Emigration	+.400 N = 54	+.274 N = 37
Immigration	+.500 N = 15	−.160 N = 10

A second important feature of the nineteenth-century political economy was the great migration of people from the Old World to the New. International migration affects the returns to factors, and thus prices and tariffs. In Europe, for example, emigration raised wages by creating labor shortages, which increased the price of exportables and therefore lowered the domestic price ratio. In the New World, immigration lowered wages and therefore lowered the price of import-competing goods, raising the price of exportables and lowering the domestic price ratio. Interestingly, it has the same effect in either case: migration leads to protection. Migration should also lead to lower openness. This means that

Hypothesis 8.5: Migration and protection. Increases in emigration from, or immigration to, a country make protection more likely.

We see this also in the contemporary world. The increases in migration in the 1970s and 1980s, for example, were associated with demands for protection in much of the industrialized world. Migration in the twenty-first century also seems to spark a backlash against globalization in much the way that increased trade and outsourcing do.

Because the data on immigration are much more spotty than the data on other variables, I do not include the migration variable in the other regressions from this chapter. Instead, I present only a suggestive simple correlation. Table 8.15 shows the results of a test of this hypothesis that uses decennial averages from 15 countries of emigration and 5 countries of immigration. The average tariff data clearly support the hypothesis. In contrast, the correlations between migration and openness are weak and of mixed sign. Again, the many other variables affecting openness generally make this a weaker measure of protection, so this difference between the tariff and openness correlations is not unexpected.

Capital flows should have broadly the same effect as these labor flows, inducing a protectionist response in both capital exporters and capital importers. The reasoning is similar, working through changes in the domestic price ratio.

Both migration and capital flows became a flood in the last part of the nineteenth century, say from 1870 to 1914. Protectionist demands also became more noticeable at this time. The conventional wisdom attributes these demands to deflation, but I think the reasoning here is suspect, at least as a general claim. Labor and capital flows, which were roughly coterminous with the depression, would have the same effect. These protectionist demands were held in check, it seems, only by the network of treaties produced by the second (1860s) and third (1890s) waves of trade cooperation discussed throughout this book.

These claims remain mere speculations, but embody a potentially important research agenda. Scholars of International Political Economy (IPE) have tended to separate trade, money, finance, and migration into separate boxes. I have done the same in this book. Yet these factors are clearly interrelated (O'Rourke and Williamson 1999), and our analyses should do a better job taking these connections into account.

Conclusions

This chapter has developed a theory that can account for variation in states' willingness to engage in trade cooperation. The central result is that low-tariff countries are more likely to cooperate than high-tariff countries. Many economic and political conditions work through this effect – though, as I have shown empirically, they may also exert independent effects. In contrast to its more ambiguous effects on the tariff, democracy makes trade cooperation more likely because support-maximizing politicians will value more heavily the welfare improvements that trade brings. This hypothesis receives clear support. Table 8.16 summarizes these hypotheses.

This chapter has also presented various tests of these hypotheses, looking both at individual countries and at regions. Hypotheses predicting a state's willingness to sign treaties obtained strong support in northern Europe, moderate support in the Mediterranean, and no support in Latin America. This pattern may reflect structural conditions outside the model. It is striking that the model predicts the core of the world system best, the periphery the worst, and the semi-periphery moderately well.

The results of this hypothesis-testing are not only interesting for their own sake but also help explain the pattern of cooperation in the century as a whole. Figure 8.5 shows the total annual treaty initiation for all countries across the century. Democracy, lower revenue constraints for some

Table 8.16. *Claims about variations in trade cooperation*

Remark 8.1: Unanticipated defection. Defection occurs only in response to unanticipated changes in the parameters of the political support function.

Remark 8.2: Discount factors and cooperation. The more a state values the future (high discount factor), the more likely it is to cooperate; the less likely it values the future (low discount factor), the less likely it is to cooperate (Axelrod 1984; M. Taylor 1976/1987).

Hypothesis 8.1: Tariffs and cooperation. Tariff treaties are less likely to be stable for high-tariff countries than for low-tariff countries.

Hypothesis 8.2: Foreign tariffs and home treaties. Tariff treaties are more likely to be stable when foreign tariffs begin high than when foreign tariffs begin low.

Conjecture 8.1: Treaty variation by good. Tariff concession are more likely on duties that are already low, whereas high-tariff goods are more likely to be excluded from a trade treaty.

Hypothesis 8.3: Treaties and the terms of trade. Tariff treaties are more likely among countries with decreasing terms of trade than for countries with increasing terms of trade.

Hypothesis 8.4: Country size and treaties. Small states are less likely to sign trade treaties than large states.

Hypothesis 8.5: Migration and protection. Increases in emigration from, or immigration to, a country make protection more likely.

Result 8.1: Endogenous revenue and cooperation. An endogenous revenue constraint makes tariff treaties more likely.

Result 8.2: Exogenous revenue and cooperation. An exogenous revenue constraint makes tariff treaties less likely than does an endogenous revenue constraint and may or may not make tariff treaties less likely altogether.

---

countries, and lower autonomous tariffs in many countries all work in the same direction, producing a secular increase in treaty initiation over the years. The figure also demonstrates the strongly wave-like pattern of cooperation, a topic I address in Chapter 12.

This chapter also examined the treaty stability condition, which predicts that countries will adhere to treaties even when underlying conditions change. I tested this proposition by seeing whether the same variables that explained treaty initiation were *not* associated with treaty maintenance, that is, the number of treaties that remained in effect each year. The evidence strongly supports this claim except for Austria-Hungary and the Netherlands, two countries that I discuss further in Chapter 9.

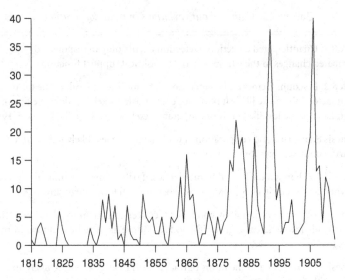

Figure 8.5. Global Treaty Initiations by Year, 1815–1913.

Unlike these latter two countries, the United Kingdom appears entirely unexceptional. This stands in marked contrast to the historiography, which has long puzzled over Britain's apparent exceptionalism. Britain remained committed to a strategy of free trade long after most other states had turned to modest protection. It also seemed unusually reluctant to join the trade treaty regime (see Howe 1997; Marsh 1999 for recent accounts). The analysis here suggests that Britain was not so unusual, at least in the sense that its policy can be explained by the same model used for other countries. A strong revenue constraint provided an important brake on trade cooperation for Britain and largely explains its relative reluctance to sign trade treaties. Democracy and other variables worked in England as elsewhere. Even when I used dummy variables for the United Kingdom, they were no larger than those for other countries, such as Spain or Sweden. Britain may have been different from other countries, but it was no more different than the others were.

Two features of this chapter's results point toward the coming chapters. As I noted, some of the hypotheses might yield mixed results because the underlying variables necessarily have opposite effects on two countries that might consider cooperating with one another. For example, low-tariff countries are more likely to cooperate and they are more likely to cooperate when foreign tariffs are high. Yet these high-tariff foreigners will be *less* likely to cooperate and less likely to cooperate with the low-tariff home countries. The best way to think about the net effects on more than one country is to look at the spread effects of treaties. A treaty between any two countries will affect all third parties similarly, a subject that I examine in Part IV.

Another finding was that democracy does not have the effects that many people would attribute to it. The most common structural theory of democracy, grounded in the theory of two-level games, emphasizes legislative ratification as a feature of democracy. It argues that democracy makes cooperation more difficult because legislatures may veto treaties that the executive would otherwise reach (see especially Milner 1997a). The evidence of this chapter does not support this claim and is consistent with Martin's (2000) claim that democracy can enhance the credibility of commitments and thus make cooperation more likely. This chapter's evidence is also consistent with recent studies showing that the relationship between democracy and cooperation is more nuanced and conditional than was previously thought (i.e., Dai 2002; Hammond and Prins 1999; Pahre, 2006). In the next chapter, I explore the problem of democracy and trade cooperation more deeply by looking at preferences, ratification, and political institutions. Chapter 9 represents an internal critique of two-level theory, showing that existing hypotheses do not follow from the premises of the theory when we consider reversion points explicitly. It also evaluates the role of legislative nonratifications, which may confound the theory's expectations for some countries.

It is also interesting that the results are much more strongly consistent with the theory in the pooled regressions than in the country-level regressions. Quantitative work in international relations generally looks at large numbers of countries over extended periods of time and yields good results. Against this, qualitative researchers offer evidence from the history of individual countries that challenges many theories. This difference in findings may not be, as generally assumed, simply a matter of looking at patterns versus looking at anomalies. Instead, the evidence here suggests that many variables have their most consistent effects only cross-nationally. Anomalous case study evidence may not reflect poor selection rules, but may point us to the weak intertemporal effects of many variables in a single country. This suggests that qualitative research may do better to focus on cross-national comparisons than historical institutional studies of a single country.

I have tried to move back and forth between the two levels, examining both individual countries and regional patterns. The pattern also suggests that understanding intertemporal change in individual countries requires much closer inspection than is common. Change may not occur from one year to the next, but may only appear as a qualitative break between periods (as the democracy findings here suggest). Three extended case studies in the next chapter attempt to explain cooperation by several important countries in exactly this way.

NINE

Ratification and Trade Treaties

" 'Constitution,' that is a separation of powers. The king does what he wants, and against this, the people do what the king wants. The ministers are responsible for seeing that nothing happens."[1]
 – Adolf Glassbrenner, 1848 (cited in Craig 1978)

I have so far treated each country's executive as the sole decision maker for trade policy. In the theory, a single actor chooses trade policy to maximize political support. This theory is parsimonious and potentially powerful, but clearly incomplete. In particular, this approach leaves out legislatures, which normally hold or share responsibility for a country's autonomous tariff. As we saw in Chapter 8, high autonomous tariffs make trade cooperation less likely, whereas low autonomous tariffs have the reverse effect. Because of their autonomous tariff-setting authority it is important to examine the legislature's role in trade cooperation.

A country's legislature may also have the ability to veto trade treaties. When treaties require legislative ratification, executives may find it harder to liberalize tariffs through international agreement. A growing literature argues that such domestic ratification institutions, combined with differences between executive and legislative preferences, explain both the tariffs chosen by the legislature and the trade agreements negotiated by the executive (Lohmann and O'Halloran 1994; Mansfield et al. 2000, 2002a; Milner 1997a; Milner and Rosendorff 1996, 1997; but Pahre 2001a).

This chapter first examines the role of ratification institutions indirectly, by looking at the set of treaties rejected by domestic legislatures. This analysis

[1] "Konschtitution, des is Teilung der Gewalt. Der Koenig dut, wat er will, un dajejen das Volk, des dut, wat der Koenig will. Die Minister sind dafür verantwortlich, dess nischt jeschieht." The flavor of this text depends on its use of Berlin dialect instead of standard German (*Hochdeutsch*).

shows that legislatures mattered for a small number of countries. Most of these are presidential republics in the New World, but France, the Netherlands, and Switzerland also saw treaties regularly blocked – or not negotiated in the first place.

The legislature only matters analytically if it has preferences that differ from the executive's preferences. This difference is often referred to as (the degree of) divided government (see Pahre 2006). Although existing theory has focused on how divided government makes a legislature less likely to ratify treaties, divided government also affects the autonomous tariff. As we have seen, this autonomous tariff has a strong effect on trade cooperation. Looking at this tariff, or reversion point, shows that divided government may make cooperation either more or less likely.

Whether divided government makes cooperation easier or harder depends in significant part on whether the executive or legislature controls the reversion point, which is a characteristic of each country's institutional setting. France under the Second Empire provides an interesting, and substantively important, illustration. In the 1850s, the French legislature lost the power to ratify trade treaties even as it retained control of the autonomous tariff. As the legislature became more independent of the executive and more protectionist, the conditions for trade cooperation became particularly favorable. In this way, a peculiar institutional setting contributed to the start of the 1860s wave of trade treaties.

Testing conditional propositions about ratification and divided government requires more information about each country than is possible in a large-n quantitative test. To test them, I have selected three cases that provide variation in the independent variable, with agenda-setting authority lodged in the legislature or executive. These cases also prove to be substantively important for the overall argument of this book. The Prussia/*Zollverein* case was central to the first wave of trade treaties in the 1820s and 1830s, whereas Austria-Hungary was a leading – if overlooked – player in the 1870s and 1890s. In both cases, the institutional setting meant that an increasing degree of divided government made institutional cooperation more likely. In contrast, Sweden-Norway did not play an important role in the regime, and the case study helps explain why its divided government inhibited cooperation.[2]

This chapter shows that we must often look inside individual countries in some detail, even within a general theoretical framework. Doing so can

---

[2] Another Dual Monarchy, Moldavia-Wallachia, did not last long in that form before becoming a unitary state. Had it lasted longer it would have provided another interesting case.

help us understand what sparks a wider wave of cooperation, as the German Confederation did in the 1830s or France in the 1860s. Examining domestic politics also explains why some countries participate actively, as did Austria-Hungary after 1867, or remain relatively aloof, such as Norway and Sweden until 1905.

Ratification and Divided Government with an Exogenous Status Quo

Over the past two decades, political scientists have increasingly explored the ways that domestic politics affects international cooperation. Many advances in domestic-level theory have built on Robert Putnam's (1988) theory of "two-level games." In this framework, chiefs of government negotiate an agreement internationally, subject to approval by one or more domestic actors. One of the strongest claims from this literature maintains that divided government makes international cooperation more difficult (Friman 1993; Iida 1993; Meunier 2000; Milner 1997a; Milner and Rosendorff 1997; Mo 1994, 1995; O'Halloran 1994; Pahre 2006). This literature has focused almost entirely on studies of the contemporary United States (but see Hug and König 2002, 2006; Pahre 1997, 2001a).

Following this literature, I use a spatial model to analyze the tariff question, a type of model that differs from those used so far in this book, but that I continue to use in Part IV.[3] Spatial theories model policy as a point in space on axes such as protectionism or free trade. In such a model, actors must decide whether to change policy away from the status quo (or reversion point). Each actor has an ideal policy, or bliss point, and evaluates policies in terms of their distance from this bliss point: the nearer, the better. For simplicity, I assume that utility is a negative function of the distance from the outcome of the game to this ideal point, so that indifference curves are circles around each player's ideal point.[4] The solution concept here is the negotiation-set, or N-set, which is the set of points that are efficient and would be accepted by all of the relevant players.

Figure 9.1 shows the logic of domestic political constraints within such a model. For simplicity of exposition, I begin with a single policy dimension along the x axis and then make it more complex. Three actors interact:

---

[3] For a formal demonstration of how one can convert a support-maximizing model into a spatial theory, see Milner and Rosendorff (1997: Appendix A).

[4] In a more elaborate model, the indifference curves would be ellipses because home tariffs are more important than foreign tariffs to each government. Although the shape of the indifference curves would affect the outcome, it does not affect the comparative statics central to the graphical analysis here.

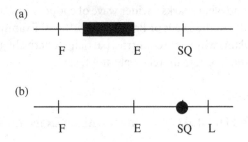

Figure 9.1. Reversion Points and International Cooperation.

Foreigners (F), the home Executive (E), and the home Legislature (L). In this basic version of a two-level game, the two states negotiate to change policy away from the status quo (SQ), with the legislature having the ability to veto any agreement reached.

To see the effects of this legislative veto, Figure 9.1a shows the case in which E and F negotiate an agreement without a legislative constraint. They may choose any point in the N-set shown, which consists of those points that are at least as close to E as to SQ. Figure 9.1b then shows that adding L may make international agreement impossible. The legislature will veto any leftward change in the policy, while E and F will never negotiate any rightward shift. With this configuration of preferences, no agreement will occur when the negotiators need the legislature's approval. This kind of institutional change occurred regularly in 1815–1913, as legislatures gained powers against monarchs and other executives.

This analysis clearly does a good job explaining some states. In Switzerland, for example, the Federal Assembly plays an important role in foreign affairs and must approve all treaties and alliances. Even if the Federal Assembly ratifies a treaty, under many circumstances the people may subject the treaty to a referendum (Coddington 1961: Chapter 5). These bodies can become stumbling blocks to Swiss participation in international cooperation. As I show later, Swiss levels of cooperation are lower than comparable countries.

The Netherlands, with a strong two-house Estates General, may provide another example in which the legislature inhibits trade cooperation. The 1815 Constitution gave the king limited power over foreign relations. Though weaker than other monarchs in Europe, the king's position was stronger than in the Napoléonic-era Batavian Republic, where "the foreign relations power was so weak that the Republic had made itself infamous for

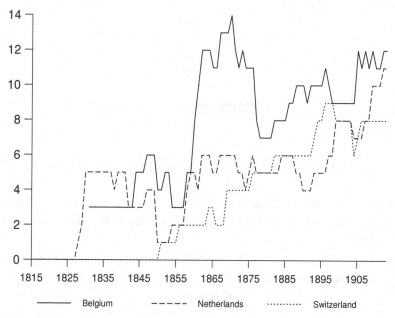

Figure 9.2. Annual Number of Treaties in Effect in Belgium, the Netherlands, and Switzerland, 1815–1913.

unbelievable dilatoriness in its relations with other states" (Vandenbosch 1944: 430). However, the king's power over foreign relations was reduced by constitutional revisions in 1848. He had to submit for parliamentary approval any treaty whose stipulations affected legal rights; in 1887 any treaty imposing financial obligations on the kingdom also required such approval (Vandenbosch 1944). The reader may recall that the Netherlands did not perform well in the quantitative tests of Chapter 8. In addition, the Netherlands had a slightly higher tariff than Belgium, which did sign many tariff treaties. Problems of domestic ratification may account for this behavior because I did not control for them.

Some simple measures yield evidence consistent with this interpretation of Switzerland and the Netherlands. Figure 9.2 shows the annual number of treaties in effect for three comparable continental small countries: Belgium, the Netherlands, and Switzerland. Belgium is almost always the most active cooperator among these three, consistent with our expectations. Dutch treaties fall especially far behind Belgium after 1848, when the strengthening of the Estates General occurred. Swiss cooperation remains low, though increasing, throughout the century. This pattern suggests that

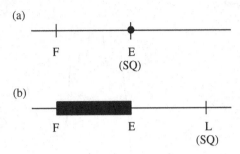

Figure 9.3. Divided Government and International Cooperation.

problems of treaty ratification may account for some of the cross-national variations among these three countries, despite their similar size and levels of development.

Ratification and Divided Government with an Endogenous Status Quo

Though the conventional wisdom provides a useful account of such countries, these results may be quite different if we model the reversion point explicitly. Figure 9.3 illustrates two possibilities, with agenda-setting lodged in the executive or legislature, respectively. Figure 9.3a presents a dictatorial system in which the executive chooses the autonomous tariff and then negotiates an international agreement. In this figure, E chooses the SQ policy and naturally chooses her ideal point. International negotiations are impossible, because E will not agree with F on any change in this policy.

Figure 9.3b shows a different situation, in which L chooses the autonomous tariff, while E negotiates international agreements. L chooses the SQ policy. In this case, divided government creates a status quo that both E and F dislike. If they can negotiate an agreement that does not require assent from L, E and F will jointly choose some point in their N-set. Here, divided government combined with legislative control over the status quo makes cooperation possible, not more difficult. (At this point, I ignore the possibility that the legislature may also have ratification powers, but return to this issue later.)

We can see the logic of Figure 9.3 at work in the 1860s, when France led the second wave of trade cooperation. Under the Restoration (1815–1830) and Orléans (1830–1848) monarchies, the legislature made the tariffs, though the executive could modify tariff lines temporarily pending ratification. As a

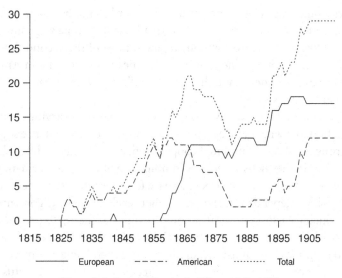

Figure 9.4. French Treaties in Effect, 1815–1913.

result, commercial negotiations often proved elusive. The most notable series of failed talks occurred with the United Kingdom before 1860 (Ratcliffe 1978). Only modest treaties with the newly independent states of Latin America were common (see Figure 9.4).

A change in institutions weakened the legislature's veto powers. Louis Napoléon's 1852 Constitution gave the emperor the power to sign commercial treaties without the assent of the Chambers. Any such treaty would have the force of law and would supersede any previous provisions of tariff law (Dunham 1930; Thompson 1983). Both executive and legislative preferences changed in the mid- to late 1850s, so divided government increased. Louis Napoléon became convinced of the advantages of tariff liberalization, whereas his legislature remained protectionist. In addition, the legislature slowly gained independence from the executive, with an increasingly strong minority opposing his governments after the elections of 1857 and 1860.

This combination of institutions and preferences closely matches Figure 9.3b. As I would predict, this increasing degree of divided government made international cooperation more likely. France reached the famous Cobden-Chevalier treaty in 1860, followed by a flurry of treaties with other European states. As Michel Chevalier had suggested, Napoléon used treaties to evade the legislature's authority over trade policy. Figure 9.4 shows a marked upswing in France's treaties with Europe in this period.

After Louis Napoléon's abdication, the Third Republic again required legislative ratification of trade treaties. Treaties with Europe stagnated until the 1890s, when the Third Republic renewed most of the Second Empire's treaties as they expired. The number of treaties in effect in Latin America seems to have declined, though this may reflect a weakness in the Trade Agreements Database (see Chapter 6).

We have seen, then, that divided government may have varying effects on cooperation. In Switzerland and the Netherlands, indirect evidence suggests that strong legislatures inhibited cooperation, as did the French legislature before 1848. In the 1860s, a peculiar combination of legislative tariff-making and executive treaty-making opened space for international cooperation in France, which depended in part on higher levels of divided government. Reintroducing a legislative ratification constraint in the 1870s proved to be problematic for cooperation. Although Figures 9.1 and 9.3 present obviously stylized examples, they illustrate an important general point: domestic politics affects not only the ratification of agreements but also the status quo. Divided government, too, can affect both the status quo and ratification of international agreements.

Ratification Failures

The analysis so far has assumed that executives will not negotiate a treaty that the legislature will reject, at least if the legislature has ratification powers. With incomplete information, however, the legislature may reject treaties outright as the executive may not anticipate rejection. This section shows that treaty rejections are rare, so that legislative ratification is unlikely to provide much variation in countries' abilities to cooperate. The following sections show that a focus on how divided government affects reversion points accounts better for substantial variations, both cross-nationally and intertemporally.

Nonratification is an uncommon event. Though countries reached more than 1000 trade treaties in this century, legislatures rejected only 43 of them. Despite this low percentage, the threat of nonratification may have exerted a powerful influence on the substance of any agreements reached and may have kept some agreements from being negotiated in the first place.[5] As I

---

[5] Interestingly, Coates and Ludema (2001) have also found conditions under which potential nonratification by foreigners contributes to home liberalization, with longer term effects encouraging foreign liberalization as well.

suggested in the previous section, this may have been true of Switzerland and the Netherlands.

It is difficult to say much about such uncommon events, for which standard statistical methods may be inapplicable (Beck et al. 2000). At the same time, these events were clearly patterned. This section outlines the patterns and also proposes some necessarily speculative explanations of them.

Because the spatial theory of two-level games maintains that incomplete information is a necessary (but not sufficient) condition for nonratification, even this low rate of nonratification suggests that information is sometimes incomplete. The executive's uncertainty about legislative preferences, perhaps because of multiple and rapidly changing cleavages in the legislature, seems a likely suspect (see Milner 1997a). We should think, then, about possible causes of this uncertainty.

If executive uncertainty about certain types of legislatures causes nonratifications, then we would expect nonratifications to be highly concentrated by country. Some countries would have the requisite uncertainty, whereas others presumably would not. The data are consistent with this claim. Table 9.1 lists the number of nonratifications by country. Because of a lack of information for many cases, each nonratification is counted twice, regardless of which legislature rejected the treaty first.

This method of counting has some theoretical foundation. A home legislature may reject a treaty because of problems with the foreign government. Without a stronger theory of nonratification it could be wrong to count, say, a Dutch nonratification of a French treaty against the Netherlands if we suspect that parliamentary uncertainty in France can cause non-French nonratifications. The logic is analogous to signaling models of the democratic peace (i.e., Bueno de Mesquita and Lalman 1992) in which peaceful democracies may nonetheless initiate conflict against nondemocracies. U.S. Senate rejection of some Mexican treaties because of uncertainty over the Mexican legislature provides one example (see Table 12.4).

More than half of all countries in the database (31 of 58) are never involved in a treaty rejection. At the other extreme, México is involved in one-third of all nonratified treaties (14 of 43). Five states (Argentina, France, México, the United States, and Uruguay) were involved in three-fourths of all nonratifications (32 of 43). Adding only four more states (Guatemala, Italy, the Netherlands, and Nicaragua) encompasses 42 of the 43 nonratifications. Only the 1869 El Salvador-Perú nonratification does not involve one of these nine states. We arrive at essentially the same rankings if we look at the rate of nonratifications, that is, the percentage of all negotiated treaties that

Table 9.1. *Nonratified trade treaties by country, 1815–1913*

Country	Nonratifications	Total initiations	Percent nonratified
México	14	56	25
France	9	73	12
Uruguay	7	36	19
Argentina	6	33	18
United States	6	86	7
Belgium	4	29	14
Guatemala	4	29	14
Italy	4	90	4
Netherlands	4	40	10
Austria	3	71	4
Prussia	4	49	8
Switzerland	3	34	9
Bolivia	2	35	6
Chile	2	29	7
Costa Rica	2	21	10
El Salvador	2	28	7
Nicaragua	2	36	6
Portugal	2	14	14
United Kingdom	2	37	5
Dominican Republic	1	27	4
Ecuador	1	23	4
Haiti	1	11	9
Honduras	1	30	3
Iran	1	4	25
Paraguay	1	14	7
Perú	1	53	2
Spain	1	32	3

Note: Each nonratified treaty is counted twice, once for each signatory.

were not ratified. Furthermore, these national nonratification counts are not Poisson-distributed, which suggests that there is *not* some underlying rate of treaty rejection common to all states. A few states were clearly different from the rest in being prone to reject treaties.

Some countries make the list only because they signed several treaties with serial nonratifiers, such as México, the United States, France, or Uruguay. Prussia's four nonratifications include three treaties rejected by México and one by the United States. Both of Portugal's nonratifications were rejected by Uruguay. The Netherlands represent a more ambiguous case. Two of the

Netherlands' four nonratifications were French treaties, though both were rejected by the Dutch Estates General (in 1881 and 1882).

Though France and the Netherlands are exceptions to the rule, this evidence weakly suggests the following inductive claim:

Finding 9.1: Treaty nonratification occurs more often in the presidential systems of the Americas than in the parliamentary systems of the Old World.

The institutional links between the legislature and executive were weaker in the Americas than in Europe, with neither affecting the selection of the other. These countries were also relatively new, with developing party systems and political norms. This less settled institutional environment would presumably increase uncertainty about the legislature's preferences, making it more difficult to negotiate an acceptable treaty.

The rate of nonratification may also have inhibited cooperation. The nonratification rate is weakly negatively correlated with the number of treaty initiations (–.21). This suggests that countries with ratification problems were slightly less likely to negotiate treaties in the first place:

Finding 9.2: Countries with higher rates of nonratification also initiate fewer treaties.

An example from two leading nonratifiers illustrates some of the dynamics at work. When the U.S. Senate rejected the 1859 agreement with México, it had hoped that withholding concessions would induce President Benito Juárez to cede territory to the United States in exchange for further trade or financial incentives. Because Juárez was holed up in Veracruz, under siege by domestic opposition forces during these negotiations, it is reasonable to assume that the United States was uncertain about Mexican preferences. When the Mexican government refused to negotiate on this basis, the United States eventually relinquished all territorial demands and successfully concluded a ratifiable commercial treaty (Lauck 1904). In this case, uncertainty about *foreign* preferences brought about a treaty's rejection.

This kind of domestic uncertainty probably explains México's problems with many countries. Figure 9.5 shows the annual number of treaties in effect for the five largest countries of Latin America from 1815 to 1913. México led the region in cooperation during the 1820s and 1830s, a period coinciding with its federalist Republic of 1824–1836. When it turned to a central system, it fell back to last place in the trade treaty standings until the 1880s. This reflected the political disorder of these years in México, which ended only under President Porfirio Diaz. Elected president in 1872 and

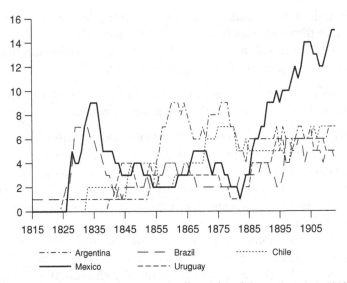

Figure 9.5. Latin American Treaties in Effect: Selected Countries, 1815–1913.

again in 1876, Diaz yielded the presidency to a close colleague, General Manuel Gonzalez, in 1880–1884, before being elected six more times in succession (and becoming increasingly dictatorial). This entire period, known as the Porfiriato, marked the consolidation of the Mexican political system and a time of relative prosperity (Krauze 1997). Diaz's dominance of the political system brought greater stability and predictability and doubtless made it easier to anticipate the legislative approval of treaties. Indeed, the number of Mexican treaties in effect jumped dramatically. The number of Mexican treaties in effect therefore seems to be well explained by variation in domestic political stability. In this case, a closer look at the institutional setting illuminates intertemporal variations more effectively than can the annual data of Chapter 8.

Yet even if we accept this argument, the relatively high rejection rates in France and the Netherlands – though small by any reasonable standard – remain unexplained. The preferences and institutional setting discussed in earlier sections are doubtless part of the story, but uncertainty about them is also necessary to explain this higher rate of nonratification.

Furthermore, the rejection rate does nothing to help us understand how divided government might affect the status quo, an issue that I began to address in Figure 9.3. This effect on the status quo may have systematic consequences for the likelihood of cooperation. I examine this issue in the next section.

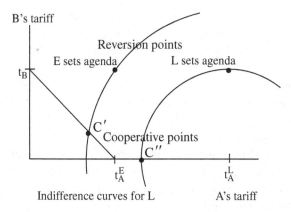

Figure 9.6. Negotiations in Two Dimensions.

Divided Government and Reversion Points in Two Dimensions

Although Figures 9.1 and 9.3 show only a single-dimensional problem and ignore the problems of enforcing cooperation, the main point generalizes to multiple dimensions and to repeated play. This section begins by adding a policy dimension and turning to repeated play in the next. Consider Figure 9.6, which follows Milner (1997a) and other standard presentations of trade policy problems in two dimensions. Two countries, A and B, each choose an autonomous trade policy. For simplicity, B is a unitary actor whose decisions are exactly modeled by the theory of political support in Chapter 3.

In contrast, either the executive (E) or the legislature (L) may set the agenda in A. E and an imaginary decisive actor in L each have an ideal tariff defined by the theory of political support, but they weigh exporters and import-competing interests differently. It is common to assume that E weighs exporters and/or consumer interests more heavily than does L (see Mansfield and Busch 1995; Rogowski 1987; Rosendorff 2006), and I follow that convention here.

Each actor's ideal foreign tariff is zero, and each desires a positive home tariff. In other words, E has the ideal point $\{t_A{}^E, 0\}$, L has the ideal point $\{t_A{}^L, 0\}$, and B has the ideal point $\{0, t_B\}$ with $t_A{}^E, t_A{}^L, t_B > 0$. For simplicity, I assume that utility is a negative function of the distance from the outcome of the game to this ideal point, so that indifference curves are circles around each player's ideal point. (If the dimensions were weighted differently, the indifference curves would be ellipses and the qualitative findings would be unchanged.) I limit attention to cases when $t_A{}^L > t_A{}^E$.

Because each government selects only its own tariff, it chooses its ideal point as that tariff.[6] I begin with L as the agenda-setter in A. Because B and L each choose their ideal domestic tariffs, the Nash equilibrium is $N = \{t_A{}^L, t_B\}$. There are mutual gains from joint action because each country's tariff imposes externalities on the other (see Remark 7.1). In particular, E and B can negotiate some cooperative agreement (C), subject to ratification by L. The possible outcomes of this game are the "N-set," agreements that E and B could rationally make when they anticipate L's ratification constraint. For simplicity in the comparisons here, I reduce the N-set to a unique point, rather than modeling the negotiation process directly. Specifically, I assume that B chooses a point as C subject to two constraints: first, an agreement must be ratifiable by L, and second, it must lie on the contract curve $t_B t_A{}^E$ if this is possible given the ratification constraint. If no point on the contract curve is ratifiable, B chooses a ratifiable point from the line segment $t_A{}^E t_A{}^L$. The points C and C' in Figure 9.6 illustrate these two possibilities. This solution concept yields a unique outcome, making the comparative statics much easier.[7]

As the legislature becomes more distant, the reversion point becomes less attractive for both E and B.[8] The N-set also changes. In Figure 9.6, moving the legislature's ideal point from $t_A{}^L$ to $t_A{}^{L'}$ shifts the N-set onto the x axis. As the legislature moves rightward, foreigners find cooperation less and less attractive. The president finds C more attractive in the range from C to $t_A{}^E$, and then less attractive from $t_A{}^E$ to C' and beyond.

The analysis in this section has modeled the trade-cooperation problem in two dimensions, looking at how changing the legislature's preferences changes the reversion point. This differs from most previous two-level analysis – presented in a stylized way in the previous sections of this

---

[6] An actor might choose a different initial tariff while anticipating negotiations. I neglect this (1) for simplicity; (2) because it produces a cycle of tariff raising without obvious net effect on the negotiations and off the single-play Nash equilibrium; and (3) because the legislature may set a tariff without knowing the executives' discount factors and thus whether they will reach agreement.

[7] This solution concept also makes the outcome a continuous function of $t_A{}^L$. Without the second requirement, B's utility off the contract curve $t_B t_A{}^E$ would be maximized by a point above the x-axis on L's indifference curve, creating a discontinuity at $t_A{}^E$; the results in the text would still follow except for points near this discontinuity. The results in the text should follow from a broad range of other solution concepts, at a considerable cost in ease of presentation. See Dai (2002) and Mansfield et al. (2002a, b) for discussion of this assumption.

[8] For simplicity I neglect B's reaction (Hypothesis 7.1, the reaction hypothesis). Adding this complication would raise the value of the reversion point to E and B, making cooperation less likely for reasons discussed later.

chapter – in that the legislature affects both the reversion point and the outcome of negotiations. Existing theory usually takes the status quo as exogenous and then examines how moving the ratifier's ideal point changes the ratification constraint on negotiators (i.e., Hammond and Prins 1998). When the reversion point changes as a result of increasing divided government (differences between E and L), the probability of cooperation also changes, as we see in the next section.

Divided Government and Cooperation in Repeated Play

The spatial model in single play predicts that cooperation always occurs with the types of preferences shown. This may change when we consider enforcement problems in repeated play. As we saw in Chapter 7, cooperation will occur if the reward for cooperation is greater than the temptation to defect. Using a standard notation for the Prisoners' Dilemma that characterizes the utility functions of Chapter 7 more simply, cooperation will occur if a state's preferences meet the condition $(T-R)/(T-P) \geq \delta$, where R represents the payoff from mutual cooperation, P the payoff when cooperation breaks down, and T the temptation to defect. Lowering the reversion point (P), raising the rewards of cooperation (R), or lowering the temptation to defect (T) make this condition more likely to hold. This synthesis of spatial models and repeated-play enforcement mechanisms makes cooperation probabilistic, allowing me to conduct comparative statics on the conditions that make cooperation more or less likely.

Consider first the problem when L controls the reversion point. We can analyze an increasing degree of divided government as a legislature moving from the executive's ideal point t_A^E to the point t_A^L in Figure 9.6. As the legislature moves increasingly to the right, the reversion point (P) grows worse for both E and B. This makes cooperation more likely for both. The rewards of cooperation have a more ambiguous effect: for some range, the cooperative outcome (R) moves toward E's ideal point, making cooperation more likely. After this, R moves rightward away from t_A^E along the x-axis, making cooperation less likely. Throughout, this shift in R always makes cooperation less likely for B because the gains of cooperation have gone down for foreigners.

It is also possible in a divided polity that the legislature might decide to defect from any agreement, especially if it has control of the reversion point. The utility of noncooperation is unchanged from t_A^L to $t_A^{L'}$, because L receives its ideal home tariff and an identical foreign tariff in either case. Given the narrow definition of the N-set used here, B will always propose an agreement (C) that leaves L indifferent between C and the reversion point, so R is also unchanged. T must also be unchanged if P and R are unchanged. As a result, increasing the degree of divided government has no effect on the legislature's condition.

In this institutional context, then,

Hypothesis 9.1: Legislative control of the reversion point. When the legislature controls the reversion point and has ratification power, divided government

(a) makes cooperation more likely for the executive up to a point and has ambiguous effects thereafter.

(b) has ambiguous effects on foreigners' willingness to cooperate, and

(c) has no effect on the legislature's willingness to accept international cooperation.

In other words, the effects of divided government on trade cooperation are context-dependent.

These effects differ when E, not L, controls the reversion point. E might have set the SQ, or it may have authority to threaten a reversion point if a treaty is not ratified, regardless of the SQ before negotiations.[9] If E, not L, chooses the autonomous tariff, the noncooperative outcome is $N = \{t_A^E, t_B\}$. Moving L rightward does not affect this, so the reversion point does not depend on L's preferences. However, divided government does affect the N-set. As L moves to the right, it will accept fewer agreements on the contract curve between E and B. This makes the rewards for cooperation greater for E but lower for B. With E unchanged, only these changes in R will affect the inequality $w \geq (T-R)/(T-P)$. Divided government raises R for E, making cooperation more likely. However, it lowers R for foreigners, making them less likely to cooperate. Because both must consent to cooperate, the net effect on international cooperation is unclear.

In contrast, the effect on L is very clear if E controls the reversion point. As divided government increases, L's utility from noncooperation (P) goes down because $t_A^{L\prime}$ becomes increasingly distant from E's ideal point. The R goes down by the same amount because, again, B leaves L indifferent between cooperation and noncooperation. Lowering both the denominator

---

[9] In some countries, the executive and the legislature jointly set the reversion point. The effects of divided government in this case lie between the effects in the pure-legislative and pure-executive control models (Pahre 2001a).

and numerator of $(T-R)/(T-P)$ by the same amount reduces the ratio because it is less than 1. This change makes cooperation more likely. T also does down, as it must given the fact that R and P have decreased. This also makes cooperation more likely. As a result, L becomes less likely to reject cooperation as divided government increases, even though L's utility from both cooperation and noncooperation decreases. This follows because L is happy to have any concession from B that E can obtain and will not reject cooperation if that leads to an undesirable reversion point.

In summary, then, E controlling the reversion point yields somewhat less ambiguous results than does L agenda-setting:

Hypothesis 9.2: Executive control of the reversion point. When the executive controls the reversion point, and the legislature has ratification power, divided government makes

(a) the executive more likely to cooperate,
(b) foreigners less likely to cooperate, and
(c) the legislature more likely to cooperate.

As these examples show, divided government has various effects on international cooperation when we model the reversion point explicitly. Institutions as well as preferences matter, especially institutional control over the reversion point. The best conclusion from this analysis is that we should always analyze the effects of divided government on the reversion point as well as on ratification. These effects depend heavily on both preferences and institutions.

The following sections provide concrete examples of such an analysis. I examine Austria-Hungary before and after 1867, Sweden-Norway before and after Norwegian independence, and two "crises" of the *Zollverein*. I chose these three cases because they vary in institutional control over the reversion point and in the degree to which ratifiers' preferences differed systematically from the executive's. Simply put, divided government made cooperation more likely in Austria-Hungary because of complementary preferences in the two halves of the monarchy, while it made cooperation more likely in the *Zollverein* because of the executive's control of the reversion point. Neither condition held in Sweden-Norway, where divided government seems to have made cooperation less likely.

These cases also provide insight into important parts of the century's trade network. As we see at greater length in Part IV, the *Zollverein* dominated the first wave of cooperation and helped spark the second wave at mid-century.

Austria-Hungary joined that second wave a few years late, but then became as important a player as any other state. In both cases, domestic politics played a critical role in explaining trade cooperation. Sweden, which we might expect to have played an important role comparable to Belgium, remained outside the main trade network because of the structure of its divided governemnt.

Reversion Points and International Cooperation in Austria-Hungary

In addition to their substantive importance, these countries also pose interesting analytical puzzles. The conventional wisdom on divided government, which has not considered changing reversion points, has argued that added ratifiers and increasing the degree of divided government between the executive and legislature make cooperation less likely. We have seen in earlier sections that this argument has force for some countries, such as Switzerland, the Netherlands, and by implication several Latin American republics.

Against this background, Austria-Hungary is puzzling. The unitary state of Austria became a deeply divided polity when the *Ausgleich* (Compromise) of 1866 took effect in 1867. This constitutional change was associated with a significant *increase* in Austro-Hungarian trade cooperation. Thus, there is a clear intertemporal puzzle to be explained.

In addition, Austria-Hungary stands out in a cross-national perspective. This is evident when we compare it to other large European countries. Figure 9.7 shows the number of European treaties in effect for the European great powers other than Russia. (The Prussian total excludes treaties with *Zollverein* members.) Austria went from being a relatively low cooperator among the great powers to being a high cooperator. The transition occurred in the late 1860s and early 1870s, that is, after the *Ausgleich* introduced permanent divided government. All the great powers were exposed to the same external stimulus – the wave of treaties resulting from the Cobden-Chevalier treaty – so some other factor must account for the dramatic change in Austro-Hungarian behavior compared to its peers.[10]

That factor lies in the domestic politics of the Dual Monarchy. The *Ausgleich* of 1866, which had to be renewed every ten years, replaced the Habsburg dynasty's unified absolutist empire with two states, the Kingdom of Hungary

---

[10] Another factor, which is not unconnected to those discussed in the text, is that Austrian trade policy was subordinated to foreign policy in general and to German policy in particular before 1867 (Vomáčková 1963). We see some of these concerns reflected in the *Zollverein*'s "crises" discussed in this chapter and in the spread of cooperation throughout Greater Germany discussed in Chapter 11.

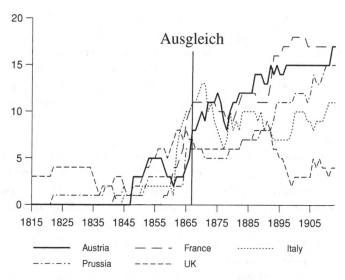

Figure 9.7. Treaties in Effect: Large European Countries, 1815–1913.

and the Austrian Empire.[11] The Dual Monarchy stemmed from the massive defeat of the Austro-Prussian War (1866) and the resulting need to put the multinational empire on a new social foundation. Although each half was formally independent and could set its own trade policy, these states were unified in the person of the King-Emperor Franz Joseph and shared a common currency, imperial bank, tariffs and many indirect taxes, railroads, army, and foreign policy. Joint ministries responsible to the Crown handled common affairs, with commercial policy falling under the authority of the foreign minister (Brauneder and Lachmayer 1980; Kann 1974; May 1951; Szíjartó 1994).

To the Hungarian mind, these were now two countries, and the trade relations between them were to be governed by treaty, not by a constitution. Article XII of the Hungarian constitution (cited in Harvey 1938: 63) was very clear on this point: "Between the lands of the Hungarian crown and the other lands of his majesty, a customs and trade pact shall be concluded. This shall be established by a treaty mutually agreed on in the manner of other agreements between independent lands."

When negotiating trade treaties with outsiders, the foreign minister consulted the two commerce ministers, and any treaty required ratification by

[11] Technically, the non-Hungarian half was known as "the lands represented in the *Reichsrat* (Imperial Council)," but were typically referred to as "Austria" or "Cisleithania," that is, the lands on the near side of the Leitha River.

both parliaments. This meant that the ratifier, the Hungarian Diet, had control over the reversion point because it could establish a separate tariff on its own authority. (The Austrian Diet had similar power, but its preferences were better reflected in the common ministries.) The theory predicts that this control would make cooperation more likely, at least in some range.

This constitutional regime mattered because the Hungarians differed with the Austrians on many issues (see Eddie 1968, 1972; Good 1981; Huertas 1977; Hunt 1974; Matis 1973: 41–45; Ránki 1964, 1981; Somogyi 1984). On trade policy, for example, Hungary favored lower tariffs, looked to Germany for export markets, and saw agricultural producers such as Serbia and Romania as potential threats. Better transportation, which saved Balkan exporters the need to drive their livestock to urban markets such as Vienna, contributed to Hungarian concerns from the 1870s on (see also Hypothesis 3.6, transportation costs). Several important trade disputes hung on the fact that Hungary always wanted a strong veterinary convention with Germany to secure that export market but seeking to deny Serbian hogs the same treatment in Austria. The political power of export-oriented ethnic Magyar estate-holders magnified the importance of these concerns.

In contrast, Austrian Germans generally favored higher tariffs, looked down the Danube for export markets in the East – in which they would not have to compete with west European industries – and feared competition in manufactured goods from Germany (see also Chapter 11). The urban market in Vienna, in particular, also imported large quantities of livestock, meat, grains, and fruits from southeastern Europe. All of these competed with Hungarian trade.

Austria had already signed some trade treaties in Germany (see Chapter 11) and joined the western European trade treaty system by signing a treaty with France in 1862 and one with England in 1865. After the *Ausgleich* this tendency became a flurry of treaties – with Belgium (February 23, 1867), the Netherlands (March 26, 1867), Italy (April 23, 1867), Prussia (March 9, 1868), and Switzerland (July 14, 1868). At first glance, these treaties could be attributed to the spread of the French treaty system as easily as to the *Ausgleich*. However, Chapter 11 shows that Austrian entry into the cooperation network predates France, reflecting the spread of the German customs union. Yet, this entry was slow before the *Ausgleich*, and the 1862 treaty with France seems not to have sparked any further negotiations.

Subsequent events also show that the *Ausgleich* provided the more important connection. Because the two halves of the empire retained the right to impose an independent tariff, negotiations with foreigners were always linked to implicit and explicit threats to reimpose a tariff boundary (*Zwischenzolllinie*) between Austria and Hungary (for other examples of such linkage, see Lohmann 1997; Pahre 1994). These threats became most visible every ten years in the negotiations leading up to the renewal of the *Ausgleich*. Hungary typically threatened to reinstall the old customs boundary if its concerns in agricultural trade were not given greater weight in negotiations with outsiders. The resulting demands on foreigners also led to occasional trade wars, which therefore coincided with the decennial *Ausgleich* renewals.

The first renewal came while protectionism was growing strong in Austria as a result of the economic difficulties of the 1870s, for reasons related to Hypothesis 3.4 (the declining prices hypothesis) and Hypothesis 3.6 (transportation costs). In late 1875 Austria floated the idea of letting the existing trade treaties expire without renewal. Hungary responded that, if Austria did that, then it wished to end the customs union with Austria and impose its own tariff. Austria backed down and renewed the treaties. Taking advantage of its evident leverage, Hungary also consented to the increases in a new Austrian tariff only on the condition that this new "autonomous" tariff for the Empire include the tariff reductions of any future treaty with Germany (von Bazant 1894: 16–17, 28–29). This condition represents one reason why this supposedly autonomous tariff was in fact negotiable (see Chapter 7).

The actions prompted Austria to pursue favorable treaties with its own natural markets in the Balkans, even as it agreed to renew the treaties in western Europe. The most important of these was an extensive treaty with Serbia in 1881, in which the empire reduced or eliminated tariffs on many agricultural goods in exchange for Serbian reductions on most of its exports. This treaty also included a strong veterinary convention (Láng 1906: 289–91).

In coming years, *Ausgleich* renewals regularly coincided with tariff wars. During the negotiations on the second renewal, Hungary closed its market to Romanian and Russian cattle, sheep, and swine after Germany had closed its market to most foreign cattle, including Hungary's (Hunt 1974). Though all sides claimed veterinary motives, Romania interpreted these closures as protective acts and imposed retaliatory tariffs. The resulting tariff war hurt Romania particularly hard, as its exports to Austria-Hungary declined from 40 to 4 million gulden in 1885–1887 (Láng 1906: 291–92).

During negotiations on the third *Ausgleich* renewal in 1895–1896, Hungary banned the import of Serbian hogs, ostensibly for veterinary reasons (Lampe and Jackson 1982: Chapter 6). Serbia was forced to grant Austria-Hungary a lopsided commercial treaty. Serbia was also a victim of the fourth

Ausgleich renewal, which produced the Pig War of 1906–1910. Like the last, this conflict was fought over veterinary regulations and led to a treaty favoring Austria-Hungary.

Protectionism, and not phytosanitary concerns, drove these conflicts. According to Michael Palairet (1997: 211), Serbia had no livestock epidemics that would warrant border closures. Ironically, Hungary did suffer from swine fever and hoof-and-mouth disease at least until 1898.

Though not part of foreign relations per se, relations with autonomous Bosnia faced similar obstacles. Bosnian livestock enjoyed free entry into Austria-Hungary in theory, but its suppliers faced Hungarian interference and occasional closures on veterinary grounds. When Hungary required incoming pigs to be slaughtered before entry in 1895, Bosnia's pig export trade fell by 90% because it had almost no meat-packing capacity. The Bosnian herd, like Hungary's, seems to have suffered from both swine fever and hoof-and-mouth disease.

Germany, which was by far the empire's largest trading partner, played a central role in Austro-Hungarian commercial policy. In the early 1890s, Vienna's imperial and royal government was divided over whether talks with Germany or the Balkan countries should be concluded first. Although Hungary was ready for immediate talks with Germany, the Austrians demanded that agreements be reached first with Serbia and Romania. Both sides feared that concluding any one treaty would make later treaties more difficult (Weitowitz 1978: 55–56). For example, if Austria-Hungary reached treaties with the Balkan states first, and if these had the lax veterinary regulations that Austria desired, this might lead Germany to break off its negotiations with the empire. If Austria-Hungary reached a treaty with Germany first, presumably with strong veterinary provisions, then it would be hard to have lower standards in the treaties with Serbia and Romania. This would make it more difficult for Austria to obtain the concessions it desired in these export markets. (Such concerns are discussed further in Chapter 12, where they provide a motive to "cluster" trade agreements in time.)

The solution lay in an informal agreement known as the "Montssche Proposition." Germany and Austria-Hungary each agreed not to negotiate any treaties without coordinating with the other state. This meant that Hungary could consent to Balkan treaties because the negotiations would be linked to Hungary's own efforts to open Germany. Similarly, Austria could make concessions to Germany while working together on the Balkans, Italy, or Switzerland. Rolf Weitowitz (1978: 56) argues that this arrangement "made it possible to appease the opposing interests of agrarians and industrialists in Austria-Hungary. This made it easier for the Viennese government to grant Germany industrial concessions, in the well-founded hope of obtaining tariff advantages in third markets."[12] This mode of negotiations would make it unnecessary for Austria to postpone closing its negotiations with Germany until after having reached treaties with Serbia and Romania. The politics of the Montssche Proposition clearly linked cooperation with divided government at home.

Germany's own motives in this deal were somewhat different. It wanted to coordinate trade negotiations with Austria-Hungary in order to increase the pressure on Switzerland, Italy, and especially Russia (Weitowitz 1978: Chapter 4). This makes most sense in terms of the pressure to "cluster" trade negotiations in an MFN regime, as analyzed in Chapter 12.

As this history shows, Austro-Hungarian cooperation with the outside world always had close links to divided government at home. Because Hungarian threats to use its tariff autonomy against Austria played a central role, my argument rests on the claim that the *Zwischenzolllinie* would have imposed significant costs on both halves of the empire. Although high duties on this boundary were unlikely, more modest dues such as those prevailing before 1850 seem a reasonable possibility.

As it turns out, the costs of a *Zwischenzolllinie* are a matter of some controversy. The traditional view maintains that such a boundary, which existed before 1850, would have been costly at late century. Certainly both Austria and Hungary suffered from a loss of traditional trading ties after World War I. Austria also lost duty-free access to points down the Danube from Hungary, important traditional markets for its goods.

Against this, Komlos (1983) presents a revisionist view, arguing that the pre-1850 barriers were a nuisance but not a major obstacle. His analysis suggests that the gains to Hungary from the customs area were about 1.5% of GNP (cf. Huertas 1977; Hunt 1974). Austria's net gain or loss, he suggests, was negligible. Although Komlos dismisses a loss of 1.5% of GNP as relatively small, this income effect exceeds the GNP gains from the NAFTA, a GATT/WTO round, and similar major trade openings among large countries today (Hamilton and Whalley 1985). Komlos's econometrics also leaves out two important features of the Austro-Hungarian economy: Austrian capital flows to Hungary and the Danubian transit trade past Hungary. His estimates of the tariff costs rely on static models of the early nineteenth-century economy

---

[12] "denn sie ermöglichte, die widerstreitenden Interessen der Agrarier und Industriellen in Österreich-Ungarn zu beschwichtigen. Der Wiener Regierung wurde es hierdurch leichter gemacht, Deutschland industrielle Konzessionen zu gewähren, in der begründeten Hoffnung, Zollvorteile auf dritten Märkten zu erlange."

and leave out dynamic effects that would presumably have made the costs of an internal boundary larger.

Certainly the Austrians viewed an internal boundary as disastrous, shutting off the urban areas of the empire from their raw materials and natural markets. Austria's and Bohemia's cotton textiles benefited from ready access to the Hungarian market, as they exported as much as 30% of their output there. Many other Bohemian industries would not have been competitive in Germany and needed preferential access to Hungary and the Danubian markets.

Many of Austria's economic advantages from the tariff union came from trade-related credit, banking, and other investments. Austria exported significant amounts of capital to Hungary after repeal of the *Zwischenzolllinie*, and these investments assumed continued free trade within the empire (Somogyi 1984). Interestingly, these patterns persist today as Austria's banks have established major positions in several post-Communist neighbors. Reflecting these industrial and financial concerns, Karl Renner – a leading Socialist writer on national questions and future president of Austria – opposed Hungarian demands for independence despite the "colonial" nature of the relationship because "the Hungarian market is incomparably more important for Austrian capital than the Moroccan market is for Germany" (cited in Taylor 1964: 193). These contemporary views of the dangers of Hungarian autonomy were decisive for policymakers.

In short, this case demonstrates a tight link between divided government and greater cooperation stemming from an undesirable reversion point and the ratifier's control over this reversion point, both of which made cooperation more likely (at least to a point). Although theoretically ambiguous, the case also suggests how increasingly divided government at home can make foreigners more willing to cooperate. Though it reduces the reward to foreigners for cooperation, divided government also makes the reversion point much worse. The tariff wars with the Balkan states show both of these effects, with one-sided treaties and dreadful reversion points. Depending on the exact payoffs in the fraction $(T-R)/(T-P)$, this protectionism may make cooperation either more or less likely.

The analysis here also has implications for some tests presented earlier in this book. Chapter 5 found that Austria was the only country for which a revenue dummy did not have a statistically significant effect on the tariff. This dummy variable also did not have a significant effect on trade treaty cooperation. As it turns out, changes in the revenue constraint exactly coincide with the constitutional changes – this revenue dummy variable equals 1 only in the *Ausgleich* years of 1867–1913. The analysis in this chapter suggests that the *Ausgleich* made trade cooperation more likely, which would *lower* the tariff. This effect would counteract the expected positive relationship stemming from an endogenous revenue constraint in the same period. In other words, this more detailed study of the country finds a confounding effect that may have masked the expected revenue effect. Again, closer study of intertemporal changes in a single country can illuminate anomalies of the seemingly more powerful cross-national analysis.

Reversion Points and International Cooperation in Sweden-Norway

The effect of divided government in the Dual Monarchy of Sweden-Norway differs significantly from the Austrian case. It seems that Sweden was more likely to cooperate with other countries after Norway broke away in 1905, that is, after the Dual Monarchy came to an end. This increase in cooperation was associated with the end of divided government in 1905–1914, in which majority governing coalitions formed to address the constitutional crisis arising from Norwegian independence. However, Yvonne Maria Werner (1989: Chapter 8) argues that negotiators' uncertainty over legislative preferences inhibited cooperation in the first round of talks with Germany in 1906.

Interestingly, Norway does not show any clear effect of divided government in either direction after independence (see Figure 9.7). In other words, divided government made cooperation less likely in Sweden-Norway, but had no apparent effect in Norway. Sweden's revenue constraint changed from exogenous to endogenous in 1885, so it cannot account for this variation; Norway's own constraint remained exogenous throughout this period and may or may not account for the lack of effect for divided government (see Table 4.4). In addition, it is not clear what theoretical expectations we should have when both halves of a dual monarchy have exogenous revenue constraints, though George Tsebelis's (2002) theory of veto actors might expect this structure to make any policy change, including cooperation, more difficult.

As in the case of Austria-Hungary, the effects of divided government become more evident when we compare a country with its peers. Accordingly, Figure 9.8 compares Sweden with the smaller trading states of Europe. As the figure shows, Sweden-Norway cooperated less than most other small states into the 1890s. After losing Norway in 1905, Sweden rapidly became the most active cooperator among the small states. This shift in Sweden's rank among the small powers rules out other plausible explanations for Sweden-Norway's earlier low levels of cooperation, such as a more isolated

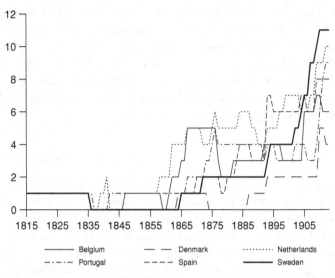

Figure 9.8. Treaties in Effect: Small European Countries, 1815–1913.

geographical position. This comparative perspective also helps rule out constitutional instability in 1905–1914 as an inhibitor of Swedish coopera-tion. Divided government provides a more plausible, theoretically grounded explanation.

Much like the *Ausgleich*, the Convention of Moss (1814) unified Sweden and Norway in the person of the Swedish king. Though each country retained its own constitution and armed forces, foreign affairs and similar matters were handled jointly. Both countries' parliaments controlled the customs and excise duties, and with few exceptions Sweden and Norway had a joint tariff from 1825 to 1897 (Lindgren 1959: Chapter 3). The cabinet (King-in-Council) could negotiate commercial treaties with foreign governments, subject to legislative ratification by both countries (Szijártó 1994; Verney 1957). The Swedish foreign service handled almost all negotiations, though Norwegian consular officials negotiated the joint trade agreements with Italy and Belgium. This structure resembles trade policy in the modern United States, in that the negotiator sets the agenda for treaties, subject to approval by two legislatures that had earlier set the agenda in the original tariff.

As in the United States, at first the legislature in Sweden-Norway did not select the executive. This changed in 1885, when parliamentary government was established. Because politically liberal agrarians increasingly dominated both legislatures in opposition to a ministry based on civil servants and the Swedish aristocracy, differences in preferences were endemic.

Unlike the complementary economies of Austria and Hungary, Norway and Sweden had very similar economic structures. Dairy products were the mainstay of both countries' agricultural sectors, and both imported grain. Both countries rapidly expanded into forest products beginning in the 1870s. Norway also expanded its merchant marine and developed new fishing, whaling, and chemical industries (Hodne 1983), whereas Sweden turned to machine industries, shipping, the steel industry, and iron ore exports. Norway continually complained that Swedish embassies and consulates gave Norway's exporters, whalers, and merchant marines less support than they deserved.

Sweden and Norway did not look to each other for trade. England and Germany were the most important trading partners for both, though each was the third or fourth most important partner for the other. In addition to competing abroad, the two countries often competed at home. Norwegian textile imports sparked domestic opposition in Sweden, whereas Norwegian millers and bakers objected to Swedish flour and bread imports (Lindgren 1959: Chapter 3). Most commerce went by sea until Norway's Narvik became the exit port for iron exports from the Swedish arctic.

Both halves of the monarchy saw agitation for tariff revision in the 1870s, reflecting pressures from declining agricultural prices and transportation costs common throughout Europe (again, see Hypotheses 3.4 and 3.6). These demands ultimately produced a higher Swedish tariff in 1888 (Lewin 1988). In part out of a desire to oppose the Swedes, many Norwegians favored freer trade – though the increasingly important agricultural party (the *Venstre*) supported tariff increases even as it opposed the Swedish union. As a result, only a narrow margin supported freer trade in the Norwegian *Storting*, just as only a narrow majority existed for protectionism in the Swedish *Riksdag*. Differences in preferences between Norway and Sweden did not play a major role in determining this status quo, nor would threats to change the reversion point have imposed major costs on either party.

With this background, there was no scope for a compromise between the two halves of Sweden-Norway as there had been in Austria-Hungary. Given their complementarities, the legislatures in Vienna and Budapest could both help and hurt each other. This lowered the reversion point and raised the rewards of cooperation in a way that encouraged them to find a way to work together. In Norway and Sweden, in contrast, the rewards for cooperation were never great, and they would remain competitors in any foreign market they opened by treaty. Hypothesis 9.1 maintains that divided government has ambiguous effects on cooperation when the legislature controls the reversion point, and our two dual monarchies nicely illustrate these varying effects.

The analysis here supplements the existing literature on Swedish trade policy. The historiography stresses Swedish desires to pursue an autonomous commercial policy (i.e., Y. M. Werner 1989: Chapter 2), though it does not give many reasons for this choice. After the end of the Dual Monarchy, Sweden successfully established early forms of corporatist institutions that brought together potentially divisive economic interests along with parties, parliamentary representatives, and the government. These were intended in part as a way to negotiate more effectively with foreigners (Lindberg 1983), and they also make sense in terms of the standard theory of small states (Katzenstein 1985). The conventional wisdom emphasizes ratification problems when arguing that divided government makes international cooperation more likely. Both the ambiguous theoretical predictions and the details of the historical case suggest that this is not too far from the mark in the case of Sweden-Norway. The same effect of divided government also seems evident in the United States, analyzed by Susanne Lohmann and Sharyn O'Halloran (1994) in terms consistent with the theory here.

Divided Government and the *Zollverein*

Like the Dual Monarchies, the German customs union (*Zollverein*) was characterized by divided government. The fact that it was an international organization and not a nation-state was not really relevant – neither Austria-Hungary nor Sweden-Norway were nation-states either, and the multinational, multistate EU today has similar control over the trade policy of its members (Pahre 2001a).

The *Zollverein* differed from the dual monarchies (and from the EU) in that the negotiator, Prussia, also controlled the reversion point. With this institutional framework, divided government made cooperation more likely for the negotiator. The negotiator was also able to use its control of the reversion point to force other members to acquiesce in treaties that they wished had not been signed. As a result, divided government made cooperation more likely in Germany, a fact that proved to have seminal importance for the European trade treaty network as a whole.

The executive's key power was that states joined the *Zollverein* by adopting the Prussian tariff by treaty (see Chapter 11). Thereafter, Prussia negotiated treaties with outsiders subject to ratification by the two houses of the Prussian legislature and of the full membership of the *Zollverein*, an institution that resembles the dual monarchies or the U.S. and EU today.

Full members included the middle powers such as Bavaria or Hannover but not the smaller states, and this status was negotiated on each state's entry into the *Zollverein*. The exact powers of each member state varied. Hesse-Darmstadt only had the right to reject treaties with states bordering it, whereas Frankfurt-am-Main was a full member, but did not have the right to reject trade treaties. All members normally retained the right to conclude commercial treaties independent of the *Zollverein* as long as they did not harm the customs union and the other members were informed (Price 1949: 245–46). The only example of this that I have found came in May 1865, when Bavaria, Württemberg, and Baden signed a treaty with Switzerland that Prussia, Saxony, Hannover, and Hesse-Darmstadt refused to accept. This sparked negotiations between the *Zollverein* and Switzerland, which provisionally agreed to grant one another the same concessions that they granted to other states until at least 1869.

Stepping back from these details, we may say that Prussia set the agenda by negotiating treaties. Berlin also had significant power over the reversion point, which was originally the Prussian tariff itself, though eventually *Zollverein* Congresses revised the common external tariff. When the *Zollverein* was reconstituted in 1867 as a treaty among the North German Confederation, Bavaria, Württemberg, Baden, and Hesse, all vetoes were eliminated and decisions made on the basis of majority rule. However, Bavaria and Saxony reserved the right to be present during any negotiations for trade treaties; Caprivi decided to consult Württemberg, Baden, and Alsace-Lorraine as well (Weitowitz 1978: 61). At this point, Germany looked increasingly like other federal states in its handling of trade policy.

Throughout the century, the other members often had different interests than the Prussians. In addition to the usual sectoral differences stemming from variation in economic structure, the south Germans favored closer ties to Austria and thus opposed Prussian maneuvers to weaken those ties. Austria encouraged the southerners' resistance to Prussia, at least until its defeat in the war of 1866 and the *Ausgleich* that transformed its own polity (see above).

Despite these differences, its agenda control in the presence of divided government meant that Prussia could propose foreign treaties that other states opposed. If they balked, Prussia could threaten an unattractive reversion point, such as higher intra-German tariffs or the creation of rival customs unions, to force the treaty through. The theory shows how divided government with negotiator control over the reversion point can make a ratifier more likely to cooperate, even if cooperation is not particularly desirable to that ratifier.

The two major crises of the *Zollverein* (1848–1853 and 1862–1865) both involved linking domestic cooperation to foreign treaties in this way. Although divided government produced each crisis, in both cases the reversion point helped Prussia force reluctant members to accept the proposed treaty. The first crisis arose when Hannover, on behalf of the Tax Union, agreed to join the *Zollverein* in exchange for union tariff reductions on coffee, tea, tobacco, syrup, cognac, and wines (Henderson 1939/1984: Chapter 6). By lowering effective tariffs further and strengthening traditionally free-trade groups in Germany, Hannover's accession spelled the end of any possibility that more protectionist Austria might join the *Zollverein* (see also Chapter 11).

Neither Hannover nor Prussia consulted the other parties of their respective unions before signing the treaty. In the Tax Union, Schaumburg-Lippe and Oldenburg acceded easily. These very small states were not in a position to pursue trade options separately from both Prussia and Hannover. In contrast, Prussia faced significant opposition from pro-Austrian states in the *Zollverein*. It responded with what we might call today its "nuclear option." Prussia simply denounced the *Zollverein* in November 1851 and said that it would renew the customs union only in conjunction with the Hannover treaty. Prussia's decision forced the middle German states to choose between a more liberal *Zollverein* oriented toward the West or trying to form a new and more protectionist union with Austria. The executive's control over the reversion point gave it a valuable tool in this case.

Austria tried to exploit the situation by introducing a lower tariff and inviting all German states to discuss a commercial treaty or customs union. These efforts brought no fruit in the end. Dividing Germany into rival unions would sacrifice the gains many states had already achieved through the *Zollverein*. For example, Saxony's Minister-President Friedrich Ferdinand Graf Beust noted that dissolution of the *Zollverein* would seriously threaten the Leipzig fair, the Leipzig book trade that dominated north Germany, and the Leipzig cigar industry, which had a large market in Prussia (Zorn 1973: 332). As a result, the Prussian threat succeeded in forcing the other states of the *Zollverein* to accept the treaty with the Tax Union.

The second crisis of the *Zollverein* (1862–1865) also ended with Prussian threats (Ashley 1926: Chapter 3; Davis 1997: Chapter 7; Henderson 1939/ 1984: Chapter 8; Marsh 1999: 40–45; Zorn 1963). Prussia signed treaties with Belgium, France, and the United Kingdom, which it submitted to the *Zollverein* at roughly the same time. The French treaty attracted immediate opposition, and only Saxony and Baden were willing to accept it.

Württemberg, Hannover, Nassau, and Hesse-Darmstadt all stood opposed, for a variety of reasons. Some feared competition, but most opposed the French treaty because they wanted to improve *Zollverein* relations with Austria first. They also believed that the MFN clauses of this treaty violated provisions of the Austro-Prussian treaty of 1853 that gave Austria preferential treatment on some goods. The Prussian government said it would treat rejection of the French treaty as a desire to dissolve the *Zollverein*. Once again, Prussia gave formal notice of the termination of the *Zollverein*, in December 1863.

Possible dissolution again threatened the smaller states with disaster. If anything, this disaster had grown more fearsome in 1863–1864 than before because of the high levels of economic integration achieved by the *Zollverein* over the preceding decade (Zorn 1963, 1973). Many German states could not really reject Prussian offers because of their small domestic markets and their dependence on sales in larger states, combined with Prussia's strong enforcement of high transit tolls. These considerations dominated the policy of Hesse-Darmstadt, Electoral Hesse, and Nassau (Hahn 1982: 27), among others. The last recalcitrants were Bavaria and Württemberg, larger states that could realistically have considered leaving the *Zollverein*. Still, King Ludwig II of Bavaria argued that even if Bavaria and Württemberg could go it alone, powerful economic interests would sooner or later force his country to rejoin the *Zollverein*. Northern Bavaria relied on the Prussian port of Hamburg for its trade with the outside world, and it depended on Saxony, Prussia's close ally, for cotton yarn exports and coal imports. Responding to such interests, Bavaria and Württemberg finally accepted the French treaty in October 1864.

These cases provide further evidence that divided government can make international cooperation more likely. Because it could make the reversion point unattractive to other states, Prussia could force through treaties that most south Germans opposed. This ability rested on institutional powers as well as the difference in preferences. Here, the same actor controlled both the reversion point and the foreign negotiations, lacking only ratification power. As the theory would expect, this made cooperation easier.

In addition, this domestic configuration forced through treaties at the heart of the international treaty network. The first crisis led to the economic unification of Germany, bringing the northern commercial states of the Tax Union into the broader *Zollverein*. Because of their close economic and political ties with the United Kingdom and other outsiders, this contributed to the broader spread of trade cooperation (see Chapter 11). The second

Table 9.2. *Findings and hypotheses on ratification*

Finding 9.1: Treaty nonratification occurs more often in the presidential systems of the Americas than in the parliamentary systems of the Old World.

Finding 9.2: Countries with higher rates of nonratification also initiate fewer treaties.

Hypothesis 9.1: When the legislature controls the reversion point and has ratification power, divided government
  (a) makes cooperation more likely for the executive up to a point and has ambiguous effects thereafter,
  (b) has ambiguous effects on foreigners' willingness to cooperate, and
  (c) has no effect on the legislature's willingness to accept international cooperation.

Hypothesis 9.2: When the executive controls the reversion point, and the legislature has ratification power, divided government makes
  (a) the executive more likely to cooperate,
  (b) foreigners less likely to cooperate, and
  (c) the legislature more likely to cooperate.

---

crisis successfully linked the German and Anglo-French networks, turning the collection of treaties of the 1860s into the century's second wave of trade cooperation.

Conclusions

Legislatures play an important role in trade policy. They may reject treaties outright, the risk of legislative rejection may keep executives from negotiating treaties in the first place, or legislatures may determine the status quo and thus affect the likelihood of cooperation. This chapter has explored each of these roles. The evidence suggests that the threat of nonratification matters for a few countries, but not for many. Most of these latter countries are in the Americas and therefore peripheral to the regime as a whole. This chapter's findings about these nonratifications are summarized in Table 9.2.

Control over the status quo may be a more important legislative power. The theory and evidence show that states may differ from their peers depending on the presence or absence of divided government. However, the evidence shows no systematic relationship between divided government and international cooperation because the cases studied here exhibit all three imaginable effects of divided government on cooperation: divided government made cooperation more likely in Second Empire France, Austria-Hungary, and the *Zollverein*, less likely in Sweden; and it had no effect in Norway. The theory presented here shows how these varying effects may occur.

It is impossible to analyze the effects of divided government on reversion points for all the countries of this study. Still, the cases analyzed here are suggestive. Divided government seems to help explain the very active commercial policy of Prussia and the *Zollverein* in the first wave of trade treaties. It also accounts for Austria-Hungary's active participation after 1867. In contrast, divided government inhibited cooperation by Sweden and Norway, two countries that might otherwise have cooperated as much as, say, Belgium.

More speculatively, divided government seems to have had other effects as well. Potential ratification problems encourage a government to list all of its tariffs in every treaty, so that rejection of one treaty will not jeopardize a network of concessions. This issue seems to have shaped Chancellor Caprivi's thinking when he presented all of his treaties to parliament as an indivisible work, treating the tariffs within them as a whole (Weitowitz 1978: 72). Such considerations also make trade treaties a kind of free-trade logroll (cf. Gilligan 1997), as well as a way to reduce domestic obstacles to liberalization by linking treaties that a group likes with other treaties that it might oppose (see also Davis 2004; Lohmann 1997).

Ratification remains a live issue in contemporary economic cooperation. The need to obtain approval from parliament or in a referendum limits cooperation in the EU (Hug and König 2006; Pahre 2001a). The U.S. president depends very much on his ability to obtain trade promotion authority as well as ratification of any agreements that he subsequently reaches (Pahre 2004). This chapter points to a closer study of executive-legislative relations, agenda-setting, and reversion points in order to understand such issues.

PART FOUR

NORMS AND COOPERATION

TEN

The Most-Favored-Nation Norm

"The most-favored-nation principle can in fact be interpreted as a convention designed to protect the third parties at the expense of whose industrial production the mutual benefits of preferential reciprocal tariff reduction are in part obtained."
– Harry G. Johnson (1965: 279)

Previous chapters have looked at the characteristics of individual states and at the two-country problem of cooperation. This part moves beyond dyads to look at the international system, especially the norms characterizing that system. I also introduce the concept of a regime, distinguishing it from both norms and behavior.

As in the rest of this book, I make a point of looking at variables that actually vary. This differs from many other theories' treatment of systemic-level characteristics, including norms. For example, Kenneth Waltz's (1979) *Theory of International Politics* examines only anarchic systems made up of nation-states, so that two of his three variables (the ordering principle and nature of the unit) do not vary; the third variable in Waltz's theory, the distribution of capabilities, does vary. Though differing from Waltz on almost every other dimension, Martha Finnemore's (1996) *National Interests in International Society* also does not study variation at the systemic level, but explicitly looks only at countries that share a given norm. Representing yet another tradition, Immanuel Wallerstein (1979, 1989) examines an international system that evolves and is internally differentiated, but his conceptual framework also does not allow central features of a world system, such as capitalism itself, to vary.

The structural features that I examine in this part – particularly the MFN norm – do vary. Unlike Waltz's principles, they do not make up *necessary* features of the international system – but, when present, they do affect behavior within it. Because the principles that I examine vary, it is easier to isolate their effects in the system.

These analytical distinctions are also important for isolating causation. Many theorists of international relations argue that norms and/or regimes facilitate international cooperation (i.e., Haggard and Simmons 1987; Jervis 1982; Keohane 1984; Milner 1992). With this chapter's analysis in hand, Chapters 11 and 12 show that the content of the norm matters and that not all norms facilitate cooperation. MFN, for example, may inhibit the spread of cooperation and reduce its depth. These conclusions differ dramatically from the generally benign view of MFN held by most analysts today, at a time when MFN is ubiquitous. Yet my claims echo the conclusions of many nineteenth-century analysts who were, after all, better familiar with systems lacking MFN.

This chapter does not derive hypotheses or present findings, but has more foundational goals. On the positive side, I show how variations between MFN and non-MFN norms fit in a general analysis of norms and regimes. More critically, this chapter also argues that our most common economic explanations of MFN do not explain these variations in norms that we observe. Political factors, though often idiosyncratic, seem to be more important than general concerns of economic efficiency. This means that variations in MFN norms are exogenous, and logically prior to, the analysis of trade cooperation at the level of the international system.

Regimes and Norms

Analyzing systemic-level norms requires a definitional excursus, for existing definitions and usage are problematic for our purposes. The important principles of the international system often go under the name of "regimes" or "norms." The regime concept generated an older literature (Krasner 1983; see Haggard and Simmons 1987 for review). Though it still resonates for many problems, the concept is not very contested today. In contrast, norms are a hotly contested concept in the study of international relations today, and the concept has many different definitions. I do not wish to propose a theory of norms here (see Finnemore 1996 for review and Goertz and Diehl 1992 for a rival, behavioralist theory). My aims are much more narrow. I wish to distinguish "norms" from "regimes" in such a way that norms retain the ability to explain behavior, especially international cooperation. Because each concept can easily be conflated with behavior, I narrow the definitions enough to make them distinct. My distinctions may not be appropriate for all theoretical purposes but they do allow the derivation and testing of explicit, falsifiable hypotheses in this book.

The main line of regime theory defines regimes as the "implicit or explicit principles, norms, rules, and decision-making procedures around which actors' expectations converge" (Krasner 1983: 2). Examples include formal institutions such as the WTO as well as less formal regimes such as the Concert of Europe. Regularized behavior – such as the nineteenth-century tariff treaty network – would meet this definition of a regime.

This definition explicitly encompasses norms as part of any regime. Because actors' expectations presumably converge around recurrent behavior, such behavior is logically part of a regime – which cannot, therefore, explain it.[1] Clearly, then, a norm cannot *explain* the existence of a regime of which it is logically a part.

This problem is also found in newer, constructivist approaches. Martha Finnemore (1996: 22; see also Arend 1999: Chapter 4; Elster 1989) defines norms as "shared expectations about appropriate behavior held by a community of actors." Here, too, the definition combines a prescriptive component ("appropriate behavior") with behavioral components ("shared expectations … held by a community"). The behavioral components of such a norm make it difficult to explain behavioral patterns consistent with the norm, both because cause and effect overlap and because the relevant community will likely share expectations about regular patterns. Norm violations are even more difficult to explain with this definition.

The challenge for analysis is to distinguish among regimes, norms, and behavior. The trade treaty networks of the nineteenth century are not only a regime, exhibiting recurrent behavior around which expectations converge, but also behavior. We need, then, a definition of norm that is distinct from this behavior. A better definition would eliminate the requirement that a norm be shared by a community, because this sharing is an aspect of behavior. A norm would therefore simply be a rule about appropriate behavior, whether or not any state holds this norm to be a guide (cf. Elster 1989). Under this definition, pacifism is a norm, even though no state seems to use it as a guide. Limiting the definition in this way severs the definitional links with behavior and allows for variations, because states need not act on the basis of the norm.

---

[1] I assume here that a proposed cause must be logically distinct from its effect – a tricky proposition in quantum mechanics but not, I think, in politics. For some of the issues here, see Cartwright (1983).

The MFN clause, which I discuss at length in the next section, fits this restricted definition of a norm. It became the common form of trade agreement by the latter decades of the nineteenth century and was held to be normatively appropriate by many states but not by all. The United States, for example, rejected the unconditional form of the MFN norm.

In contrast, the trade treaty network did not have this normative component – few people, and no states, argued for an ethical obligation to sign treaties. The dominant school of thought on the subject, protectionist reciprocity (see Chapter 7), made a pragmatic, not a normative case for the network. Though not a norm, the network meets the definition of a regime. However, the term "regime" is only useful descriptively because it includes both norms and behavior and therefore can neither explain nor be explained by either concept.

Without making any general definition, then, I have carved out enough space so that the MFN norm and trade cooperation behavior are logically distinct from each other. My approach simply reduced the domain of each concept enough so that each concept only applies to one of the variables of interest in this study. By narrowing existing definitions, instead of proposing new ones, this application may prove to be useful for those who develop more precise definitions of these concepts in the future.

The MFN Clause

Trade cooperation may take place under one of at least two norms (for an excellent review of the issues that is sensitive to the economic, legal, and political issues, see Horn and Mavroides 2001). The first is preferential bargaining, in which each preference given exclusively to a single nation constitutes discrimination against every other nation. Economists generally dislike such as system, which "means a constant shifting of the channels of world trade, not in response to the operation of the fundamental economic forces of supply and demand, but in accordance with the arbitrary and political decisions of governmental officials" (Sayre 1939: 415; see also Tasca 1938/1967: Chapter 6; Viner 1924). Germany in the 1930s is a well-known example of this system (Hirschman 1945/1980).

The second ideal type is MFN, by which any concession given to one MFN partner is given to all. Policymakers have historically been wary of using this norm because it gives free concessions without reciprocity. For example, the Austrian protectionist Neuwirth (cited in von Bazant 1894: 35) argued against MFN because it represented "a gift to all states that neither can nor want to make mutual concessions, a clause through which every tariff reduction granted to one state immediately and *ipso facto* becomes applicable to all other states."[2] In Germany, Chancellor Caprivi's 1891 review of earlier policies argued that "the most-favored-nation clause gradually became a cause of general detriment and injury" (cited in Dawson 1904: 112). One result is that policymakers may refrain from making concessions in the first place for fear that they will be granted to other states in the future without compensation (Viner 1924: 105). Mansfield and Reinhardt (2003) have argued that such concerns drive the spread of PTAs today, which provide a way to gain bargaining leverage within a global MFN regime.

In part to address such concerns, the MFN clause comes in two variants, an unconditional and a conditional form (Jones 1908; Willis 1911). One example of the conditional clause is the Prusso-American treaty of 1828 (cited in Fisk 1903: 220), which states, "If either party shall hereafter grant to any other nation any particular favor in navigation or commerce, it shall immediately become common to the other party, freely, when it is freely granted to such other nation, or on yielding the same compensation, when the grant is conditional."

Concerns over the bargaining implications of MFN provide the traditional justification in American writing for the conditional interpretation of the MFN clause (Hornbeck 1910). Though associated with the United States, conditional MFN treaties include many British treaties, including those with Portugal (1810), Austria (1838), Russia (1843), and many smaller powers between 1849 and 1853 (Liberia, Costa Rica, Dominica, Perú, Hawaii, Sardinia, Ecuador, and Paraguay).

Unconditional MFN is a variant of conditional MFN, freely granting the favors of future treaties to other most-favored nations. Unconditional MFN first appeared in Britain's treaties with Sweden and Russia in 1766 (Williams 1972: 145), and is associated especially closely with the Cobden-Chevalier wave of the 1860s (Lazer 1999; Marsh 1999). It ultimately became the dominant form of the treaty.

However, even unconditional MFN treaties often come with exceptions. The Austro-Russian treaty of February 15, 1906, is noteworthy for its relatively long list of such exceptions: the Austrian customs unions with Liechtenstein and Bosnia-Herzegovina, border traffic favors, national fishing and the coasting trade, import and export favors to Archangel and the northern and eastern shores of Siberia, the clauses of the 1838 Russian agreement with

---

[2] "als eine Gratisprämie für alle Staaten, die Gegenkonzessionen nicht machen können oder wollen, eine Klausel, durch welche jede Zollverabsetzung, die irgend einem Staate für irgend eine Konzession gewährt wird, sofort und *ipso facto* auch allen anderen Staaten zugute kommt."

Sweden, and Russian trade with bordering Asian states. This treaty is reminiscent of the Southern Cone customs union (MERCOSUR) today, whose supposedly common external tariff includes many hundreds of exceptions.

We have, then, three different principles by which states may organize their trade policy. Pure discrimination maximizes bargaining leverage, but has economic welfare losses. Unconditional MFN avoids the welfare losses of discrimination, but gives away future concessions without receiving anything in exchange. Conditional MFN combines elements of each of these approaches, perhaps mitigating each kind of problem somewhat, but retaining some disadvantages of each pure approach.

Explanations of MFN

Variation between discriminatory and nondiscriminatory rules plays a central role through this part of the book. This section argues that this variation reflected political concerns and was not endogenous to trade cooperation. This distinction has important implications for theorizing about MFN. If MFN is endogenous, then a theory should model both MFN and cooperation simultaneously. If it is exogenous, then we can study the consequences of regimes for behavior both with and without MFN.

Almost all economists and many political scientists share the assumption that the MFN clause is endogenous, representing an institutional solution to some tariff-bargaining problem. The most common claim maintains that MFN addresses a problem of incomplete contracting by protecting a country's exporters against "opportunism," that is, all unforeseen bargains in the future by which today's partner gives better concessions to others (Bagwell and Staiger 1999, 2005; Caplin and Krishna 1988; Choi 1995; Ethier 2001; cf. Johnson 1965; Snyder 1940). MFN means that if France and England sign a treaty today, France need not fear that England will make greater concessions on Portuguese wines tomorrow, effectively closing the English market to France. With MFN, any reduction on Portuguese wines will be extended to French wines, allowing both to compete.

Another explanation is that MFN is an efficient form of intervention in markets, once a state has decided to impose a tariff in the first place. Without MFN, a country may find itself importing from high-cost producers that receive lower tariffs, rather than from lower cost producers, as Viner (1924: 105) explains:

From the economic point of view, moreover, it is not a source of loss to A if its unconditional most-favored-nation treaties force it to generalize the tariff concessions which it had by special arrangement granted to particular countries. A remission of import duties on a specific commodity, if confined to imports from one country not capable of supplying the entire import needs, will reduce the customs revenue and will impair the protection to domestic industries without substantially lowering the price to the domestic consumer.[3]

Efficiency considerations also affect the government's revenue from the tariff. With differentiated tariffs and a uniform price in the importing market, countries that pay lower tariffs earn rents that do not accrue as revenue to the importing country. This entails revenue loss to the government without any benefit to home consumers or producers. Instead, this policy acts like a subsidy from the importing treasury to the foreign producer. Using the MFN clause, in contrast, guarantees that the government can capture all the rents from protection.

A final reason for MFN could be enforcement. By multilateralizing trade concessions, a state increases the number of offended parties if it were to raise its tariff. In this way, a state increases the potential punishment it faces, making its trade liberalization more credible (Pahre 1994).

These are all persuasive reasons for adopting the MFN norm – so persuasive, it seems, that they are unable to explain why states would ever fail to include an MFN clause. Economic concerns reflect a functionalist analysis in which MFN exists because it performs some function. Like most functionalist arguments, these claims are ahistorical and fail to account for the origin or spread of the MFN clause. Preferential bargaining, conditional MFN, and unconditional MFN were all available to trade negotiators in the second half of the eighteenth century. Despite the apparent advantages, states did not always sign MFN treaties, and they did not sign such treaties in much of the nineteenth century. As a result, a functionalist theory cannot explain the variations in MFN that we observe.[4]

Second, many trading areas go further than MFN treatment as normally defined. Members of a customs union or free trade area, for example, grant

---

[3] The analysis is more complicated with differentiated goods. If country B produces a less desirable good than some substitute from C, an unprotected market would find some consumers purchasing B's goods at lower cost. MFN protection would normally keep the market divided, but the exact effect would depend on the height of the tariff because a high tariff might keep consumers of low-quality goods from demanding B's goods at all. If country A gives preferences to B, some consumers will presumably shift from C's goods to B's. In a distorted market, evaluating the consequences of this discrimination is a problem of the second-best.

[4] Cebi and Ludema (2001) provide an interesting exception. Under the particular conditions of bilateral MFN between two rich countries that both grant nonreciprocal MFN to developing countries, the costs and benefits of MFN may vary over time in a way that explains variations in the norm itself. This approach may be rewarding for understanding the General System of Preferences (GSP) in the GATT/WTO, but I cannot think of any nineteenth-century parallels.

one another treatment better than that they give to their MFN partners. This discrimination leads to welfare-reducing trade diversion and does not make sense in incomplete contracting terms.[5] The "noodle bowls" of preferential trading arrangements in Asia and Europe today, in which different sets of goods are covered on different timetables in different PTAs, represent another form of better-than-MFN treatment (see Bhagwati, Greenaway, and Panagariya 1998; Sapir 2000). Regionalism in the twenty-first century, which violates the MFN norm, also seems unexplained by the functionalist approach.

To understand variations in MFN, we need to step outside economics. States often chose to use MFN for political reasons, as a token of disinterestedness, and in support of an ethical principle of equal treatment. For example, France had political reasons for wanting a conditional MFN clause included in the Franco-American commercial convention of February 6, 1778. To keep Britain isolated from the rest of Europe, France wanted to avoid the suggestion that it was fighting a war of aggrandizement. It preferred to pose as a protector of the colonies against British oppression. One negotiator stated that his king "was eager to give to Europe as well as America on this occasion an example of disinterestedness, by asking of the United States only such things as it might suit them to grant equally to any other power whatsoever" (cited in Setser 1933: 323).

Great Britain pursued a similar policy in the 1820s when negotiating with the newly independent countries of Latin America. Unwilling to offend Spain gratuitously, Britain negotiated MFN commercial treaties with Gran Colombia and México in the early 1820s, thereby renouncing any special privileges for itself (Williams 1972: 260–61). Foreign Minister George Canning's "Polignac Memorandum" of October 1823 extended this policy, stating that Britain would assist in negotiations between Spain and the rebellious colonies on the basis of neutrality (Dixon 1976: 228).[6]

Latin America's own policies further encouraged nondiscrimination. When México declared independence in 1821, it opened its ports to all nations on equal terms. In 1822, Gran Colombia offered commerce, free residence, and full reciprocity to all countries that would recognize it (Williams 1972: 257–58). Following these examples, Latin American treaties generally included MFN clauses through the century.

---

[5] Possible explanations include the new international economics (Mansfield and Milner 1999; Milner 1997b). Whatever their importance today, oligopolistic markets, economies of scale, and the like were irrelevant to the nineteenth-century customs unions.

[6] French intervention in Spain continued, contributing to Britain's support for the Monroe Doctrine of December 1823.

These concerns were largely lacking in Europe. As a result, MFN did not become a part of regular British or French practice in Europe until the 1860s, even though it was common in the Western Hemisphere. Economic theories of MFN could not explain this variation. Presumably, the problems of future opportunism among Europeans were no less than those among Latin Americans or between Latin Americans and Europeans, yet the Europeans did not originally insert MFN clauses in their treaties to guard against this opportunism. Economic theories also struggle to explain either non-MFN treaties or better-than-MFN treatment such as customs unions and free-trade areas. For example, they would also face difficulties explaining the German customs union (*Zollverein*) in this century (see Chapter 11). This customs union protected Germans from opportunism by other Germans, but did not protect French or Dutch interests, among others. Moreover, its purposes were primarily administrative and political. Chapter 11 shows that these differences in rules help account for the regional differences in the spread between the New World and the Old and between Germany and the rest of Europe.

Although it is easy to generalize that New World MFN represented a response to the challenges of independence, European MFN often stemmed from more idiosyncratic concerns. One important MFN clause in Europe is quite obscure in its origins, though they were undoubtably political in some way. Article 11 of the 1871 Treaty of Frankfurt guaranteed Germany the same tariffs as a list of other French trading partners, a clause that worked exactly like MFN. This article may have taken this form to allow France to form a Latin customs union or favorable treaties with small countries such as Morocco or Tunis, though none of these things occurred in the event. It seems that the main purpose of the clause was simply that "Bismarck was determined that France should not be at liberty to commence a tariff war, declaring that he preferred a war with cannons" (Harvey 1938: 14). Bismarck's particular views on politics, it seems, were decisive.

In addition to these political motivations, MFN can be self-reinforcing when it appears within a network of other MFN treaties. To see this effect, suppose that France and Belgium sign an MFN treaty, after which Belgium and Germany also sign an MFN treaty. If France denounces its treaty with Belgium, then some of Belgium's duties that Germany expected to be bound by the French treaty may no longer be bound. For this reason, Belgium and Germany will likely agree to bind *all* their tariffs at existing levels even if those tariffs are not reduced by treaty, as protection against the effects of French denunciation. The logic is similar to the packaging of treaties that require legislative ratification, so that the tariffs will remain in effect even

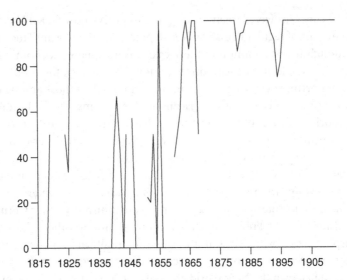

Figure 10.1. MFN Treaty Initiations as a Percentage of All Initiations.

if the legislature rejects one of them, as discussed in Chapter 9. This logic only applies if the Franco-Belgian and Belgian-German treaties both provide MFN, that is, if they exist within a network of MFN treaties. Such concerns were a real issue for Belgium and Germany when France renounced its treaty with Belgium, and they help explain Austria's and Germany's subsequent desires to bind all treaty duties in every treaty. When established in this way, "the denunciation of a single trade treaty would not fundamentally endanger the tariff, as long as other treaties with the same tariff remained in effect"[7] (Weitowitz 1978: 71). Thanks to such logic, binding MFN treaties will spread from one treaty to the next.

Figure 10.1 provides evidence with which to evaluate this claim about the spread of MFN. It shows that the proportion of MFN treaties as a share of all treaties did indeed increase over time, eventually becoming near- universal. We may propose, then, the following finding:

Finding 10.1:   Use of the MFN norm spreads.

The network effects discussed earlier probably explain how this norm came to be part of the shared expectations of the system. This norm diffusion occurred through strategic calculation, not information dissemination as

---

[7] "Durch die Kündignung eines Handelsvertrages würden die Zollsätze nicht grundsätzlich gefährdet, solange andere Verträge mit den gleichen Tarifen in Kraft blieben."

in Simmons and Elkins (2004), and would therefore be subject to change if the underlying strategic calculation changed. Indeed, MFN itself altered the strategic environment, for universal MFN has negative consequences that help explain why countries would move to PTAs within such a system, as Chapters 11 and 12 will show.

In summary, functional explanations of MFN cannot explain the variations we observe. In contrast, political concerns, especially a European interest in appearing disinterested in the New World, can explain the regional variations we observe. Finally, the logic of MFN means that, once established in a network, its use is likely to spread through that network. This explains how the clause slowly became general throughout the trade treaty network. Though political in origin, economic concerns do help explain the spread of the MFN norm.

Additional Implications of MFN

The next two chapters examine the effects of MFN for the spread of cooperation and for the clustering of cooperation in time. This section explores several additional implications of the MFN norm in a more informal way.

First, it has long been recognized that MFN encourages greater tariff differentiation. If English textiles and French textiles can be differentiated in some way, such as weight, then Germany can receive separate concessions in exchange for reductions on each. If all textiles pay the same tariffs under MFN, then Germany could only obtain a concession from one of these countries, for the other would benefit from this concession through MFN. As Arthur Graf von Posadowski-Wehner, who handled trade policy under von Bülow, argued, "The more specialized the customs act, the more compensation material there would be for treaties; and, the more general, the less there would be" (cited in Dietzel 1903: 376). Such differentiation became common in central and eastern Europe, leading France to respond in kind in 1910 (Ashley 1926: 348). This differentiation also characterizes today's tariff codes, which require thousands of pages to list in the annexes of the Uruguay Round treaty.

A second consequence of MFN is the problem of free-riding. A country may remain aloof from the give-and-take of trade concessions if it can rest easily within a network of MFN treaties. The hard-won concessions of others will then be extended to it through MFN. As many have noted, trade concessions even take on the characteristics of a public good within an MFN network (Conybeare 1987; Pahre 1994). A state such as Sweden could free-ride on concessions obtained by others.

Yet, free-riding was not an unmixed blessing even for the free-rider. One would-be free-rider, Louis Mallet of the UK Board of Trade, had hoped that the MFN would enable Britain to rely on France to make concessions to third parties from which Britain would benefit without making further concessions itself (Howe 1997: 93). Domestic critics argued that France would prove to be a very imperfect agent of Britain's interests. If another textiles producer, such as Belgium, failed to obtain concessions on textiles that were of interest to British producers, these producers were helpless against foreign protectionism (Howe 1997: 179–80). Marsh (1999: 36) argues that this is exactly how the treaty network worked in practice, as the tariffs that France was to negotiate with others did not serve British interests hoping to free-ride on those negotiations through MFN.

These points remind us that the MFN norm has interesting strategic implications, and politicians are well aware of them. It may also lead to consequences such as tariff differentiation and free-riding that run counter to the liberal predispositions of many MFN advocates. We see more such examples in the next two chapters. In all these cases, it helps to remember that the choice to use an MFN is one made in a world of the second-best, where first-best efficiency considerations may not be the best guide.

Summary

Against the functionalist logic underlying most accounts of MFN, this chapter has argued that we should see the origins of MFN in political choices. At least one signatory of each early MFN treaty wished to avoid the appearance of favoritism. These concerns became especially important in the Western Hemisphere, but were also found in Europe for a variety of reasons.

These political goals may also account for postwar MFN. MFN in the GATT is an embodiment of the American value of multilateralism. The United States took a doctrinaire position in favor of multilateralism when negotiating the GATT, whereas the Europeans were far less supportive.

Once established, the logic of MFN encourages its spread through the practice of tariff bindings. This accounts for its spread throughout Europe in the 1860s and 1870s, alongside the growth of the French trade treaty network. Again, this is evident in the GATT/WTO system, which has grown to encompass most countries in the world.

In this way, past cooperation and the norms governing such cooperation structure future cooperation. Specifically, Chapter 11 shows that discriminatory networks spread to encompass new countries more readily than do nondiscriminatory networks. This does not provide a general policy recommendation for trade discrimination, but does suggest that in a world of the second-best, discrimination has its uses. Chapter 12 then shows that MFN treaties lead states to cluster their negotiations in time and that this clustering reduces the concessions that participants make to one another. Even if global free trade is the goal, in the real world of tariffs and trade negotiations, some discrimination may be preferable to the nondiscrimination of the MFN.

ELEVEN

The Spread of the Trade Treaty Network

"Every new Commercial Treaty was at once a model and a starting point, a pattern for imitation and a basis for further development."
   – Lord Napier, 1865 (cited in Lazer 1999: 470)

Any network of international cooperation has some history, and we can trace how it has changed over time. One interesting kind of change is the spread of a network. Some international cooperation spreads, whereas other cooperation does not. This chapter extends the theory of Part III to explain such variations in spread among networks of trade treaties. The main principles of the analysis would extend to cooperation in other issue areas as well.

The key independent variable is the most-favored-nation (MFN) clause discussed in Chapter 10. MFN discourages the spread of cooperation by generalizing concessions even to nonsignatories. Generalizing concessions reduces the gains from cooperation and improves the reversion point, making cooperation by new actors, if they receive MFN, less likely. In contrast, trade regimes lacking MFN encourage the spread of cooperation. Excluded countries typically face trade diversion, lowering their reversion point and thereby making cooperation more likely. These discriminatory regimes provide incentives both for third parties to join the regime and for third parties to cooperate with one another to build an alternative network.

Whether or not they use MFN, this analysis also applies to customs unions and similar preferential trading agreements (PTAs). A customs union has a single tariff against outsiders and free trade within. Examples include the German customs union (*Zollverein*) and the Austro-Hungarian Empire in the nineteenth century or the European Union (EU) and MERCOSUR today. Because customs unions discriminate against outsiders, they tend to spread. Some customs unions expand to add new members, whereas others induce the creation of rival customs unions. As a result, we see a steady increase in the number of trade treaties throughout the century, a fact that accounts for my use of YEAR as a control variable in much of Parts II and III.

The workings of PTAs and discriminatory, non-MFN treaties provide a motor force for the growth of the trade network. Nondiscriminatory trade policies, such as MFN, provide a brake. To show this, I focus on cooperation in greater Germany (*Grossdeutschland*), especially the *Zollverein* and its competitors. Discrimination against nonmembers made *Zollverein* membership attractive to German states that were reluctant to join at first and also encouraged trade cooperation between Germany and the rest of the world. The result proved to be very significant for global trade cooperation, for the evidence demonstrates that German cooperation from the 1820s on, and not the Cobden-Chevalier Treaty of 1860, provides the fount of the nineteenth-century trade cooperation network.

Domestic Politics, Economic Discrimination, and MFN

The analysis here rests on a nonformal extension of the model developed in Part III. In particular, I apply Hypothesis 7.1 (the reaction hypothesis) to an n-country setting in which some countries' tariffs are held constant but affecting outsiders' tariffs. Instead of modeling directly the effects of a customs union on trade, I apply the results of standard customs union theory (for some recent reviews of related issues, see Abrego, Riezman, and Whalley 2004; Olarreaga, Soloaga, and Winters 1999). In other words, my argument takes the form of statements such as "when trade diversion away from country 1's exports occurs in country 2's market, this diversion has the following political effects." Obviously, modeling the customs union directly is one possible extension of this research.

Recall first how one state will react to changes in the foreign tariff. Without cooperation, home tariffs will increase when foreign tariffs decline, and home tariffs will decline when foreign tariffs increase (Hypothesis 7.1, the reaction hypothesis). This analysis implicitly assumed the absence of MFN and yields the first hypothesis:

Hypothesis 11.1: Without MFN, foreign cooperation leads to home liberalization; with MFN, foreign cooperation leads to home protection or no change in tariffs.

With MFN, cooperation among foreigners may lower the tariff that home exporters face, though it may not address the goods that home producers export. If this cooperation does lower foreign tariffs, then the home country will raise its tariffs in response. Without MFN, foreign cooperation may divert foreign customers away from home exporters, raising the effective barriers they face. Politicians will spread the costs of this change among groups at home by lowering the tariff.

Russia's decision to enter the trade treaty network in the 1890s is an excellent example of these forces at work. Russia had long refused to negotiate its tariff downward, but had a change of heart in the 1890s. The cause was the Caprivi cluster of treaties, according to Walter Harvey (1938: 85). German-Russian

economic relations had become worse because of the trade treaties Caprivi had concluded with Austria-Hungary and other states early in 1891. These treaties probably hurt Russia more than the previous raising of the German duties. As long as the German duties were general, their chief effects were to raise prices in Germany....
With the coming into effect of the treaties with Austria-Hungary and Rumania [sic], however, prices in Germany would be brought down to the Austro-Hungarian level (plus the transportation charges and the small German duty) and Russian exporters had to bear the full burden of the tariff or seek a market elsewhere.

Percy Ashley (1926: 69–70) notes that this price difference was substantial, for Russian corn paid a duty 43% higher than did Germany's MFN partners. Indeed, Germany anticipated these effects, and one of Germany's major goals in its negotiations with Austria-Hungary in 1891 was to put pressure on Russia (Weitowitz 1978: Chapter 4). After a tariff war beginning in August 1893, Germany and Russia came to terms in February 1894.

Tariff treaty networks are only one form of cooperation that discriminates against outsiders. Customs unions represent another and typically lead to trade diversion, raising the effective tariff faced by nonmembers. This implies the following corollary:

Corollary 11.1: Customs unions lead to foreign liberalization.

This corollary follows from Hypothesis 7.1, according to which a higher home tariff will lead to foreign liberalization.

These changes in the home autonomous tariff also affect cooperation. Without MFN, foreign cooperation lowers the home tariff by reducing the market for home exports. By lowering the home tariff, foreign cooperation makes the home country more likely to cooperate because low-tariff countries are more likely to cooperate. The home country might cooperate either with the foreign cooperators or with third parties that have also seen their own tariffs decrease.

With MFN, in contrast, foreign cooperation may lower the tariffs faced by home exporters, raising the reversion point (in the notation of Chapter 9, P). Taken by itself, this makes cooperation less likely. However, MFN occurs in an environment of tariff bindings and other cooperation that the home country may be unwilling to break. In this case, foreign liberalization will not affect home cooperation. This reasoning yields the second major hypothesis:

Hypothesis 11.2: Without MFN, foreign cooperation makes home cooperation more likely, both with the two initial cooperators and with fourth parties; with MFN, foreign cooperation may make home cooperation less likely or have no effect.

This logic was a factor for the second wave of cooperation after the Cobden-Chevalier treaty. Indeed, Percy Ashley (1926: 301; see also Lazer 1999) argues that France had intended to set off a treaty network:

> Napoleon and his advisers had hoped from the first that once Great Britain had set the example of a treaty, other nations would not be slow to follow it. The expectation was justified; and, indeed, the industrial powers had no alternative if they did not wish Great Britain to enjoy marked advantages over them in the French market.

As we have seen throughout this book, the resulting group of treaties was substantial in both number and effect. After Cobden-Chevalier, France signed its next treaty with Belgium, followed by the *Zollverein* in 1862; Italy in 1863; Switzerland in 1864; Hannover and Bremen, the Netherlands, Spain, and Sweden and Norway in 1865; Austria in 1866; and Portugal in 1867. Countries were forced to respond in part because, without a treaty, British and Belgian manufacturers would enjoy a large advantage in the French market (Henderson 1939/1984: 274).

Customs unions are a form of foreign cooperation that eliminates internal duties without generalizing these concessions to outsiders through MFN. As argued above, this leads to a lower home tariff, which also encourages home countries to seek to cooperate with the customs union. This implies the following corollary:

Corollary 11.2: Customs unions spread to encompass new members.

In addition to the reasoning so far, the potential to join a customs union probably also raises the rewards of cooperation. By joining, a country gains access to a larger market with zero internal tariffs. Increasing the rewards of cooperation also makes cooperation more likely.

Of course, a customs union also raises the reversion point for its members when they consider cooperating with outsiders, because countries will only form a customs union if it raises their utility. This makes them less likely to cooperate with outsiders by adding new members. In other words, trade diversion provides the accelerator for customs unions by attracting new members, whereas trade creation provides the brakes by reducing the need to cooperate with outsiders.

If outsiders cannot join a customs union, they may find solace in one another's arms. Each outsider is in the same position, with a lower reversion point. As a result:

Corollary 11.3: Customs unions induce the formation of other customs unions.

As we will see, the proliferation of customs unions in Germany accords well with this prediction.

Taken together, these hypotheses state that a country faced with a foreign customs union – or other discriminatory cooperation – will respond in three ways. First, it will liberalize its own tariff, compensating its exporters for the loss of foreign markets. Second, the lower reversion point makes it more likely that a country will cooperate with the customs union; the larger tariff area within the union also increases the rewards of cooperation. Third, the lower reversion point encourages cooperation with third parties. The first of these reactions, liberalization, should always occur. The hypotheses about cooperation are probabilistic, because a state's shadow of the future may be too low to support cooperation, no matter what happens to foreign markets (see Chapter 8).

If the home country enjoys the benefits of foreign cooperation through MFN provisions, none of these effects will occur. Protectionism and less cooperation are likely – but not inevitable, because the tariff bindings associated with any MFN treaties may preclude them.

These hypotheses can explain a wide range of observed patterns. Plateaus are likely within a network of MFN cooperation. Spread, either linear or S-shaped, occurs in a non-MFN environment. Starts and stops occur as a discriminatory network spreads to encompass its major trading partners and then stops. A new wave might begin either with changes in the shadow of the future, in the underlying economy, or in erosion of the MFN norm within the network.[1] In this way, these hypotheses comprise a richer set of propositions than the existing literature. Baldwin (1993) and Lazer (1999), for example, predict only accession to an existing network and not home liberalization or the formation of rival networks. The neofunctionalist theory of European integration likewise argues that spread depends only on the process of "spillover," and it does not consider how spread might vary by regime norm.

---

[1] For example, the Tokyo Round Codes on nontariff barriers represented a derogation of the MFN norm because only code signatories could claim their benefits (Winham 1986: 355). The Uruguay Round subsequently generalized these provisions on MFN terms to all WTO members.

By letting the form of relations between nations vary, the theory here can account for more than one pattern of observed behavior.

Testing the Argument

I now test the argument of the preceding section both quantitatively and qualitatively. The quantitative tests should show that the patterns predicted by the model exist and that these patterns are general to many different kinds of countries. Because such correlations do not prove a causal relationship, I also examine a case study. In addition to testing the hypotheses in a more detailed setting, a case study lets me determine whether policymakers exhibit motives and reasoning consistent with the logic of my theory. Taken together these two kinds of evidence should give us substantial confidence in the theory.

This section presents some simple quantitative tests of the theory. First, signing nondiscriminatory treaties should have little effect on third parties' own willingness to sign trade treaties, whereas discriminatory treaties make foreign treaties more likely. For example, if Prussia and the Netherlands have not granted each other MFN status, any treaties that Prussia signs with Saxony or Austria will discriminate against the Netherlands, making the Dutch more likely to sign treaties of their own. In this case, the number of future Prussian treaties should be positively correlated with the number of Dutch treaties. With MFN, Dutch exporters benefit from any Prussian concessions to Austria, so the Netherlands is no more likely to sign further treaties. This means that Prussian and Dutch treaty totals will be negatively correlated or unrelated.

To test this, I use the annual number of treaties in effect for each country. This is the appropriate measure because the extent of foreigners' existing cooperation induces home cooperation. Then I correlate this count with the counts for other countries before and after each dyad granted each other MFN status. I use only simple correlations, because neither my theory nor a wider literature predicts an effect for any other variables, and adding control variables without theoretical foundation can introduce omitted variable bias as easily as it reduces it (Clarke 2005). I have used only the counts for treaties with other European countries because of difficulties in finding end dates for many Latin American treaties.

The theory predicts three kinds of correlations: positive, negative, and none. The important distinction, however, is between positive and nonpositive correlations. Testing the theory requires setting some boundary between positive and nonpositive correlations inside the range of possible correlation

Table 11.1. *European trade treaties in effect before and after MFN: simple correlations*

Dyad	Date of MFN	Before MFN	After MFN
Prussia-UK	1824	1.00	−.004
Sweden-UK	1826	–	−.067
Netherlands-UK	1837	–	.131
Netherlands-Prussia	1841	.545	−.077
Portugal-UK	1842	.767	.053
France-Russia	1846	–	.633
France-UK	1860	.406	−.774
Belgium-France	1861	.099	.046
Italy-Ottomans	1861	−.117	.404
Belgium-UK	1862	.479	−.339
Netherlands-Ottomans	1862	.657	.076
Netherlands-Switzerland	1862	.442	.661
France-Italy	1863	.837	−.090
Belgium-Italy	1863	.719	−.163
Italy-UK	1863	.690	.014
Italy-Russia	1863	.748	.148
Italy-Netherlands	1863	.743	.204
Austria-UK	1864	.558	−.526
Denmark-Italy	1864	.647	.155
France-Switzerland*	1864	.814	.392
France-Netherlands	1865	.812	.673
France-Spain	1865	.668	.660
Italy-Prussia	1865	.488	−.061
Austria-France	1866	.421	.827
France-Portugal	1866	.124	.245
Austria-Belgium	1867	.701	.470
Austria-Netherlands	1867	.535	.610
Austria-Italy	1867	.581	−.144
Italy-Spain	1870	.855	.078
Austria-Spain	1870	.693	.866
Austria-Portugal	1872	.685	.273
Austria-Sweden	1873	.187	.674
Greece-Italy	1872	.712	−.021
Italy-Switzerland	1879	.824	−.161
Austria-Denmark†	1887	.400	.610
Germany-Switzerland	1891	.919	−.027
Germany-Russia	1894	.644	.794
France-Switzerland*	1895	.778	.332

* France and Switzerland had a tariff war in 1892–1895, so the 1864 row shows 1815–1892 and the last row 1892–1913.
† I have no evidence that the Austro-Danish treaty of 1887 lasted more than ten years; if it lapsed, we would again expect a positive correlation.

Table 11.2. *European trade treaties for non-MFN dyads: simple correlations*

Dyad	Correlation
Belgium-Denmark	.719
Belgium-Russia	.789
Denmark-France	.777
Denmark-Netherlands	.775
Denmark-Prussia	.955
Denmark-Sweden	.888
Germany-Norway	.860
Netherlands-Russia	.825

coefficients (−1 to +1). The choice of threshold is arbitrary. I consider any correlation of .40 or greater as the positive correlation that we should expect without MFN. With MFN, I expect no systematic relationship, which I operationalize as any "nonpositive" correlation – a negative correlation or a positive correlation less than .40.

I chose the .40 cut-off because of the way the data are distributed. In the first 26 dyads I checked, there were no correlation coefficients between .30 and .40 and only two of the 45 coefficients are between .20 and .30; in the data reported here only two correlations lie between .30 and .40. Thus, there is a natural break in the set of correlation coefficients. All these coefficients between .20 and .40 are in the "after MFN" column. I examine alternative thresholds, such as .20, as a check on the robustness of these findings.

Table 11.1 presents the results, which are strongly consistent with the theory. Thirty-one of the 35 dyads with data show the expected positive correlation before MFN, whereas 26 of the 38 dyads show a nonpositive correlation after MFN. Changing the threshold to .20 would change the results to 22 correctly predicted and 16 incorrectly predicted, which is still significantly better than chance. The theory also gets both of a dyad's coefficients correct in 22 of 35 cases. In addition, eight dyads that did not sign an MFN treaty during the entire century all behave as predicted, as shown in Table 11.2. All these are much better than one would expect by chance with a 0.5 null hypothesis, though given the asymmetric standard (.40 cut-off) perhaps a different null would be appropriate. Table 11.3 summarizes these results.

We can have further confidence in these results because the data exhibit a range of initial MFN dates. The different correlations before and after MFN do not reflect any periodization in the European treaty system, at least into the 1870s.

Table 11.3. *European spread, conditional on MFN*

	Before MFN	After MFN
Dyads correctly predicted	31	26
Dyads incorrectly predicted	4	12

Interestingly, those dyads that only began to grant each other MFN in 1887 or later do exhibit a stronger tendency for a positive correlation even after MFN. This finding suggests that a change in behavior occurs when MFN is particularly widespread, as it is at this time (recall Figure 10.1). I offer one explanation, the relationship between clustering and MFN, in Chapter 12. If states cluster their negotiations in a year or two, a pattern that I have found occurred around 1892 and 1905, then we would observe positive correlations among all cluster members. Because the change in behavior occurs after 1887, the theoretical expectation and the empirical pattern coincide.

Although the results are impressive in both columns, the results are especially strong for non-MFN treaties. The somewhat weaker performance for the post-MFN dyads probably reflects the fact that the mere presence or absence of MFN status is insufficiently informative for our theoretical purposes. Even if Britain grants both France and Portugal MFN treatment in wine duties, it might still treat their wines differently because they have different quality characteristics and alcohol content (see Marsh 1999; Weitowitz 1978). In these cases, MFN Anglo-Portuguese treaties might still lead to diversion away from French wines, making French cooperation more – not less – likely.

The results also give a wide range of estimates for the substantive importance of the spread effects. Before MFN, correlations tend to be high, with two-thirds of them greater than .60 (more than 70% fall above this threshold if we include the dyads in Table 11.2). This finding suggests that discrimination exerts strong effects indeed, with each non-MFN treaty associated with more than three-fifths of a treaty in response. In contrast, the correlation coefficients for MFN dyads are widely dispersed. The dynamics of nondiscriminatory networks, it seems, depends on more than just MFN. This would make the analysis here less useful for understanding the dynamics of an extensive nondiscriminatory system, such as the contemporary WTO.

The theory is agnostic about whether conditional MFN clauses behave like unconditional clauses. For many countries, a conditional clause is a distinction without a difference, because they import different goods from

Table 11.4. *Selected dyads with conditional MFN*

	Date of MFN		Correlations		
	Conditional	Unconditional	Before MFN	Conditional	Unconditional
Austria-UK	1838	1864	N.A.	.643	−.524
Netherlands-UK	1837	1851	N.A.	−.258	−.391
Portugal-UK	1810	1842	N.A.	.767	.053
U.S.-Denmark	1826	–	N.A.	−.190	N.A.
U.S.-France	1831	–	.830	−.070	N.A.
U.S.-Prussia	1828	–	N.A.	.410	.037
U.S.-*Zollverein**	1827	–	.751	.354	N.A.

* The U.S. signed treaties with Bremen, Hamburg, and Lübeck in 1827; given the rarity of treaties for these powers, I use the *Zollverein* total for the correlation.
The correlations for the UK dyads use only European treaties; those for the U.S. dyads, use global treaties.

different trading partners. With others, conditional MFN is effectively not MFN at all. Table 11.4 examines this question for selected dyads. It is hard to draw any firm inferences, but most of the time conditional MFN in the United Kingdom acts as if it is not MFN at all, whereas conditional MFN in the United States usually behaves like unconditional MFN. This finding suggests that other states held the United States to a standard of unconditional MFN that looked much like their interactions with others. Qualitative evidence from American interaction with Prussia/Germany (Fisk 1903) is consistent with this claim. In contrast, Britain's choice of conditional MFN apparently sent a strong signal to its partners that they would receive discriminatory treatment, and they responded accordingly.

A final kind of quantitative evidence is more impressionistic and relies on patterns at the aggregate level instead of the dyadic level. Corollary 11.2 states that customs unions spread by adding new members. Figure 11.1 shows that the spread of a customs union was the most important spread dynamic in Europe until 1870, with the *Zollverein* responsible for about half of all European treaties. It is possible, following the logic of Corollary 11.3, that this customs union also encouraged cooperation among other European states, producing some increase in non-*Zollverein* treaties as well. I provide some evidence below that this form of spread was important for Austria, the Netherlands, the United States, and perhaps other states.

The figures also suggest that the MFN clause inhibits treaty formation. Cooperation between Europe and the new countries of Latin America was important through the century, often consisting of small tariff concessions alongside broad agreements on commercial relations. Integrating these

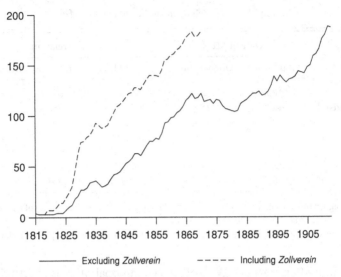

Figure 11.1. Global Trade Treaties in Effect, 1815–1913.

new countries into the transatlantic economy, a process that lies outside my theory, was therefore important – European-American treaties remain more common than non-*Zollverein* intra-European treaties into the 1870s (see Figures 11.2 and 11.3).

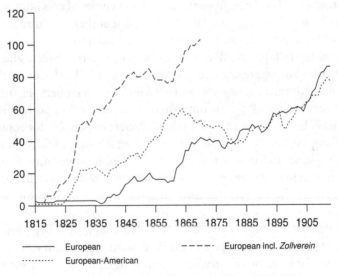

Figure 11.2. European Trade Treaties in Effect, 1815–1913.

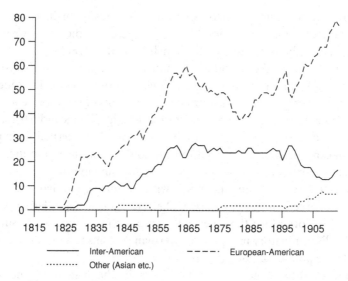

Figure 11.3. Non-European Trade Treaties in Effect, 1815–1913.

Despite this activity across the Atlantic, treaties between countries in the Western Hemisphere remained at a low but steady level. The standard explanation is that trade between American countries was itself small, with most countries oriented toward European export. Revenue considerations may also be a factor, because many Latin American countries faced exogenous revenue constraints (see Chapter 4). Though both of these may be factors, many dyads cooperated despite revenue constraints and despite having export orientations elsewhere (examples from the 1830s include Argentina-Chile, Colombia-Ecuador, Ecuador-México, México-Perú, and Venezuela-United States). Hypothesis 11.2 would explain the American pattern by pointing to the MFN clause common among treaties in the hemisphere. Latin American cooperation did not spread because Latin American treaties included the MFN clause (see also Table 12.4). Because either explanation is consistent with the evidence, clearly more work needs to be done to learn which of these causes better explains the variation.

The *Zollverein* and the Spread of Trade Treaties

The correlations in the preceding section certainly establish the empirical plausibility of my claims. This section examines the spread of cooperation in Germany more closely to confirm the causal logic at work. I chose Germany in part because it exhibits abundant variation in the independent variable of cooperation (multiple customs unions), but mostly for its substantive importance. Germany provides the major impetus for the century's treaty network, including even the Anglo-French wave of the 1860s.

I concentrate on the hypotheses concerning customs unions (Corollaries 11.1–11.3), in which rival explanations of cooperation exist. Modern political economy explains customs unions in terms of imperfect competition – industries subject to economies of scale, oligopolistic industries, and businesses characterized by learning-by-doing or other externalities in production can gain most from a customs union. A customs union increases the market for such firms, while still providing an environment that can be protected from foreign oligopolies, with advantages familiar to the new international economics (Abrego et al. 2004; Krugman 1986; Olarreaga et al. 1999). If important for the nineteenth century, these issues would suggest that the discriminatory norms of the German customs union were endogenous to the politics of trade negotiations.

None of these concerns can be found in the history of the *Zollverein* (Dumke 1978; Hahn 1982: Chapter 1; Henderson 1984; Price 1949; Vomáčková 1963), except that Friedrich List's (1844/1966) arguments for infant industry protection may anticipate learning-by-doing effects. Instead, administrative problems and then political concerns dominated Prussian policy. After the Napoleonic Wars, Prussia faced two important administrative problems. First, Prussia was divided into two parts: the historic kingdom of Brandenberg-Prussia and regions bordering this kingdom in the East, and newer western provinces, mostly along the Rhine. As a matter of state-building, Prussia wanted to encourage transit through the smaller German states that lay between West and East Prussia (Láng 1906: 132–33).

Second, all Germany was a patchwork of disconnected states, provinces, and towns, many of which were surrounded by foreign territory. These enclaves and mini-territories forced traders to submit to a profusion of border controls and to pay multiple duties even over short distances. Their existence encouraged merchants to use routes with fewer boundaries and lower duties. All these obstacles were more salient to traders after 1815, because Napoléon Bonaparte's Continental System had largely abolished them (E. Heckscher 1922), but the Restoration states had mostly reimposed tariffs (Crouzet 1964).

Prussia could address these problems by consolidating and lowering tariffs, as it did in 1818. This legislation set different tariffs for the two halves of the kingdom, which were slightly higher in the East, until a single tariff was introduced in 1821. It also eliminated almost all nontariff restrictions and could be called the most liberal tariff in Europe. Reformers also had to address the enclaves. Eight enclaves in the East, with a population of 166,000, could serve as a center for smuggling or as a source of revenue through transit duties, and each required border controls.

Prussia decided to treat the enclaves as part of its own customs territory, thereby reducing the length of the Prussian frontier and saving administrative costs. Doing so effectively imposed its consumption taxes on the citizens of other states, which Prussia probably did not have the legal right to do. Of course, Prussia could relabel its customs duties "transit duties" for goods destined to the enclaves, adding administrative complexity at the border in exchange for the simplification of eliminating the enclave boundaries. Alternatively, it could consolidate its tariff system and offer to share the revenue with the enclaves. The Prince of Schwarzburg-Sondershausen formally consented to this latter proposal in 1819, entering the Prussian customs system in exchange for a share of the revenue proportional to the population. Prussian discrimination against outsiders was thus born of exogenous administrative problems and was not endogenous to political economy problems (cf. Chapter 10).

The reasons for states' decisions to join the *Zollverein* vary. Many found the administrative consolidation helpful and welcomed a steady source of revenue. Reactionary states also welcomed it, because they could then avoid going to their legislatures for revenue (Dumke 1978). Others resisted these developments for political reasons. For example, the South German states had opposed German economic union at the Congress of Vienna in 1814/1815. They had just regained their sovereignty from Bonaparte, and most had gained substantial territory. They were little disposed to give up their own tariff levels in favor of a greater middle European economic order.

The Anhalt duchies of Bernburg, Dessau, and Köthen also protested the Prussian tariff instead of joining the customs union. Prussia leveled duties at the Anhalt frontier in 1822 anyway, forcing all three to accede to its customs system by 1828. This expansion of the Prussian customs area alarmed many other states in Germany, enclaves or not: "it became ever more clear that the Prussian tariff system had a great effect not only on the Prussian economy but on the Germany economy as a whole"[2] (Hartung 1923: 452). Bavaria, Württemberg, Hesse-Darmstadt, Hesse-Kassel, Nassau, and Austria, among others, reassessed their trade policy in response to Prussian actions (Hahn 1982; J. Schmidt 1973; Vomáčková 1963). The theory predicts three possible

---

[2] "... erwies es sich aber auf der andern Seite immer mehr, daß das preußische Zollsystem großen Einfluß auf das gesamte nicht nur preußische, sondern deutsche Wirtschaftsleben ausübte."

reactions: these states could lower their own tariffs (Corollary 11.1), cooperate with Prussia by acceding to its customs system (Corollary 11.2), or
cooperate with other states outside the Prussian network (Corollary 11.3).

Many states acceded. Though alarmed by Prussia's offensive against the
Anhalt duchies, the King of Württemberg admitted that "sooner or later we
shall be forced to follow this example" (cited in Henderson 1939/1984: 53).
The small states of Hesse felt similar pressure, because even the low tariff
of 1818 was higher than the free trade they had enjoyed in the Continental
System. The Grand Duchy of Hesse joined in 1828, Baden in 1835, Waldeck
in 1838, and many others along the way.

As the theory predicts, others tried to form rival customs unions. In 1822,
13 smaller states (Hannover, Saxony, Hesse-Kassel, Brunswick, Oldenburg,
Frankfurt, Bremen, Saxony-Meiningen, Hesse-Homburg, Schwarzburg-
Rudolstadt, Schwarzburg-Sondershausen, Reuß-Greitz, and Reuß-Schleitz)
signed the Treaty of Arnstadt to establish a Thuringian customs union.
This customs union was an entirely defensive response to the *Zollverein*
(Hartung 1923: 452–54; Henderson 1939/1984: 64–69). It never became
effective, however, because its members could not develop a common tariff.

Many of these states formed a new body, the Middle German Customs
Union, in 1828. Specifically, Saxony, Hannover, Electoral Hesse, Weimar,
Altenburg, Koburg, Nassau, Schwarzburg-Rudolstadt, and Frankfurt were
all founding members; later accessions were Meiningen, Brunswick,
Schwarzburg-Sondershausen, both Reuss principalities, Bremen, Oldenburg, and Hesse-Homburg. Prussia began almost immediately to attract
its members away. Saxony-Meiningen and Saxony-Coburg-Gotha came to
an agreement with Prussia in 1829 by which they would build roads with
Prussian subsidies; the Reuß Principalities followed suit.[3] The 1829 Kassel
treaty was intended to extend the Middle German Customs Union to 1840,
but many states ratified it only with reservations or not at all. Its members
had joined the *Zollverein* by 1833.

South Germany also developed its own customs union. Hohenzollern-
Hechingen and Hohenzollern-Sigmaringen acceded to the Württemberg
customs system in 1824, much as other states were acceding to the Prussian.
Württemberg and its partners then formed the South German Customs
Union with Bavaria in 1828. This union also sought to cooperate with
Prussia, signing a treaty in 1829 and joining the *Zollverein* in 1833.

---

[3] This is an interesting counterpart to my analyses of transportation costs in Chapter 3.
That chapter argued that transportation costs work like tariffs; here, reciprocal lowering of
transportation costs substitutes for reciprocal tariff reductions. Foreign aid today plays a
similar role by building transportation infrastructure for developing countries that refuse
to lower their tariffs.

The last rival union to form was the longest-lived. Hannover and Brunswick formed the *Steuerverein* (Tax Union) in 1834, joined by Oldenburg in 1836 and Schaumburg-Lippe in 1838. It lasted until 1854, when its members joined the *Zollverein*.

The historiography clearly identifies these rival unions as responses to the *Zollverein*. Each German state was threatened by the loss of markets as the *Zollverein* expanded. They could respond by liberalizing – or by engaging in programs of road and water transport improvement, which had similar effects (see Chapter 3). They might join the *Zollverein*, or they could form rival unions. No one, it seems, stood still.

Reactions of Austria to the *Zollverein*

Among the major powers, Austria was the most concerned about the growth of the *Zollverein*. The conventional wisdom attributes this concern to Austria's rivalry with Prussia for leadership of Germany, a struggle it ultimately lost in the war of 1866 (see also Chapter 9). Because of its high tariffs, the story goes, Austria was unable to build a rival customs union and therefore saw its political ties to Germany weaken (Ashley 1926; Beer 1891; Henderson 1939/1984; Láng 1906: 168–70; Price 1949).

Without denying the political overtones of Austria's reaction, this section highlights three features of Austrian economic policy that are consistent with the predictions of the model. First, Prussia's growing customs union put pressure on Austria to liberalize its high tariffs (Corollary 11.1). The Austrian bureaucracy favored such a move, though political opposition from Bohemian and Lower Austrian industry allowed only minor measures until after the revolution of 1848. Second, the customs union encouraged Austria to cooperate with it (Corollary 11.2). The most important of such acts were Austrian treaties with Prussia in 1847 and 1853. Third, the growth of the *Zollverein* induced Austria to cooperate with other outsiders (Corollary 11.3). In addition to treaties of commerce and navigation with Russia and the Netherlands, and treaties covering navigation on the Rhine and the Danube, Austria signed tariff treaties with Belgium, Britain, Greece, the Ottoman Empire, Russia, Sardinia, and the Two Sicilies.

These trade treaties came against the background of a strongly mercantilist system, with prohibitions on the import of goods competing with domestic manufactures. It was also a highly fragmented system. Because the Habsburg Empire had grown as a patchwork of political units, it also retained a bewildering array of different tariff units (two of which, Jungholz and Mittelberg, joined the *Zollverein*). As Chapter 9 discussed, the most important division was the customs barrier (*Zwischenzolllinie*) between Austria and

Hungary. Chapters 4, 8, and 9 have showed that this tariff provided an exogenous revenue constraint that affected both the autonomous tariff and Austrian trade cooperation.

Austria initially responded to extension of the Prussian customs area by trying to discourage additional members from joining. At the same time, the government liberalized its own tariff. First, it made some reductions in export duties in 1824 and 1829 (Láng 1906: 174–78). During talks with Britain that eventually led to a navigation treaty, Austria went further, with a new tariff in 1836 that replaced prohibitions with duties on several articles (Williams 1972). It also revised some duties downward.

Before the Revolution of 1848–1849, Austria's most important response to the *Zollverein* emerged out of discussions in the court in 1840–1842 (Beer 1891: Chapter 2; Láng 1906: 178–81; Vomáčková 1963: 119–21). Karl Friedrich, Freiherr von Kübeck von Kübau, president of the Exchequer (*Hofkammer*) in Vienna, believed that the *Zollverein*'s continued success showed that the Austrian system of prohibitions could not be maintained. The *Zollverein*'s lower tariff had raised revenue and encouraged industrial development, whereas high tariffs and export prohibitions in Austria led merely to an increase in smuggling. He found written support from at least two other members of the *Hofkammer*, who also favored better relations with the *Zollverein*, domestic industrial development, repeal of the *Zwischenzolllinie*, and the conclusion of trade treaties. Vice President Ritter von Breyer was eventually to go farther still and advocate joining the *Zollverein* outright.[4]

Kübeck then wrote a long memorandum to Prince Klemens von Metternich recommending major changes in trade policy. His reasoning and his recommendations are consistent with Hypothesis 11.2 and its corollaries. Kübeck argued that the *Zollverein* made Austrian exports more difficult and that Austria's existing prohibitive system encouraged smuggling. He recommended replacing the prohibitive system with protective tariffs and repealing the *Zwischenzolllinie*. While joining the *Zollverein* would be too dangerous for domestic industry, a treaty with the *Zollverein* was consistent with a protective system. We recognize these beliefs from Chapter 9 as protectionist reciprocity. Austria should also look toward cooperation with

[4] One can imagine Austria joining the *Zollverein* without Hungary in the 1840s, without this divide being anomalous for a nineteenth century political organization. Even after German unification in 1871, the empire did not coincide with its own customs area. Luxemburg was part of the customs union but not of the empire, as were the Austrian districts of Jungholz in Tirol and Mittelberg in Vorarlberg. Hamburg and Bremen were inside the empire, but outside the customs union (Henderson 1939/1984: 319–29).

third parties, he argued. Stronger trade ties with Italy would give Austrian industry an additional export market, although Kübeck believed that the future of Austrian trade lay in the Orient and transatlantic markets. Treaties in the Orient would also support Austria's foreign policy, which sought to loosen the ties between the Sublime Porte and its vassals in southeastern Europe (Antonescu 1915).

Kübeck obtained initial approval for this policy, thanks no doubt to Metternich's support. Metternich feared that German economic union could isolate Austria politically, and he favored lower autonomous tariffs and closer ties to the *Zollverein* as countermeasures. After Kübeck's proposal passed, administrative work began, much of it in secret to avoid stirring up immediate opposition. A fact-finding commission found that Austrian industry had reached a sufficiently high level to compete with the Germans in all but a few branches.

When invited to Vienna, most regional governments discussed only the particular interests of their area. However, Graf Karl von Chotek of Bohemia – whose granddaughter would be assassinated in Sarajevo in 1914 – argued for much slower implementation of reform. He had support from Bohemian industry, which lobbied the government before the final reading of the reform bill in May 1843. This opposition effectively killed reform (Vomáčková 1963: 119–21). Though Kübeck continued to have Metternich's support, the conference of state (*Staatskonferenz*) decided that his recommendations could not be carried out for the time being. It did recommend minor relaxation in the prohibitive system.

Most of Kübeck's other reforms also reached a standstill. Efforts to repress smuggling failed. They would require agreements with neighboring states, but Prussia and Saxony would not negotiate until Austria's prohibitive system had been reformed. Tariff union with Hungary proved impossible as the aristocracy would not consent to the domestic tax reform necessary to replace revenue from the *Zwischenzolllinie*. Cooperation with third parties, on the other hand, was a success. Austria moved toward developing its transatlantic, Italian, and oriental markets through treaties of commerce, navigation, and trade (see Table 11.5). These were exactly the regions that Kübeck had identified as compensation to Austrian exporters for loss of *Zollverein* markets.

Further moves in trade policy had to await the domestic political changes that followed the Revolution of 1848–1849. More prohibitions were changed to tariffs, and other tariffs were lowered in 1851 and 1853 (Komlos 1983: Chapter 1). The tariff revisions of 1853 also converted tariffs based on Viennese weights to the *Zollverein* weights. The reforms significantly lowered

Table 11.5. *Austrian treaties, 1838–1859*

Date	Party	Type
1838	Ottoman Empire	Treaty of commerce
1838	Britain	Treaty
1840	Russia	Danubian trade and shipping convention
1841	Belgium	Treaty of commerce
1842	México	Treaty of friendship, commerce, and navigation
1844	Two Sicilies	Trade treaty
1844	Russia	Treaty of commerce and navigation
1846	Russia	Additional convention on commerce and navigation
1847	Ottoman Empire	Tariff agreement
1847	Prussia	Trade agreement
1848	Modena	Customs convention
1849	Parma	Accession to Austria-Modena treaty
1851	Sardinia	Treaty renewal
1851	Two Sicilies	Additional convention to 1844 treaty
1852	Liechtenstein	Customs union
1852	Modena and Parma	Customs treaty
1853	Prussia	Commerce and customs convention
1854	Belgium	Treaty of commerce and navigation
1855	Netherlands	Treaty of commerce and navigation
1856	Greece	Additional articles to 1835 treaty
1857	Modena	Customs union

duties on cotton yarn, pig iron, and a range of industrial raw materials, but raised the tariff on linen and woolen yarn.

Important acts of cooperation also came after the revolution. The first was repeal of the *Zwischenzolllinie* in 1850. As Chapter 9 argued, we should consider this repeal as a form of trade cooperation with a non-German party. Austria also formed customs unions with three non-German states – Parma (1848), Modena (1849), and Liechtenstein (1852) – among others (see Table 11.5). All these moves are consistent with the theory's Corollary 11.3.

In the following year, Austria had its last major adventure with the *Zollverein* before the war of 1866 (Henderson 1939/1984: 213–28). Prussia and Hannover had signed a treaty unifying the *Zollverein* and the Tax Union, but neither consulted the other parties to these treaties first. Because both customs unions were due to expire in 1853, Prussia and Hanover simply made acceptance of the 1851 treaty a condition of renewal (see Chapter 9). Schaumburg-Lippe and Oldenburg acceded easily in the Tax Union, but Prussia faced more opposition in the *Zollverein* (see Chapter 9). Prussia had agreed to reduce the *Zollverein* tariffs on many transport goods, such as coffee, tea, tobacco, syrup, cognac, and wines. This action effectively created a wall against Austrian accession, because Austria was unlikely to reduce its duties to these lower levels.

After announcing a new tariff of 1851, Austria invited all German states to a conference to discuss a commercial treaty or rival customs union. The smaller states avoided the Vienna conference, but the larger states, including Hannover, did not. These efforts looked promising at first. During separate discussions in Darmstadt, the Middle German states refused to renew the *Zollverein* if Prussia refused to negotiate with Austria.

The Prussian king then sent an obscure young diplomat, Otto von Bismarck, to Vienna. After Bismarck failed to reach agreement with the Austrians, perhaps intentionally, Russia put political pressure on Austria and Prussia to resolve their political differences. Russia wanted the legitimate monarchies to present a united front against Louis Napoléon, who had just carried out his coup of December 1851.

Austria and Prussia eventually reached a treaty in February 1853 (Henderson 1984: 213–28; Huertas 1977: Chapter 2). Austria gave up most import prohibitions and lowered its duties on certain raw materials and semi-manufactured goods. Its total reductions in duty were about 25% *ad valorem*, though a requirement that the new duties be paid in silver and not paper currency reduced the effect of this liberalization. The treaty gave Austria preferential access to the *Zollverein*. By blocking Austria's attempts to detach the South German states from the *Zollverein*, Prussia secured adhesion of the Tax Union and made it virtually certain that the *Zollverein* treaties would be renewed (see Chapter 9).

In short, Austria responded to the *Zollverein* much as the theory would expect and for much the same reasons. Liberalization, cooperation with Prussia, and cooperation with third parties all resulted from the *Zollverein*. Austria continued to feel pressed into the trade regime from the 1860s. As Austrian Deputy Minister of Finance Carl Freiherr von Hock put it (cited in Howe 1997: 102),

Austria for the most serious political, fiscal and economic reasons, cannot isolate herself from the general movement towards Free Trade, which has spread from the West of Europe right up to her own borders, without inviting the enmity of those States, without suffering grievous losses of customs revenue, without harming her trade, and without surrendering her industry to the monopoly power of a few.

Though reluctant, Austria did join the treaty network as it deepened and widened, raising the costs to Austria of staying outside. This reluctant cooperation provides an illustration of how a wave of cooperation works, beginning with the most willing and then spreading to those who had been unwilling to cooperate at first.

My findings here represent not only an exercise in hypothesis testing but also a reinterpretation of Austrian trade policy from the 1830s to the 1850s. Not merely reflecting a power struggle in Germany, Austrian policy follows naturally from a theory of political economy. My analysis highlights a change in the direction of Austrian policy in the 1840s and 1850s, well before the conventional dating of the 1860s. It also brings out Austria's modest role in the spread of the German trading network and connects Austria's extra-German customs unions to German affairs.

Reactions of Outsiders to the *Zollverein*

Austria was not the only outsider to respond to the *Zollverein*. In this section, I trace the major responses that took the form of trade cooperation. Figure 11.2 shows a modest upswing in European cooperation in the 1840s, which I attribute in large part to a response to the *Zollverein*. European-American treaties also took off at this time, as shown in Figure 11.3. Some autonomous liberalization could probably also be judged a reaction to the *Zollverein*, but a lack of data makes this claim difficult to test. In any case, both liberalization (Corollary 11.1) and cooperation (Corollary 11.3) are consistent with the theory.

Britain and France each had close trade relationships with particular German states. Hamburg, Hannover, and Bremen were pro-British because they served as Germany's entrepôts for the Atlantic trade; Hannover and England also had dynastic ties. Each feared that the growth of the *Zollverein* would create barriers to their import and export trades, and they preferred free trade with the outside world. Britain offered modest support by signing a navigation treaty with Hannover in 1844.

Britain feared that internal free trade in Germany might lead to higher tariffs against British coal, iron, and textiles. This is exactly the reaction that I would expect based on the analysis in this chapter, and this implicit increase in the effective tariff facing England demanded a response. Its first reaction was a quiet effort to keep German states out of the *Zollverein* (Kennedy 1980: 43). When this failed, Britain turned to Prussia. They signed a minor treaty in 1841 and a more important one in 1862. In this way, the *Zollverein* network spread to include the United Kingdom among its nonmember trading partners.

France disapproved of the *Zollverein* on both economic and political grounds. It responded by signing treaties with a few German states with which it had particular relations. France and Nassau signed a treaty in 1833. This treaty lowered the French tariff on mineral water, whereas Nassau bound its duties on wines and silks for five years. Although it had originally sought external support against the Prussians, Nassau soon denounced this treaty to join the *Zollverein*. France also signed a treaty with Mecklenberg in 1836. As the German customs union grew, French relations with the *Zollverein* became strained. After the failed negotiations of 1839, France imposed some very high duties on German goods, and the *Zollverein* retaliated in 1843 with duties on gloves, brandy, and other items.

The Netherlands also bordered Germany and served as the major port for many German states. A German customs union could encourage interior states to use other routes to the outside world, either overland or through the Hansa ports. Faced with this threat to its livelihood, the Netherlands sought to cooperate with the Germans. An 1837 treaty of navigation between Prussia and the Netherlands provided for reciprocal national treatment for all shipping on rivers and the seas, as well as national treatment of goods regardless of the country of origin. A treaty of commerce in 1839 extended this to include reciprocal MFN, with specified tariff reductions.

As in Austria and Britain, the major response came in the early 1840s when the Netherlands sought to cooperate with third parties. Most of these treaties were intimately linked to shipping concerns, with reciprocal lowering of duties secondary to their purpose. An exchange of notes between Luxemburg and the Netherlands in late 1840 fixed and lowered duties between them until 1842, unless Luxemburg were to enter the *Zollverein* before then. The Netherlands signed a treaty of commerce and navigation with France in 1840, which accorded reciprocal MFN treatment in all trade restrictions and navigation regulations and specified certain duty reductions. Despite a history of political antagonism stemming from their days as the United Provinces, Belgium and the Netherlands also signed a similar treaty in 1846, providing reciprocal national treatment of navigational affairs and reducing selected tariffs.

Like Britain, the United States had a substantial trade through the Hansa cities. Among the countries of the Western Hemisphere, United States was unusual in signing treaties with many *Zollverein* members. As a result, I can test to see if spread of the *Zollverein* made it more likely that the United States would sign these treaties, consistent with Hypothesis 11.2. Using the same method as in the quantitative section above, I find a correlation of .945 between U.S. treaties with *Zollverein* members and the sum of all non-U.S. *Zollverein* treaties. Consistent with the theory, the sum of non-U.S. *Zollverein* treaties was also associated with increases in U.S. treaties with third parties, with a correlation of .747. This is consistent with Corollary 11.3, which states that customs unions induce outsiders to cooperate with one another. With or without the *Zollverein*, the antebellum United States was one of the most active cooperators in the world, with 22 treaties in effect in 1856. About a third of these were signed with German states. The *Zollverein*'s treaties had a similarly high correlation (0.5818) with the number of Mexican treaties (see also Table 12.4). The *Zollverein*'s effect even in the New World, this suggests, was far from negligible.

In this way, the *Zollverein* may have been a catalyst for the entire nineteenth-century trade regime. Though its motives were only partly economic, it created facts on the ground that induced third parties to sign treaties both with Prussia and with each other. Though it had the greatest impact on Austria, its effects can also be seen in the Americas.

National Unifications and the Spread of Cooperation

Another important impetus for the trade network was the unifications of Germany and Italy over the years from 1848 to 1870. Consistent with Hypothesis 8.2 (foreign tariffs and cooperation), this provided an incentive for cooperation, especially in Germany. The traditional customs union of the *Zollverein* morphed into a national state after the wars of 1866 and 1870. This unification effectively implied discrimination against outsiders, though in most cases the *Zollverein* had already introduced such discrimination.

Italian unification had similar effects. First it extended the Piedmont tariff to the rest of Italy and created free trade within the country. We may think of these actions as having created a customs union in Italy. This new tariff area raised the effective protection that outsiders faced in Piedmont and Sardinia. Foreigners who exported goods to these territories now faced tariff-free competition from the rest of Italy. Because the Piedmontese tariff was lower than most other Italian tariffs, it is not clear whether foreigners faced a higher or lower tariff with, say, Tuscany than they had previously. Countries that had special trading relationships with Italian states, as Austria did with Parma and Modena, doubtless faced higher effective tariffs in those territories after unification.

Because these new nations were also customs unions, Corollary 11.2 suggests that they should make cooperation more likely for foreigners. Figure 11.4 shows global treaty initiation both before and after this period. Clearly 1848–1870 represents one of the active periods of the global treaty system. The figure cannot show this, but many of the later treaties, especially around 1877–1881, were renegotiations and renewals of the treaties in this unification period.

Of course, other events also characterize these years. It is difficult to determine whether the German and Italian unifications were more decisive

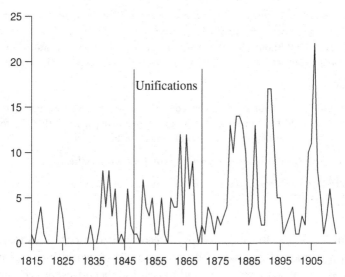

Figure 11.4. National Unifications and Treaty Initiation.

than the Cobden-Chevalier treaty, though the importance of German cooperation before 1860 suggests that Cobden-Chevalier cannot be the whole
story. The 1830s, in particular, represent an imporant early wave of treaty
initiation, one clearly associated with German events. Moreover, French
motives in the 1860 negotiations included political concerns about British
and French interests in Italy (Iliasu 1971), so we should probably see this as
an additional force for economic cooperation in these years. Whatever the
relative weight of causes, the national unifications of Germany and Italy are
certainly associated with an upswing of cooperation.

Conclusions

This chapter has examined the substantively important question of how
international cooperation may or may not spread. Its hypotheses state that
a country faced with a foreign customs union will respond by liberalizing
its own tariff, cooperating with the customs union, and cooperating with
third parties. If the home country enjoys the benefits of foreign cooperation
through MFN provisions, none of these effects will occur. In theoretical
terms, these claims show how past cooperation conditions present and future
cooperation, mediated by variation in norms.

Table 11.6 summarizes these hypotheses. Taken as a whole, they yield
the ironic conclusion that economic discrimination is a major force in
the spread of trade cooperation. Again, this does not imply that economic

Table 11.6. *Summary of propositions concerning the spread of cooperation*

Hypothesis 11.1: Without MFN, foreign cooperation leads to home liberalization; with MFN, foreign cooperation leads to home protection or no change in tariffs.

Corollary 11.1: Customs unions lead to foreign liberalization.

Hypothesis 11.2: Without MFN, foreign cooperation makes home cooperation more likely, both with the two initial cooperators and with fourth parties; with MFN, foreign cooperation may make home cooperation less likely or have no effect.

Corollary 11.2: Customs unions spread to encompass new members.

Corollary 11.3: Customs unions induce the formation of other customs unions.

---

discrimination is a first-best solution – economic theory tells us that unilateral free trade is optimal – but in a second-best world in which other states, as well as one's own, respond to political incentives, discrimination has some positive effects on trade cooperation and thus on liberalization.

Both quantitative and qualitative evidence from this period confirm this argument. Simple correlations between the levels of cooperation exhibited by European states demonstrate the claim that, when two states have an MFN treaty in effect between them, cooperation with third parties does not spread from one partner to the next. Without an MFN treaty, in contrast, one state's increase in cooperation will induce the other state to follow suit. Evidence on global trade treaties also suggests that the MFN clause common to Western Hemisphere treaties inhibited spread of the trade treaty regime within the New World.

I established the causal link with a case study of cooperation in Germany. Although most scholars trace the nineteenth-century trade regime to those treaties signed in the wake of the 1860 Cobden-Chevalier treaty, I show that the *Zollverein* and Austro-German cooperation served as ground zero for the regime. The *Zollverein* was responsible for more than half of Europe's trade treaties until the 1850s, and it helped spark a European upswing in the 1840s and perhaps also an American increase in the 1850s. Understanding this process is essential, for this expansion of trade cooperation obviously precedes the Cobden-Chevalier treaty of 1860.

This German cooperation is also important counterfactually. With the reduction in transportation costs in the 1820s and 1830s, we would have expected an upswing in protection as states sought to insulate their import-competing sectors from cheaper imports (Hypothesis 3.6, transportation costs). Yet, German cooperation, with motives both political and administrative, worked to counteract this upswing. Inside the *Zollverein*, it lowered tariffs. Outside, by raising tariffs, it created an incentive for other countries to cooperate. As a result, the 1830s looked very different politically than the 1870s.

Another impetus for the second wave of cooperation was the national unifications of Germany and Italy that occurred from 1848 to 1870. This predates the conventional dating of the mid-century wave of cooperation, suggesting that spread effects were important in addition to whatever domestic political changes in France spurred activity in the 1860s.

My analysis generally follows the historiography on the *Zollverein*, but represents a reinterpretation of Austrian foreign economic policy in the 1840s and 1850s. I have also discussed the reactions of other countries to German cooperation, from the Netherlands to the Americas, but these remain more speculative. I have not discussed trade policy in European colonies, which generally lacked tariff autonomy. Some colonial networks were similar to free-trade areas or customs unions, as was France's; Britain's began as a PTA, but moved to nondiscrimination. Changes in French trade policy therefore demanded a response, whereas changes in Britain's policy did not. For example, a move away from free trade in French West Africa in the late 1870s closed off those markets to foreigners and encouraged them to respond with closer ties of their own. However, a full discussion of colonialism would require a separate project, and I do not enter further into the topic.

Finally, the analysis here has implications for the modern trading system. It shows how regional cooperation in one area can produce regionalism elsewhere (cf. Mansfield and Milner 1997). Corollary 11.3 suggests that it is causally meaningful to talk of the spread of regionalism, as cooperation in one area encourages similar cooperation in other regions. Even so, these regional networks should not be seen as rivals, because the theory here shows that regionalism also encourages each network to cooperate with one another.

TWELVE

Clustering Negotiations in Time

Chapter 11 examined the spatial configuration of trade cooperation through the process of spread. In this chapter, I show that the MFN norm also shapes the organization of the treaty network in time as well as in space: when each pair of countries negotiates over different tariff lines, negotiations will be randomly distributed over time: but when each pair negotiates over the same lines, that is, when bound by (effective) MFN, these negotiations will "cluster" in time. Interestingly, states did not agree to centralize their trade bargaining, yet negotiations nonetheless occurred simultaneously. This centralized bargaining, or "clustering," provides the central topic of investigation for this chapter.

Clustering may characterize an individual country's trade negotiations, as a country signs a flurry of treaties at once. Examples of such clusters for México, the Ottoman Empire, and Russia are shown in Tables 12.2, 12.4, and 12.5. For reasons developed here, these country-level clusters create incentives for other countries to cluster at the same time, that is, clustering spreads to a country's trading partners. The result is a multicountry cluster, which attracts most of our attention here. The causal processes behind these mega-clusters help explain why trade cooperation often comes in waves.

Clustering among groups of countries can be found as early as 1863–1866, but became a central feature of the network in 1881–1884, 1890–1891, and 1904–1906. From a theory-testing standpoint, clustering makes life difficult by cramming treaties into a few years. Smoothly changing economic and political data series may not be statistically related to treaty initiation if a clustered year such as 1905 is surrounded by zero-initiation years. These issues may help explain the weak results in parts of Chapter 8 for many countries with short data series concentrated in the last quarter of our period. In contrast, the results were stronger for Britain and France with their long treaty series, which predates the confounding effects of clustering.

Because of MFN, nonclustered bilateral negotiations can have some undesirable distributional effects. After a state makes politically costly concessions in its negotiations with one country, MFN may force it to make still more concessions on the same issue with another country. Clustering avoids this problem by packaging concessions with many states simultaneously. As a result, clustering occurs when countries grant each other MFN status and negotiate with several countries over the same tariff lines.

Clustering also has substantively important effects. Most important, it is associated with smaller concessions than nonclustered negotiations. Clustering also provides the basic rhythm of the trade network in the last 25 years of our period, a pattern continued in WTO rounds. Today, as a hundred years ago, trade negotiations are clustered in rounds and not scattered evenly through time.

Clustering

The temporal organization of cooperation has not been a topic of research, so it requires some attention to definitions. I define clustering as a state's simultaneous negotiations with two or more countries on the same issue. Because the negotiations address the same issue, each bilateral negotiation will be linked implicitly or explicitly to the other negotiations. Like the definition of nominal multilateralism (see Keohane 1990; Pahre 1994; Ruggie 1993a, b), this definition only requires three states.

Empirically, we can see clusters by looking at the treaties signed by a single state. Figure 12.1 provides an example. It graphs the number of non-*Zollverein* treaties that Prussia/Germany signed in each year from 1815 to 1913.[1] Before the 1890s, Prussian treaties are infrequent and scattered in time, with no more than one treaty reached in any year except 1865. The spikes in later years reflect a flurry of treaties in 1890–1891 and 1904–1906, whereas tariff treaties remained uncommon between these years. The secondary literature identifies these two clusterings with Chancellors Caprivi and Bülow, respectively (Barkin 1970; Marsh 1999: Chapter 8; Weitowitz 1978; Werner 1989).

In contrast to Germany, Belgium and the United Kingdom did not cluster their treaties. Figure 12.2 shows that each country negotiated only one or

---

[1] The figure distinguishes MFN treaties from non-MFN treaties for reasons I explain below. Although it excludes *Zollverein* treaties between, say, Prussia and Bavaria, it does include Prussia's treaties with outside states that had territories within the German Confederation, such as Austria, Denmark (Holsten), Luxemburg/Netherlands, and for a time the United Kingdom (Hannover).

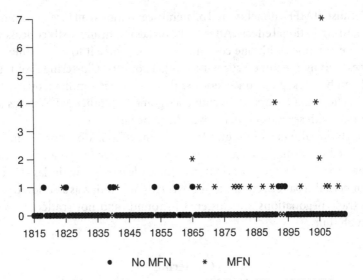

Figure 12.1. Prussian/German Treaty Signings by Year, 1815–1913.

two treaties a year over the course of the century. Both the treaties and the gaps between them appear to be randomly distributed, not clustered. With very few exceptions, such as Britain's simultaneous negotiations with France and Spain in the 1870s, the secondary literature confirms this picture

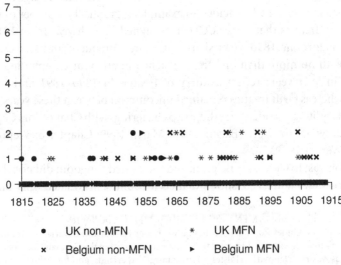

Figure 12.2. Belgian and British Treaty Signings by Year, 1815–1913.

(see Marsh 1999 for Britain; see Augier 1906, Mahaim 1892, and Marsh 1999 for the scattered treatment of Belgium).

We may also see several countries cluster simultaneously, creating a mega-cluster or wave (see Table 12.4). In contrast, some years exhibit a seemingly random collection of treaties, as was true of the treaties of 1888 shown in Table 6.1.

Although such visual inspections help identify clustering, apparent clustering may reflect random processes when a country occasionally negotiates several simultaneous agreements simply by chance. As explained below, I rule out random processes by testing whether a country's annual treaty initiations are Poisson-distributed. A case study of the Caprivi cluster at the end of this chapter provides evidence that these clusters linked treaty negotiations both causally and intentionally.

Distribution and MFN

Like much of the literature on international cooperation, Part III gave primary attention to the monitoring and enforcement of bargains. Yet, distributional concerns are also highly salient in bargaining. Negotiators will always disagree about how to divide the joint gains from agreement. Each negotiator faces the same problem in that foreign concessions benefit exporters, but come at the price of concessions that harm one's own import-competers (see Chapter 7). MFN exacerbates this strategic situation. Any concessions negotiated between two countries will be generalized to all other countries granted MFN treatment. As a result, a tariff reduction granted as a concession to one state today becomes a new, lower starting point for negotiations with another state tomorrow.

States anticipate these consequences. In the 1860s, Prussia wanted to negotiate a treaty with France before it negotiated with the United Kingdom. It feared that concessions to the United Kingdom would put it in a weak position against France because France would have already received Britain's concessions through MFN. Concessions to France, in contrast, would not harm any future negotiations with the United Kingdom (see Davis 1997: Chapter 7; Henderson 1939/1984). Negotiating the French and British treaties at the same time would also avoid giving away too much to the United Kingdom before turning to France.

The renewal and renegotiation of these treaties in the late 1870s supply a further illustration. France had timed all its tariff treaties to expire in 1877, though they could be extended from year to year (M. S. Smith 1980: 182–95). The government temporarily extended these treaties several times while negotiating with the other countries of Europe. Negotiations with Britain, France's chief trading partner, received priority. Commerce Minister Pierre Tirard, a free trader in the otherwise protectionist ministry of 1881, offered concessions on metals and machinery but not textiles, for he anticipated protectionist opposition to any British treaty. Because they insisted on obtaining concessions on cotton textiles, the British broke off talks in June 1881. They hoped that a Franco-Belgian treaty would yield Britain the tariffs they desired through MFN. This made the Belgian treaty a bellwether for the treaty system; "the conventional duties embodied in the Belgian treaty, if ratified, would single-handedly extend the liberal tariff system of the Second Empire" (M. S. Smith 1980: 191; see also Marsh 1999: Chapters 6 and 7).

These examples show that states were certainly aware of the distributional consequences of MFN treaties. This awareness made them attentive to the sequence by which they negotiated treaties with multiple other states. The next two sections treat this problem formally, after which I turn to the evidence.

Tariff-Making With and Without MFN

Without MFN, every nation can impose a separate tariff on the same good from each foreign country. This requires extensions of the model used so far in this book to allow for multiple tariffs. As in Chapter 9, I use a spatial model. Instead of providing full analytical solutions to these problems, I use illustrations to generate the hypotheses.

Each country A will have a tariff t_{A1B} on good 1 from country B, a different tariff t_{A1C} on good 1 from country C, and so on. Tariff negotiations with country B over t_{A1B} need have no relation to t_{A1C}, nor would A's negotiations with C over t_{A1C} have any necessary implications for t_{A1B}. Each country could have in principle $m(n-1)$ tariff lines for m importable goods in a system of n countries. In contrast, MFN makes identical the tariff on imports from B and C for each good i, or $t_{AiB} = t_{AiC}$ for each good i.

These tariffs affect the domestic political problem confronting a government. As in the models used so far in this book, states face a trade-off between exporting and import-competing interests. Each government favors some nonzero domestic tariff (t_{Ai}) on each good, and the home government's ideal foreign tariff is zero.

With these interests in mind, consider a simple model with three countries and only one imported good in each country. State A has the ideal point $\{t_A, 0, 0\}$, B has the ideal point $\{0, t_B, 0\}$, and C has the ideal point $\{0, 0, t_C\}$

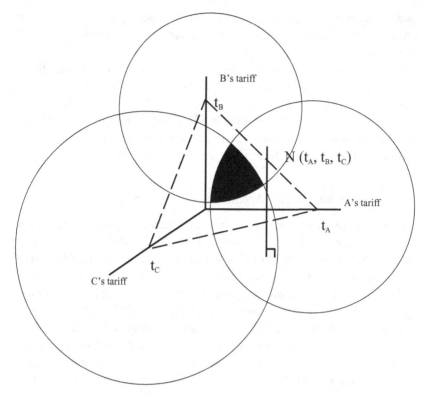

Figure 12.3. Tariff Negotiations Among Three States.

with t_A, t_B, $t_C > 0$. As in Chapter 9, utility is a negative function of the distance from the outcome of the game to this ideal point, and indifference curves are spheres around each player's ideal point. Rather than show all of these spheres, Figure 12.3 shows a slice of each, a circle through the $t_A t_B t_C$ plane.

Because each government selects only its own tariff, each chooses its ideal point. With A choosing t_A, B choosing t_B, and C choosing t_C, the noncooperative outcome N is the point $\{t_A, t_B, t_C\}$. Figure 12.3 shows this point N in three-dimensional space. There are joint gains to liberalization, so all three states prefer any point that lies inside the three indifference spheres to the reversion point N. Any of these points on the plane defined by these three ideal points (inside the triangle in Figure 12.3) are Pareto-efficient. Inside this triangle, moving the policy toward t_A and t_B simultaneously can only occur by moving away from t_C, whereas moving policy toward t_B and t_C simultaneously moves policy away from t_A, and moving policy toward t_A

and t_C moves it away from t_B. There are many possible points of agreement on the $t_A t_B t_C$ plane that are also within the indifference curves; Figure 12.3 shades this set.

This analysis implies that distributing the joint gains among these three states will present a salient problem in this strategic setting. How the states negotiate over this set of possible agreements will depend in part on the negotiating agenda that they choose. In effect, different negotiating agendas decide how states move from N to an efficient point that all prefer to N. I examine this problem in the next section.

Choosing the Agenda for Tariff Negotiations

When states can negotiate tariffs with many foreign countries, they have a choice between negotiating with one state at a time or with many simultaneously. To understand this procedural choice, this section considers tariff negotiations under two different rules: "clustered" and "seriatim."

For ease of presentation, I assume that the outcome of any bargaining game is the Nash Bargaining Solution, or NBS (Nash 1950). The NBS maximizes the product of the two parties' gains from agreement, that is, the product of the differences between each negotiator's payoff from the agreement and that negotiator's payoff from the reversion point or status quo. Whenever the game is symmetric, the NBS splits the difference between the two bargainers. Because the NBS is unaffected by monotonic transformations of the utility functions, any game that can be made symmetric through such a transformation will also have a split-the-difference outcome after being transformed. This feature makes the NBS very useful for the presentation here, though the results of the analysis do not require the NBS.

As discussed earlier, each state's bliss point is a positive home tariff and zero foreign tariffs. Because the initial tariff levels do not matter for the subsequent analysis, I define the axes such that each state's ideal tariff equals 1, or $t_A^* = t_B^* = t_C^* = 1$. For simplicity of exposition, I continue to assume that utility functions use an unweighted distance, that is, that indifference functions are spherical. Negotiations among three states, A, B and C, might occur under two possible agendas:

1. *Seriatim:* First, A and B negotiate over tariffs. Next, A and C negotiate over tariffs. (B and C may also negotiate, but the issues surrounding this choice are best raised in the case study that follows.)
2. *Clustering:* A, B, and C negotiate simultaneously over tariffs.

I assume that state A can choose between the two agendas regardless of B's and C's interests. This is simply a notational convenience: clearly, whichever state finds itself in the position to choose the agenda, for whatever historically contingent reasons, can be labeled A. In the case study below, Germany's market power, British aloofness from trade treaties, and the negotiating inflexibility of France's governing coalitions combined to make Germany the focal point of trade negotiations in the early 1890s.

Sequence has an important effect on the outcomes. If states cluster the negotiations, the three-player NBS is $\{\frac{1}{2}, \frac{1}{2}, \frac{1}{2}\}$. This solution simply splits the difference between each state's ideal point and that of its interlocutors among each dimension.

Negotiating in a seriatim manner poses a more subtle problem without a single, fully satisfactory analytical solution. To illustrate the issues, I discuss two different ways of thinking about the solution to the seriatim negotiation game. Though they vary in their assumptions about rational behavior, they yield the same results.

Consider first what would happen if the states approached each bargain myopically.[2] This might occur if the first states did not accurately anticipate C's willingness to negotiate. The NBS at the AB node is $\{\frac{1}{2}, \frac{1}{2}, 1\}$, splitting the difference between A and B. This agreement at the AB node changes the reversion point for the subsequent AC negotiations. Because the NBS depends on the reversion point, the AB negotiations change the NBS for A and C. As a result, the NBS at the AC node is $\{\frac{1}{4}, \frac{1}{2}, \frac{1}{2}\}$. If A myopically negotiates one agreement after the other, then it makes greater concessions than it would if it had clustered.

Now suppose that A does not negotiate myopically, but reasons through this problem with the aid of backward induction. Though backward induction is the normal way of solving an extensive-form game such as this, it yields an odd result. The NBS at the AC node is $\{\frac{1}{2}, 1, \frac{1}{2}\}$, splitting the difference between A and C. However, this agreement at the AC node changes the reversion point for the AB negotiations, which occur first. As a result, the NBS at the AB node is $\{\frac{1}{4}, \frac{1}{2}, \frac{1}{2}\}$. This result strikes most people as strange because A gives B concessions right away out of the knowledge that C will get these concessions eventually. Odd as it is, however, it produces the same result in the end as myopia.

[2] It is ironic that A might rationally anticipate the outcome of its own myopic behavior. One way to square this circle is to suppose that a rational institutional designer anticipates that subordinate organizations will behave in a boundedly rational way; another is that today's government might anticipate myopia on the part of a successor government.

These very different approaches to the seriatim game therefore yield qualitatively the same result: state A makes more concessions under seriatim negotiations than it does under clustering. For this reason, A will prefer clustering to seriatim negotiations. Because labeling any state as A is simply a notational convenience, this means that every state will prefer clustering over negotiating seriatim.

Though all states prefer to cluster themselves, they also want others to choose seriatim negotiations. In the above analysis, states B and C clearly prefer that A pursue seriatim negotiations. Yet, if they were given the chance, they would clearly choose to cluster themselves. Given this strategic setting, it seems reasonable to suppose that states find clustering an attractive focal point solution (Schelling 1960) to the agenda-setting problem – any other solution produces asymmetric distributional consequences, and there is no reason to expect these asymmetric effects in what is essentially a symmetric game. Symmetry results easily when everyone clusters.

The conclusion that states will cluster when they negotiate MFN tariffs is also affected by economic structure. Economic structure matters because A's preference for clustering depends on the fact that A negotiates the same tariff line with both B and C. If A imports good 1 from B and good 2 from C, then there are two relevant tariffs in A, t_{A1B} and t_{A2C}. The reversion point is now $\{t_{A1B}^*, t_{A2C}^*, t_B^*, t_C^*\} = \{1, 1, 1, 1\}$. As in my analysis of MFN above, t_{A1B} is of interest solely to B's exporters, whereas t_{A2C} is only of interest to C's exporters. With clustered negotiations, the three-player NBS is $\{\frac{1}{2}, \frac{1}{2}, \frac{1}{2}, \frac{1}{2}\}$, which splits the difference among all tariff dimensions.

Now consider seriatim negotiations with backward induction (myopia is similar). Here, the NBS at the AC node is $\{t_{A1B}^*, \frac{1}{2}, t_B^*, \frac{1}{2}\}$, because A and C negotiate only over t_{A1C} and t_C. These tariffs are not part of the negotiations between A and B, who split the difference on the remaining tariffs. As a result, the NBS at the AB node is $\{\frac{1}{2}, \frac{1}{2}, \frac{1}{2}, \frac{1}{2}\}$.

This means that when A negotiates different tariff lines with B than with C, the clustered and seriatim outcomes are identical. Anticipating negotiations between A and C does not change the reversion point between A and B for any of the variables over which A and B negotiate and thus does not affect the outcome.[3] If A negotiates over a different tariff line with B than with C, A is indifferent between clustered and seriatim negotiations. Whether

---

[3] To see that the concessions in the AC negotiations do not affect the NBS, consider the fact that the outcome of the AC negotiations can be washed away with a monotonic transformation of A's and B's utility functions without affecting the AB negotiation problem. Because the NBS is resistant to monotonic transformations of the utility functions, this has no effect.

this occurs is an empirical question of economic structure, not a subject of theory. There is no reason to expect clustering, especially if – as seems likely – the transaction costs of multilateralized clustering are greater than the transaction costs of bilateralism (Deardorff and Stern 1992).[4]

In each of the analyses above, A reduces its tariff from 1 to $\frac{1}{2}$ when it clusters, but from 1 to $\frac{1}{4}$ when it does not cluster. In other words, its concessions are much smaller when it clusters:

Hypothesis 12.1: Clustering leads to smaller concessions by states that cluster.

This is, after all, why states cluster (see Pahre 2001b; for an analogous result in a different model, see Caplin and Krishna 1988).

In short, when each pair of countries negotiates over different tariff lines, we would expect seriatim negotiations. When they negotiate over the same lines, however, we expect clustering. MFN makes the tariff lines on each good identical for all countries and therefore opens up the possibility of clustering. When states cluster, they will make smaller concessions than when they do not.

Testing the Relationship Between Clustering and MFN

The preceding section argues that the norm of MFN structures the distributional problem for states and thus leads to decision-making rules, such as clustering or seriatim negotiations, and is causally linked to clustering:

Hypothesis 12.2: MFN is a necessary condition for clustering.

MFN is *necessary* because when it is absent, state A would always negotiate different tariff lines with states B and C. When A negotiates different tariff lines, it will negotiate seriatim because of the greater transaction costs of clustering. At the same time, MFN is *not sufficient* because MFN could fail to lead to clustering if A negotiated different tariffs with B than it negotiated with C because of differences in economic structure. For example, Austria-Hungary might reduce its grain tariffs for Romania, but cut its tariffs on fruit for Italy. In this case, lower tariffs from A's negotiations with B would not lead to a new starting position for negotiations with C, which would necessarily focus on different tariff lines. Yet if A negotiates the same tariff lines with B and with C, then these two variables (MFN and economic structure)

---

[4] Multilateral bargains have higher transaction costs because they include irrelevant negotiations; A could participate in matters that affect only B and C.

are jointly sufficient for clustering. Conditional MFN has ambiguous status here. The ostensible American insistence on additional concessions in exchange for generalizing each MFN reduction often did not matter, because the United States had a single-column tariff. Even under the Dingley two-column tariff, all trading partners received the lower tariff within a few years (Fisk 1903; Lake 1988, O'Halloran 1994; Viner 1924). Recall that Chapter 11 found that U.S. conditional MFN resembled unconditional MFN in practice.

Although both MFN and economic structure are easily observed in a case study, it is a straightforward matter to test the necessity portion of this claim even in a large-n setting.[5] This test requires some operationalization of clustering. First, I might operationalize clustering by visual inspection of a country's pattern of trade negotiations (as in Figures 12.1–12.2). An alternative operationalization would capture clustering by looking at the distribution of treaty initiations over time. Seriatim negotiations should be Poisson-distributed. This assumes that the observed number of treaties in a given year will depend on some underlying rate of treaty initiation whose realization as a count variable will vary from year to year. In contrast, clustered negotiations will not be Poisson-distributed.

To test this, I run a Poisson regression for each country's annual treaty initiations using only a constant and an error term. The goodness-of-fit χ^2 tells us whether we can reject the null hypothesis that the data are Poisson-distributed. Table 12.1 reports a summary of these tests, showing the confidence level at which we can reject the null hypothesis. For example, we can reject the null hypothesis at the $p < .01$ level that Austro-Hungarian MFN treaties are Poisson-distributed.

Because the null hypothesis of this test is that the data are Poisson-distributed, the test might wrongly code some actual clustering as Poisson-distributed when it is in fact clustered. However, for almost all cases in Table 14.1 the confidence level for rejecting the Poisson null is either less than .10 or greater than .90 (these latter levels are not shown as such in the table). For these data, then, wrongly accepting the null is unlikely to be a problem. Only Serbia presents a serious question of inference in these data.

Hypothesis 12.1 states that MFN is a necessary condition for clustering. We should observe that all non-MFN treaty initiations are Poisson-distributed. If this is a nontrivial necessary condition, we should also observe

---

[5] Braumoeller and Goertz (2000) and Verkuilen (2005) have recently proposed techniques for testing necessary conditions quantitatively; the dichotomous variables here allow for a simpler approach.

Table 12.1. *Distribution of European treaty signings by year*

	MFN treaties			Other treaties	
Austria(-Hungary)	Not Poisson	(48)	$p < .01$	Poisson	(23)
Bulgaria	Not Poisson	(23)	$p < .01$	N.A.	(0)
France	Not Poisson	(62)	$p < .01$	Poisson	(11)
Italy	Not Poisson	(88)	$p < .01$	Poisson	(2)
Prussia/Germany	Not Poisson	(37)	$p < .05$	Poisson	(12)
Romania	Not Poisson	(16)	$p < .10$	Poisson	(2)
Serbia	Not Poisson	(12)	$p = .33$	Poisson	(3)
Spain	Not Poisson	(32)	$p < .05$	N.A.	(0)
Switzerland	Not Poisson	(34)	$p = .16$	N.A.	(0)
Belgium	Poisson	(22)		Poisson	(7)
Denmark	Poisson	(9)		Poisson	(5)
Greece	Poisson	(15)		N.A.	(0)
Montenegro	Poisson	(6)		N.A.	(0)
Netherlands	Poisson	(29)		Poisson	(11)
Portugal	Poisson	(14)		N.A.	(0)
Russia	Poisson	(20)		Poisson	(13)
Sweden	Poisson	(18)		N.A.	(0)
Turkey	Poisson	(5)		Poisson	(6)
United Kingdom	Poisson	(26)		Poisson	(11)

Note: The probabilities shown are the level at which I can reject the null hypothesis that the data are Poisson-distributed. I can always reject this null at the .90 level or better for those cases labeled "Poisson."

The number of treaties signed in each category is in parentheses.

that some MFN treaties are *not* Poisson-distributed (Braumoeller and Goertz 2000). Although this necessary condition would not be falsified even if none of the MFN treaties were non-Poisson distributed, such a condition would not be very interesting or useful. Because the hypothesis does not state a sufficient condition, we need not expect that all MFN treaties will be non-Poisson-distributed.

Table 12.1 shows the result of such a test for the countries of Europe. As expected, all non-MFN treaties are Poisson-distributed. This is consistent with the necessary condition. The fact that about half of the MFN observations exhibit clustering also means that MFN is substantively important and nontrivial.

Visual inspection catches some cases that the statistical tests miss. One such case is Russia, whose treaties are summarized in Table 12.2. There are MFN "clusters" of two treaties each in 1846 and 1874, as well as more significant clusters in 1893–1895 and 1904–1907. The low overall number of

Table 12.2. *Russian trade treaties, 1840–1913*

Date	Party	Summary of terms
January 1843	Britain	Reciprocal trade and navigation with conditional MFN
1844	Prussia	Russia reduces its tariffs on Prussian silk, wool, and iron, and Prussia reduces its transit dues on Russian cereals by river
September 1, 1846	Netherlands	Reciprocal freedom of commerce and navigation, with MFN on import duties
September 4, 1846	France	Reciprocal freedom of commerce and navigation, with MFN on import duties
June 14, 1857	France	Reciprocal freedom of commerce and navigation, with MFN on import duties
March 20, 1874	France	Reciprocal freedom of commerce and navigation, with MFN on import duties and some concessions in French colonies
May 16, 1874	Perú	Reciprocal unconditional MFN
November 2, 1876	Romania	Russia grants MFN with exceptions, Romania grants concessions of the 1876 Austrian treaty
June 5, 1893	France	MFN, with listed concessions
January 29, 1894	Germany	Reciprocal tariff reductions
May 18, 1894	Austria	Replaces certain articles of 1860 treaty, which otherwise remains in force
February 7, 1895	Spain	Modus vivendi including reciprocal MFN
July 15, 1904	Germany	Convention on commerce
September 16, 1905	France	Reciprocal MFN for imports, renews itemized concessions of 1893 agreement
1905	Bulgaria	Reciprocal MFN in trade and navigation except fishing and coasting trades
February 15, 1906	Austria	Reciprocal MFN, with listed tariff concessions, and some exceptions
March 1, 1906	Germany	Reciprocal MFN
July 27, 1906	Sweden	Extension of 1838 treaty with modifications including reciprocal MFN with exceptions for Archangel, Siberia, and Norway
February 15, 1907	Serbia	
June 15, 1907	Italy	Reciprocal MFN, with listed tariff reductions

Dates are Western dates.

Russian treaties and the way that these clusters are spread across several years make the statistical test miss what is evident to the human eye. The latter two, more significant clusters, also coincide with European-wide clusters. The first is a little delayed, however, dating to the end of the Russo-German tariff war sparked by the Caprivi cluster (see above).

Table 12.3. *Annual treaty distribution in the Americas*

	Poisson?	Number
Argentina	ambiguous (yes)	33
Bolivia	ambiguous (yes)	35
Brazil	ambiguous	30
Chile	ambiguous (yes)	29
Colombia	ambiguous (no)	34
Costa Rica	yes	21
Ecuador	yes	23
El Salvador	ambiguous (yes)	28
Guatemala	ambiguous (yes)	29
Honduras	ambiguous (yes)	30
México	no	56
Perú	no	53
United States	no	86
Uruguay	ambiguous	36
Venezuela	ambiguous	24

I assume that all Latin American treaties, even when no information is available, are MFN.

If we would accept or reject the Poisson null at the .25 level, but not the .10 level, I code it as ambiguous (yes) or ambiguous (no).

Table 12.3 presents the same statistical exercise for the Americas. Unfortunately, there is very little variation in the independent variable, as virtually all of these treaties included the MFN clause. The distribution of these treaty initiations was also more difficult to classify as either Poisson- or non-Poisson-distributed. Though no test of the hypothesis is possible here, I have included these data for informational purposes. I speculate about the reason for this pattern in a later section, when I argue that the metropole-centered pattern of Latin American trade affects the incentives for clustering.

As in the European cases, visual inspection picks up some clustering where statistical techniques do not. There would seem to be a strong cluster focused on Brazil, México, and the United States in 1826–1827. This is clearly associated with Latin American independence from Spain and the reactions of Britain, France, and the United States to those events. México's treaties, listed in Table 12.4, suggest some of the processes here, recalling earlier chapters. México's first cluster came in 1826–1827, consisting of MFN treaties with the United States and several European countries. German states are prominent here – Prussia (*Zollverein*), Hannover, and we might also count Denmark and the Netherlands as German because both were also members of the German Confederation. Spread from the *Zollverein* to the Americas, identified in Chapter 11, seems to have interacted with American events.

Table 12.4. *Summary of Mexican treaties, 1820–1913*

Date	Country	Summary
April 6, 1825	Britain	Reciprocal MFN treatment
December 26, 1826	Britain	Reciprocal MFN commerce and navigation
1826–1828	Prussia/*Zollverein*	Reciprocal MFN treatment; not ratified
July 10, 1826	United States	Reciprocal MFN treatment; not ratified
June 20, 1827	Hannover	Extends provisions of UK treaty to Hannover
June 15, 1827	Netherlands	Reciprocal MFN commerce and navigation
May 9, 1827	France	Reciprocal MFN customs treatment
July 19, 1827	Denmark	Reciprocal MFN customs treatment
March 13, 1831	France	Reciprocal MFN treatment
February 18, 1831	Prussia/*Zollverein*	Reciprocal unconditional MFN treatment
March 7, 1831	Chile	Reciprocal unconditional MFN treatment, with exceptions for former Spanish colonies
April 5, 1831	United States	Reciprocal unconditional MFN treatment
October 4, 1831	Saxony	Reciprocal unconditional MFN treatment
December 31, 1832	Switzerland	Reciprocal unconditional MFN, not ratified
November 16, 1832	Perú	Reciprocal MFN treatment
October 15, 1832	France	Reciprocal MFN treatment
April 7, 1832	Prussia/*Zollverein*	Reciprocal unconditional MFN treatment
June 21, 1838	Ecuador	Reciprocal MFN treatment
November 19, 1839	Belgium	Reciprocal MFN treatment; not ratified
July 30, 1842	Austria	Reciprocal unconditional MFN treatment
February 2, 1848	United States	Renews 1831 treaty with modifications
August 24, 1854	Belgium	Reciprocal MFN treatment; not ratified
July 10, 1855	Prussia/*Zollverein*	Reciprocal unconditional MFN treatment
July 10, 1855	Italy	Reciprocal MFN treatment
February 19, 1858	El Salvador	National treatment, with exceptions
September 14, 1859	United States	Trade agreement; rejected by U.S. Senate
July 20, 1861	Belgium	Reciprocal MFN treatment
October 27, 1866	Britain	Treaty of friendship, commerce, and navigation
May 6, 1866	Turkey	Treaty of friendship, commerce, and navigation
August 28, 1869	Prussia/*Zollverein*	Reciprocal unconditional MFN treatment
December 17, 1870	Italy	Reciprocal MFN commerce, navigation, reexport, and transit
July 10–11, 1882	Italy	Extend 1870 treaty with minor modifications
December 5, 1882	Germany	Reciprocal MFN treatment
December 26, 1882	Italy	Extend 1870 treaty of commerce
June 14–15, 1883	Italy	Extend 1870 treaty of commerce until conclusion of treaty negotiations
January 20, 1883	United States	Reciprocal tariff concessions
July 29, 1885	Sweden-Norway	Reciprocal MFN customs treatment
July 17, 1885	Argentina	Treaty of amity, commerce, and navigation
November 27, 1886	France	Reciprocal MFN customs treatment
July 10, 1888	Ecuador	Reciprocal MFN treatment

Date	Country	Summary
November 27, 1888	Britain	Reciprocal MFN in commerce, navigation, and duties
November 30, 1888	Japan	Reciprocal MFN customs treatment
March 8, 1888	Guatemala	Freedom of commerce, with the exception of wheat; not ratified
April 16, 1890	Italy	Reciprocal MFN in commerce, navigation, and duties
March 29, 1890	Dominican Rep.	Reciprocal MFN treatment
April 24, 1893	El Salvador	Reciprocal MFN customs treatment
July 7, 1895	Belgium	Reciprocal MFN customs treatment
September 22, 1897	Netherlands	Reciprocal MFN customs treatment
December 14, 1899	China	Reciprocal MFN treatment
November 6, 1900	Nicaragua	Treaty of commerce and navigation
September 17, 1901	Austria	Reciprocal MFN customs treatment
May 14, 1902	Iran	Reciprocal MFN customs treatment
March 24, 1908	Honduras	Reciprocal MFN on import and export duties and taxes, with selected tariff reductions
October 2, 1909	Russia	Reciprocal MFN treatment of import and export tariffs
May 3, 1910	Denmark	Reciprocal MFN

México failed to ratify several of these treaties, for reasons seen in the analysis of divided government in Chapter 9. These treaties also tended to have similar provisions, not shown in Table 12.4. For example, they each bound, reduced, or eliminated trade prohibitions in addition to providing for MFN treatment in tariffs and other trade matters. Germany, the United States, and France remain prominent in later clusters of 1831 and 1882–1883, and ratification problems also recur. Listed tariff concessions tended to be small, reflecting the MFN-based Latin American treaty network.

There is also a cluster in 1855–1857 involving Argentina, Colombia, México, Uruguay, and possibly Brazil and El Salvador. I do not know what the origins of this latter cluster were, but it is striking that it included the largest economies of the region (plus El Salvador). Finally, it is worth noting that the United States exhibits a very strong cluster in 1891–1892 at the same time as the Caprivi cluster in Europe. The historiography rightly identifies this flurry of activity with the McKinley tariff.

The evidence suggests that clustering plays an important role in the trade regime. Those countries that cluster are central to the nineteenth-century system. Austria, France, and Italy sign more treaties with more countries than anyone else. They are also central to the case study below. Denmark,

Greece, and Montenegro were much more incidental to the regime. In this way, the necessary condition explains the behavior we find in the most important players in the regime.

Clustering and the "Comet Year" of 1892

Although the Poisson tests uncovered a nonrandom distribution of treaties, no statistical test can show that states *intended* to cluster. Showing intentionality requires more qualitative evidence, which I provide in this section.

My central claim is that MFN is necessary for clustered negotiations. Testing this hypothesis requires selecting on the dependent variable (Dion 1998) – that is, finding a case of clustered negotiations and then looking to see if the MFN clause was necessary for it. Of course, the case should also reveal that decentralized negotiations between many states can be causally linked, that is, clustered. In a strategic model such as mine, showing causality further requires evidence that decision makers understood the dangers of seriatim negotiations under MFN. I also need to show that decision makers intended to cluster negotiations, recognizing that doing so would avoid the problems of MFN.

The case selection issue comes first. Several clusters present themselves, including France's clusters of 1863–1866 and 1881–1884, the Caprivi-Méline cluster of 1890–1892, and the Bülow cluster of 1904–1907. Minor powers also clustered their negotiations, but these generally coincided with major power clusters and are derived from them. The most substantively interesting one is the 1890–1892 cluster because it stemmed from contemporaneous but causally distinct decisions in Austria-Hungary, France, and Germany.

The French had arranged for their existing treaties to expire together in 1892, a date the German speakers labeled the *Kometenjahr* (Comet Year). Domestic debates over the treaties and rising protectionism led France to adopt the Méline tariff of 1892, which established a supposedly non-negotiable minimum tariff. In fact these duties could be negotiated downward and were. France concluded treaties with 16 countries from 1891 to 1893, though the concessions exchanged were much less significant than in earlier treaties.

Although aware of French debates (Harvey 1938: 25), German clustering occurred in a different context. Chancellor Leo von Caprivi sought a new foreign policy (*Neue Kurs*) distinct from Otto von Bismarck's. Trade treaties would mark his government's greater concern with economic issues. Treaty negotiations also posed an opportunity to attract labor support for the government, support that was especially attractive after the repeal of the *Sozialistengesetz* (anti-Socialist law) in 1890.

In contrast to France and Germany, Austria-Hungary did not have domestic political reasons for treaty negotiations in 1890–1892. The Caprivi-Méline cluster thus occurred when the Dual Monarchy would not otherwise have negotiated treaties, for Austro-Hungarian negotiations typically occurred around the decennial renewal years of the *Ausgleich* (see Chapter 9). This makes Austria-Hungary a useful control case, for its decision to cluster in 1890–1892 must follow exclusively from MFN bargaining considerations and not merely domestic political calculations.

Politicians were well aware of the distributional effects of MFN identified here. Because of the MFN clause, according to Foreign Minister Baron Adolf Hermann Marschall von Bieberstein (cited in Weitowitz 1978: 144), most of Germany's "concessions in cooperative treaty negotiations with Italy are obtained not only through concessions made directly to Italy but also with an eye on those concessions obtained indirectly through the Austro-Italian treaty."[6]

Wine tariffs, which played an important role in many negotiations, provide a good illustration of how these concerns manifested in practice. Britain knew that the MFN wine duties that it had given to France also gave cheap Italian wines low-tariff access to the British market. Instead of being grateful, Italy's government could – and did – ask for still more reductions in these wine duties in exchange for lower tariffs on English exports. Spain had similar views. It was willing to trade reductions in its tariffs only for still more concessions on wines, particularly a structure of duties that treated heavier Iberian wines more favorably than the existing system based on alcohol content. The seriatim model developed in this chapter nicely captures this concern, whereby earlier concessions to one party become a new baseline for negotiations with third parties.

Germany, another wine importer, faced the same strategic problem. The Interior Ministry in Berlin opposed lowering any wine tariffs for Austria-Hungary because they would reduce the basis for future negotiations with Italy, Spain, and France (Marsh 1999: Chapters 5 and 6; Weitowitz 1978: 58–59). As argued above, MFN negotiations covering the same tariff lines

---

[6] "daß bei kooperativen Handelsvertragsverhandlungen mit Italien...das Maß unserer Konzessionen, nicht nur durch die uns direkt angebotenen italienischen Konzessionen, sondern auch durch die Aussicht bestimmt wird, weitere Konzessionen indirekt durch den österreichisch-italienischen Vertrag zu erhalten."

are sufficient for clustering. These conditions are met here, and wine did indeed provide an important subject matter throughout the Caprivi cluster.

Concerns about MFN are also found in negotiations over industrial tariffs. The problems of MFN concessions were especially important for Belgium, a centrally located small country. It was always careful during the Austro-German-Belgian negotiations to see that France could not take advantage of the treaty tariffs. Anticipating an eventual MFN treaty with France, Belgium also sought to limit its concessions to Germany on the iron and textile tariffs that would be the focus of Franco-Belgian negotiations. The same concerns led Belgium to negotiate with France and Britain at essentially the same time, delaying the easier British talks until the outline of the French treaty was established (Marsh 1999: Chapter 8; Weitowitz 1978: 115–16).

Perhaps the most important example of clustering came as a result of explicit coordination between Austria-Hungary and Germany in 1890–1892. The impetus came from interaction between the coming expiration of Germany's treaties and the recurrent differences of opinion between Austria and Hungary inside the Dual Monarchy (see Chapter 9). The Austrians (and Bohemians) sought a very different set of trading partners than did the Hungarians. The German chargé in Vienna, Anton Graf Monts, proposed a way to square the circle, with Austria-Hungary and Germany each agreeing not to renew any trade treaties with outsiders without coordinating with one another first. This Montssche Proposition made possible a cluster of treaties in which Hungary obtained cheaper manufactured imports from Germany, Austria obtained cheaper agricultural imports from the Balkans, and everyone obtained higher veterinary standards for livestock imports (Weitowitz 1978: 54–84). The provisions of the initial treaties were kept secret, so that the same concessions could be offered anew in MFN negotiations with France, Italy, Spain, and Switzerland. Weitowitz (1978: 154–55) summarizes the powerful advantages of this clustering:

> The central powers' cooperative mode of negotiation was of great importance for the widening of the trade treaty zone. Common negotiations weakened the opposition and secret arrangements made it possible for concessions that had already been given once to be exchanged for new trade advantages. In the later trade treaties Austria-Hungary and Germany were only forced to make unsubstantial concessions that went beyond the content of the first trade treaty and secret protocol.[7]

---

[7] "...[daß] die kooperative Handlungsweise der mittelmächte für die Erweiterung der Handelsvertragszone von größter Wichtigkeit war. Gemeinsames Handeln schwächte die Opposition, und geheime Absprachen ermöglichten es, bereits gemachte Konzessionen für neue Handelsvorteile einzutauschen. In den späteren Handelsverträgen waren Österreich-Ungarn und Deutschland deshalb nur zu unwesentlich Zusatzkonzessionen

As a result, both Austria-Hungary and Germany obtained significant distributional advantages from coordinating negotiations with one another. This is consistent with Hypothesis 12.1.

This tactic depended in part on maintaining secrecy – once the first group of Austro-German treaties were made public in December 1891, there was a danger that third states would simply demand MFN treaties with Germany and Austria-Hungary in order to obtain the already given treaty tariffs. These partners addressed this problem by putting their tariff-line concessions in a secret protocol. After reaching this secret agreement, these two then presented a common front in negotiations with Italy, Switzerland, and Belgium in the summer of 1891. By keeping these tariff lines secret, concessions that these states had already made to each other could be offered to this second group of countries (Weitowitz 1978: 83–84).

Such secrecy was only one reason why other states did not want a government to cluster its negotiations with them. As the theory predicts, a country should oppose, on distributional grounds, being brought into a cluster. Austria-Hungary and Germany had various means to bring reluctant interlocutors along. The size of the German market, in particular, posed a potent source of power (for its effects on Sweden, see Lindberg 1983). Although Switzerland did not want to negotiate simultaneously with Vienna and Berlin, it feared exclusion from the treaty network, especially if Italy were to sign a treaty whose benefits would be denied the Swiss. When this exclusion seemed a real possibility, Bern commenced common negotiations with Austria-Hungary and Germany in the fall of 1891 (Weitowitz 1978: 91, 104). The Belgian negotiator, Baron Jules Greindl, apparently did not even know about Austro-German coordination at first. After receiving common demands from the partners, he naively asked whether it might not be more advantageous for Belgium to receive separate lists of demands from Germany and Austria-Hungary. This objection was met by referring to the political friendship of the Dual Alliance countries and their wish for common negotiations (Weitowitz 1978: 114–15).

Because this alliance excuse was not available, Austro-German coordination against Italy presents evidence that distributional concerns were important. Out of respect for its partner in the Triple Alliance, the Dual Alliance had decided not to give Italy the same treatment as Switzerland, Belgium, and the Balkan countries. When given a choice in August 1891 between separate Austrian and German negotiations or a conference *á trois*, Italy

gezwungen, die über den Inhalt des ersten Handelsvertrages und des Geheimprotokolls hinausgingen."

naturally chose separate talks. The logic behind this choice follows directly from the earlier analysis. However, Italy's decision did not keep the German and Austrian commissioners from consulting each other in secret, a deception made easier by the fact that Italy had agreed to conduct all these negotiations in Munich (Weitowitz 1978: 136, 143).

When Prime Minister Antonio di Rudinì discovered his partners' deceit, he threatened to break off negotiations. Caprivi calmed him in telegrams explaining that common negotiations were necessary because of German domestic politics and the tightness of the Dual Alliance; linking any Austro-Italian trade treaty to foreign policy would help ratification of the Italian treaty in Germany. Rudinì satisfied himself with a paraphrase of their secret treaty of October 1891 – though Austria-Hungary and Germany did not give Italy a copy of the treaty itself. The Germans' account of these negotiations makes the connection to MFN clear (cited in Weitowitz 1978: 144): "What he [Rudinì] calls 'pressure' and 'threats' is just nothing but the indivisible connection between the various treaties, created by the idea of cooperation and MFN, which he has himself recognized by accepting our condition."[8] Again, this follows the logic of the theory.

Austria-Hungary and Germany used the same technique against Switzerland that they had previously used against Italy. As Italy had before it, Switzerland thought it disadvantageous to negotiate simultaneously with Vienna and Berlin (Weitowitz 1978: 91, 100). The German negotiator pressed Switzerland to negotiate immediately so that it would not face a unified front of three powers (including Italy). Bern acquiesced.

Finally, the theory predicts that all this clustering would lead to treaties that make smaller concessions than nonclustered treaties. As we would expect, the concessions made in the Caprivi cluster were not particularly far reaching. In the German case, Barkin (1970: 249) argues that "the treaties presented to the Reichstag for approval on 5 February 1905 were on the whole favorable to Germany, although not to the extent of the earlier ones." The same was true of the French treaties of this period.

Belgium's concessions can stand for many others. Germany received 24 tariff-line concessions in the Belgian treaty, mostly on industrial goods, and obtained 18 additional tariff bindings. Belgium reduced only seven tariff line items, two of which responded to Austro-Hungarian demands. German agriculture was particularly disappointed in its hopes for greater

[8] "Was er 'Pression' und 'Drohung' nennt, ist also nichts anderes als der durch die Kooperationsidee und die Meistbegünstigung geschaffene, untrennbare Zusammenhang der verschiedenen Verträge, den er selbst mit Annahme unserer Bedingung anerkannt hatte."

access to the Belgian market. All these concessions were sufficiently small that an upward revision of the Belgian tariff in 1895 was consistent with the letter of these treaties.

In summary, this case study strongly confirms both the hypotheses and the underlying logic of the model. This case also shows some of the steps that practical statesmen take in response to the strategic problems highlighted by the model. Although these tactics are richer than those found in any model could be, they reflect the same strategic logic. The resulting policies of nondiscrimination, combined with threats of exclusion, careful attention to sequence and timing, and efforts at secrecy, play important roles in the negotiations of the early 1890s. As events showed, states facing a clusterer have few choices available to them, making it easier for a state to cluster when MFN gives it the incentive to do so.

Clustering and the Turkish Capitulations

As a further test of the logic of the argument, consider the Turkish general tariff. The generally low Turkish tariff provided the same import, export, and transit duties to all foreigners, who eventually achieved national treatment in these duties through treaties. This general tariff creates the same incentives as an MFN norm because, like MFN, it treats all countries equally. Conceding a lower general tariff to Britain and then negotiating further reductions with France a few years later would give a disadvantage to the Ottomans, who should prefer clustering.

Table 12.5 summarizes the terms of Turkish trade treaties in this century. Because Turkish treaties are infrequent and clusters often extend across more than one calendar year, the statistical test could not reject the Poisson null. However, inspection of this table shows clear clusters in 1838 (or 1838–1840) and 1861–1862. The first cluster reduced the Ottoman tariff to 9%, the second to 8%. These treaties also granted Europeans identical terms in many nontariff areas, such as internal transit and excise duties, though such matters lie outside my theory. The Turks apparently clustered their negotiations with Europe to avoid granting concession after concession in the same general tariff to different countries.[9] The major additional concessions that the Ottomans made were the end of prohibitions on the exports of foodstuffs

---

[9] The Ottomans initiated these discussions as part of fiscal reform. These treaties also coincide with Mahmud II's *Tanzimat*, a program of internal reform that summarized its goals in the *Gülhane* (Rose Garden) rescript of November 1839. A committee of foreign commissioners helped write the tariff because it was based on official values of goods, not invoice values (Williams 1972: 294–95).

Table 12.5. *Ottoman trade treaties in Europe, 1815–1913*

Date	Party	Summary of terms
August 16, 1838	Austria	Treaty of commerce.
August 16, 1838	Great Britain	Grants reciprocal MFN treatment of ships and tariff parity to British traders. Abolishes Turkish agricultural monopolies, and replaces transport duties in Turkey with a 9% *ad valorem* duty and 3% export duty.
November 25, 1838	France	Abolishes Turkish agricultural monopolies and purchase permits for French importers.
September 2, 1839	Sardinia	Convention on commerce.
March 14, 1840	Netherlands	Guarantees Dutch ships all advantages granted vessels from third countries in Turkish ports. The Dutch pay the same internal duties as Muslims, with a 9% duty on exports on arrival in port and a further 3% exit duty. Dutch merchandisers pay a 3% import duty in Turkey.
1840	Prussia	Prussia receives treatment equal to the other European states.
January 1, 1847	Austria	MFN customs treatment.
April 29, 1861	Great Britain	Reduces and fixes duties for imports and exports and grants MFN treatment for warehousing imports.
July 10, 1861	Italy	Applies all commercial treaties between former Italian states and Turkey to the new Kingdom of Italy and abolishes Turkish buyer monopolies. Grants reciprocal MFN for all export and import duties. Turkish articles bought by Italians within Turkey pay an 8% duty.
February 15, 1862	Netherlands	Extends Turkish trade or navigational concession made to third parties to the Netherlands and abolishes Turkish buyer monopolies. Dutch traders pay an 8% export duty on Turkish articles bought for export. Grants reciprocal MFN on import duties.
March 13, 1862	Austria	Revision of tariff for imports, based on current prices.
May 22, 1862	Austria	Guarantees that Turkish concessions made to third parties will be extended to Austria and eliminates Turkish monopolies on its agriculture and other products.
August 26, 1890	Germany	Treaty of commerce.
May 15, 1906	Serbia	Reciprocal tariff reductions.
April 25, 1907	Germany	Additional terms to 1890 treaty.
February 6, 1911	Bulgaria	Provisionally grants MFN on all import, export, reexport, transit, and warehousing duties.

and raw materials. Marxists see these primary product exports as part of Turkey's peripheralization, but from a neoclassical standpoint these policy changes must have been welfare-increasing (see Pamuk 1987: 195; I. Wallerstein, Decdeli, and Kasaba 1987).

The Turkish evidence, along with the more formal Poisson data, strongly confirm the hypothesis. The evidence also suggests that clustering plays an important role in the trade regime. Those countries that cluster are central to the nineteenth-century system. Austria, France, and Italy (and Bulgaria!) sign more treaties with more countries than anyone else. Denmark, Greece, Montenegro, and even the United Kingdom are much more incidental to the regime. In this way, the necessary condition explains the behavior we find in the most important players in the regime.

Further Implications

This section explores some additional implications of the analysis in the preceding two sections. These implications show some ways in which clustering is substantively important for the international trading system and help further distinguish the approach here from alternative theoretical approaches.

The preceding analysis shows how a state will cluster negotiations over import concessions with its trading partners. The analysis has no implications for demands for tariff concessions from those states to whom it exports. In other words,

Hypothesis 12.3: States cluster as a result of pressures on the import side, not the export side.

In contrast, if clustering stemmed from either regime norms or transaction costs, we would not expect this asymmetry between import and export pressures. Transaction cost problems should be similar on both the import and export side, and I can see no reason why a regime norm approach should even distinguish the two sources of pressure.

Another way to test Hypothesis 12.3 is to see whether coordination is a decreasing function of import concentration by country, but is unrelated to export concentration by country. If a country tends to import from a single country, clustering is unlikely; if it imports from many, clustering is likely.

Figure 12.4 shows the number of treaties signed each year by European countries with each other and of treaties signed each year between a European country and a Latin American country. The historiography emphasizes the core-periphery trading patterns between Europe and the Western Hemisphere, stemming originally from colonialism and restrictive navigation

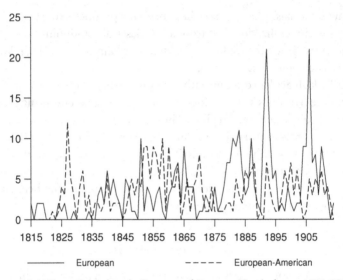

Figure 12.4. Treaty Initiations in Europe and Between Hemispheres, 1815–1913.

laws. Even after independence, many countries retained only a narrow range of trading partners, though Britain generally replaced Spain or Portugal as the main partner.

I would expect, then, that Latin American countries would not cluster because they did not import the same goods from multiple sources. In contrast, many European countries should cluster. Inspection of Figure 12.4 shows this pattern. European-American treaties look randomly distributed through time; they are, in fact, Poisson-distributed. As discussed earlier, the only clear clusters in the Americas are an independence cluster of 1826–1827 and an unexplained cluster of some larger countries in 1855–1857. In contrast, European treaties become clustered in the second half of the period, especially in the years 1893 and 1906. A formal test strongly rejects the hypothesis that these treaty initiations are Poisson-distributed in the last decades of this period (exact results vary by the cut-off year chosen, of course).

One way to test Hypothesis 12.3 is to see whether coordination is a decreasing function of import concentration by country, but is unrelated to export concentration by country. If a country tends to import from a single country, clustering is unlikely; if it imports from many, clustering is likely. However, testing this hypothesis is difficult because of a lack of good data for all but the largest partners. It is also complicated by the many examples of secondary clustering. A small state whose imports come from a few countries might not be expected to cluster. If its trading partners cluster and if they negotiate

Table 12.6. *Hypotheses on the clustering of trade cooperation*

Hypothesis 12.1: Clustering leads to smaller concessions by states that cluster.

Hypothesis 12.2: MFN is a necessary condition for clustering.

Hypothesis 12.3: States cluster as a result of pressures on the import side, not the export side.

---

at the same time for any reason, this small state's treaties will themselves cluster. Bulgarian-Romanian-Serbian clustering in the 1890s in response to the Austro-German Montssche Proposition provides an example of this clustering.

The analysis here may also help explain Britain's failure to cluster. The Netherlands and the United Kingdom stand out for importing goods from a wide range of countries. On these grounds, they might be expected to cluster. However, both imported many goods from their colonies, with which they hardly need negotiate trade treaties. British colonial goods regularly made up 15 to 20% of its imports, whereas Dutch imports from Indonesia were as high as 30% of all imports, declining to about 5% in 1880 and then increasing to about 15% from 1890 on. This reduced the need to make concessions to many other countries and therefore also reduced the incentive to cluster.

Conclusions

This chapter has argued that MFN is a necessary condition for clustering and that clustering became more likely as the number of states in the trade network increases. These hypotheses are summarized in Table 12.6. The argument also implies that states that cluster make fewer concessions than states that do not. For example, France clustered its negotiations in the early 1880s by imposing a renegotiation deadline of November 18, 1881, on all its partners. This action is closely associated with its efforts to increase its tariff without breaking away from the treaty network. In other words, France wanted its partners in cooperation to agree to a higher French tariff in the 1880s than they had negotiated in the 1860s or 1870s (Marsh 1999: 137).

Examples of such treaties, which accompanied *higher* duties, abound. The Swiss-Italian treaty of 1904 entailed an increase in Swiss duties on wine, livestock, slaughtered animals, and preserved meats over the levels in the treaty of 1892. The treaty kept the old duties for 56 million lire of exports, lowered duties on 63 million lire of exports, and allowed higher duties on only 48 million lire of Italian exports (Coppa 1971: 76–77). Most important, it guaranteed stability: the Italians reckoned that it safeguarded 168 million of 181 million lire of their exports.

The result of such pressures was continued treaties but less progress in lowering tariffs. Walther Lotz (1907: 275) noted the consequences at the time:

It is true that Germany was able successfully to conclude new treaties, or, more correctly speaking, to prolong Caprivi's treaties until the end of December, 1917, by introducing important alterations in the duties. But what was the nature of these alterations? Germany raised her duties, but other countries granted higher duties in exchange. Prince Bülow's government considered that it had won a success if the foreign duties were not much enhanced by the treaties of 1905, and the official introduction to the new treaties tells us that better concessions could not be got from foreign countries because Germany was not willing to concede more.

A different mechanism by which clustering induced higher tariffs was the widespread practice of introducing tariffs in advance of a cluster of major renegotiations. Many countries raised their tariffs in advance of the renewals and renegotiations in 1903–1905. This became common later in our period, and Austria, Romania, Russia, and even Switzerland raised their tariffs before beginning a round of treaty negotiations (Lotz 1907: 275). Though I have not modeled the incentives for such tariff-setting, the logic is fully consistent with the model. At times this exercise appeared to be coercive. A large state such as Austria-Hungary might raise its duties on Serbian goods, knowing that it was difficult for Serbia to retaliate, and then extract concessions from Serbia in exchange for returning to something near the status quo ante.

Another trick that states used to combine protectionism with MFN treaties was greater tariff differentiation. Sweden used differentiation of iron export duties to good effect to force Germany to make major concessions (Lindberg 1983; Y. M. Werner 1989: Chapter 1). Bismarck had done the same thing in 1889 in anticipation of the Comet Year of 1892. Apparently, most of the Continental trading states – including Austria-Hungary, Belgium, Germany, Italy, Romania, Serbia, and Switzerland – increased the differentiation of their tariffs in advance of the 1905–1906 renegotiations, and all but Belgium and Italy had also raised their autonomous manufacturing tariffs before negotiating them back down (Ashley 1926: 109–13).

The analysis here helps reconcile contending views of the last 25 years before World War I. Historians typically describe 1890–1914 as a period of increased protectionism in Europe, which eventually included even liberal Switzerland in 1906 (examples of the historiography include Coppa 1970, 1971; Friedman 1978; Lindberg 1983; Howe 1999; Marsh 1999; Platt 1968; Rogowski 1989; M. S. Smith 1980; Weitowitz 1978; Y. M. Werner 1989).

Recent historians have notice that this alleged protectionism was accompanied by an increase in trade treaty negotiations (examples include Marsh 1999; Weitowitz 1978). Some countries, notably France, used these treaties as part of an effort to revise tariffs upward, while retaining market access in a few sectors. Likewise, Germany and Sweden signed two significant treaties that guaranteed each country some protection, while liberalizing only a few sectors, such as iron ore, paving stones, and timber. Clustering made these treaties less liberal than their often nonclustered predecessors. These treaties were nonetheless more liberal than autonomous tariffs would have been, as we have seen throughout this book.

These consequences of MFN clustering seem to have had systemic-wide negative effects. Accominotti and Flandreau (2006) and O'Rourke and Williamson (1999) have found that the MFN trade treaties from the 1860s onward did not contribute to trade expansion. If these findings hold up in future analyses, this would imply that the major effects of the MFN waves were counterfactual – though they did not contribute to further trade expansion, they at least prevented protectionism and a contraction of trade that would have otherwise happened. Still, these positive effects were weaker under MFN and a clustered regime than they might have been in a different regime.

The analysis here can also help us better understand the contemporary trade regime. The WTO is central to the international trading system. Among other things, the WTO system (and its predecessor GATT) coordinates trade negotiations between countries and across time by packaging negotiations and concessions into "rounds." Therefore, negotiations are clustered in a few periods with longer periods of no negotiations between them. These rounds have made remarkable progress in reducing tariffs among industrialized countries, but this task took decades and a half-dozen rounds to achieve. This chapter poses the question whether a different regime than MFN might have achieved more or achieved the same goal more quickly.

Most who study the international trade regime have treated clustering as unexceptional. Finlayson and Zacher (1981) argue that clustering follows from regime norms of nondiscrimination, liberalization, and reciprocity. Clustering occurs especially at the end of a negotiating round, when third-party beneficiaries of some bilaterally negotiated tariff reduction would be pressured to make additional concessions to "pay" for these benefits. Others might see clustering as a decision rule that follows from the multilateral principles of the postwar order (i.e., Ruggie 1993a).

Such a view neglects the history of the international trade regime. Even in the postwar period, multilateral coordination became an important feature of the trading system only in the 1960s (Curzon and Curzon 1976; Finlayson and Zacher 1981; Pahre 1999: Chapter 10). Such clustering cannot follow merely from the postwar regime because similar clustering characterized years, such as 1892–1893 and 1905–1906. Moreover, clustering did not last long, even in the postwar period. It became less important for the better part of a decade after the Tokyo Round (1979), as the major trading nations negotiated bilaterally with one another on market opening, voluntary export restraints (VERs), and other issues. These effects are normally seen as evidence of regime breakdown (i.e., Aggarwal 1985) and not a change of rules within a regime.

Rather than viewing clustering as a decision rule within a single international regime, I have argued that this clustering should be seen as a dependent variable. Under MFN, bilateral negotiations have undesirable distributional effects – a state makes politically costly concessions in its negotiations with one state and then turns around and makes still more concessions on the same issue with another state. Clustering avoids this, packaging concessions with many states simultaneously. As a result, clustering has distributional benefits for those who cluster.

The theory and the historical evidence presented here both show that clustering has important distributional effects in a trade regime. These effects are evident historically, and the explanation offered here suggests that these effects help explain the slowness of GATT/WTO liberalization.

PART FIVE

CONCLUSIONS

THIRTEEN

Explaining Trade Cooperation in 1815–1914

"State intervention is like the little girl who had a little curl right in the middle of her forehead: when she was good, she was very, very good; and when she was bad, she was horrid."

– David Landes (1998: 520)

This book has been built on a theoretical scaffolding, with each chapter presenting both a piece of the theory and a test of that part. The flow of the argument has been theoretical and not driven by substantive puzzles as much as by a desire for theoretical elaboration. The central task has been a desire to explain variation between cooperation and noncooperation, for which I used a bottom-up theory of trade policy. Because the central result is that low-tariff countries are more likely to cooperate than high-tariff countries, examining the domestic political reasons for high tariffs has played an important role in the analysis. At the same time, each state's policy conditions the policies of other states, pointing to an analysis of reactions as well as international-level norms such as MFN.

The first half of this chapter summarizes the theoretical claims of the book. Beyond providing a mere summary, I also develop some suggestions for a research agenda on international cooperation. The second half uses this theory to provide a synthetic account of the nineteenth-century trade treaty network, providing an alternative narrative of nineteenth-century trade policy. For those interested in the nineteenth century, it points to greater Germany as central to the regime. For the contemporary world, I join others in emphasizing the critical role of international regimes in constraining protectionism. At the same time, the organizing principles of these regimes, most particularly MFN, pose challenges of their own. The theory and history here point to a more benign view of regionalism and trade discrimination in a political world of the second-best. This differs from the more critical view of regionalism found in most economists' analyses of optimal policies.

The Theory of Political Support

This book rests on a political-support theory of trade policy, albeit one modified by a study of revenue concerns, democratic institutions, and divided government. The foundations of this approach are hardly new, dating to around 1970, and the first pure application to trade policy came in 1981. The approach is perhaps used most widely in the study of regulation in both economics and political science. It is attractive for its analytic simplicity, for it assumes only that politicians maximize support from, and thus income to, several different groups, subject to trade-offs between them. Though well-established elsewhere, it has never caught on in the study of international political economy – nor, as far as I have found, has it ever been explicitly rejected.

This lack of application probably reflects the peculiar discourses of international relations in the 1970s, 1980s, and 1990s. The theory of political support does not fit easily into debates among proponents of interdependence theory, neo-Realists, neoliberal institutionalists, and constructivists. There seems to have been little professional incentive for scholars interested in those meta-theoretical debates to use it, and these scholars may still see no meta-theoretical value in the theory of political support. Whether or not it contributes to interparadigmatic battles, however, the theory does help us understand reality a little better.

Political-support theory finds surprising resonance in nineteenth-century politics and in many political systems today. The theory focuses on the executive's interests, subject to the needs of obtaining multifaceted support from a heterogeneous population. In the historiography, this maps well into the literature on Bonapartism. It also accords with the integrative thesis used to explain many nineteenth-century political economies. The approach also echoes an older literature in political science on the politics of mass society.

This kind of theory also seems to fit well many transitional regimes, such as Italian fascism, Wilhelmine Germany, or Vladimir Putin's Russia today. The support-maximization features of the theory also correspond tolerably well to plebiscitarian political systems, such as Alberto Fujimori's Perú (Roberts 1995), and to quasi-democracies, such as México under the PRI (Partido Revolucionario Instituciona, Institutional Revolutionary Party).

The theory of political support also enjoys substantial analytical power not found in many rival approaches. Its highly general assumptions make it easier to derive hypotheses that apply across countries and over time. In this it resembles Realism and perhaps Marxism. Though partly a rival to these, the theory is not obviously inconsistent with either – support maximization could be the domestic counterpart of security maximization abroad, for example. I have already mentioned the theory's similarities to the mostly – Marxist literature on Bonapartism, which dates, after all, to the master's *Class Struggles in France*. In these ways, political-support theory provides a scaffolding on which to build in many different directions, in many different styles.

Theoretical Summary

This book has sought a theoretical understanding of international cooperation, using trade cooperation as its focus. I argued first that traditional cooperation theory was inadequate to explain variations in cooperation from one country to another or within the same country over time. Most of this failure consisted of sins of omission – cooperation theory provides a few answers, mostly correct, to these questions. For example, the theory's focus on the "shadow of the future" is reasonable enough, but it is difficult to test. When I tested it in Chapter 7, the one measure that I found gave unusual results. Only continental European states were affected by interest rates, and they were affected only by those rates in Paris.

An example of what existing theory leaves out is whether each state's choices are influenced by the trade policies of other states. There has also never developed a literature examining reversion points, though the standard Prisoners' Dilemma theory of cooperation makes reversion points an essential part of the model.

This book differs from many other works in developing a model to understand political economy outcomes. This model enables me to derive 47 interrelated propositions, summarized in Tables 13.1–13.3, concerning trade policy and trade cooperation. Of these, 23 are deductive hypotheses, 8 are corollaries derived from these hypotheses, 1 is conjecture, and 2 are remarks. These propositions are all eminently falsifiable. Nine other propositions I classified as findings, inductively derived from the data. Like other inductive propositions, these are not falsifiable within this dataset (though they could be falsified against other datasets). Finally, four results, which synthesize hypotheses and findings, are also falsifiable.

The point of these counts is not mere chest-thumping. Instead, I wish to argue that developing several dozen hypotheses requires a focus that is uncommon in the field of IPE today. An unscientific scan of the nonformal books on my shelf suggest that most yield three or four distinct hypotheses at most. This means that people argue over the validity of individual hypotheses, often from incompatible theoretical frameworks. Those kinds of debates cannot really be resolved.

Scholars trained in more philosophical traditions evidently find these debates congenial, which is apparently why they persist. If we must have interparadigmatic debates – and it is not obvious in the philosophy of science that we must – let them take place between well-specified theories with a multitude of interconnected hypotheses, each with some empirical support. Having several dozen claims here challenges rival theories to respond in kind. If many of my claims ultimately prove wrong, perhaps they will at least spark a detailed alternative set of claims.

The theory of political support provides a simple framework within which to derive a surprisingly rich set of propositions, without specifying a lot of detail about individual countries in advance. For example, I argued that state preferences rest on domestic politics, though the specifics of this process naturally vary. Understanding these preferences does not require a detailed study of each individual country, but can be captured in a broad theory of political-support maximization. At the same time, case studies of several countries show that one *can* extend the theory into more detailed analyses when desired. This deceptively simple theory emerges from endogenous tariff theory, though I focus on cross-national and intertemporal variation in policy instead of explaining variation in tariffs by good within a single country.

In the more general framework here, domestic politics produces an autonomous tariff. Table 13.1 summarizes the propositions of the theory concerning this tariff. Except for those on volatility, the propositions from Chapter 3 are familiar to the literature on endogenous tariff theory. They therefore supply a firm, empirically grounded foundation for the latter parts of the book.

Compensation is central to this theory. States react to the outside world in a way that compensates domestic actors for change. Extensive anecdotal evidence suggests that many nineteenth-century leaders thought about their roles in this way. In contrast, modern political economists often think in winner-take-all terms, an assumption that leads to dramatically different predictions in many ways.

This logic of compensation leads to several hypotheses about the treaty system. Economic conditions also influence politicians' support-maximization problem and thus affect both tariffs and tariff treaties. For example, declining terms of trade reduce tariffs and make trade treaties more

Table 13.1. *Propositions concerning the autonomous tariff*

Hypothesis 3.1: The balancing hypothesis. The domestic price for protected goods is always less than the autarky price would be.

Hypothesis 3.2: The partial compensation hypothesis. Compensation is always partial in that no group receives a policy that fully compensates it for disadvantageous exogenous changes.

Hypothesis 3.3: The group influence hypothesis. Any increase in the marginal valuation of a group will change equilibrium prices in its favor.

Hypothesis 3.4: The declining prices hypothesis. Decreasing world prices (i.e., increasing terms of trade) lead to increased protection, and increasing world prices (decreasing terms of trade) lead to decreased protection.

Hypothesis 3.5: Large states and tariffs. Large states will have higher autonomous tariffs than small states.

Hypothesis 3.6: Transportation costs. Declining transportation costs leads to higher tariffs, whereas increasing transportation costs leads to lower tariffs.

Corollary 3.1: Tariff volatility. High tariffs are more volatile than low tariffs.

Corollary 3.2: Price volatility. As the world price of an imported good increases, tariffs imposed on that good will be less volatile; as the world price of an imported good decreases, tariff volatility will increase. (Equivalently, worsening terms of trade reduce tariff volatility; improving terms of trade increase tariff volatility.)

Result 3.1: Tariff volatility decreases as tariffs decrease over time in Europe.

Result 3.2: Small countries have less volatile tariffs than large countries.

Finding 4.1: In Europe, exogenous revenue constraints characterize only Denmark, Norway, Portugal, Sweden to 1885, and Switzerland.

Finding 4.2: Endogenous revenue constraints characterize Austria from 1867, France, Germany, Italy from 1877, and perhaps Bulgaria and Romania.

Finding 4.3: The limited data available support the claims of exogenous revenue constraints throughout Latin America, except in the more developed Southern Cone (Argentina, Brazil, Chile, and Uruguay).

Finding 4.4: High exogenous revenue dependence in North America apparently give way to endogenous considerations after the American Civil War (1861–1865) and Canadian Confederation (1866).

Finding 5.1: Democracy raises the tariff in northwest Europe, lowers the tariff in the Mediterranean, and has no effect elsewhere.

Finding 5.2: Austria and Italy exhibit increasing tariffs over time, even after controlling for other variables; tariffs decline over time in Latin America and northern Europe.

---

likely. Increasing terms of trade have the reverse effect, raising tariffs, causing tariffs to be more volatile, and making tariff treaties less likely. The basic logic here would extend easily to other issue areas, as politicians choose policy to counteract economic change.

Domestic institutional arrangements affect the support-maximization problem. Some (exogenous) revenue concerns limit tariff reductions, whereas other (endogenous) concerns encourage tariff reductions and thus also encourage trade cooperation. Democracy, too, could have effects that vary by country, raising the tariff in Northern Europe and lowering it in the Mediterranean. These political changes are not subject to the logic of compensation, as they directly change the weighting of variables in politicians' support functions, rather than changing the choices politicians make for a given weighting.

No matter how they value import-competers and exporters, however, all states have an incentive to cooperate. Politicians cooperate in trade because the political gains from helping exporters outweigh the political losses from reducing protection. This is hardly a novel argument. Nineteenth-century political economists and policymakers were well aware of the logic behind reciprocity, and it also lies behind modern economic theories of reciprocity.

The model predicts that low-tariff countries will be more likely to sign trade treaties than high-tariff countries. As a result, economic and political conditions associated with low tariffs will also be associated with greater cooperation. Democracy has unambiguous effects at this cooperation stage, making cooperation more likely. More speculatively, it appears that migration of persons also had unambiguous effects, making cooperation less likely both in countries of origin and in countries of immigration. Propositions stating the conditions under which cooperation is more or less likely are summarized in Table 13.2. These kinds of propositions are likely to extend well to other nontrade forms of economic cooperation.

It was striking that these propositions tended to perform better cross-nationally than intertemporally. Because institutional changes occurred only intermittently in each country, there was insufficient variation to account for variation in trade policy over time. Institutional differences were much more visible cross-nationally and had significant effects on variation in cooperation. The hypotheses also performed better for larger countries than for smaller countries and for European countries than for Latin American countries. This pattern suggests that more powerful countries with an incentive to cooperate are able to induce otherwise reluctant, less powerful countries to join them.

Moving beyond the theory of political support per se, I also explored how interaction between the executive and the legislature may affect cooperation.

Table 13.2. *Propositions concerning cooperation*

Hypothesis 7.1: The reaction hypothesis. Increasing protection in one country reduces protection in the other country, and vice versa.

Hypothesis 7.2: Liberalizing treaties. Two countries can always sign a reciprocity treaty reducing tariffs, but not one increasing tariffs.

Hypothesis 7.3: Treaty correlation. When two countries sign a tariff agreement, their tariffs will be positively correlated. (Thus, Hypothesis 8.1 does not apply.)

Hypothesis 7.4: Treaty support. Governments that sign reciprocity agreements receive more political support than those that do not.

Corollary 7.1: Democracy and treaties. Democracies are more likely to cooperate.

Corollary 7.2: Reciprocity and liberalization. Reciprocity makes possible tariff concessions that are impossible unilaterally.

Corollary 7.3: Mixed interests and reciprocity. Some groups that oppose unilateral liberalization will favor reciprocal liberalization.

Hypothesis 7.5: Treaty stability. When two countries sign a tariff agreement, Hypotheses 3.4 through 3.6 do not hold up to some point.

Remark 8.1: Unanticipated defection. Defection occurs only in response to unanticipated changes in the parameters of the political-support function.

Remark 8.2: Discount factors and cooperation. The more a state values the future (high discount factor), the more likely it is to cooperate; the less it values the future (low discount factor), the less likely it is to cooperate.

Hypothesis 8.1: Tariffs and cooperation. Tariff treaties are less likely to be stable for high-tariff countries than for low-tariff countries.

Hypothesis 8.2: Foreign tariffs and home treaties. Tariff treaties are more likely to be stable when foreign tariffs begin high than when foreign tariffs begin low.

Conjecture 8.1: Treaty variation by good. Tariff concession are more likely on duties that are already low, whereas high-tariff goods are more likely to be excluded from a trade treaty.

Hypothesis 8.3: Treaties and the terms of trade. Tariff treaties are more likely among countries with decreasing terms of trade than for countries with increasing terms of trade.

Result 8.1: Endogenous revenue and cooperation. An endogenous revenue constraint makes tariff treaties more likely.

Result 8.2: Exogenous revenue and cooperation. An exogenous revenue constraint makes tariff treaties less likely than does an endogenous revenue constraint and may or may not make tariff treaties less likely altogether.

(continued)

Table 13.2 *(continued)*

Hypothesis 8.4: Country size and treaties. Small states are less likely to sign trade treaties than large states.

Hypothesis 8.8: Migration and protection. Increases in emigration from, or immigration to, a country make protection more likely.

Hypothesis 9.1: When the legislature controls the reversion point, and it has ratification power, divided government makes cooperation
  (a) more likely for the executive up to a point, and has ambiguous effects thereafter,
  (b) has ambiguous effects on foreigners' willingness to cooperate,
  (c) and has no effect on the legislature's willingness to accept international cooperation.

Hypothesis 9.2: When the executive controls the reversion point and the legislature has ratification power, divided government makes
  (a) the executive more likely to cooperate,
  (b) foreigners less likely to cooperate, and
  (c) the legislature more likely to cooperate.

Finding 9.1: Treaty nonratification occurs more often in the presidential systems of the Americas than in the parliamentary systems of the Old World.

Finding 9.2: Countries with higher rates of nonratification also initiate fewer treaties.

Following the conventional wisdom, I examined how divided government may increase the risks of treaty nonratification, inhibiting cooperation. These problems may be found in some countries, from México to Switzerland. However, they are not general to all countries. As a result, a focus on ratification problems alone can provide only a partial explanation of variation in cooperation.

Figuring out the other effects of divided government requires looking beyond ratification problems. Ratification models neglect the effects of divided government on the reversion point. Because these effects may make cooperation more likely, the net effects of divided government on cooperation can be ambiguous. They depend on whether the executive or legislature sets the agenda for that reversion point and for cooperation, as well as the distance between the preferences of the two.

After looking at the politics of individual countries, I turned to the interaction of trade policies in the system as a whole. At times the regime fed on itself through spread effects. Anything that causes foreign tariffs to increase makes home trade treaties more likely. Because discriminatory trade treaties have trade diversion effects, third parties will face higher effective protection. In

Table 13.3. *Propositions concerning trade treaty norms*

Finding 10.1: Use of the MFN norm spreads.

Hypothesis 11.1: Without MFN, foreign cooperation leads to home liberalization; with MFN, foreign cooperation leads to home protection or no change in tariffs.

Corollary 11.1: Customs unions lead to foreign liberalization.

Hypothesis 11.2: Without MFN, foreign cooperation makes home cooperation more likely, both with the two initial cooperators and with fourth parties; with MFN, foreign cooperation may make home cooperation less likely or have no effect.

Corollary 11.2: Customs unions spread to encompass new members.

Corollary 11.3: Customs unions induce the formation of other customs unions.

Hypothesis 12.1: Clustering leads to smaller concessions by states that cluster.

Hypothesis 12.2: MFN is a necessary condition for clustering.

Hypothesis 12.3: States cluster as a result of pressures on the import side, not the export side.

---

this way, discriminatory trade treaties make treaties more likely among third parties. They may either seek treaties of their own with the discriminators or pursue treaties with other states left outside the discriminatory tariff area. These propositions are summarized in Table 13.3. Though MFN is specific to trade, these implications will likely extend to other issue areas in which states can choose between discriminatory and nondiscriminatory norms.

Because changes in the terms of trade and spread effects hit western European countries at the same time, with effects working in a similar direction, the theory helps explain why changes occurred in a wave pattern. A coincidence of major domestic institutional changes in the 1860s spurred the middle of the three waves. A partial move to protection in the 1880s contributed to the wave in the next decade, reinforced by worsening terms of trade for many countries in the 1890s.

The most strongly focused waves were characterized by "clusters" of negotiations, especially in 1892–1893 and 1905–1906. These clusters only occurred when states negotiated treaties using the MFN clause, and they had the effect of reducing the concessions that each country would make to others. As a result, the clustered negotiations in the last 25 years of the period rarely yielded substantial liberalization, though they did prevent a return to protectionism. I return to this account in the historical summary later in this chapter.

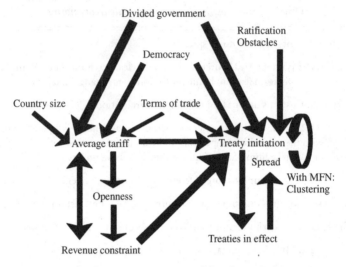

Figure 13.1. Diagrammatic Summary of the Theoretical Argument.

A Bottom-up Theory of Cooperation

The theory presents a bottom-up explanation of cooperation. It begins with the autonomous trade policy of the state and then moves to cooperation, which requires at least a pair of states. After this I looked at regime-wide rules, most notably MFN, to see how they affected cooperation within the system. Figure 13.1 shows this argument diagrammatically.

Critics of domestic-level theorizing often argue that systemic-level theory is much more parsimonious and provides a better starting point for the discipline. I am sympathetic to this claim, having written a systemic-level book myself. Yet, the force of this argument seems to lie more in the intellectual history of the discipline than in its present. Indeed, systemic-level theory did provide us with a parsimonious starting point and did yield many hypotheses about international relations. However, our tools now allow us to begin at either the systemic or domestic level or to combine parts of each. This book, like many others written over the last decade or so, contributes to this latter project. It treats the levels of analysis as a purely taxonomic issue, not a fundamental problem for theory.

Even so, some features of the levels-of-analysis "problem" remain. At each level, the next level confounds some of the explanation. For example, some hypotheses concerning the autonomous tariff do not apply when countries negotiate over the tariff (see Chapters 3, 7, and 8). Sometimes I was able to test for these differences explicitly, but in other cases we had to be content with the conjecture that the single-country tests obtained weak results because of interactions between states. Similarly, some of the hypotheses on trade treaty initiation were probably confounded by system-wide clusters and/or spread effects. It was harder to control for these systemic-level effects (see Chapters 8, 11, and 12), though they doubtless help explain why some hypotheses on cooperation had only modest empirical success.

These confounding relationships remind us that the levels-of-analysis problem in political science is real, if exaggerated. At the same time, this book shows that a theory can work across multiple levels. Future research can better explicate the relationships between levels, deriving the conditions under which hypotheses at one level will not hold because of contrary forces at a different level. The future may also see more fully synthetic theories instead of the distinct, but compatible, models used here in different parts.

Political Economy and History

Whereas the levels-of-analysis debate divides political scientists, questions of both theory and method divide the disciplines of economics, history, and political science. Economists and political scientists, who are overwhelmingly positivists, argue that theories and laws apply to any period of history. Historians maintain that even if social scientific laws have some validity they must be applied with attention to context and sequence (i.e., Carr 1961). Because the positivists rarely study historical events and historians rarely attempt to develop strong theory, all can point to evidence in their support.

Several decades ago, the "new economic history" began with the observation that one could use the tools of modern economics to analyze economic history theoretically. This marked an advance on the tradition of more descriptive economic history found in the disciplines of economics and history. This book is a contribution toward a growing field of "new political history" or, in my case, new historical political economy. The most obvious locus of the new political history has been a group of scholars who use formal theory and/or quantitative techniques to examine nineteenth-century Britain and the United States. Notable examples of this research include Gary Cox's *The Efficient Secret* (1987), Doug Dion's *Turning the Legislative Thumbscrew* (1997), Fiona McGillivray et al., *International Trade and Political Institutions* (2001), Cheryl Schonhardt-Bailey's *From the Corn Laws to Free Trade* (2006), and articles by Douglas Irwin (1989, 1991, 1993, 1995), Timothy McKeown (1991), Iain McLean (1998, 2001; McLean and Bustani 1999; McLean and Foster 1992), and others. These works vary substantially in the extent to which they use historical color in support of their arguments, but all share an interest in bringing historiography and theoretical political science into dialogue.

Without going into any of the contextual detail one would normally find in history, this chapter provides an overview of my account of the nineteenth-century trade regime. My claims are grounded in the theory presented in earlier chapters, but I present them here with minimal reference to that theory. I return to the three waves of trade cooperation described in Chapter 1, waves that correspond roughly with the 1820s–1830s, 1860s, and 1890s. The first and last of these centered on Germany, the middle wave on France.

The Three Waves of Trade Treaties

Accounting for the three waves of treaties in this period required that I paint with a broad brush because each wave depended on the choices of many states with a variety of interests. Here I focus almost entirely on Europe, as the evidence from Latin America remains too incomplete to provide more than a guide to further research. Recall too that the hypotheses on trade cooperation performed best for the core states, and most poorly for the periphery (Chapter 8).

First Wave

The first wave of treaties centered on the German *Zollverein* and foreigners' reactions to it. Prussia and other North German states responded both to the chaos of the post-Napoleonic period in Germany and to important changes in their terms of trade. Lower prices for their grain exports induced liberalization and made them more eager to cooperate with others. Grain importers such as Britain raised their tariffs, inducing further liberalization in Prussia and making cooperation still more attractive. The patchwork of customs enclaves and exclaves throughout Germany provided a further incentive for liberalization.

This liberalization resonated elsewhere in Germany in part because of early forms of democratization. The rules of the German Confederation encouraged constitutionalism, and popular protests in 1830 pushed the process along still further. The effects of this early democratization varied widely by region, but supported free-trade interests more often than not because the more democratic parts of Germany tended to have a working class and other popular forces that favored freer trade. A mix of constitutionalism, republicanism, and democracy in the Americas also encouraged the hemisphere's newly independent states to cooperate with one another and with some European countries. Relations among México, the United States, and the *Zollverein* seem particularly important in this nexus.

Each German state also affected the others. In particular, fears of being shut out of the growing *Zollverein* led many German states to join Prussia and others to form their own regional customs unions. Once they joined the *Zollverein*, Prussia used its control of the union tariff to encourage cooperation with outsiders, even over the opposition of members.

The German network also had important spread effects on the rest of Europe. Most countries did not have MFN treaties with the *Zollverein* and feared being shut out of German markets. These fears even began to bring autocratic Austria into the German trade treaty network. Austria took hesitant steps toward liberalization and toward cooperation with Germany and third parties. However, these tendencies only reached fruition after the revolutions of 1848–1849 and the ensuing constitutional reforms in Austria. These spread effects may have encouraged cooperation among some outsiders, including Britain, France, and the United States.

Though important in Germany, this was the least important of the three waves for the global political economy. The century's first transportation revolution probably played a role in inhibiting the growth of the treaty network. Railroads and steamships emerged, and most countries built new road or canal networks. Many countries, such as France and the United Kingdom, responded to increased trade with compensatory protection. This also made them less willing to sign trade treaties, especially during the economic disruptions of the post-Napoleonic period. Only their concerns about losing access to the growing German market overcame these protectionist impulses.

The unreformed political systems of many countries also reduced cooperation, though they had mixed effects on tariffs. Recognizably democratic institutions were limited to Norway and some small German states, to which Belgium may be added in 1830. Britain's reform act in 1832, the revolution of 1830 in Germany, and an expanding franchise in the Netherlands added a few more countries, but fuller democratization in Europe had to await the revolutions of 1848. Though this democratization had ambiguous effects on autonomous trade policy, trade cooperation was increasingly dominated by democratic states cooperating with one another.

Second Wave
The second wave is the most well known in both history and political science. Sparked by the Cobden-Chevalier treaty of 1860, this wave depended most visibly on France's commercial diplomacy under the Emperor Louis

Napoléon. This activity reflected Napoléon's changing beliefs about trade policy, a strong deterioration in France's terms of trade, and a particular set of domestic institutions in which the legislature set tariffs, while the emperor could negotiate trade treaties without requiring legislative ratification. Yet, it also grew out of existing cooperation in Germany and the relations between the *Zollverein* and its neighbors.

The wave was also marked by the unifications of Italy and Germany. Each had the effect of raising effective tariffs against outsiders, giving these outsiders an incentive to cooperate with one another as well as with the unifiers. This effect was strongest on Austria, which saw itself facing an economically and politically unified Germany, but also losing territory in northern Italy. Austria's traumatic loss to Germany in 1866 then led to a new constitutional settlement that lasted to the end of the dynasty. The divided government that characterized this *Ausgleich* had a strong positive effect on Austria's willingness to sign trade treaties, and these treaties helped hold the two halves of the empire together.

This wave of treaties accelerated a massive expansion of trade at mid-century. Ronald Rogowski (1989: 21) describes the period as having

recorded history's swiftest and most comprehensive expansion of international commerce. Between 1840 and 1895, world trade roughly sextupled in nominal terms; from then to 1913 it more than quintupled. In real terms – that is, taking into account price movements – it appears that international trade increased by between 135 and 150% between 1800 and 1840, more than quadrupled between 1840 and 1870, more than doubled between 1870 and the end of the century, and grew by about half again between 1901 and 1913.

The secondary literature generally finds that this increase in trade depended both on the trade treaty network and the transportation and communication revolutions. Trade treaties led to unprecedented prosperity for French farmers in the 1860s, in part because of greater exports of foodstuffs to Great Britain. Italy's treaties with Austria, Germany, and Switzerland secured important export markets for southern agricultural produce, which prospered as a result. The reciprocal tariff elimination of the *Zollverein*, alongside the railroad building of the period, was critical to German industrialization in the nineteenth century.

MFN also played an important role in this wave. As the wave sputtered to a close, most countries in the network had MFN treaties in effect with everyone else in the network. Those left outside the treaty network increasingly found themselves facing high effective tariffs, which could be reduced only by joining the system themselves. This effect was most obvious in

Latin America, where major expansion in the first wave had slowed down by the time of the second wave. Russia too was largely excluded, and this contributed to its new direction under Witte in the 1890s.

The wave ended with the transportation revolution of the 1870s. The explosion of steamships and railroads and the start of refrigeration opened Europe to large-scale imports of wheat, beef, and other foodstuffs. Prices fell, threatening most of Europe's agriculture and leading to demands for protection across the continent.

The trade treaty system played an important role in avoiding a descent to mutual protectionism. Most countries hesitated to denounce these treaties, which made it more difficult for them to raise tariffs against imports. As a result, the move toward protectionism in the 1880s was constrained by the existing treaties. Most countries continued to increase their openness even if tariffs also went up a little, and most of the rest remained on a plateau in both tariffs and openness (see Figures 2.11–2.20).

Third Wave

The third wave arose in response to this limited protectionism, encouraged by recovery in agricultural prices. It began as a reaction to domestic demands to denounce the trade treaties, notably in Austria-Hungary and France. Politicians redirected these demands toward a policy of treaty renegotiation, which came to characterize the third wave. This allowed politicians to respond not only to the demands of import-competing interests for greater protection but also to exporters' desires to open foreign markets for their goods.

Though France saw the strongest demands for renegotiation, leading to the Méline tariff of 1891, Germany became the center of these negotiations. This reflected its declining terms of trade as well as political openings after the fall of Bismarck. As world grain prices recovered, German grain tariffs slowly decreased again, which opened fissures in the protectionist coalition and created political space for Caprivi's active commercial diplomacy. The Socialist Party, rapidly growing after being relegalized, gave tacit support to this policy along with much of the political center.

These negotiations occurred in an international environment very different from the first German wave. Most European countries had treaties in effect with one another, and these generally included the MFN clause. Because any concession given to one state would then be generalized to all, the timing of negotiations became critically important. Germany's solution, joined by Austria-Hungary and others, was to cluster negotiations into a narrow period and to keep concessions secret for as long as feasible.

MFN within the network also encouraged the system's final phase of expansion. The third wave saw the entry of a few formerly reluctant states, such as Russia and Sweden. Their entry coincided with other domestic developments, included Witte's reforms in Russia and the end of divided government in Sweden after Norwegian independence in 1905. The United States was also a significant player, thanks to the McKinley tariff.

In contrast to these new members, the United Kingdom stood mostly aloof from the third wave of treaties. The analysis here agrees with others who emphasize the revenue constraint faced by the United Kingdom. Paradoxically, Britain's renunciation of a protective tariff was accompanied by comparatively high dependence on the tariff for revenue, and this limited cooperation.

The argument of this book helps reconcile two contending views of the nineteenth-century trade system. Many historians view the 1890s as a return to protectionism, evidenced by the Méline tariff and the supposed breakdown of the 1860s treaty system. In contrast, political scientists see continued openness under hegemony, led by Britain's refusal to engage in tariff reform. My analysis suggests a middle ground – continued openness undergirded by new treaties that did not reduce tariffs by as much as previous treaties had. Severe distributional conflicts within a cooperative regime limited the openness that was achieved.

As this account suggests, this wave saw an increasing role of the state in negotiating the ground rules for trade. This pattern mirrors the increasing role of the state in other spheres, such as the nascent welfare state, social imperialism, or what German Marxists have called *organisierter Kapitalismus* (Magnusson 2000: Chapter 7; Offe and Wiesenthal 1980; Winkler, 1974). This greater role of the state laid the foundation for more extensive interventionism in the 1930s and beyond. Outside Germany, some have argued that Giolittismo anticipated the New Deal in Italy (Coppa 1971), whereas Sweden's trade negotiations helped establish a pattern of interest intermediation that laid the foundations for corporatism (Lindberg 1983).

Trade policy also has implications for political and economic history. Tariffs are historically important because they were a major line of cleavage in the party systems of most European countries in the nineteenth century. Labor and socialist parties generally favored free trade. After steamships opened Europe to low-cost competition from the Western Hemisphere and Australian grain and beef, agricultural parties were invariably protectionist. Business parties varied, from free-trading smaller liberal parties in Germany and the large Liberal Party of Victorian England to protectionist bourgeois parties in France and elsewhere.

These trade treaties also played an important role in domestic affairs, as part of the breakup of classical Liberalism. Although they served Liberal goals of freer trade, increasingly detailed treaties put liberalization in the hands of the state. Indeed, this state role in treaties was one reason English Liberals rejected such treaties, and this view remained important in England through 1914.

Finally, trade policy was important in idiosyncratic ways for most countries of Europe. Robert Peel's repeal of the Corn Laws, in opposition to a majority of his own party, broke the Conservatives for a generation. Free trade gave the German Social Democrats a wedge with which to break open the apparent unity of the bourgeois parties in Wilhelmine Germany. Although they were unsuccessful at the national level, the Social Democrats found several bourgeois allies in individual states, such as Bavaria, Baden, and Württemberg, in part because of their position on trade. Tariffs were an important cleavage issue in the French Third Republic, as in the Second Empire and before.

In short, trade cooperation presents not only an interesting theoretical problem in the study of international relations but also a substantively important subject for historians. The historiography has traditionally seen the trading regime of the nineteenth century as centered on either Britain or France, whereas this book moves this center substantially eastward. Germany played the key role in both the first and third waves, and Austria-Hungary and Italy were both major players in the system from the late 1860s on.

Substantive Implications

The model has implications for several different problems, from the understanding of certain historical events to the analysis of some trade policy problems. I briefly review some of these implications here.

Unilateral Liberalization

As I discussed earlier, economists have long advocated a policy of free trade, regardless of the policies that other nations choose. When faced with the unfortunate fact that politicians have not listened to this advice, economists have argued that politicians are too confined by political interests to pursue economic rationality. The model here shows that politicians may be right to hesitate even on welfare grounds. If *foreign* politicians worry about political support, then unilateral home liberalization will induce increases in foreign tariffs.

Failing to think about foreign responses was the error of most nineteenth-century British political economists, who believed that unilateral liberalization would lead the rest of the world to follow suit. Though they usually did not draw the correct inferences, they learned that liberalization of British imports soon led to greater British exports, threatening import-competers abroad and encouraging protectionism.

European liberalization ultimately resulted not from the British example, but from a network of reciprocal commercial treaties, many embodying the MFN principle. The most famous of these was negotiated by Richard Cobden and Maurice Chevalier and signed in 1860. France alone signed about a dozen more MFN treaties after that.

Although there was some return to protectionism after 1873 in unilateral tariffs, reciprocity agreements restrained this tendency. States tended to respect these treaties, implying that the threat of tariff war must generally have been effective (for exceptions, see Conybeare 1987). Most interestingly, governments that depended on protectionist coalitions signed and observed these agreements: France under the Méline tariff, Caprivi and, to some extent, Bülow in Germany, Taft and Roosevelt in the United States. This suggests that a world without reciprocity treaties could not constrain tariff increases, whereas a world with such agreements could.

The WTO

The practical politicians of the post-1945 era seem to have learned this lesson better. Trade liberalization has occurred not only in a network of trade treaties but under the auspices of a formal international organization, first the GATT and now the WTO. This international organization is based on a series of norms, including the MFN.

Despite its successes, the GATT/WTO system has been dogged by problems that reached a head in the collapse of the Doha Development Round in 2006. This study of the nineteenth century highlights the MFN norm as one reason for this collapse. Nondiscrimination helps explain why GATT/WTO trade liberalization has been so slow. Comparable liberalization was achieved in much of Western Europe in the 1860s alone (Marsh 1999). A historical perspective raises the question of whether the GATT somehow encouraged states to make small concessions or to liberalize only in a series of small steps.

Though this claim must remain speculative for now, the theory suggests that the GATT's slow pace stemmed from clustering MFN negotiations. The first three rounds (Annecy, Torquay, and Geneva) made especially slow progress under conditions closest to those of the model. Gilbert Winham argues that MFN forced each state to attempt simultaneous negotiations with all the relevant players simultaneously (Winham 1986, 62–63). These negotiations made concessions more difficult because they would be generalized to third parties. Andrew Shonfield (1976: 47) even labels this the "explosive mixture" of MFN and reciprocity:

It is worth noting that the dominant place accorded to the m.f.n. principle in postwar international trade relations tended to make them even more fragile and subject to the accidents of bargaining than they had been before. M.f.n. is in fact a ready-made instrument for setting in motion a downward spiral in the process of bargaining, once nations begin to adopt an adversary posture towards one another, for a dispute between two countries which leads one of them to withdraw a trade concession originally made as part of a general bargain between them is almost bound to inflict some injury on the trading interests of other countries who happen to be exporters of the products affected.

According to Winham (1986: 355), the Kennedy Round avoided these problems by moving to linear tariff reductions. This focused negotiations on exceptions to the basic cuts and not on the basic offer. It therefore represents a novel agenda-setting rule, one that poses an alternative to clustering in its nineteenth-century form. With the Tokyo Codes, the GATT norm in practice became much closer to conditional MFN because the benefits of these codes were granted only to other code signatories and not to all GATT members.

Despite these similarities in tariff-cutting, the WTO performs two tasks that make it differ from the nineteenth-century system. First, it has an elaborate dispute resolution mechanism, and dispute panels can now make binding resolutions of disputes by majority vote. These mechanisms can be analyzed in terms broadly consistent with the theory of political support (see Busch 2000; Milner and Rosendorff 2001; Reinhardt 2001), but fall outside the analysis of this book.

Second, beginning with the Tokyo Round (1973–1979) the GATT and WTO have addressed many trade-related issues, such as investment, intellectual property, and phytosanitary standards. Many of these represent more subtle problems than nondiscriminatory tariff-cutting under MFN rules. The political dynamics of these issues has pushed the regime forward and calls out for future analysis using the theory of political support.

Explicit modeling of policy instruments might produce results congruent with the "spillover" logic of functionalist theories of economic integration. Reciprocal liberalization of trade policy decreases the marginal political support attainable from future policies benefitting export sector industries. This makes reciprocal liberalization of other sectors, such as factor markets, more attractive because the marginal political support available there is (almost) unchanged. By the same logic, liberalizing factor markets might reach a point where reciprocal support gains are only attainable in sectors such as government procurement. It is easy to see how this logic might illuminate a cascade of liberalization such as the Single European Act and Maastricht Treaty or the complexities of NAFTA, no less than the steady expansion of issues covered by the WTO.

Analyzing these effects in the model here is difficult because the model is limited by my failure to model the international economy explicitly. Explicit modeling of trade flows would clearly affect the analysis of both clustering and spread, as noted in Chapters 11 and 12. Using a full model of the economy, instead of bracketing the topic, would also make for better analysis of country size, tariff differentiation, transport costs, and the effects of comparative advantage on the choice of cooperation partners. Such extensions would also make it possible to move the theory of political support into areas of the new international economics, such as economies of scale, imperfect competition, and strategic trade theory (Brander 1996; Spencer 1986).

Economic variables have played only a superficial role in most empirical theories of political economy, including mine. Although price levels and comparative advantage have attracted substantial attention, the level of economic detail in most theories is disappointing. Consider the trade policy implications of having two substitute goods, such as long-haul trucks and railroad equipment, produced in noticeably different sectors – the first relatively competitive, subject to only modest economies of scale and no network effects, and the second differing on each of these points. Theory would expect higher tariffs on railroad equipment, but that makes railroad users more likely to switch to long-haul trucking, raising the demand for trucks and lowering that for railroad equipment even more than protection in a partial equilibrium model. This lobbying story ignores political coalitions, however, and truckers might form a coalition with railroads, or they might choose to compete them out of business. Theory provides no guide to understand the politics of protection in such cases, yet both transport equipment and transport services have become salient sectors in international trade negotiations. Future research should provide more guidance. Both lobbying and coalitional behavior will differ depending on industrial structure.

This book focuses on the cross-national environment for such questions, but clearly the intersectoral issues and the economics behind them deserve more attention. They also affect the cross-national differences: the United States relies on many industries with scale economies, whereas Chinese manufacturing exports generally do not have such economies.

Behind all these details, stability remains an important goal of the contemporary regime, as it was in the nineteenth century. The WTO's Web page asserts that its main function

is to ensure that trade flows as smoothly, predictably and freely as possible. The result is assurance. Consumers and producers know that they can enjoy secure supplies and greater choice of the finished products, components, raw materials and services that they use. Producers and exporters know that foreign markets will remain open to them.[1]

Stability in trade barriers is apparently as important as lowering them. Any criticism of the WTO must remember its stability-inducing effects.

Regional Integration

Many analysts have argued that the WTO is also threatened by increasing regionalism in the international trading system. Global regimes treat all countries equally. In contrast, regional agreements typically grant their members better-than-MFN treatment, representing explicit exceptions to the MFN norm of the GATT/WTO system. When we look at the political consequences of discrimination, the theory of political support leads to more optimistic conclusions about the interrelationship between globalism and regionalism.

Chapter 11 showed that liberalization among a group of countries reduces the market access enjoyed by third-party exporters. The governments of these third parties will want to compensate their citizens who are harmed by this reduced access, redirecting income to their exporters either through unilateral liberalization or through commercial agreements with the regional bloc. Such concerns may help explain the spread of the European Economic Community from 6 countries to 27 or the growth of the US-Canada Free Trade Area into NAFTA and beyond.

Contemporary regionalism should affect clustering. Preferential trading areas such as the EU, NAFTA, or MERCOSUR, grant members better-than-MFN treatment. In effect, this removes MFN between members and outsiders, though each outsider still receives the same treatment as every other outsider. This discrimination between members and nonmembers pulls the rug out from under centralized bargaining. I would expect clustering within these institutions, where all members are treated equally. The important role of intergovernmental conferences (IGCs) in the EU in the 1990s is a good example of such clustering.

---

[1] See http://www.wto.org/wto/inbrief/inbr00.htm, accessed February 29, 2000. Oddly, only the first sentence appears on the Web site now (as of August 28, 2005).

This clustering would be less attractive between regions. In this way, re-gionalization takes away an important motive for global negotiations, nego-tiations that make progress more slowly than regional trade agreements. At the same time, regionalism spreads, and it encourages negotiations between regions. All these processes should encourage reciprocal liberal-ization of the global economy.

This analysis suggests that we should tell the history of regional agree-ments only with reference to other regions. The creation of EFTA in 1959, for example, only makes sense as part of a history including the European Economic Community. Regional blocs feed on each other. The failure of the Doha Round's globalism stands in contrast to ongoing expansion and deepening of the EU. We can expect regionalism to continue to flourish in the twenty-first century.

Conclusions

One studies international cooperation to see how peoples can jointly solve the problems they face. Cooperation can be a central part of global manage-ment. Trade has been the most important facet of globalization for centuries, though it has now been joined by the globalization of money, finance, migra-tion, and other economic processes. Trade cooperation therefore presents an especially relevant subject of analysis.

The theory of political support offers both parsimony and productivity, using a few simple assumptions to generate a large number of propositions. The logic can be extended indefinitely to particular economic or political contexts. Moreover, the propositions derived from this theory enjoyed sub-stantial empirical support throughout this book, suggesting that even more detailed propositions can clear up the anomalies found here. I have sketched some of these directions here, which point us toward a more detailed under-standing of the world as we find it and not toward meta-theoretical debates over ontology and perspectives.

The nineteenth-century trade treaty network provides grounds for opti-mism in the twenty-first century. Left to their own devices, countries choose trade policies that harm other countries. Trade treaties provide a solution, contributing to the hitherto unprecedented prosperity of the nineteenth century. The post-1945 regime built on this success with global economic management of its own. Yet the nineteenth century differed dramatically from the post-World War II pattern. The last half-century has seen globaliza-tion undergirded by the Cold War, military alliances, and all-encompassing institutions. Security concerns supposedly tempered economic conflict for nearly five decades. This book explores a different type of global economic cooperation, no less deep and no less successful. The nineteenth-century regime provides a model for regulating the international economy in the face of domestic backlash against globalization. Both its robustness in the face of economic change and its ability to compensate those who lose from trade, while retaining the advantages of openness should encourage free traders today.

References

Abbott, Kenneth W. and Duncan Snidal. 1998. "Why States Act Through Formal International Organizations." *Journal of Conflict Resolution* 42(1): 3–32 (February).

Abrego, Lisandro, Raymond Riezman, and John Whalley. 2004. "Computation and the Theory of Customs Unions." Unpublished Manuscript.

Accominotti, Olivier and Marc Flandreau. 2006. "Does Bilateralism Promote Trade? Nineteenth Century Liberalization Revisited." London: Centre for Economic Policy Research Discussion Paper No. 5423.

Aggarwal, Vinod K. 1985. *Liberal Protectionism: The International Politics of Organized Free Trade.* Berkeley: University of California Press.

Alapuro, Risto. 1988. *State and Revolution in Finland.* Berkeley: University of California Press.

Allen, Deborah L., Leslie Lewis, and Edward Tower. 1980. "U.S. Concessions in the Kennedy Round and Short-run Labor Adjustment Costs: Still Further Evidence." *Quarterly Review of Economics and Business* 20: 108–10 (Autumn).

Anderson, Gary M. and Robert D. Tollison. 1985. "Ideology, Interest Groups, and the Repeal of the Corn Laws." *Zeitschrift für die gesamte Staatswissenschaft* 141(2): 197–212.

Anderson, Kym. 1980. "The Political Market for Government Assistance to Australian Manufacturing Industries." *The Economic Record* 56(153): 132–44 (June).

Angell, James B. 1901. "The Turkish Capitulations." *American Historical Review* 6(2): 254–59 (January).

Ankli, Robert E. 1971. "The Reciprocity Treaty of 1854." *Canadian Journal of Economics* 4(1): 1–20 (February).

Antonescu, Cornelius G. 1915. *Die Rumänische Handelspolitik von 1875–1910.* Leipzig: Wilhelm Schunke Verlag.

Arend, Anthony Clark. 1999. *Legal Rules and International Society.* Oxford: Oxford University Press.

Ashley, Percy. 1926. *Modern Tariff History. Germany – United States – France* (3rd ed.). New York: E. P. Dutton & Company.

Augier, Charles. 1906. *La France et les traités de commerce: Étude sur les tarifs des douanes de la France et de l'étranger.* Paris: Librairie Chevalier et Riviere.

Austen-Smith, David. 1981. "Voluntary Pressure Groups." *Economica* 48(190): 143–53 (May).

Avery, William P., ed. 1993. *World Agriculture and the GATT.* Boulder: Lynne Rienner Publishers.

Axelrod, Robert. 1984. *The Evolution of Cooperation.* New York: Basic Books.

Axelrod, Robert and Robert O. Keohane. 1986. "Achieving Cooperation under Anarchy: Strategies and Institutions." in Oye, ed. 1986: 226–54.

Bac, Mehmet, and Horst Raff. 1997. "A Theory of Trade Concessions." *Journal of International Economics* 42(3): 483–504 (May).

Bagwell, Kyle and Robert W. Staiger. 1990. "A Theory of Managed Trade." *American Economic Review* 80(4): 779–95 (September).

Bagwell, Kyle and Robert W. Staiger. 1999. "Multilateral Trade Negotiations, Bilateral Opportunism and the Rules of GATT." Cambridge, MA: National Bureau of Economic Research Working Paper 7071.

Bagwell, Kyle and Robert W. Staiger. 2005. "Multilateral Trade Negotiations, Bilateral Opportunism and the Rules of GATT/WTO." *Journal of International Economics* 67(2): 268–94 (December).

Bairoch, Paul. 1972. "Free Trade and European Economic Development in the 19th Century." *European Economic Review* 3(3): 211–45 (November).

Bairoch, Paul. 1989. "European Trade Policy 1815–1914." in *Cambridge Economic History of Europe*, Vol. 13, edited by Peter Mathias and Sidney Pollard. New York: Columbia University Press, pp. 1–160.

Bairoch, Paul. 1993. *Economics and World History: Myths and Paradoxes.* Chicago: University of Chicago Press.

Baldwin, Robert E. 1976. "Trade and Employment Effects in the United States of Multilateral Tariff Reductions." *American Economic Review Papers and Proceedings* 66: 142–48 (May).

Baldwin, Robert E. 1985. *The Political Economy of U.S. Import Policy.* Cambridge: MIT Press.

Baldwin, Richard E. 1990. "Optimal Tariff Retaliation Rules." In *The Political Economy of International Trade*, ed. R. Jones and A. Krueger. Oxford: Blackwell, pp. 108–21.

Baldwin, Richard. 1993. "A Domino Theory of Regionalism." NBER Working Paper No. 4465, September.

Bale, Malcolm D. 1977. "United States Concessions in the Kennedy Round and Short-Run Labour Adjustment Costs: Further Evidence." *Journal of International Economics* 7(2): 145–48 (May).

Barkin, Kenneth D. 1970. *The Controversy over German Industrialization 1890–1902.* Chicago: University of Chicago Press.

Basevi, Giorgio. 1966. "The United States Tariff Structure: Estimates of Effective Rates of Protection of United States Industries and Industrial Labor." *Review of Economics and Statistics* 48(2): 147–60 (May).

Bastiat, Frédéric. 1862. "Démocratie et libre-échange." In *Œuvres complètes de Fréderic Bastiat, mises en ordre, rev. et annotées d'après les manuscrits de l'auteur.* 2nd ed., vol. 2, *Le Libre-Échange.* Paris: Guillaumin, 1862–64.

Bazant, Johann von. 1894. *Die Handelspolitik Österreich-Ungarns 1875 bis 1892 in ihrem Verhältnis zum Deutschem Reiche und zu dem westlichen Europa.* Leipzig: Verlag von Dunker & Humblot.

Beck, Nathaniel and Jonathan N. Katz. 1995. "What to do (and not to do) with Time-Series Cross-Section Data." *American Political Science Review* 89(3): 634–47 (September).

Beck, Nathaniel, Gary King, and Langche Zeng. 2000. "Improving Quantitative Studies of International Conflict: A Conjecture." *American Political Science Review* 94(1): 21–35 (March).

Becker, Gary S. 1983. "A Theory of Competition Among Pressure Groups for Political Influence." *Quarterly Journal of Economics* 98(3): 371–400 (August).

Becker, Gary S. 1985. "Public Policies, Pressure Groups, and Dead Weight Costs." *Journal of Public Economics* 28(3): 329–47 (December).

Beckett, Grace Louis. 1941. *The Reciprocal Trade Agreements Program.* New York: Columbia University Press.

Beer, Adolf. 1891. *Österreichische Handelspolitik im neunzehnten Jahrhundert.* Vienna: Manz'sche k.u.k. Hof-Verlags und Universitäts-Buchhandlung.

Bergstrom, Theodore, Lawrence Blume, and Hal Varian. 1986. "On the Private Provision of Public Goods." *Journal of Public Economics* 29(1): 25–49 (March).

Bhagwati, Jagdish. 1990. "Departures from Multilateralism: Regionalism and Aggressive Unilateralism." *Economic Journal* 100 (403): 1304–17 (December).

Bhagwati, Jagdish, David Greenaway, and Arvind Panagariya. 1998. "Trading Preferentially: Theory and Policy." *Economic Journal* 108(449): 1128–48 (July).

Black, D. E. 1943. *The Establishment of Constitutional Government in Bulgaria.* Princeton: Princeton University Press.

Bordo, Michael D., Barry Eichengreen, and Douglas A. Irwin. 1999. "Is Globalization Today Really Different than Globalization a Hundred Years Ago?" Cambridge, MA: NBER Working Paper 7195. http://www.nber.org/papers/w7195 (June).

Brainard, S. Lael and Thierry Verdier. 1997. "The Political Economy of Declining Industries: Senescent Industry Collapse Revisited." *Journal of International Economics* 42(1): 221–37 (Febraury).

Brander, James A. 1996. "Rationales for Strategic Trade and Industrial Policy." In *Strategic Trade Policy and the New International Economics*, ed. Paul R. Krugman, pp. 23–46.

Braumoeller, Bear F. and Gary Goertz. 2000. "The Methodology of Necessary Conditions." *American Journal of Political Science* 44(4): 844–58 (October).

Brauneder, Wilhelm and Friedrich Lachmayer. 1980. *Österreichische Verfassungsgeschichte* (2d ed.). Wien: Manzsche Verlags- und Universitätsbuchhandlung.

Brawley, Mark R. 1993. *Liberal Leadership: Great Powers and Their Challengers in Peace and War.* Ithaca: Cornell University Press.

Bueno de Mesquita, Bruce and David Lalman. 1992. *War and Reason: Domestic and International Imperatives.* New Haven: Yale University Press.

Bueno de Mesquita, Bruce, Alastair Smith, Randolph M. Siverson, and James D. Morrow. 2003. *The Logic of Political Survival.* Cambridge, MA: MIT Press.

Bulmer-Thomas, Victor. 1994. *The Economic History of Latin America Since Independence.* Cambridge: Cambridge University Press.

von Bülow, Heinrich August Ernst. 1902. *Österreich-Ungarns Handels- und Industrie-Politik.* Berlin: Wilhelm Süsserott.

Busch, Mark L. 2000. "Democracy, Consultation, and the Paneling of Disputes under GATT." *Journal of Conflict Resolution* 44(4): 425–46 (August).

Busch, Marc L. and Eric Reinhardt. 2000a. "Geography, International Trade, and Political Mobilization in U.S. Industries." *American Journal of Political Science* 44(4): 703–19 (October).

Busch, Marc L. and Eric Reinhardt. 2000b. "Bargaining in the Shadow of the Law: Early Settlement in GATT/WTO Disputes." *Fordham International Law Journal* 24(1–2): 158–72 (November-December).

Busch, Marc L. and Eric Reinhardt. 2001. "Testing International Trade Law: Empirical Studies of GATT/WTO Dispute Settlement." In *The Political Economy of International Trade Law: Essays in Honor of Robert E. Hudec*, ed. Daniel L. M. Kennedy and James D. Southwick. Cambridge: Cambridge University Press.

Cahan, Steven F. and William H. Kaempfer. 1992. "Industry Income and Congressional Regulatory Legislation: Interest Groups vs. Median Voter." *Economic Inquiry* 30(1): 47–57 (January).

Calvo, Carlos. 1862. *Recueil Complet des Traités, Conventions, … de Tous les Etats d'Amérique Latine (1493–1862)*. Paris: A. Durand.

Caplin, A. and K. Krishna. 1988. "Tariffs and the Most-Favored-Nation Clause: A Game Theoretic Approach," *Seoul Journal of Economics* 1(3): 267–89.

Cardoso, Fernando Henrique and Enzo Faletto. 1979. *Dependency and Development in Latin America*, trans. Marjory Mattingly Urquidi. Berkeley: University of California Press.

Cardoso de Oliveira, José Manuel. 1912. *Actos diplomáticos do Brasil: Tratados do período colonial e varios documentos desde 1493*. Río de Janeiro: Typografía do Jornal do Commercio, de Rodrígues.

Cariola, Carmen and Osvaldo Sunkel. 1985. "The Growth of the Nitrate Industry and Socioeconomic change in Chile, 1880–1930." In *The Latin American Economies: Growth and the Export Sector, 1880–1930*, ed. Roberto Cortés Conde and Shane J. Hunt. New York: Holmes and Meier, pp. 237–54.

Carr, Edward Hallett. 1961. *What is History?* New York: Vintage Books.

Cartwright, Nancy. 1983. *How the Laws of Physics Lie*. Oxford: Clarendon Press.

Cassing, James H. and Arye L. Hillman. 1985. "Political Influence Motives and the Choice Between Tariffs and Quotas." *Journal of International Economics* 19(3): 279–90 (November).

Cassing, James, Timothy J. McKeown, and Jack Ochs. 1986. "The Political Economy of the Tariff Cycle." *American Political Science Review* 80(3): 843–62 (September).

Caves, Richard E. 1976. "Economic Models of Political Choice: Canada's Tariff Structure." *Canadian Journal of Economics* 9(2): 278–300 (May).

Cheh, John H. 1974. "United States Concessions in the Kennedy Round and Short-Run Labor Adjustment Costs." *Journal of International Economics* 4(4): 323–40 (November).

Cheh, John H. 1976. "A Note on Tariffs, Nontariff Barriers, and Labor Protection in United States Manufacturing Industries." *Journal of Political Economy* 84(2): 389–94 (April).

Choi, J. P. 1995. "Optimal Tariffs and the Choice of Technology: Discriminatory Tariffs, v. the 'Most Favored Nation' Clause." *Journal of International Economics* 38(3): 143–60 (February).

Church, Clive H. 1983. *Europe in 1830: Revolution and Political Change*. London: George Allen & Unwin.

Clark, Don P. 1980. "Protection of Unskilled Labour in the United States Manufacturing Industries: Further Evidence." *Journal of Political Economy* 88(6): 1249–54 (December).

Clark, Martin. 1996. *Modern Italy 1871–1995* (2d ed.). London and New York: Longman.

Clarke, Kevin A. 2005. "The Phantom Menace: Omitted Variable Bias in Econometric Research." *Conflict Management and Peace Science* 22(4): 341–52 (Winter).

Clogg, Richard. 1992. *A Short History of Greece.* Cambridge: Cambridge University Press.

Coates, Daniel E. and Rodney D. Ludema. 2001. "A Theory of Trade Policy Leadership." *Journal of Development Economics* 65(1): 1–29 (June).

Cobden Club. 1875. *Free Trade and the European Treaties of Commerce.* London: Cassell Petter & Galpin.

Cochrane, D. and G. H. Orcutt. 1949. "Application of Least Squares Regression to Relationships Containing Auto-Correlated Error Terms." *Journal of the American Statistical Association* 44(245): 32–61 (March).

Coddington, George Arthur, Jr. 1961. *The Federal Government of Switzerland.* Boston: Houghton Mifflin Company.

Collier, David. 1978. "Industrial Modernization and Political Change." *World Politics* 30(4): 593–614 (June).

Conybeare, John A. C. 1984. "Politicians and Protection: Tariffs and Elections in Australia." *Public Choice* 43(2): 203–09 (January).

Conybeare, John A. C. 1987. *Trade Wars: The Theory and Practice of International Commercial Rivalry.* New York: Columbia University Press.

Conybeare, John A. C. 1991. "Voting for Protection: An Electoral Model of Tariff Policy." *International Organization* 45(1): 57–82 (Winter).

Coppa, Frank J. 1970. "The Italian Tariff and the Conflict Between Agriculture and Industry: The Commercial Policy of Liberal Italy, 1860–1922." *Journal of Economic History* 30(4): 742–69 (December).

Coppa, Frank J. 1971. *Planning, Protectionism, and Politics in Liberal Italy: Economics and Politics in the Giolittian Age.* Washington, DC: Catholic University of America Press.

Cornes, Richard and Todd Sandler. 1986. *The Theory of Externalities, Public Goods, and Club Goods.* Cambridge: Cambridge University Press.

Cortés Conde, Roberto. 1985. "The Export Economy of Argentina, 1880–1920." In Cortés Conde and Hunt, ed., pp. 319–81.

Cortés Conde, Roberto and Shane J. Hunt, ed. 1985. *The Latin American Economies: Growth and the Export Sector, 1880–1930.* New York: Holmes and Meier.

Cowhey, Peter F. and Edward Long. 1983. "Testing Theories of Regime Change: Hegemonic Decline or Surplus Capacity?" *International Organization* 37(2): 157–83 (Spring).

Cox, Gary W. 1987. *The Efficient Secret: The Cabinet and the Development of Political Parties in Victorian England.* Cambridge: Cambridge University Press.

Craig, Gordon A. 1978. *Germany 1866–1945.* New York: Oxford University Press.

Crampton, R. J. 1997. *A Concise History of Bulgaria.* Cambridge: Cambridge University Press.

Crosby, Travis L. 1976. *Sir Robert Peel's Administration, 1841–1846.* Newton Abbot, Devon: David and Charles Ltd.

Crouzet, F. 1964. "Wars, Blockade, and Economic Change in Europe, 1792–1815." *Journal of Economic History* 24(4): 567–88 (December).

Culbertson, William S. 1937. *Reciprocity: A National Policy for Foreign Trade*. New York: McGraw-Hill.

Curzon, Gerard and Victoria Curzon. 1976. "The Management of Trade Relations in the, GATT." In *International Economic Relations of the Western World 1959–1971, vol. 1: Politics and Trade*, ed. Andrew Shonfield et al. London: Oxford University Press for the Royal Institute of International Affairs, pp. 143–286.

Dai, Xinyuan. 2002. "Political Regimes and International Trade: The Democratic Difference Revisited." *American Political Science Review* 96(1): 159–66 (March).

Das, S. P. 1990. "Foreign Lobbying and the Political Economy of Protection." *Japan and the World Economy* 2(2): 169–79 (June).

Davis, Christina L. 2004. "International Institutions and Issue Linkage: Building Support for Agricultural Trade Liberalization." *American Political Science Review* 98(1): 153–69 (February).

Davis, John R. 1997. *Britain and the German Zollverein, 1848–66*. Houndmills, Basingstoke, Hampshire, UK: Macmillan Press Ltd.

Dawson, William Harbutt. 1904. *Protection in Germany: A History of German Fiscal Policy During the Nineteenth Century*. London: P. S. King & Son.

Deardorff, Alan V. 1984. "Testing Trade Theories and Predicting Trade Flows." In *Handbook of International Economics*, vol. 1, ed. R. W. Jones and P. B. Kenen. New York: Elsevier Science Publishers, pp. 467–517.

Deardorff, Alan V. and Robert M. Stern. 1992. "Multilateral Trade Negotiations and Preferential Trading Arrangements." Ann Arbor: University of Michigan Institute of Public Policy Studies Discussion Paper No. 344.

Destler, I. M. and John Odell. 1987. *Antiprotection: Changing Forces in United States Trade Politics*. Washington, DC: Institute for International Economics.

Dietzel, H. 1903. "The German Tariff Controversy." *Quarterly Journal of Economics* 17(3): 365–416 (May).

Dion, Douglas. 1997. *Turning the Legislative Thumbscrew: Minority Rights and Procedural Change in Legislative Politics*. Ann Arbor: University of Michigan Press.

Dion, Douglas. 1998. "Evidence and Inference and the Comparative Case Study." *Comparative Politics* 30(2): 127–45 (January).

Dixon, Peter. 1976. *Canning: Politician and Statesman*. London: Weidenfeld and Nicolson.

D'Lugo, David and Ronald Rogowski. 1993. "The Anglo-German Naval Race and Comparative Constitutional 'Fitness.'" In *The Domestic Bases of Grand Strategy*, ed. Richard Rosecrance and Arthur A. Stein. Ithaca: Cornell University Press, pp. 65–95.

Donnenfeld, S. and S. Weber. 1985. "Lobbying for Tariffs and the Cost of Protection." *Recherches economiques de Louvain* 51(1): 21–27 (March).

Downs, George W. and David M. Rocke. 1995. *Optimal Imperfection? Domestic Uncertainty and Institutions in International Relations*. Princeton: Princeton University Press.

Downs, George W., David M. Rocke, and Peter N. Barsoom. 1998. "Managing the Evolution of Multilateralism." *International Organization* 52(2): 397–419 (Spring).

Dumke, Rolf H. 1978. "The Political Economy of German Economic Unification: Tariffs, Trade and Politics of the Zollverein Era." *Journal of Economic History* 38(1): 277–78 (March).

Dunham, Arthur Louis. 1930. *The Anglo-French Treaty of Commerce of 1860 and the Progress of the Industrial Revolution in France*. Ann Arbor: University of Michigan Press.

Dunlop, Kathleen Edith. 1946. "The Policy of the Canadian Protective Tariff 1859–1914." Urbana, Illinois: MA Thesis.

East, Maurice. 1973. "Size and Foreign Policy Behavior: A Test of Two Models." *World Politics* 25(4): 556–76 (July).

Eddie, Scott M. 1968. "Agricultural Production and Output per Worker in Hungary, 1870–1913." *Journal of Economic History* 28(2): 197–222 (June).

Eddie, Scott M. 1972. "The Terms of Trade as a Tax on Agriculture: Hungary's Trade with Austria, 1883–1913." *Journal of Economic History* 32(1): 298–315 (March).

Eddie, Scott M. 1977. "The Terms and Pattern of Hungarian Foreign Trade, 1882–1913." *Journal of Economic History* 37(2): 329–58 (June).

Edwards, Richard C. 1970. "Economic Sophistication in Nineteenth Century Congressional Tariff Debates." *Journal of Economic History* 30(4): 802–38 (December).

Eicher, Theo and Thomas Osang. 2002. "Protection for Sale: An Empirical Investigation: Comment." *American Economic Review* 92(5): 1702–10 (December).

Elman, Colin, Miriam Fendius Elman, and Paul W. Schroeder. 1995. "History vs. Neo-Realism: A Second Look." *International Security* 20(1): 182–95 (Summer).

Elster, Jon. 1989. "Social Norms and Economic Theory." *Journal of Economic Perspectives* 3(4): 99–117 (Fall).

Ethier, Wilfred. 2001. "Theoretical Problems in Negotiating Trade Liberalization." *European Journal of Political Economy* 17(2): 209–32 (June).

Evangelista, Matthew. 1990. "Cooperation Theory and Disarmament Negotiations in the 1950s." *World Politics* 42(4): 502–28 (July).

Evans, Peter B., Dietrich Rueschemeyer, and Theda Skocpol, ed. 1985. *Bringing the State Back In.* Cambridge: Cambridge University Press.

Evans, Peter J., Harold K. Jacobson, and Robert D. Putnam, ed. 1993. *Double-Edged Diplomacy.* Berkeley: University of California Press.

Fabella, Raul V. 1991. "The Bias in Favor of Pro-Tariff Lobbies." *Journal of Public Economics* 44(1): 87–93 (February).

Fay, H. Van V. 1927. "Commercial Policy in Post-War Europe: Reciprocity Versus Most-Favored Nation Treatment." *Quarterly Journal of Economics* 41(3): 441–70 (May).

Fearon, James D. 1998. "Bargaining, Enforcement, and International Cooperation." *International Organization* 52(2): 269–305 (Spring).

Finger, J. M. and DeRosa, Dean A. 1979. "Trade Overlap, Comparative Advantage and Protection." In *On the Economics of Intra-Industry Trade*, ed. H. Giersch. Tübingen: J. C. B. Mohr, pp. 213–40.

Finger, J. M., H. Keith Hall, and Douglas R. Nelson. 1982. "The Political Economy of Administered Protection." *American Economic Review* 72(3): 452–66 (June).

Finger, J. M. and S. Laird. 1987. "Protection in Developed and Developing Countries: An Overview." *Journal of World Trade Law* 21(1): 9–23.

Finlayson, Jock A. and Mark W. Zacher. 1981. "The GATT and the Regulation of Trade Barriers: Regime Dynamics and Functions." *International Organization* 35(4): 561–602 (Autumn).

Finnemore, Martha. 1996. *National Interests in International Society.* Ithaca: Cornell University Press.

First International American Conference. 1889–1890. *Reports and Recommendations.* Washington, DC: Government Printing Office.

Fischer, Ronald D. 1992. "Endogenous Probability of Protection and Firm Behavior." *Journal of International Economics* 32(1–2): 149–63 (February).

Fisk, George M. 1903. "German-American 'Most Favored Nation' Relations." *Journal of Political Economy* 11(2): 220–36 (March).

Fletcher, R. A. 1983. "Cobden as Educator: The Free-Trade Internationalism of Eduard Bernstein, 1899–1914." *American Historical Review* 88(3): 561–78 (June).

Frankel, Jeffrey A. and Shang-Jin Wei. 1997. "Regionalization of World Trade and Currencies: Economics and Politics." In *The Regionalization of the World Economy*, ed. Jeffrey A. Frankel. Chicago: University of Chicago Press, pp. 189–226.

Ford, Worthington Chauncey. 1902. "The Economy of Russia." *Political Science Quarterly* 17(1): 99–124 (March).

Friedberg, Aaron L. 1988. *The Weary Titan: Britain and the Experience of Relative Decline, 1895–1905*. Princeton: Princeton University Press.

Frieden, Jeffry A. and Ronald Rogowski. 1996. "The Impact of the International Economy on National Policies: An Analytical Overview." In *Internationalization and Domestic Politics*, ed. Helen V. Milner and Robert O. Keohane. Cambridge: Cambridge University Press, pp. 25–47.

Friedman, Philip. 1978. "An Econometric Model of National Income, Commercial Policy and the Level of International Trade: The Open Economies of Europe, 1924–1938." *Journal of Economic History* 38(1): 148–80 (March).

Friman, H. Richard. 1993. "Side-Payments Versus Security Cards: Domestic Bargaining Tactics in International Economic Negotiations." *International Organization* 47(3): 387–410 (Summer).

Fry, Michael G. and Arthur N. Gilbert. 1982. "A Historian and Linkage Politics: Arno Mayer." *International Studies Quarterly* 26(3): 425–44 (September).

Fudenberg, Drew and Eric Maskin. 1986. "The Folk Theorem in Repeated Games with Discounting or with Incomplete Information." *Econometrica* 54(3): 533–54 (May).

Fuller, Steve. 1988. *Social Epistemology*. Bloomington: Indiana University Press.

Gall, Lothar. 1976. "Bismarck und der Bonapartismus." *Historische Zeitschrift* 223: 618–37.

Gallagher, John and Ronald Robinson. 1953. "The Imperialism of Free Trade." *Economic History Review*, 2nd series, 6(1): 1–15.

Garrett, Geoffrey. 1992. "International Cooperation and Institutional Choice: The European Community's Internal Market." *International Organization* 46(2): 533–60 (Spring).

Garrett, Geoffrey and George Tsebelis. 1996. "An Institutional Critique of Intergovernmentalism." *International Organization* 50(2): 269–99 (Spring).

Gash, Norman. 1972. *Sir Robert Peel. The Life of Sir Robert Peel After 1830*. London: Longman Group Limited.

Gerschenkron, Alexander. 1943/1989. *Bread and Democracy in Germany*. Ithaca: Cornell University Press.

Gilligan, Michael J. 1997. *Empowering Exporters: Reciprocity, Delegation, and Collective Action in American Trade Policy*. Ann Arbor: University of Michigan Press.

Gilpin, Robert. 1981. *War and Change in World Politics*. Cambridge: Cambridge University Press.

Godek, Paul E. 1985. "Industry Structure and Redistribution Through Trade Restrictions." *Journal of Law and Economics* 28(4): 687–703 (October).

Goertz, Gary and Paul F. Diehl. 1992. "Toward a Theory of International Norms: Some Conceptual and Measurement Issues." *Journal of Conflict Resolution* 36(4): 634–64 (December).

Goldberg, Pinelopi Koujianou, and Giovanni Maggi. 1999. "Protection for Sale: An Empirical Investigation." *American Economic Review* 89(5): 1135–55 (December).

Goldstein, Judith. 1993. *Ideas, Interests, and American Foreign Policy*. Ithaca: Cornell University Press.

Gollwitzer, Heinz. 1952. "Der Cäserismus Napoleons III. Im Widerhall der öffentlichen Meinung Deutschlands." *Historische Zeitschrift* 173: 23–75.

Good, David F. 1981. "Economic Integration and Regional Development in Austria-Hungary, 1867–1913." In *Disparities in Economic Development since the Industrial Revolution*, ed. Paul Bairoch and Maurice Lévy-Leboyer. New York: St. Martin's Press, pp. 137–50.

Gordon, Barry J. 1979. *Economic Doctrine and Tory Liberalism, 1824–1830*. London: Macmillan.

Gourevitch, Peter Alexis. 1977. "International Trade, Domestic Coalitions, and Liberty: Comparative Responses to the Crisis of 1873–1896." *Journal of Interdisciplinary History* 8(2): 281–313 (Autumn).

Gourevitch, Peter. 1986. *Politics in Hard Times: Comparative Responses to International Economic Crises*. Ithaca: Cornell University Press.

Gowa, Joanne. 1989. "Bipolarity, Multipolarity, and Free Trade." *American Political Science Review* 83(4): 1245–56 (December).

Gowa, Joanne. 1994. *Allies, Adversaries, and International Trade*. Princeton: Princeton University Press.

Gowa, Joanne and Edward D. Mansfield. 1993. "Power Politics and International Trade." *American Political Science Review* 87(2): 408–20 (June).

Gowa, Joanne and Edward D. Mansfield. 2004. "Alliances, Imperfect Markets, and Major-Power Trade." *International Organization* 58(4): 775–805 (Fall).

Grieco, Joseph. 1988. "Realist Theory and the Problem of International Cooperation. Analysis with an Amended Prisoner's Dilemma Model." *Journal of Politics* 50(3): 600–24 (August).

Grieco, Joseph M. 1990. *Cooperation Among Nations: Europe, America, and Non-Tariff Barriers to Trade*. Ithaca: Cornell University Press.

Grossman, Gene and Elhanan Helpman. 1994. "Protection for Sale." *American Economic Review* 84(4): 833–50 (September).

Grossman, Gene M. and Elhanan Helpman. 1995. "Trade Wars and Trade Talks." *Journal of Political Economy* 103(4): 675–707 (August).

Grossman, Gene M. and Elhanan Helpman. 2002. *Interest Groups and Trade Policy*. Princeton: Princeton University Press.

Grossman, Gene M. and James A. Levinsohn. 1989. "Import Competition and the Stock Market Return to Capital." *American Economic Review* 79(5): 1065–87 (December).

Grossman, Herschel I. and Taejoon Han. 1993. "A Theory of War Finance." *Defence Economics* 4(1): 33–44.

Gstöhl, Sieglinde. 2002. *Reluctant Europeans: Norway, Sweden, and Switzerland in the Process of Integration*. Boulder: Lynne Riemer.

Haggard, Stephan and Beth A. Simmons. 1987. "Theories of International Regimes." *International Organization* 41(3): 491–517 (Summer).

386   *References*

Hahn, Hans-Werner. 1982. *Wirtschaftliche Integration im 19. Jahrhundert.* Göttingen: Vandenhoeck & Ruprecht. Number 52 in the series *Kritische Studien zur Geschichtswissenschaft,* ed. Helmut Berding, Jürgen Kocka, and Hans-Ulrich Wehler.

Haight, Frank Arnold. 1941. *A History of French Commercial Policies.* New York: Macmillan Company.

Hall, Richard L. 1995. "Empiricism and Progress in Positive Theories of Legislative Institutions." In *Positive Theories of Congressional Institutions,* ed. Kenneth A. Shepsle and Barry R. Weingast. Ann Arbor: University of Michigan Press, pp. 273–302.

Hallerberg, Mark. 1996. "Tax Competition in Wilhelmine Germany and its Implications for the European Union." *World Politics* 48(3): 324–57 (April).

Hamilton, Bob and John Whalley. 1985. "Geographically Discriminatory Trade Arrangements." *Review of Economics and Statistics* 67(3): 446–55 (August).

Hammond, Thomas H. and Brandon Prins. 1998. "Domestic Veto Institutions, International Negotiations, and the Status Quo: A Spatial Model of Two-Level Games with Complete Information." Political Institutions and Public Choice Working Paper 98-05. East Lansing: Michigan State University, Institute for Public Policy and Social Resarch.

Hammond, Thomas H. and Brandon C. Prins. 2006. "Domestic Veto Institutions, Divided Government, and the Status Quo: A Spatial Model of Two-Level Games with Complete Information." In Pahre 2006a: 21–82.

Hansen, Wendy L. 1990. "The International Trade Commission and the Politics of Trade Protectionism." *American Political Science Review* 84(1): 21–46 (March).

Hardach, Karl W. 1967. *Die Bedeutung wirtschaftlicher Faktoren bei der Weidereinführung der Eisen- und Getreidezölle in Deutschland 1879.* Berlin: Duncker und Humblot.

Harley, C. Knick. 1982. "The Antebellum American Tariff: Food Exports and Manufacturing." *Explorations in Economic History* 29(4): 375–400 (October).

Hartung, Fritz. 1923. *Das Großherzogtum Sachsen unter der Regierung Karl Augusts 1775–1828.* Weimar: Hermann Böhlaus Nachfolger.

Harvey, Walter Bennett. 1938. *Tariffs and International Relations in Europe.* University of Chicago: PhD Dissertation.

Heckscher, Eli F. 1922. *The Continental System: An Economic Interpretation.* Oxford: Clarendon Press.

Heckscher, Eli F. 1954. *An Economic History of Sweden,* trans. Goran Ohlin. Cambridge, MA: Harvard University Press.

Heckscher, Gunnar. 1966. "The Role of Small Nations – Today and Tomorrow." (Fiftieth Anniversary Lecture of the School of Slavonic and East European Studies of the University of London, given on October, 19, 1965.) London: University of Athlone Press.

Helleiner, G. K. 1973. "Manufactured Exports from Less-Developed Countries and Multinational Firms." *Economic Journal* 83(329): 21–47 (March).

Helleiner, G. K. 1977. "The Political Economy of Canada's Tariff Structure: An Alternative Model." *Canadian Journal of Economics* 10(2): 318–26 (May).

Henderson, William O. 1939/1984. *The Zollverein.* Cambridge: Cambridge University Press.

Hertslet, Sir Edward. 1875–. *Treaties and Tariffs Regulating the Trade Between Great Britain and Foreign Nations.* London: Butterworth's.

Hillman, Arye L. 1982. "Declining Industries and Political-Support Protectionist Motives." *American Economic Review* 72(5): 1180–87.

Hirschman, Albert O. 1945/1989. *National Power and the Structure of Foreign Trade.* Berkeley: University of California Press.

Hiscox, Michael J. 2001. "Class Versus Industry Cleavages: Inter-Industry Factor Mobility and the Politics of Trade." *International Organization* 55(1): 1–46 (Winter).

Hiscox, Michael J. 2002. "Commerce, Coalitions, and Factor Mobility: Evidence from Congressional Votes on Trade Legislation." *American Political Science Review* 96(3): 593–608 (September).

Hobson, John M. 1997. *The Wealth of States: A Comparative Sociology of International Economic and Political Change.* Cambridge: Cambridge University Press.

Hodne, Fritz. 1983. *The Norwegian Economy 1920–1980.* New York: St. Martin's Press.

Horn, Henrik, and Petros C. Mavroidis. 2001. "Economic and Legal Aspects of the Most-Favored-Nation Clause." *European Journal of Political Economy* 17(2): 233–79 (June).

Hornbeck, Stanley K. 1910. *The Most-Favored-Nation Clause in Commercial Treaties.* Madison: University of Wisconsin Press.

Howe, Anthony. 1997. *Free Trade and Liberal England 1846–1946.* Oxford: Clarendon Press.

Hueckel, Glenn. 1981. "Agriculture During Industrialization." In *The Economic History of Britain Since 1700. vol. I: 1700–1860*, ed. R. C. Floud and D. N. McCloskey. Cambridge: Cambridge University Press, pp. 182–92.

Huertas, Thomas F. 1977. *Economic Growth and Economic Policy in a Multinational Setting. The Habsburg Monarchy, 1841–1865.* New York: Arno Press.

Hug, Simon and Thomas König. 2002. "The Dimensionality of European Integration in the Ratification Stage." Paper presented at the Annual Meeting of the Midwest Political Science Association.

Hug, Simon and Thomas König. 2006. "Divided Government and the Ratification of the Amsterdam Treaty." In Pahre, ed. 2006a: 133–50.

Hunt, James C. 1974. "Peasants, Grain Tariffs, and Meat Quotas: Imperial German Protectionism Reexamined." *Central European History* 7(4): 311–31 (December).

Huth, Paul K. 1988. "Extended Deterrence and the Outbreak of War." *American Political Science Review* 82(2): 423–43 (June)

Huth, Paul K. 1996. *Standing Your Ground. Territorial Disputes and International Conflict.* Ann Arbor: University of Michigan Press.

Iida, Keisuke. 1993. "When and How Do Domestic Constraints Matter? Two-Level Games with Uncertainty." *Journal of Conflict Resolution* 34(3): 403–26 (September).

Iliasu, Asaana. 1971. "The Cobden-Chevalier Commercial Treaty of 1860." *Historical Journal* 14(1): 67–98 (March).

Imlah, Albert H. 1958. *Economic Elements in the Pax Britannica. Studies in British Foreign Trade in the Nineteenth Century.* Cambridge, MA: Harvard University Press.

Imlah, Ann G. 1966. *Britain and Switzerland 1845–1860.* London: Longmans.

Irwin, Douglas A. 1988. "Welfare Effects of British Free Trade: Debate and Evidence from the 1840s." *Journal of Political Economy* 96(6): 1142–64 (December).

Irwin, Douglas. 1989a. "Political Economy and Peel's Repeal of the Corn Laws." *Economics and Politics* 1: 41–59.

Irwin, Douglas. 1989b. "The Political Economy of Free Trade: Voting in the British General Election of 1906." *Journal of Law and Economics*, 37(1): 75–108 (April).

Irwin, Douglas A. 1991. "Challenges to Free Trade." *Journal of Economic Perspectives* 5(2): 201–08 (Spring).

Irwin, Douglas A. 1993. "Free Trade and Protection in Nineteenth-Century Britain and France Revisited: A Comment on Nye." *Journal of Economic History* 53(1): 146–52 (March).

Irwin, Douglas A. 1995. "Industry or Class Cleavages over Trade Policy? Evidence from the British General Election of 1923." Cambridge: National Bureau of Economic Research Working Paper No. 5170.

Irwin, Douglas A. 1996. *Against the Tide: An Intellectual History of Free Trade.* Princeton: Princeton University Press.

James, John A. 1981. "The Optimal Tariff in the Antebellum United States." *American Economic Review* 71(4): 726–34 (September).

Jelavich, Barbara. 1983. *History of the Balkans. Eighteenth and Nineteenth Centuries.* Cambridge: Cambridge University Press.

Jervis, Robert. 1983. "Security Regimes." In Krasner, ed. 1983: 173–94.

Johnson, Harry G. 1965. "An Economic Theory of Protectionism, Tariff Bargaining, and the Formation of Customs Unions." *Journal of Political Economy* 73(3): 256–83 (June).

Jones, Kent. 1984. "The Political Economy of Voluntary Export Restraints." *Kyklos* 37(1): 82–101.

Kadar, Bela. 1970. *Small States in the World Economy* Budapest: Center for Afro-Asian Research of the Hungarian Academy of Sciences.

Kaempfer, William H., J. Harold McClure, Jr., and Thomas D. Willett. 1989. "Incremental Protection and Efficient Political Choice Between Tariffs and Quotas." *Canadian Journal of Economics* 22: 228–36 (May).

Kann, Robert A. 1974. *A History of the Habsburg Empire, 1526–1918.* Berkeley: University of California Press.

Katzenstein, Peter J. 1976. *Disjoined Partners: Austria and Germany Since 1815.* Berkeley: University of California Press.

Katzenstein, Peter J. 1985. *Small States in World Markets: Industrial Policy in Europe.* Ithaca: Cornell University Press.

Keegan, John. 1999. *The First World War.* New York: Alfred A. Knopf.

Kehr, Eckart. 1965. *Der Primat der Innenpolitik,* ed. Hans-Ulrich Wehler. Berlin: W. de Gruyter.

Kennedy, Paul M. 1980. *The Rise of the Anglo-German Antagonism 1860–1914.* London: The Ashfield Press.

Keohane, Robert O. 1980. "The Theory of Hegemonic Stability and Changes in International Economic Regimes, 1967–1977." In *Change in the International System,* ed. Ole Holsti et al. Boulder: Westview Press, pp. 131–62.

Keohane, Robert O. 1984. *After Hegemony: Discord in the World Political Economy.* Princeton: Princeton University Press.

Keohane, Robert O. 1986. "Reciprocity in International Relations." *International Organization* 40(1): 1–27 (Winter).

Keohane, Robert O. 1990. "Multilateralism: An Agenda for Research." *International Journal* 45: 731–64 (Autumn).

Kindleberger, Charles P. 1951. "Group Behavior and International Trade." *Journal of Political Economy* 59(1): 30–46 (February).

Kindleberger, Charles P. 1973. *The World in Depression 1929–1939.* Chicago: University of Chicago Press.

Kindleberger, Charles P. 1975. "The Rise of Free Trade in Western Europe, 1820–1875." *Journal of Economic History* 35(1): 20–55 (July).

King, Gary. 1989. "Event Count Models for International Relations: Generalizations and Applications." *International Studies Quarterly* 33(2): 123–47 (June).

King, Gary, Robert O. Keohane, and Sidney Verba. 1994. *Designing Social Inquiry.* Princeton: Princeton University Press.

Kitson Clark, G. S. R. 1951. "The Electorate and the Repeal of the Corn Laws." *Transactions of the Royal Historical Society*, 5th series, I: 109–26.

Kiyono, Kazuharu, Masahiro Okuno-Fujiwara, and Kaoru Ueda. 1991. "Industry Specific Interests and Trade Protection: A Game Theoretic Analysis." *Economic Studies Quarterly* 42(4): 347–59 (December).

Knorr-Cetina, Karin and Michael Mulkay, ed. 1983. *Science Observed: Perspectives on the Social Study of Science.* London: Sage Publications.

Komlos, John. 1983. *The Habsburg Monarchy as a Customs Union. Economic Development in Austria-Hungary in the Nineteenth Century.* Princeton: Princeton University Press.

Komorita, S. S. and James K. Esser. 1975. "Frequency of Reciprocated Concessions in Bargaining." *Journal of Personality and Social Psychology* 32(4): 699–705 (April).

Koremenos, Barbara. 2001. "Loosening the Ties that Bind: A Learning Model of Agreement Flexibility." *International Organization* 55(2): 289–325 (June).

Koremenos, Barbara, Charles Lipson, and Duncan Snidal. 2001. "The Rational Design of International Institutions." *International Organization* 55(4): 761–800 (Fall).

Krasner, Stephen D. 1976. "State Power and the Structure of International Trade." *World Politics* 28(3): 317–413 (April).

Krasner, Stephen D. 1977. *Defending the National Interest: Raw Materials Investment and U.S. Foreign Policy.* Princeton: Princeton University Press.

Krasner, Stephen D., ed. 1983. *International Regimes.* Ithaca: Cornell University Press.

Krasner, Stephen D. 1991. "Global Communications and National Power: Life on the Pareto Frontier." *World Politics* 43(3): 336–66 (April).

Krauze, Enrique. 1997. *Mexico: Biography of Power.* New York: HarperCollins.

Kreider, Carl. 1943. *The Anglo-American Trade Agreement. A Study of British and American Commercial Policies, 1934–1939.* Princeton: Princeton University Press.

Kreps, David, Paul Milgrom, John Roberts, and Robert Wilson. 1982. "Rational Cooperation in the Finitely Repeated Prisoners' Dilemma." *Journal of Economic Theory* 27(2): 245–52 (August).

Krishna, Pravin, and Devashish Mitra. 2005. "Reciprocated Unilateralism in Trade Policy." *Journal of International Economics* 65(2): 461–87 (July).

Krugman, Paul R. 1986. "Introduction: New Thinking About Trade Policy." In *Strategic Trade Policy and the New International Economics*, ed. Paul R. Krugman. Cambridge, MA: MIT Press, pp. 1–22.

Laird, Sam and Alexander Yeats. 1990. *Quantitative Methods for Trade-Barrier Analysis.* New York: New York University Press.

Lakatos, Imre. 1970. "The Methodology of Scientific Research Programmes." In *Criticism and the Growth of Knowledge*, ed. Imre Lakatos and Alan Musgrave. Cambridge: Cambridge University Press, pp. 91–196.

Lake, David A. 1988. *Power, Protection, and Free Trade. International Sources of U.S. Commercial Strategy, 1887–1939.* Ithaca: Cornell University Press.

Lamborn, Alan C. 1983. "Power and the Politics of Extraction." *International Studies Quarterly* 27(2): 125–46 (June).

Lampe, John R. and Marvin R. Jackson. 1982. *Balkan Economic History, 1550–1950: From Imperial Borderlands to Developing Nations.* Bloomington: Indiana University Press.

Landes, David. 1998. *The Wealth and Poverty of Nations. Why Some Are So Rich and Some So Poor.* New York: W. W. Norton and Company.

Láng, Ludwig. 1906. *Hundert Jahre Zollpolitik,* trans. Alexander Rosen. Vienna: Kaiserliche und königliche Hof-Buchdruckerei und Hof-Verlags-Buchhandlung Carl Fromme.

LaPalombara, Joseph. 1971. "Penetration: A Crisis of Government Capacity." In *Crisis and Sequence in Political Development,* ed. Leonard Binder et al. Princeton: Princeton University Press, pp. 205–32.

Lauck, W. Jett. 1904. "The Political Significance of Reciprocity." *Journal of Political Economy* 12(4): 495–524 (September).

Laughlin, J. Laurence and H. Parker Willis. 1903. *Reciprocity.* New York: Baker & Taylor Co.

Lavergne, Réal P. 1983. *The Political Economy of U.S. Tariffs: An Empirical Analysis.* Toronto: Academic Press Canada.

Lazer, David. 1999. "The Free Trade Epidemic of the 1860s and Other Outbreaks of Economic Discrimination." *World Politics* 51(4): 447–83 (July).

Leamer, Edward E. 1990. "Latin America as a Target of Trade Barriers Erected by the Major Developed Countries in 1983." *Journal of Development Economics* 32(2): 337–68 (April).

Lebow, Richard Ned and Janice Gross Stein. 1990. "Deterrence: The Elusive Dependent Variable." *World Politics* 42(3): 336–69 (April).

Leff, Nathaniel H. 1982. *Underdevelopment and Development in Brazil. Vol. I: Economic Structure and Change, 1822–1947.* London: George Allen & Unwin.

Levasseur, Emile. 1892. "The Recent Commercial Policy of France." *Journal of Political Economy* 1(1): 20–49 (December).

Levinsohn, James A. 1989. "Strategic Trade Policy When Firms Can Invest Abroad: When Are Tariffs and Quotas Equivalent?" *Journal of International Economics* 27(1–2): 129–46 (August).

Lévy-Leboyer, Maurice and François Bourguignon. 1985. *L'économie française au XIXe siècle: Analyse macro-économique.* Paris: Economica.

Lewin, Leif. 1988. *Ideology and Strategy: A Century of Swedish Politics.* Cambridge: Cambridge University Press.

Li, Chien-pin. 1994. "Trade Negotiation Between the United States and Taiwan: Interest Structure in Two-Level Games." *Asian Survey* 34(8): 692–705 (August).

Li, Quan. 2000. "Institutional Rules of Regional Trade Blocs and Their Impact on Trade," in *The Political Consequences of Regional Trade Blocs,* edited by R. Switky and B. Kerremans. London: Ashgate, pp. 85–118.

Lindberg, Anders. 1983. *Småstat mot Stormakt. Beslutssystemet vid tillkomsten av 1911 års svensk-tyska handels- och sjöfartstraktat.* Lund: CWK Gleerup.

Lindgren, Raymond E. 1959. *Norway-Sweden: Union, Disunion, and Scandinavian Integration.* Princeton: Princeton University Press.

Lipson, Charles. 1984. "International Cooperation in Economic and Security Affairs." *World Politics* 37(1): 1–23 (October).

Lipson, Charles. 1985. "Bankers' Dilemmas: Private Cooperation in Rescheduling Sovereign Debts." *World Politics* 38(1): 200–25 (October).

Lipson, Charles. 1991. "Why are Some International Agreements Informal?" *International Organization* 45(4): 495–538 (Autumn).

List, Friedrich. 1844/1966. *The National System of Political Economy.* New York: A. M. Kelley.

Lohmann, Susanne. 1997. "Linkage Politics." *Journal of Conflict Resolution* 41(1): 38–68 (February).

Lohmann, Susanne and Sharyn O'Halloran. 1994. "Divided Government and U.S. Trade Policy: Theory and Evidence." *International Organization* 48(4): 595–632 (Autumn).

Long, Ngo Van and Neil Vousden. 1991. "Protectionist Responses and Declining Industries." *Journal of International Economics* 30(1–2): 87–103 (February).

Long, William O. 1989. *U.S. Export Control Policy: Executive Autonomy vs. Congressional Reform.* New York: Columbia University Press.

Long, William J. 1996. "Trade and Technology Incentives and Bilateral Cooperation." *International Studies Quarterly* 40(1): 77–106 (March).

Lotz, Walther. 1907. "The Commercial Policy of Germany." *Journal of Political Economy* 15(5): 257–83 (May).

Macgregor, John. 1846. *Commercial Tariffs and Regulations, Resources, and Trade of the Several States of Europe and America, Together with the Commercial Treaties Between England and Foreign Countries (Part XVI: States of Mexico).* London: Charles Whiting, Beaufort House, Strand.

Magee, Christopher. 2003. "Endogenous Tariffs and Trade Adjustment Assistance." *Journal of International Economics* 60(1): 203–22 (May).

Magee, Stephen. 1971. "Three Simple Tests of the Stolper-Samuelson Theorem." In Magee et al. 1999: Chapter 7.

Magee, Stephen P. 1997. "Endogenous Protection: The Empirical Evidence." In *Perspectives on Public Choice*, ed. Dennis E. Mueller. Cambridge: Cambridge University Press, pp. 526–61.

Magee, Stephen, William Brock, and Leslie Young. 1989. *Black Hole Tariffs and Endogenous Policy Theory.* Cambridge: Cambridge University Press.

Magnusson, Lars. 2000. *An Economic History of Sweden.* London and New York: Routledge.

Mahaim, E. 1892. "La politique commerciale de la Belgique." *Handelpolitik* 1: 197–238.

Mansfield, Edward D. 1998. "The Proliferation of Preferential Trading Arrangements." *Journal of Conflict Resolution* 42(5): 523–43 (October).

Mansfield, Edward D. 1994. *Power, Trade, and War.* Princeton: Princeton University Press.

Mansfield, Edward D. and Rachel Bronson. 1997. "Alliances, Preferential Trade Arrangements, and International Trade." *American Political Science Review* 91(1): 94–107 (March).

Mansfield, Edward D. and Marc L. Busch. 1995. "The Political Economy of Nontariff Barriers: A Cross-National Analysis." *International Organization* 49 (3): 723–49 (Autumn).

Mansfield, Edward D. and Helen V. Milner, ed. 1997. *The Political Economy of Regionalism.* New York: Columbia University Press.

Mansfield, Edward D. and Helen V. Milner. 1999. "The New Wave of Regionalism." *International Organization* 53(3): 589–627 (Summer).

Mansfield, Edward D., Helen V. Milner, and B. Peter Rosendorff. 2000. "Free to Trade: Democracies, Autocracies, and International Trade." *American Political Science Review* 94(2): 305–21 (June).

Mansfield, Edward D., Helen V. Milner, and B. Peter Rosendorff. 2002a. "Why Democracies Cooperate More: Electoral Control and International Trade Agreements." *International Organization* 56(3): 477–513 (August).

Mansfield, Edward D., Helen V. Milner, and B. Peter Rosendorff. 2002b. "Replication, Realism, and Robustness: Analyzing Political Regimes and International Trade." *American Political Science Review* 96(1): 167–69 (March).

Mansfield, Edward D. and Eric Reinhardt. 2003. "Multilateral Determinants of Regionalism: The Effects of GATT/WTO on the Formation of Preferential Trading Arrangements." *International Organization* 57(4): 829–62 (Fall).

Marcy, G. 1960. "How Far Can Foreign Trade and Customs Agreements Confer upon Small Nations the Advantages of Large Nations?" In *Economic Consequences of the Size of Nations. Proceedings of a Conference Held by the International Economic Association,* ed. E. A. G. Robinson. London: Macmillan & Co. Ltd., pp. 265–81.

Marks, Stephen V. and John MacArthur. 1990. "Empirical Analyses of the Determinants of Protection: A Survey of Empirical Studies and Some New Results." In *International Trade Policy: Gains from Exchange Between Economics and Political Science,* ed. John S. Odell and Thomas D. Willett. Ann Arbor: University of Michigan Press, pp. 105–40.

Marsh, Peter T. 1999. *Bargaining on Europe: Britain and the First Common Market, 1860–1892.* New Haven: Yale University Press.

Martin, Lisa L. 1992. *Coercive Cooperation: Explaining Multilateral Economic Sanctions.* Princeton: Princeton University Press.

Martin, Lisa L. 2000. *Democratic Commitments: Legislatures and International Cooperation.* Princeton: Princeton University Press.

Marvel, Howard P. and Edward J. Ray. 1983. "The Kennedy Round: Evidence on the Regulation of International Trade in the United States." *American Economic Review* 73(1): 190–97 (March).

Marvel, Howard P. and Edward John Ray. 1987. "Intraindustry Trade: Sources and Effects on Protection." *Journal of Political Economy* 95(6): 1278–91 (December).

Marx, Karl. 1854/1963. *The Class Struggles in France, 1848–1850.* New York: International Publishers.

Mastanduno, Michael. 1988. "Trade as a Strategic Weapon: American and Alliance Export Control Policy in the Early Postwar Period." In *The State and American Foreign Economic Policy,* ed. G. John Ikenberry, David A. Lake, and Michael Mastanduno. Ithaca: Cornell University Press, pp. 121–50.

Mastanduno, Michael, David A. Lake, and John G. Ikenberry. 1989. "Toward a Realist Theory of State Action." *International Studies Quarterly* 33(4): 457–74 (December).

Matis, Herbert. 1973. "Leitlinien der österreichischen Wirtschaftspolitik." In *Die Habsburgermonarchie, 1848–1918. Im Auftragen der Kommission für die Geschichte der*

Österreichisch-Ungarischen Monarchie, ed. Peter Urbanitsch and Adam Wandruszka. Vienna: Österreichische Akademie der Wissenschaften, I: 29–67.

Matis, Herbert. 1984. "Österreichs Wirtschaft im Zeitalter Franz Josephs I." In *Das Zeitalter Kaiser Franz Josephs. 1. Teil: Von der Revolution zur Gründerzeit*, ed. Harry Kühnel and Adam Wandruszka. St. Pölten: Kulturabteilung der Niederösterreichischen Landesregierung, pp. 113–20.

May, Arthur J. 1951. *The Habsburg Monarchy 1867–1914.* Cambridge: Harvard University Press.

Mayer, Arno. 1969. "Internal Causes and Purposes of War in Europe, 1870–1956: A Research Assignment." *Journal of Modern History* 41(3): 291–303 (September).

Mayer, Frederick W. 1992. "Managing Domestic Differences in International Negotiations: The Strategic Use of Internal Side-Payments." *International Organization* 46(4): 793–818 (Autumn).

Mayer, Wolfgang. 1981. "Theoretical Considerations on Negotiated Tariff Settlements." *Oxford Economic Papers* 33(1): 135–53 (March).

Mayer, Wolfgang. 1984. "Endogenous Tariff Formation." *American Economic Review* 74(5): 970–85 (December).

Mayer, Wolfgang and Jun Li. 1994. "Interest Groups, Electoral Competition, and Probabilistic Voting for Trade Policies." *Economics and Politics* 6(1): 59–77 (March).

Mayer, Wolfgang and Raymond Riezman. 1987. "Endogenous Choice of Trade Policy Instruments." *Journal of International Economics* 23(3–4): 377–81 (November).

McGillivray, Fiona. 1997. "Party Discipline as a Determinant of the Endogenous Formation of Tariffs." *American Journal of Political Science* 41(2): 584–607 (April).

McGillivray, Fiona. 2004. *Privileging Industry: The Comparative Politics of Trade and Industrial Policy.* Princeton: Princeton University Press.

McGillivray, Fiona, Iain McLean, Robert Pahre, and Cheryl Schonhardt-Bailey, eds. 2001. *International Trade and Political Institutions.* Edward Elgar Publishing.

McGillivray, Fiona and Alastair Smith. 1997. "Institutional Determinants of Trade Policy." *International Interactions* 23(2): 119–43 (April-June).

McGinnis, Michael. 1986. "Issue Linkage and the Evolution of Cooperation." *Journal of Conflict Resolution* 30(1): 141–70 (March).

McGreevey, William Paul. 1985. "The Transition to Economic Growth in Colombia." In *The Latin American Economies: Growth and the Export Sector, 1880–1930*, ed. Roberto Cortés Conde and Shane J. Hunt. New York: Holmes and Meier, pp. 23–81.

McKeown, Timothy J. 1983. "Hegemonic Stability Theory and 19th Century Tariff Levels in Europe." *International Organization* 37(1): 73–92 (Winter).

McKeown, Timothy J. 1984. "Firms and Tariff Regime Change: Explaining the Demand for Protection." *World Politics* 36(2): 215–33 (January).

McKeown, Timothy J. 1989. "The Politics of Corn Law Repeal and Theories of Commercial Policy." *British Journal of Political Science* 19(3): 353–80 (July).

McKeown, Timothy J. 1991. "The Foreign Policy of a Declining Power." *International Organization* 45(2): 257–79 (Spring).

McLean, Iain. 1995. "Railway Regulation as a Test-bed of Rational Choice." In *Preferences, Institutions, and Rational Choice*, ed. Keith Dowding and Desmond King. Oxford: Clarendon Press, pp. 134–61.

McLean, Iain. 1998. 'Irish Potatoes, Indian Corn, and British Politics: Interests, Ideology, Heresthetics, and the Repeal of the Corn Laws.' In *Contemporary Political Studies 1998*, ed. A. Dobson and J. Stanyer. Nottingham: PSA, vol. 1, pp. 124–41.

McLean, Iain. 2001. "Irish Potatoes, Indian Corn, and British Politics: Interests, Ideology, Heresthetics, and the Repeal of the Corn Laws." In McGillivray et al. 2001: 99–145.

McLean, Iain and Camilla Bustani. 1999. "Irish Potatoes and British Politics: Interests, Ideology, Heresthetics and the Repeal of the Corn Laws." *Political Studies* 47(5): 817–36 (December).

McLean, Iain and Christopher Foster. 1992. "The Political Economy of Regulation: Interests, Ideology, Voters, and the UK Regulation of Railways Act 1844." *Public Administration* 70(3): 313–31 (Fall).

McPherson, Charles P. 1972. "Tariff Structures and Political Exchange." University of Chicago: PhD Dissertation.

Messerlin, Patrick A. 1996. "France and Trade Policy: Is the 'French Exception' Passée?" *International Affairs* 72(2): 293–309 (April).

Meunier, Sophie. 2000. "What Single Voice? European Institutions and EU-U.S. Trade Negotiations." *International Organization* 54(1): 103–35 (Winter).

Millbourn, Ingrid. 1992. "Swedish Social Democracy, Crises and Tariffs Before 1900." *Scandinavian Journal of History* 17(4): 271–93 (December).

Milner, Helen V. 1988. *Resisting Protectionism: Global Industries and the Politics of International Trade.* Princeton: Princeton University Press.

Milner, Helen. 1992. "International Theories of Cooperation Among Nations." *World Politics* 44(3): 466–96 (April).

Milner, Helen V. 1997a. *Interests, Institutions, and Information. Domestic Politics and International Relations.* Princeton: Princeton University Press.

Milner, Helen V. 1997b. "Industries, Governments, and the Creation of Regional Trading Blocs." In Mansfield and Milner, 1997: 77–106.

Milner, Helen V. 1988. *Resisting Protectionism: Global Industries and the Politics of International Trade.* Princeton: Princeton University Press.

Milner, Helen V. and B. Peter Rosendorff. 1996. "Trade Negotiations, Information, and Domestic Politics." *Economics and Politics* 8(2): 145–89.

Milner, Helen V. and B. Peter Rosendorff. 1997. "Democratic Politics and International Trade Negotiations." *Journal of Conflict Resolution* 41(1): 117–46 (February).

Milner, Helen V. and David B. Yoffie. 1989. "Between Free Trade and Protectionism: Strategic Trade Policy and a Theory of Corporate Trade Demands." *International Organization* 43(2): 239–72 (Spring).

Milward, Alan S. 1984. *The Reconstruction of Western Europe, 1945–51.* Berkeley: University of California Press.

Milward, Alan S. 1992. *The European Rescue of the Nation-State.* Berkeley: University of California Press.

Ministerio degli Affari Esteri. 1865–99. *Trattati e convenzioni fra il Regno d'Italia ed i governi esteri.* Roma: Tipografia Bencini.

Mitra, Devashish. 1999. "Endogenous Lobby Foundation and Endogenous Protection: A Long-Run Model of Trade Policy Determination." *American Economic Review* 89(5): 1116–34 (December).

Mitchell, Brian R. 1975. *European Historical Statistics 1750–1970.* (Abridged ed.) New York: Columbia University Press.

Mitchell, Brian R. 1979. *European Historical Statistics 1750–1950.* New York: Columbia University Press.

Mjøset, Lars, ed. 1986. *Norden dagen derpå: De nordiska økonomisk-politiske modellene og deres problemer på 70- og 80- tallet.* Oslo: Universitetsforlaget.

Mjøset, Lars. 1987. "Nordic Economic Policies." *International Organization* 41(3): 403–56 (Summer).

Mo, Jongryn. 1994. "The Logic of Two-Level Games with Endogenous Domestic Coalitions." *Journal of Conflict Resolution* 38(3): 402–22 (September).

Mo, Jongryn. 1995. "Domestic Institutions and International Bargaining: The Role of Agent Veto in Two-Level Games." *American Political Science Review* 89(4): 914–24 (December).

Modelski, George. 1978. "The Long Cycle of Global Politics and the Nation-State." *Comparative Studies in Society and History* 20(2): 214–35 (April).

Modelski, George. 1982. "Long Cycles and the Strategy of U.S. International Economic Policy." In *America in a Changing World Political Economy,* ed. William P. Avery and David P. Rapkin. New York: Longman, pp. 97–118.

Modelski, George. 1987. *Long Cycles in World Politics.* Seattle: University of Washington Press.

Molina Enríquez, Andrés. 1909. *Los grandes problemas nacionales.* México: Carranza.

Mommsen, Wolfgang J. 1995. *Imperial Germany 1867–1918. Politics, Culture, and Society in an Authoritarian State,* trans. Richard Deveson. London: Arnold.

Moneta, Carmellah. 1959. "The Estimation of Transportation Costs in International Trade." *Journal of Political Economy* 67(1): 41–58 (February).

Moravcsik, Andrew. 1998. *The Choice for Europe: Social Purpose and State Power from Messina to Maastricht.* Ithaca: Cornell University Press.

Morrow, James D. 1997. "When do 'Relative Gains' Impede Trade?" *Journal of Conflict Resolution* 41(1): 12–37 (February).

Morrow, James D., Randolph M. Siverson, and Tressa E. Tabares. 1998. "The Political Determinants of International Trade: The Major Powers, 1907–90." *American Political Science Review* 92(3): 649–61 (September).

Morrow, James D., Randolph M. Siverson, and Tressa E. Tabares. 1999. "Correction to 'The Political Determinants of International Trade.'" *American Political Science Review* 93(4): 931–33 (December).

Moser, Peter, Arye L. Hillman, and Ngo Van Long. 1995. "Modelling Reciprocal Trade Liberalization: The Political-Economy and National-Welfare Perspectives." *Swiss Journal of Economics and Statistics* 131(3): 503–15.

Mouzelis, Nicos P. 1986. *Politics in the Semi-Periphery. Early Parliamentarism and Late Industrialisation in the Balkans and Latin America.* London: Macmillan.

Mueller, John E. 1999. *Capitalism, Democracy, and Ralph's Pretty Good Grocery.* Princeton: Princeton University Press.

Mugomba, Agrippah T. 1979. "Small Developing States and the External Operating Environment." *Yearbook for World Affairs* 33: 201–16.

Munck, Gerardo L. and Jay Verkuilen. 2002. "Conceptualizing and Measuring Democracy: Evaluating Alternative Indices." *Comparative Political Studies* 35(1): 5–34.

Mussa, Michael. 1974. "Tariffs and the Distribution of Income: The Importance of Factor Specificity, Substitutability, and Intensity in the Short and Long Run." *Journal of Political Economy* 82(6): 1191–203 (November/December).

Mussa, Michael. 1982. "Imperfect Factor Mobility and the Distribution of Income." *Journal of International Economics* 12(1–2): 125–41 (February).

Nash, John F., Jr. 1950. "The Bargaining Problem." *Econometrica* 18(2): 155–62 (April).

Nelson, Douglas. 1988. "Endogenous Tariff Theory: A Critical Survey." *American Journal of Political Science* 32(3): 796–837 (August).

Nordlinger, Eric A. 1981. *On the Autonomy of the Democratic State.* Cambridge, MA: Harvard University Press.

North, Douglass. 1981. *Structure and Change in Economic History.* London: Norton.

Nye, John Vincent. 1990. "Revisionist Tariff History and the Theory of Hegemonic Stability." St. Louis: Washington University Political Economy Working Paper, April.

Nye, John Vincent. 1991. "Changing French Trade Conditions, National Welfare, and the 1860 Anglo-French Treaty of Commerce." *Explorations in Economic History* 28(4): 460–77 (October).

Oatley, Thomas and Robert Nabors. 1998. "Redistributive Cooperation: Market Failure, Wealth Transfers, and the Basle Accord." *International Organization* 52(1): 35–54 (Winter).

Ocampo, José-Antonio. 1981. "Export Growth and Capitalist Development in Colombia in the Nineteenth Century." In *Disparities in Economic Development since the Industrial Revolution*, ed. Paul Bairoch and Maurice Lévy-Leboyer. New York: St. Martin's Press, pp. 98–109.

Odell, John S. 2000. *Negotiating the World Economy.* Ithaca: Cornell University Press.

O'Donnell, Guillermo A. 1973. *Modernization and Bureaucratic-Authoritarianism.* Berkeley: Institute of International Studies.

Offe, Claus and Helmut Wiesenthal. 1980. "Two Logics of Collective Action: Theoretical Notes on Social Class and Organizational Form." In *Political Power and Social Theory*, ed. Zeittin. New York: Elsevier, vol. I: 67–115.

O'Halloran, Sharyn. 1994. *Politics, Process, and American Trade Policy.* Ann Arbor: University of Michigan Press.

Olarreaga, Marcelo and Isidro Soloaga. 1998. "Endogenous Tariff Formation: The Case of Mercosur." *World Bank Economic Review* 12(2): 297–320.

Olarreaga, Marcelo, Isidro Soloaga, and L. Alan Winters. 1999. "What's Behind Mercosur's Common External Tariff?" Unpublished manuscript.

Olson, Mancur, Jr. 1965. *The Logic of Collective Action.* Cambridge, MA: Harvard University Press.

Olson, Mancur. 1982. *The Rise and Decline of Nations.* New Haven: Yale University Press.

O'Rourke, Kevins H. and Jeffrey G. Williamson. 1999. *Globalization and History: The Evolution of a Nineteenth-Century Atlantic Economy.* Cambridge, MA: MIT Press.

Owen, Thomas C. 1985. "The Russian Industrial Society and Tsarist Economic Policy, 1867–1905." *Journal of Economic History* 45(3): 587–606 (September).

Oye, Kenneth A., ed. 1986. *Cooperation Under Anarchy.* Princeton: Princeton University Press.

Oye, Kenneth A. 1993. *Economic Discrimination and Political Exchange: World Political Economy in the 1930s and 1980s.* Princeton: Princeton University Press.

Paarlberg, Robert L. 1993. "Why Agriculture Blocked the Uruguay Round: Evolving Strategies in a Two-Level Game." In *World Agriculture and the GATT*, ed. William P. Avery. Boulder: Lynne Rienner Publishers, pp. 39–54.

Pahre, Robert. 1994. "Multilateral Cooperation in an Iterated Prisoners' Dilemma." *Journal of Conflict Resolution* 38(2): 326–52 (June).

Pahre, Robert. 1995a. "Wider and Deeper: The Links Between Expansion and Enlargement in the European Communities." In *Towards a New Europe: Stops and Starts in Regional Integration*, ed. Gerald Schneider, Patricia A. Weitsman, and Thomas Bernauer. Boulder: Praeger/Greenwood, pp. 111–36.

Pahre, Robert. 1995b. "Positivist Discourse and Social Scientific Communities: Towards an Epistemological Sociology of Science." *Social Epistemology* 9(3): 233–55 (July-September).

Pahre, Robert. 1996. "Mathematical Discourse and Crossdisciplinary Communities: The Case of Political Economy." *Social Epistemology* 10(1): 55–73 (January-March).

Pahre, Robert. 1997. "Endogenous Ratification in Two-Level Games and Parliamentary Oversight of the European Union." *Journal of Conflict Resolution* 41(1): 147–74 (February).

Pahre, Robert. 1998. "Reactions and Reciprocity: Tariffs and Trade Liberalization in 1815–1914." *Journal of Conflict Resolution* 42(4): 467–92 (August).

Pahre, Robert. 1999. *Leading Questions: How Hegemony Affects the International Political Economy*. Ann Arbor: University of Michigan Press.

Pahre, Robert. 2001a. "Divided Government and International Cooperation in Austria-Hungary, Sweden-Norway, and the European Union." *European Union Politics* 2(2): 131–62 (Spring).

Pahre, Robert. 2001b. "Most-Favored-Nation Clauses, Domestic Politics, and Clustered Negotiations." *International Organization* 55(4): 861–92 (Summer).

Pahre, Robert. 2004. "House Rules: Institutional Choice and United States Trade Negotiations." *Conflict Management and Peace Sciences* 21(3): 195–213 (Fall).

Pahre, Robert and Paul Papayoanou. 1997. "Using Formal Theory to Link International and Domestic Politics." *Journal of Conflict Resolution* 41(1): 4–11 (February).

Pahre, Robert. 2005. "Formal Theory and Case-Study Methods in EU Studies." *European Union Politics* 6(1): 113–46 (January).

Pahre, Robert, ed. 2006a. *Democratic Foreign Policy Making: Problems of Divided Government and International Cooperation*, Palgrave.

Pahre, Robert. 2006b. "Divided Government and International Cooperation: An Overview." In Pahre 2006: 1–20.

Palairet, Michael. 1979. "Fiscal Pressure and Peasant Impoverishment in Serbia Before World War I." *Journal of Economic History* 3(3): 719–40 (September).

Palairet, Michael. 1997. *The Balkan Economies c. 1800–1914. Evolution without Development*. Cambridge: University of Cambridge Press.

Pamuk, Şevket. 1987. "Commodity Production for World-Markets and Relations of Production in Ottoman Agriculture, 1840–1913." in *The Ottoman Empire and the World-Economy*, ed. Huri İslamoğlu-İnan. Cambridge: Cambridge University Press, pp. 178–202.

Patterson, G. D. 1968. *The Tariff in the Australian Colonies 1856–1900*. Melbourne: P. W. Cheshire.

Peltzman, Sam. 1976. "Toward a More General Theory of Regulation." *Journal of Law and Economics* 19(2): 211–39 (August).

Perez-Brignoli, Hector. 1989. *A Brief History of Central America*, trans. Ricardo B. Sawrey A. and Susana Stettri de Sawrey. Berkeley: University of California Press.

Pincus, Jonathan J. 1975. "Pressure Groups and the Pattern of Tariffs." *Journal of Political Economy* 83(4): 757–78 (August).

Pincus, Jonathan J. 1977. *Pressure Groups and Politics in Antebellum Tariffs*. New York: Columbia University Press.

Platt, D. C. M. 1968. *Finance, Trade, and Politics in British Foreign Policy 1815–1914*. Oxford: Clarendon Press.

Polanyi, Karl. 1944. *The Great Transformation*. Boston: Beacon Press.

Pollard, Sidney. 1997. "The Integration of European Business in the 'Long' Nineteenth Century." *Vierteljahrschrift für Sozial- und Wirtschaftsgeschichte* 84(2): 156–170.

Pollins, Brian M. 1989. "Does Trade Still Follow the Flag?" *American Political Science Review* 83(2): 465–80 (June).

Prest, John. 1996. "A Large Amount or a Small? Revenue and the Nineteenth-Century Corn Laws." *The Historical Journal* 39(2): 467–78 (June).

Price, Arnold H. 1949. *The Evolution of the Zollverein. A Study of the Ideas and Institutions Leading to German Economic Unification between 1815 and 1833*. Ann Arbor: University of Michigan Press.

Putnam, Robert. 1988. "Diplomacy and Domestic Politics: The Logic of Two-Level Games." *International Organization* 42(3): 427–60 (Summer).

Ránki, György. 1964. "Problems of the Development of Hungarian Industry." *Journal of Economic History* 24(2): 204–28 (June).

Ránki, György. 1981. "On the Economic Development of the Habsburg Monarchy." In *Disparities in Economic Development since the Industrial Revolution*, ed. Paul Bairoch and Maurice Lévy-Leboyer. New York: St. Martin's Press, pp. 165–74.

Ratcliffe, Barry M. 1978. "The Tariff Reform Campaign in France, 1831–1836." *Journal of European Economic History* 7(1): 61–138 (Spring).

Ray, Edward John. 1974. "The Optimum Commodity Tariff and Tariff Rates in Developed and Less Developed Countries." *Review of Economics and Statistics* 56(3): 369–377 (August).

Ray, Edward John. 1981a. "The Determinants of Tariff and Nontariff Trade Restrictions in the United States." *Journal of Political Economy* 89(1): 105–21 (February).

Ray, Edward John. 1981b. "Tariff and Nontariff Barriers to Trade in the United States and Abroad." *Review of Economics and Statistics* 63(2): 161–68 (May).

Ray, Edward John. 1987. "The Impact of Special Interests on Preferential Tariff Concessions by the United States." *Review of Economics and Statistics* 69(2): 187–93 (May).

Ray, Edward J. and Howard P. Marvel. 1984. "The Pattern of Protection in the Industrialized World." *Review of Economics and Statistics* 66(3): 452–58 (August).

Razin, Assaf and Andrew Rose. 1994. "Business Cycle Volatility and Openness: An Exploratory Cross-Section Analysis." NBER Working Paper No. 4208, August.

Recueil des Traités et Conventions Conclus par le Royaume des Pays-Bas avec les Puissances Etrangères, depuis 1813 jusqu'a nos jours. Amsterdam: Belinfante Frères, 1858–.

Reinhardt, Eric. 2001. "Adjudication Without Enforcement in GATT Disputes." *Journal of Conflict Resolution* 45(2): 174–95 (April).

Remmer, Karen. 1998. "Does Democracy Promote Interstate Cooperation? Lessons from the Mercosur Region." *International Studies Quarterly* 42(1): 25–51 (March).

Rhodes, Carolyn. 1993. *Reciprocity, U.S. Trade Policy, and the GATT Regime.* Ithaca: Cornell University Press.

Richardson, Martin. 1993. "Endogenous Protection and Trade Diversion." *Journal of International Economics* 34(3–4): 309–24 (May).

Riker, William H. 1962. *The Theory of Political Coalitions.* New Haven: Yale University Press.

Roberts, Kenneth M. 1995. "Neoliberalism and the Transformation of Populism in Latin America: The Peruvian Case." *World Politics* 48(1): 82–116 (October).

Robinson, ed., E. A. G. 1960. *The Economic Consequences of the Size of Nations.* London: Macmillan.

Rodrik, Dani. 1986. "Tariffs, Subsidies and Welfare with Endogenous Policy." *Journal of International Economics* 21(3–4): 285–99 (November).

Rodrik, Dani. 1997. *Has Globalization Gone Too Far?* Washington: Institute for International Economics.

Rogowski, Ronald. 1987. "Trade and the Variety of Democratic Institutions." *International Organization* 41(2): 203–23 (Spring).

Rogowski, Ronald. 1989. *Commerce and Coalitions: How Trade Affects Domestic Political Alignments.* Princeton: Princeton University Press.

Rogowski, Ronald and Mark Andreas Kayser. 2002. "Majoritarian Electoral Systems and Consumer Power: Price-Level Evidence from the OECD Countries." *American Journal of Political Science* 46(3): 526–39 (July).

Rokkan, Stein. 1975. "Dimensions of State Formation and Nation-Building: A Possible Paradigm for Research on Variations Within Europe." In *The Formation of the National States in Western Europe,* ed. Charles Tilly. Princeton: Princeton University Press, pp. 562–600.

Rosenberg, Hans. 1978. "Wirtschaftskonjunktur, Gesellschaft und Politik in Mitteleuropa, 1873–1918." In *Machteliten und Wirtschaftskonjunkturen: Studien zur neueren deutschen Sozial- und Wirtschaftsgeschichte.* Göttingen: Vandenhoeck und Ruprecht, pp. 173–97.

Rosendorff, B. Peter. 1996. "Voluntary Export Restraints, Antidumping Procedure, and Domestic Politics." *American Economic Review* 86(3): 544–561 (June).

Rosendorff, B. Peter. 2005. "Stability and Rigidity: Politics and Design of the WTO's Dispute Settlement Procedure." *American Political Science Review* 99(3): 389–400 (August).

Rosendorff, B. Peter. 2006. "Do Democracies Trade More Freely?" In Pahre, ed. 2006a: 83–106.

Rosendorff, B. Peter and Helen Milner. 2001. "The Optimal Design of International Trade Institutions: Uncertainty and Escape." *International Organization* 55(4): 829–57 (October).

Ruffin, Roy J. 1969. "Tariffs, Intermediate Goods, and Domestic Protection." *American Economic Review* 59(3): 261–69 (June).

Ruffin, Roy and Ronald Jones. 1977. "Protection and Real Wages: The Neoclassical Ambiguity." *Journal of Economic Theory* 14(2): 337–48 (April).

Ruggie, John Gerard, ed. 1993a. *Multilateralism Matters: The Theory and Practice of an Institutional Form.* New York: Columbia University Press.

Ruggie, John Gerard. 1993b. "Multilateralism: The Anatomy of an Institution." In Ruggie 1930a:3–47.

Russett, Bruce. 1993. *Grasping the Democratic Peace: Principles for a Post-Cold War World*. Princeton: Princeton University Press.

Russett, Bruce and Joel Slemrod. 1993. "Diminished Expectations of Nuclear War and Increased Personal Savings: Evidence from Individual Survey Data." *American Economic Review* 83(4): 1022–33 (September).

Sapir, André. 2000. "Trade Regionalism in Europe: Towards an Integrated Approach." *Journal of Common Market Studies* 38(1): 151–62 (March).

Saunders, Ronald S. 1980. "The Political Economy of Effective Tariff Protection in Canada's Manufacturing Sector." *Canadian Journal of Economics/Revue Canadienne d'Economique* 13(2): 340–48 (May).

Sayre, Francis B. 1939. "The Most-Favored-Nation Policy in Relation to Trade Agreements." *American Political Science Review* 33(3): 411–23 (June).

Schattschneider, E. E. 1935. *Politics, Pressures and the Tariff*. New York: Prentice-Hall.

Schelling, Thomas C. 1960. *The Strategy of Conflict*. Cambridge: Harvard University Press.

Schmidt, Jochen. 1973. *Bayern und das Zollparlament: Politik und Wirtschaft in den letzten Jahren vor der Reichsgründung (1866/67–1870)*. Munich: Kommissionsbuchhandlung R. Wölfle.

Schmidt, Manfred G. 1981. "Politische Steuerung der Ökonomie in Kleinstaaten: Eine vergleichende Analyse." *Österreichische Zeitschrift für Politikwissenschaft* 1981(1): 77–89.

Schmoller, Gustav. 1900. "Die Wandlungen in der europäischen Handelspolitik des 19en Jahrhunderts. Eine Säkularbetrachtung." *Jahrbuch für Gesetzgebung, Verwaltung und Volkswirtschaft im Deutschen Reiche* 24: 373–82.

Schneider, Gerald. 2000. "The Two-Level Dilemma of European Politics: The Empirical Relevance of Threats and Promises in Interstate Negotiations." Universität Konstanz, unpublished manuscript, October.

Schneider, Gerald and Lars-Erik Cederman. 1993. "The Change in Tide in Political Cooperation: A Limited Information Model of European Integration." *International Organization* 48(4): 633–62 (Autumn).

Schonhardt-Bailey, C. 1991a. "Specific Factors, Capital Markets, Portfolio Diversification, and Free Trade: Domestic Determinants of the Repeal of the Corn Laws." *World Politics* 43(4): 545–69 (July).

Schonhardt-Bailey, C. 1991b. "Lobbying for Free Trade in 19th Century Britain: To Concentrate or Not." *American Political Science Review* 85(1): 37–58 (March).

Schonhardt-Bailey, Cheryl. 1994. "Linking Constituency Interests to Legislative Voting Behavior: The Role of District Economic and Electoral Composition in the Repeal of the Corn Laws." *Parliamentary History* 13: 86–118.

Schonhardt-Bailey, Cheryl, ed. 1997. *Free Trade: The Repeal of the Corn Laws*. Bristol: Thoemmes Press.

Schonhardt-Bailey, Cheryl. 1998a. "Parties and Interests in the 'Marriage of Iron and Rye.'" *British Journal of Political Science* 28(2): 291–330 (April).

Schonhardt-Bailey, Cheryl. 1998b. "Interests, Ideology and Politics: Agricultural Trade Policy in Nineteenth-Century Britain and Germany." In *Free Trade and Its Reception, 1815–1960, Freedom and Trade*, ed. Andrew Marrison. London: Routledge.

Shonhardt-Bailey, Cheryl. 2001. "The Strategic Use of Ideas: Nationalizing the Interest in the Nineteenth Century." In *International Trade and Political Institutions: Instituting Trade in the Long Nineteenth Century*, edited by Fiona McGillivray, Iain McLean, Robert Pahre, and Cheryl Schonhardt-Bailey. Edward Elgar Publishing.

Schonhardt-Bailey, Cheryl. 2006. *From the Corn Laws to Free Trade: Interests, Ideas, and Institutions in Historical Perspective.* Cambridge, MA: MIT Press.

Schonhardt-Bailey, Cheryl and Andrew Bailey. 1995. "The Buck in Your Bank is not a Vote for Free Trade: Financial Intermediation and Trade Preferences in the United States and Germany." In *Preferences, Institutions, and Rational Choice*, ed. Keith Dowding and Desmond King. Oxford: Clarendon Press, pp. 179–210.

Schoppa, Leonard J. 1993. "Two-Level Games and Bargaining Outcomes: Why *Gaiatsu* Succeeds in Japan in Some Cases but Not Others." *International Organization* 47(3): 353–86 (Summer).

Schroeder, Paul W. 1995. "Correspondence: History vs. Neo-realism: A Second Look." *International Security* 20(1): 193–95 (Summer).

Schuyler, Robert Livingston. 1945. *The Fall of the Old Colonial System: A Study in British Free Trade, 1770–1870.* London: Oxford University Press.

Schwartz, Herman. 1994. "Small States in Big Trouble: State Reorganization in Australia, Denmark, New Zealand, and Sweden in the 1980s." *World Politics* 46(4): 527–55 (July).

Sebenius, James K. 1983. "Negotiation Arithmetic: Adding and Subtracting Issues and Parties." *International Organization* 37(2): 281–316 (Spring).

Semmel, Bernard. 1970. *The Rise of Free Trade Imperialism: Classical Political Economy, the Empire of Free Trade and Imperialism, 1750–1850.* Cambridge: Cambridge University Press.

Setser, Vernon G. 1933. "Did Americans Originate the Most-Favored-Nation Clause?" *Journal of Modern History* 5(3): 319–23 (September).

Shonfield, Andrew. 1976. "International Relations of the Western World: An Overall View." In *International Economic Relations of the Western World 1959–1971*, ed. Andrew Shonfield, Gerard and Victoria Curzon, T. K. Warley, and George Ray. London: Oxford University Press for the Royal Institute of International Affairs, vol. 1, pp. 1–142.

Simmons, Beth A. 1994. *Who Adjusts? Domestic Sources of Foreign Economic Policy During the Interwar Years.* Princeton: Princeton University Press.

Simmons, Beth A., and Zachary Elkins. 2004. "The Globalization of Liberalization: Policy Diffusion in the International Political Economy." *American Political Science Review* 98(1): 171–89 (February).

Skocpol, Theda. 1979. *States and Social Revolutions: A Comparative Analysis of France, Russia and China.* Cambridge: Cambridge University Pres.

Smith, Adam. 1776. *An Inquiry into the Nature and Causes of the Wealth of Nations.* Indianapolis: Liberty Fund.

Smith, Michael Stephen. 1980. *Tariff Reform in France 1860–1900: The Politics of Economic Interest.* Ithaca: Cornell University Press.

Snidal, Duncan. 1985a. "Coordination Versus Prisoners' Dilemma: Implications for International Cooperation and Regimes." *American Political Science Review* 79(4): 923–42 (December).

Snidal, Duncan. 1985b. "The Limits of Hegemonic Stability Theory." *International Organization* 39(4): 579–614 (Autumn).

Snidal, Duncan. 1986. "The Game *Theory* of International Politics." In Oye 1986: 25–57.

Snidal, Duncan. 1991. "Relative Gains and the Pattern of International Cooperation." *American Political Science Review* 85(3): 701–26 (September).

Snyder, Richard C. 1940. "The Most Favored Nation Clause and Recent Trade Practices." *Political Science Quarterly* 55(1): 77–97 (March).

Somogyi, Éva. 1984. "Ungarn in der Habsburgmonarchie." In *Das Zeitalter Kaiser Franz Josephs. 1. Teil: Von der Revolution zur Gründerzeit*, ed. Harry Kühnel and Adam Wandruszka. St. Pölten: Kulturabteilung der Niederösterreichischen Landesregierung, pp. 269–276.

Spencer, Barbara J. 1986. "What Should Trade Policy Target?" In *Strategic Trade Policy and the New International Economics*, ed. Paul R. Krugman, Cambridge, MA: MIT University Press, pp. 69–89.

Stein, Arthur A. 1983. "Coordination and Collaboration: Regimes in an Anarchic World." In Krasner, ed., 1983: 115–40.

Stein, Arthur A. 1984. "The Hegemon's Dilemma: Great Britain, the United States, and the International Economic Order." *International Organization* 38(2): 355–86 (Spring).

Stein, Arthur A. 1991. *Why Nations Cooperate: Circumstance and Choice in International Relations*. Ithaca: Cornell University Press.

Stern, Robert. 1973. "Tariff and Other Measures of Trade Control: A Survey of Recent Developments." *Journal of Economic Literature* 11(3): 857–88 (September).

Stewart, Robert. 1969. "The Ten Hours and Sugar Crises of 1844: Government and the House of Commons in the Age of Reform." *Historical Journal* 12(1): 35–57.

Stigler, George J. 1971. "The Theory of Economic Regulation." *Bell Journal of Economic and Management Science* 2(1): 3–21 (Spring).

Stigler, George J. 1974. "Free Riders and Collective Action: An Appendix to Theories of Economic Regulation." *The Bell Journal of Economics and Management Science* 5(2): 359–65 (Autumn).

Stimson, James A. 1985. "Regression in Space and Time: A Statistical Essay." *American Journal of Political Science* 29(4): 914–47 (November).

Stone, Joe A. 1978. "A Comment on Tariffs, Nontariff Barriers, and Labor Protection in United States Manufacturing Industries." *Journal of Political Economy* 86(5): 969–62 (October).

Storing, James A. 1963. *Norwegian Democracy*. Boston: Houghton Mifflin Company.

Sykes, Alan. 1979. *Tariff Reform in British Politics 1903–1913*. Oxford: Clarendon Press.

Szijártó, István M. 1994. "Playing Second Fiddle: The Role of Hungary and Norway in the Foreign Policies of the Austro-Hungarian Monarchy and the Swedish-Norwegian Union: A Comparison." *Scandinavian Journal of History* 19(2): 143–63.

Takacs, Wendy E. 1981. "Pressures for Protection: An Empirical Analysis." *Economic Inquiry* 19: 687–93 (October).

Takacs, Wendy E. 1985. "More on Protectionist Pressure and Aggregate Economic Conditions: A Reply." *Economic Inquiry* 23(1): 183–84 (January).

Tarar, Ahmer. 2005. "Constituencies and Preferences in International Bargaining." *Journal of Conflict Resolution* 49(3): 383–407 (June).

Tarrow, Sidney. 1996. "Social Movements in Contentious Politics: A Review Article." *American Political Science Review* 90(4): 874–83 (December).

Tasca, Henry J. 1938/1967. *The Reciprocal Trade Policy of the United States: A Study in Trade Philosophy*.

Taylor, A. J. P. 1964. *The Habsburg Monarchy 1809–1918*. London: Penguin Books.

Taylor, Michael. 1976/1987. *The Possibility of Cooperation* (revised edition of *Anarchy and Cooperation*.) Cambridge, MA: Cambridge University Press.

Thompson, J. M. 1983. *Louis Napoleon and the Second Empire*. New York: Columbia University Press.

Tollison, Robert D. and Thomas D. Willett. 1979. "An Economic Theory of Mutually Advantageous Issue Linkages in International Negotiations." *International Organization* 33(4): 425–49 (August).

Travis, William Penfield. 1964. *The Theory of Trade and Protection*. Cambridge, MA: Harvard University Press.

Trebilcock, Clive. 1981. *The Industrialization of the Continental Powers 1780–1914*. London: Longman.

Treitschke, Heinrich von. 1879–1894. *Deutsche Geschichte im neunzehnten Jahrhundert*. Leipzig: S. Hirzel.

Triepel, Heinrich. 1900–1945. *Nouveau Recueil Genéral de Traités et Autres Actes Relatifs aux Rapports de Droit International (Martens)*. Leipzig: Librairie Dieterich.

Tsebelis, George. 2002. *Veto Players: How Political Institutions Work*. Princeton: Princeton University Press.

Turunen-Red, Arja H. and Alan D. Woodland. 1991. "Strict Pareto-Improving Multilateral Reforms of Tariffs." *Econometrica* 59(4): 1127–52 (July).

Twain, Mark. 1869/1966. *The Innocents Abroad, or The New Pilgrims Progress*. New York: Signet Classics.

Twain, Mark. 1880/1977. *A Tramp Abroad*, abridged and ed. Charles Neider. New York: Perennial Library.

Twain, Mark. 1880. "The Awful German Language." In *The Complete Humorous Sketches and Tales of Mark Twain*, ed. Charles Neider. New York: Doubleday & Company, Inc., pp. 438–55.

U.S. Department of State. 1890. *Reciprocity Treaties with Latin America*. Washington, DC: Government Printing Office.

United States Tariff Commission (USTC). 1920. *Reciprocity with Canada: A Study of the Arrangement of 1911*. Washington: Government Printing Office.

United States Tariff Commission (USTC). 1940. *Reference Manual of Latin American Commercial Treaties*. Washington, D.C.

Vaccara, Beatrice. 1960. *Employment and Output in Protected Manufacturing Industries*. Washington, DC: Brookings Institution.

Vandenbosch, Amry. 1944. "Formulation and Control of Foreign Policy in the Netherlands: A Phase of Small Power Politics." *Journal of Politics* 6(4): 430–52 (November).

Verdier, Daniel. 1994. *Democracy and International Trade: Britain, France, and the United States, 1860–1990*. Princeton: Princeton University Press.

Verkuilen, Jay. 2005. "Assigning Membership in a Fuzzy Set Analysis." *Sociological Methods and Research* 33(4): 462–96 (May).

Verney, Douglas V. 1957. *Parliamentary Reform in Sweden 1866–1921*. Oxford: At the Clarendon Press.

Vial Solar, Javier. 1903. *Los tratados de Chile*. Santiago: Imprenta, Litografía y Encuadernación Barcelona.

Vicens Vives, Jaime, with Jorge Nadal Oller. 1969. *An Economic History of Spain*, trans. by Frances M. Lopez-Morillas. Princeton: Princeton University Press.

Viner, Jacob. 1924. "The Most-Favored-Nation Clause in American Commercial Treaties." *Journal of Political Economy* 32(1): 101–29 (February).

Viner, Jacob. 1951. *International Economics*. Glencoe: Free Press.

Vogel, Hans. 1979. "Ein theoretischer Versuch zur Analyse kleinstaatlichen Verhaltens im internationalen System." *Annuaire suisse de science politique/Schweizerisches Jahrbuch für politische Wissenschaft* 19: 71–80.

Vomáčková, Vera. 1963. "Österreich und der Deutsche Zollverein." *Historica* 5: 109–46.

Vousden, Neil. 1990. *The Economics of Trade Protection*. Cambridge: Cambridge University Press.

Wallerstein, Immanuel. 1974a. *The Modern World-System I*. New York: Academic Press.

Wallerstein, Immanuel. 1974b. "The Rise and Future Demise of the World Capitalist System: Concepts for Comparative Analysis." *Comparative Studies in Society and History* 16(4): 387–415 (September).

Wallerstein, Immanuel. 1979. *The Capitalist World Economy*. Cambridge: Cambridge University Press.

Wallerstein, Immanuel. 1988. "Feudalism, Capitalism, and the World-System in the Perspective of Latin America and the Caribbean: Comments on Stern's Critical Tests." *American Historical Review* 93(4): 873–85 (October).

Wallerstein, Immanuel. 1989. *The Modern World System III: The Second Era of Great Expansion of the Capitalism World-Economy, 1730–1840s*. New York: Academic Press.

Wallerstein, Immanuel. 1994. *Unthinking Social Science: The Limits of Nineteenth-Century Paradigms*. Philadelphia: Temple University Press.

Wallerstein, Immanuel, Hale Decdeli, and Reşat Kasaba. 1987. "The Incorporation of the Ottoman Empire into the World-Economy." In *The Ottoman Empire and the World-Economy*, ed. Huri İslamoğlu-İnan. Cambridge: Cambridge University Press, pp. 88–100.

Wallerstein, Michael. 1987. "Unemployment, Collective Bargaining and the Demand for Protection," *American Journal of Political Science* 31(4): 729–52 (November).

Waltz, Kenneth N. 1967. *Foreign Policy and Democratic Politics: The American and British Experience*. Boston: Little, Brown and Company.

Waltz, Kenneth N. 1979. *Theory of International Politics*. Chicago: Addison-Wesley.

Warr, Peter G. 1983. "The Private Provision of a Public Good is Independent of the Distribution of Income." *Economics Letters* 13(2–3): 207–11.

Webb, Steven B. 1982. "Agricultural Protection in Wilhelminian Germany: Forging an Empire with Pork and Rye." *Journal of Economic History* 42(2): 309–26 (June).

Wehler, Hans-Ulrich. 1974. "Der Aufstieg des Organisierten Kapitalismus und Interventionsstaates in Deutschland." In *Organisierter Kapitalismus: Voraussetzungen und Anfänge*, ed. Heinrich August Winkler. Göttingen: Vandenhoeck & Ruprecht, pp. 36–57.

Weiller, Jean Sylvain. 1971. "Long-Run Tendencies in Foreign Trade: With a Statistical Study of French Trade Structure 1871–1939." *Journal of Economic History* 31(4): 804–21 (December).

Weiner, Myron. 1971. "Political Participation Crises of the Political Process." In Binder et al.: 159–204.

Weitowitz, Rolf. 1978. *Deutsche Politik und Handelspolitik unter Reichskanzler Leo von Caprivi 1890–1894*. Düsseldorf: Droste Verlag.

Wellisz, Stanislaw and John D. Wilson. 1986. "Lobbying and Tariff Formation: A Dead-weight Loss Consideration." *Journal of International Economics* 20(3–4): 367–75 (May).

Werner, Karl Heinz. 1949. "Österreichische Industrie- und Außenhandelspolitik 1848 bis 1948." In *Hundert Jahre Österreichischer Wirtschaftsentwicklung 1848–1948.* Vienna: Springer-Verlag, pp. 359–479.

Werner, Yvonne Maria. 1989. *Svensk-tyska förbindelser kring Sekelskiftet 1900. Politik och ekonomi tid tillkomsten av 1906 års svensk-tyska handels- och sjöfartstraktat.* Lund: Lund University Press.

Williams, Judith Blow. 1972. *British Commercial Policy and Trade Expansion, 1750–1850.* Oxford: Clarendon Press.

Willis, H. Parker. 1911. "The International Aspects of Reciprocity." *Journal of Political Economy* 19(7): 527–541.

Winham, Gilbert R. 1986. *International Trade and the Tokyo Round Negotiation.* Princeton: Princeton University Press.

Winkler, Heinrich August, ed. 1974. *Organisierter Kapitalismus: Voraussetzungen und Anfänge.* Göttingen: Vandenhoeck & Ruprecht.

Wonnacott, Paul and Ronald Wonnacott. 2005. "What's the Point of Reciprocal Trade Negotiations? Exports, Imports, and Gains from Trade." *World Economy* 28(1): 1–20 (January).

Wuorinen, John H. 1965. *A History of Finland.* New York: Columbia University Press.

Yarbrough, Beth V. and Robert M. Yarbrough. 1986. "Reciprocity, Bilateralism, and Economic 'Hostages': Self-enforcing Agreements in International Trade." *International Studies Quarterly* 30(1): 7–21 (March).

Zeng, Ka. 2004. *Trade Threats, Trade Wars: Bargaining, Retaliation, and American Coercive Diplomacy.* Ann Arbor: University of Michigan Press.

Zorn, Wolfgang. 1963. "Wirtschafts- und sozialgeschichtliche Zusammenhänge der Reichsgründungszeit (1850–1879)." *Historische Zeitschrift* 197: 313–42.

Zorn, Wolfgang. 1973. "Die wirtschaftliche Integration Kleindeutschlands in der 1860er Jahren und die Reichsgründung." *Historische Zeitschrift* 216: 304–34.

Index

wheat (UK "corn"), 38, 68, 85, 86, 92, 95, 112, 193, 214, 367. *See also* corn; Corn Laws; grains; rye
Wilhelm II, Kaiser, 92. *See also* Germany; Prussia
Witte, Sergei, 75, 367, 368. *See also* Russia
World Bank, 130
World Trade Organization (WTO), 3, 12, 14, 24, 28, 33, 34, 44, 81, 131, 202, 211, 215, 240, 269, 285, 294, 304, 323, 349, 350, 370–373. *See also* General Agreement on Tariffs and Trade (GATT); globalization; tariffs; trade; Trade-Related Intellectual Property (TRIPs); Trade-Related Investment Measures (TRIMs); veterinary regulations
Doha Development Round, 14, 33, 34, 370, 374

disputes, 41, 371
Generalized System of Preferences, 44
World War I, 15, 24, 33, 77, 78, 127, 171, 173, 269, 348
World War II, 3, 14, 19, 77, 134, 374

yarn, 277, 314. *See also* textiles
Yoffie, David B., 45, 46

Zollverein (German Customs Union), 16, 17, 20–22, 27, 32, 33, 49, 94, 105, 110, 111, 167–169, 183, 215, 217, 248, 263, 264, 274–277, 279, 291, 296, 297, 299, 305–323, 335, 364–366. *See also* Germany
Zollanschlüße (tariff accessions), 108
Zwischenzolllinie (tariff boundary), 267, 269, 270, 311–314. *See also* Austria; Austria-Hungary; Hungary

Printed in the United States
By Bookmasters